Further praise for A Line in the Sand

'James Barr's new book, *A Line in the Sand*, adds s⸺ ⸺ ⸺ ⸺ the usual accounts of this decisive moment in the history of the Middle East . . . He has scoured the diplomatic archives of the two powers as well ⸺ ⸺ ⸺ te papers of most of the leading officials of the tim⸺ ⸺ and has come up with a rich haul that ⸺ ⸺ ading' *Financial Times*

'With superb rese⸺ ⸺ ⸺ ⸺ered the whole shabby story . . . The conv⸺ ⸺ ⸺ l being felt today – not only in the Middle⸺

'Racy . . . Barr des⸺ ⸺ ⸺ ⸺ ⸺ mplexities of Anglo-French intrigues against each other and – in 1941 – outright war in Syria . . . he is right to assert that few British readers grasp the ferocity of Anglo-French antagonism in the Levant' *Sunday Times*

'[Barr] plunges us straight into the mindset of two relatively junior officials, François Georges-Picot and Mark Sykes, in the maelstrom of 191 . . . And there he keeps us for the next 30 years, not hovering with the historians in high Olympic judgement on the fates of nations, but with the journalists and spies at the very grubby coalface of foreign policy, made up of threat and counter-threat, hidden dreams, desire for revenge, inter-departmental rivalry and the jealousy of the bureaucratic chiefs in the capitals for their men on the ground. I found the entire book most horribly addictive, even if the ultimate picture it paints of the actions of the two Western powers is sordid, muddled and hypocritical' *Independent*

'James Barr's history of imperial machinations in the Middle East offers a revelatory slant on the continuing crisis in that area . . . an outstanding piece of research and a damning take on what stoked current Middle Eastern woes . . . Barr's lively account introduces plenty of larger-than-life characters jostling for position, capturing their paranoia and scheming' *Metro*

'Barr lays out in detail how between the wars the two countries sought to undermine one another in the Middle East . . . Barr is particularly good at identifying and portraying officials and agents engaged in these tit-for-tat reprisals that blurred the distinction between patriotism and crime' *Literary Review*

'It is one that has been often and well told before, but Barr brings a new slant, with each twist seen through the prism of Anglo-French rivalry. He has done some very thorough research and provided himself with some wonderfully rich material with which to work . . . One of the unexpected responses to reading this masterful study is amazement at the efforts the British and French each put into undermining the other . . . there is enough here to have even the most jingoistic readers shaking their heads and, in the light of 60 years of conflict that has followed, wondering whether the region would now be more resolved and peaceful had the British and French never been allowed to take control' *The Spectator*

ALSO BY JAMES BARR

*Setting the Desert on Fire: T. E. Lawrence and
Britain's Secret War in Arabia, 1916–1918*

A LINE IN THE SAND

Britain, France and the Struggle for the
Mastery of the Middle East

JAMES BARR

SIMON &
SCHUSTER

London · New York · Sydney · Toronto · New Delhi

A CBS COMPANY

First published in Great Britain by Simon & Schuster UK Ltd, 2011
This edition published in Great Britain by Simon & Schuster UK Ltd, 2012
A CBS COMPANY

7 9 10 8 6

Simon & Schuster UK Ltd
1st Floor
222 Gray's Inn Road
London WC1X 8HB

www.simonandschuster.co.uk

Simon & Schuster Australia, Sydney
Simon & Schuster India, New Delhi

Maps on pp. vii–ix © Reginald Piggott

A CIP catalogue record for this book
is available from the British Library.

ISBN: 978-1-84739-457-6

Typeset in Sabon by M Rules

Printed and bound by CPI Group (UK) Ltd, Croydon, CR0 4YY

CONTENTS

PART THREE
THE SECRET WAR: 1940–1945

PART FOUR
EXIT: 1945–1949

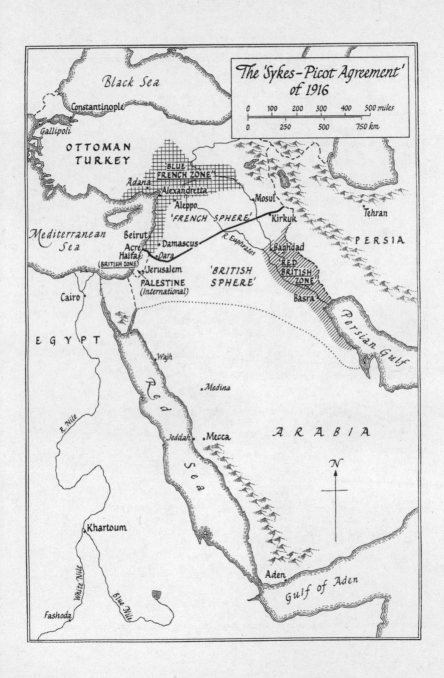

The 'Sykes–Picot Agreement'
of 1916

| 0 | 100 | 200 | 300 | 400 | 500 miles |

| 0 | 250 | 500 | 750 km |

Black Sea

Constantinople

Gallipoli

OTTOMAN
TURKEY

Adana

BLUE
FRENCH ZONE

Alexandretta

Aleppo

Mosul

'FRENCH SPHERE'

Kirkuk

Tehran

Mediterranean
Sea

Beirut

Acre
Haifa
(BRITISH ZONE)

Damascus

Dara

R. Euphrates

PERSIA

Baghdad

RED
BRITISH
ZONE

Jerusalem

'BRITISH
SPHERE'

PALESTINE
(International)

Cairo

Basra

EGYPT

Persian Gulf

Wajh

R. Nile

Red

Medina

Sea

ARABIA

Jeddah

Mecca

N

Khartoum

White Nile

Blue Nile

Fashoda

Aden

Gulf of Aden

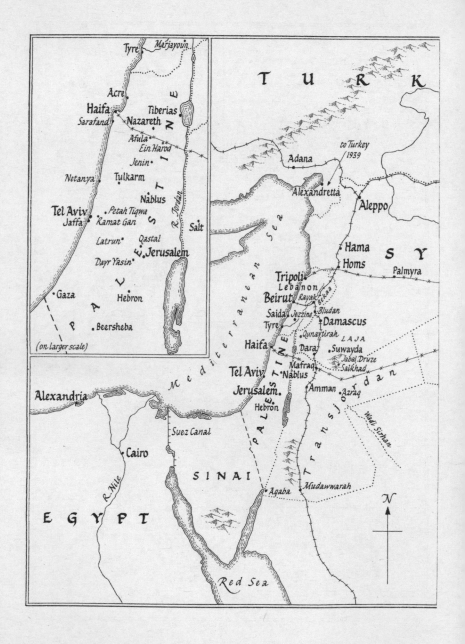

TURK

to Turkey
1939

Adana

Alexandretta

Aleppo

SY

Hama
Homs   Palmyra

Tripoli
Lebanon
Beirut   Rayak
Saida Jezzine Bludan
Tyre   Damascus
            Qunaytirah
Haifa   Dara   LAJA
                    Suwayda
Tel Aviv   Mafraq   Jabal Druze
        Nablus   Salkhad
Jerusalem
                Amman   Azraq
    Hebron

Alexandria   Transjordan

            Suez Canal   Wadi Sirhan

    Cairo

    R. Nile   SINAI

EGYPT   Mudawwarah
                Aqaba

            Red Sea   N

Mediterranean Sea

PALESTINE

Inset map (on larger scale):

Tyre   Marjayoun

Acre

Haifa   Tiberias
Sarafand   Nazareth

        Afula
        Ein Harod
        Jenin

Netanya   Tulkarm

            Nablus

Tel Aviv
Jaffa   Petah Tiqwa
        Ramat Gan   Salt
    Latrun   Qastal
            Jerusalem
    Dayr Yasin

                R. Jordan

. Gaza
        Hebron

    P

        . Beersheba

(on larger scale)

PALESTINE

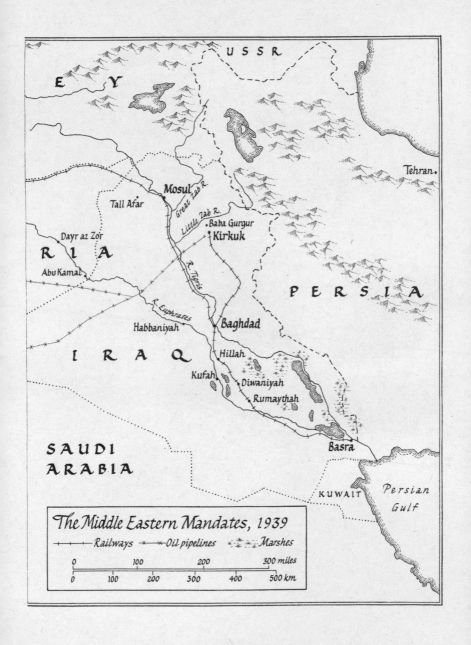

U S S R

E Y

Mosul

Tall Afar

Great Zab R.

Little Zab R.

Dayr az Zor

•Baba Gurgur

Kirkuk

R I A

Abu Kamal

R. Tigris

Tehran.

P E R S I A

R. Euphrates

Habbaniyah•

Baghdad

I R A Q

•Hillah

Kufah•

•Diwaniyah

•Rumaythah

SAUDI
ARABIA

Basra

KUWAIT

*Persian
Gulf*

The Middle Eastern Mandates, 1939

+—+—+ *Railways*   ×—×—× *Oil pipelines*   *Marshes*

| 0 | | 100 | | 200 | | 300 miles |
| 0 | 100 | 200 | 300 | 400 | 500 km |

PROLOGUE

IN THE SUMMER OF 2007 I CAME ACROSS A SENTENCE IN A
newly declassified British government report that made my eyes
bulge. Written by an officer in the British security service, MI5, in
early 1945 but never published until now, it solved a mystery that
had been puzzling the government. Who was financing and arming
the Jewish terrorists who were then trying to end British rule in
Palestine? The officer, just back from a visit to the Middle East, provided an answer that was astonishing. The terrorists, he reported,
'would seem to be receiving support from the French'.

Adding that he had spoken to his counterparts in Britain's secret
intelligence service, MI6, the officer continued: 'We ... know from
"Top Secret" sources that French officials in the Levant have been
clandestinely selling arms to the Hagana* and we have received
recent reports of their intention to stir up strife within Palestine'. In
other words, while the British were fighting and dying to liberate
France, their supposed allies the French were secretly backing Jewish
efforts to kill British soldiers and officials in Palestine.

France's extraordinary move marked the climax of a struggle for
the control of the Middle East that had been going on for thirty
years. In 1915 Britain and France, wartime allies then too, tried to
resolve the tensions that their rival ambitions in the region were
causing. In the secret Sykes–Picot agreement they split the Ottomans'
Middle Eastern empire between them by a diagonal line in the sand

* A Jewish militia

that ran from the Mediterranean Sea coast to the mountains of the Persian frontier. Territory north of this arbitrary line would go to France; most of the land south of it would go to Britain, for the two powers could not agree over the future of Palestine. The compromise, which neither power liked, was that the Holy Land should have an international administration.

Crude empire-building of this type had been common in the nineteenth century, but it was already unpopular by the time that the Sykes–Picot agreement was signed. Chief among its critics was the American president Woodrow Wilson. When the United States declared war on Germany in 1917 he criticised European imperialism and proposed that, when the war was over, subject and stateless peoples should be able to choose their own destinies instead.

In this new atmosphere, the British urgently needed a new basis for their claim to half the Middle East. Already in control of Egypt, they quickly realised that, by publicly supporting Zionist aspirations to make Palestine a Jewish state, they could secure the exposed east flank of the Suez Canal while dodging accusations that they were land-grabbing. What seemed at the time to be an ingenious way to outmanoeuvre France has had devastating repercussions ever since.

The British knew from the outset that this move risked causing deep anger in the Muslim world, but they were confident that they could overcome it. They believed that the Arabs would recognise the economic advantages of Jewish immigration and that the Jews would long be grateful to Britain for helping them realise their dream. Both assumptions proved to be wrong. When Jewish immigration triggered Arab outrage, British attempts to keep the peace by slowing change swiftly exasperated the Jews.

Under mandates granted by the League of Nations, Britain took control of Palestine, Transjordan and Iraq; France, Lebanon and Syria. Both powers were supposed to steer these embryonic countries to rapid independence, but they immediately began to drag their feet. The Arabs reacted angrily as the freedom they had been promised continually receded before them like a mirage. The British and the French blamed one another's policies for the opposition they each began to face. Each refused to help the other address violent Arab opposition because they knew that they would only make themselves more unpopular by doing so. For almost two years in the 1920s, the British ignored frequent French requests to stop the rebels who were fighting their forces inside Syria from using neighbouring, British-controlled, Transjordan as a base. The French in turn shrugged when the British asked them to clamp down on the Arabs who were taking sanctuary in Syria and Lebanon during their insurgency in Palestine in the second half of the 1930s. Lacking neighbourly support, both France and Britain resorted to violent tactics to crush protest that only enraged the Arabs further.

The French had long believed that the British were actively aiding Arab resistance to their rule, but up until the outbreak of the Second World War this suspicion was unfounded. The fall of France in 1940, and the subsequent decision by the French in the Levant to back the Vichy government, ended both sides' reluctance to interfere in one another's problems. In June 1941 British and Free French forces invaded Syria and Lebanon to stop the Vichy administration providing Germany with a springboard for an offensive against Suez. After the Vichy French surrendered a month later, the British government entrusted the government of Lebanon and Syria to the Free French. When that move caused Arab anger British officials decided that the best way to divert attention away from Palestine was to help both Syria and Lebanon gain their independence at French expense. With significant British assistance the Lebanese did so in 1943. The French found out that the British were plotting with the Syrians to the same end the following year.

The French discovered that the Zionists shared their appetite for revenge, for by now Jewish opinion had moved decisively against the British. In 1939 the British, in a bid to placate the Arabs, had imposed tight immigration restrictions that prevented large numbers of Jews fleeing Nazi Germany from reaching safety in Palestine. When news of the systematic nature and the scale of the Holocaust emerged, many Jews decided that it was time to throw the British out. Britain's appeasement of the Arabs' terrorism before the war had shown that violence worked. As this book reveals, the French now secretly offered support to Zionist terrorists who shared their determination to drive the British out of Palestine.

What makes this venomous rivalry between Britain and France so important is that it fuelled today's Arab–Israeli conflict. Britain's use of the Zionists to thwart French ambitions in the Middle East led to a dramatic escalation in tensions between the Arabs and the Jews. But it was the French who played a vital part in the creation of the state of Israel, by helping the Jews organise the large-scale immigration and devastating terrorism that finally engulfed the bankrupt British mandate in 1948. This book tries to explain how matters came to such a pass.

PART ONE

THE CARVE-UP: 1915–1919

The British proclaim martial law in Jerusalem, 11 December 1917. Days earlier their government had declared its support for a Jewish national home as a way of advancing British interests across the region. © Imperial War Museum, HU 69886

I

VERY PRACTICAL POLITICS

LATE IN THE MORNING OF 16 DECEMBER 1915, A PROMISING young politician named Sir Mark Sykes hurried into Downing Street for a meeting. The prime minister had summoned the thirty-six-year-old baronet to advise him and his war cabinet on how they might resolve a row about the future of the Ottoman Empire that looked as if it could tear Britain's fragile alliance with France apart. 'By extraordinary luck,' Sykes put it afterwards, 'I was allowed to make a statement to the war council.'[1] What he said was to shape the modern Middle East.

Sykes's surprise at being called to Number 10 was genuine, for he had managed to carve himself a role as the government's chief adviser on Middle Eastern matters in the space of just four years.[2] Elected as the Conservative Member of Parliament for the Yorkshire port of Hull in 1911, he staked his claim to be an expert on the Ottoman Empire in his maiden speech. In it he described a recent visit to North Africa, then still in Ottoman hands, and declared that he believed 'a strong and united Turkish Empire' was 'as important to English commerce and strategy now' as it had been in Disraeli's time, thirty years before.[3] But when war broke out in 1914, the Ottomans had joined Germany to fight Britain and France, and Sykes had been forced to change his mind.

To the meeting with the war council Sykes brought a map and a three-page précis of what he was about to say. This document survives among the paperwork he left when, three years later, he died from influenza at the age of just thirty-nine. His distinctive, muscular but juvenile handwriting gives it the look of a schoolboy's last-minute revision notes, but it was by far the most significant thing he ever wrote. For the *tour d'horizon* it sketched helped him convince the cabinet that they must urgently reach agreement with France on how they should divide the Ottoman Empire between them, and that he was the man to mastermind that deal.

'He is certainly a very capable fellow, with plenty of ideas, but at the same time painstaking and careful,' one minister reported afterwards of Sykes.[4] But in truth the genial MP was less expert on his subject than he led the cabinet to believe. Sykes's reputation as an authority on the Middle East rested on a series of books that he had written on the region, the latest being a two-inch-thick tome that he had published earlier that year. *The Caliphs' Last Heritage* was part history of the rise of Islam as a political force, part dyspeptic diary of his pre-war travels through the Ottoman Empire. Spiced with Arabic phrases and comical dialogue, the book implied a deeper understanding than its author truly had. Sykes did not try to puncture that illusion. That day he left the prime minister and his colleagues under the impression that he was fluent in both Arabic and Turkish. In fact he could speak neither.[5]

The book and its author's breezy self-assurance were both the fruit of an extraordinary upbringing. Sykes had been born into a dysfunctional landed Yorkshire family and made his first visit to the Middle East with his parents, the eccentric Sir Tatton and the alcoholic Lady Jessica, at the age of just eleven. Sir Tatton, obsessive about church architecture, the maintenance of his body at a constant temperature and milk pudding, was sixty-four; Lady Jessica, who was barely half his age, was having an affair with their tour guide. Mark Sykes was their only child.

The year was 1890. The Sykes family visited Egypt, which Britain had seized from the Ottomans eight years earlier, and then went on to Jerusalem and the Lebanon, still then in Turkish hands. For Sykes, the sense of travelling back in time was mesmerising. It was also a distraction from his parents' unhappy marriage, which culminated in 1897 with a toe-curling court case that revealed their respective peccadilloes. During this period, Sykes escaped to the Middle East repeatedly, first as an undergraduate, then as a young honorary attaché at the British embassy in the Ottoman capital, Constantinople. Recounting how he had shot the lock off the door of an abandoned caravanserai so that he could stay there overnight, he gained a reputation as an intrepid, if rather free-spending, tourist. When he bumped into another traveller, Gertrude Bell, in Jerusalem and admitted what he had paid for horses, she made a mental note to arrange her journey 'so as not to fall in with him, bless him, for if I know the East, prices will double all along his route'.[6]

Like many travel writers, Sykes liked to pretend that he was going into unknown territory. He chose his routes, he claimed, by 'following his nose over those portions of the map which were the whitest or most rich in notes of interrogation and dotted lines'.[7] The sight of other Europeans spoiled the view. While Bell, like many other contemporaries, found Sykes 'most amusing', Sykes was much less pleased to come across Miss Bell. 'Confound the silly chattering windbag of conceited, gushing, flat-chested, man-woman, globetrotting, rump-wagging, blethering ass,' he ranted to his wife.[8]

The Ottoman Empire was by then 'going downhill', as Sykes had put it in that first parliamentary speech. After the sultan's government went bankrupt in 1876 the British government abandoned a fifty-year-old policy of supporting the Ottomans' integrity and independence as a bulwark against other powers' ambitions. In 1878 Britain seized Cyprus and, four years later, Egypt and the Suez Canal in order to secure the route to India. As the canal turned into the major artery for Britain's growing eastern commerce, Egypt became the fulcrum of the British Empire.

While British investors took what was left of their money and ran, following the Ottoman default, the French moved in to replace them. The French already enjoyed significant prestige within the Ottoman Empire through their religious institutions, which ran dozens of schools that were better and more popular than their Ottoman equivalents. In an attempt to take advantage of the Turks' decrepitude, they now bought up most of the Ottoman government debt, gambling more than their own government's annual revenue on the Ottomans' survival.[9] But the 'Young Turks', who seized power in a coup in 1909, failed to stop the rot. They lost Libya and the empire's remaining European possessions in the Balkans three years later.

The Ottoman Empire's centre of gravity now shifted significantly eastwards. Besides Turkey itself, the Ottomans now controlled only Syria and Palestine, Iraq and the coastal fringes of the Arabian peninsula. And yet, despite the Ottomans' decay, the sultan remained influential across the wider Sunni Muslim world as the caliph, or successor, to the Prophet Muhammad and guardian of the three holiest cities in Islam: Mecca, Medina and Jerusalem. This was the caliphs' last heritage, but even there the Ottomans faced discontent from increasingly self-confident Arabs who wanted greater autonomy or even independence from the dynasty that had ruled them for four hundred years.

Sykes's travels through the empire coincided exactly with this era and, not surprisingly, in his latest book he portrayed the Ottomans as moribund. To reinforce his argument he included sublime descriptions of the squalor that he encountered in the famous cities of the Ottomans' eastern lands. In Aleppo, a city where 'ruinous modern buildings clung for support to the ancient and more solid edifices', he found that 'dirt and disease reigned in its crowded and crumbling bazaars; decay and poverty were the most notable characteristics'.[10] In Damascus he was assailed by 'packs of filthy dogs . . . ragged soldiers, yelling muleteers, greedy antika sellers', and dismayed by the 'ill-appointed hotels, tough mutton and rank butter'.[11] He saved his deepest opprobrium for Mosul, a 'foul nest of corruption, vice, disorder and disease', in which 'the new houses are as ramshackle, as insanitary, as stinking as the old; the old as ugly, as uninteresting, and as repulsive as the new'.[12] The souks there were 'ankle deep in decaying guts and offal; the kennels run with congealing blood and stinking dye in sluggish and iridescent streams, nauseous to behold and abominable in odour'.

Sykes sounded appalled, and yet in truth he did not want this colourful, decaying society to disappear, depriving him of the glimpse into the medieval world it gave him on his holidays. As the influence of jockeying foreign powers began to manifest itself, he was delighted that 'the dividers, T-square, and drawing board of the French engineer have been unable to crush out the originality of the illiterate Syrian Arab'.[13] He ignored the fact that the railways, which the Ottomans were building with German help, were making cheap travel a possibility for Arabs whose horizons had previously been limited by how far they could walk or ride. Instead, he claimed, the steam engine had brought 'not a single virtue' and only a 'host of new vices' that included 'alcohol, dirty pictures, phonographs and drinking saloons'.[14] How a postal service, the telegraph, the railway, a thriving newspaper industry and growing literacy were about to change the Arab world for ever, he either could not see or did not want to say.

Sykes 'allows his prepossessions to run away with his judgement', wrote one critic, but beyond academic circles the shortcomings of his book – in particular its underestimation of the Turks – were largely overlooked.[15] As another reviewer commented, 'the facts which he has collected will be of the highest value when the settlement of the Eastern question comes to be undertaken'.[16] *The Caliphs' Last Heritage* helped earn Sykes the nickname 'the Mad Mullah' across Whitehall, a place on a committee considering the future of the Middle East, and now a summons to Number 10 to address the 'Eastern question', the long-running argument over who would take over when finally the Ottomans collapsed, and to which the British and the French were each certain they were the only answer.

Inside Number 10, four men in particular took a close interest in what Sykes had to say. The prime minister, Asquith, who was recovering from a nervous breakdown, did not want the row with the French to escalate. Kitchener, the minister for war, whose face and finger were now emblazoned on recruiting posters on streets across the land, had previously run Egypt. Lloyd George, the quicksilver minister for munitions, was violently anti-Turkish and liked the idea of further imperial expansion at the Ottomans' expense. Balfour, the former Conservative prime minister, now at the Admiralty, felt the British Empire had reached its limits, and did not.

'I feel we ought to settle with France as soon as possible, and get a definite understanding about Syria,' Sykes proposed.[17]

'What sort of an arrangement would you like to have with the French?' asked Balfour.

'I should like to retain for ourselves such country south of Haifa,' replied Sykes, gesturing to his map.

Balfour looked sceptical. 'We have always regarded this 90 or 100 miles of desert upon her eastern side as a stronghold of Egypt; now you propose still further east of that to give us a bit of inhabited and cultivated country for which we should be responsible. At first sight it looks as if that would weaken and not strengthen our position in Egypt.'

Kitchener came to Sykes's defence. 'I think that what Sir Mark Sykes means is that the line will commence at the sea-coast at Haifa. These Arabs' – he jabbed at the Arabian peninsula – 'will then come under our control.'

'What do you mean to give exactly?' pressed Balfour, referring to the French.

Sykes sliced his finger across the map that lay before them on the table. 'I should like to draw a line from the "e" in Acre to the last "k" in Kirkuk,' he said.

Lloyd George was enthusiastic about the destruction of the Ottoman Empire. 'Do you propose that this should be the first step before you take any military action?'

Sykes did not want to tread on Kitchener's toes. 'I think it is essential that we should know where we are.'

Asquith had already warned of the dangers of disturbing 'a hornet's nest of Arab tribes' by intervening in the Middle East but, exhausted, he was happy to delegate the matter and liked the simple line in the sand that Sykes had drawn.[18] 'We must have a political deal,' he said, to end the meeting. 'We must come to terms with the French, which means we must come to terms diplomatically.'

'I think I carried the day,' an exhilarated Sykes wrote afterwards to a colleague; 'you will observe I did not soar beyond very practical politics.'[19]

The fact that Britain and France had almost come to blows over a similar territorial dispute less than twenty years before was what made Asquith and his colleagues so anxious to resolve the question of what would happen to the Ottoman Empire, assuming that they won the war. During the closing stages of the scramble for Africa in the 1890s it had been the ownership of the headwaters of the river Nile that was at stake. As a junior minister at that time, the current foreign secretary, Sir Edward Grey, had warned the French in 1895 that the British government would interpret any move to claim the river's source as 'an unfriendly act'.[20] The French had mistakenly thought this threat was empty, because the British had lost control of the Sudan to the Mahdi* a decade earlier. Soon afterwards they dispatched an expedition from west Africa to claim the upper reaches of the Nile. Its aim was to render British rule downstream in Egypt unsustainable.

Aware of French ambitions, the British embarked on the reconquest of the Sudan. In August 1898, just as Kitchener was nearing Khartoum, the French reached Fashoda, a flyblown outpost on the upper Nile in the far south of the country, where they planted the *tricolore*. There was outrage in London when the news broke that 'eight French adventurers' had 'claimed a territory twice as large as France', to quote Winston Churchill, then a reporter with Kitchener's force. The British government hurriedly sent Kitchener south to confront the French, and mobilised the fleet.[21] The French government was forced into a climbdown that was all the more humiliating because it had engineered the crisis in the first place.

Unnerved by how the Fashoda incident had brought them to the brink of war, both sides reached an 'Entente Cordiale' in 1904. The French reluctantly acknowledged Britain's rule in Egypt and the Sudan and, in exchange, the British recognised French claims in Morocco. In deference to French sensibilities they also renamed the site of the unfortunate encounter, expunging Fashoda from the map.

As its prim sound suggests, the Entente Cordiale was a shotgun marriage made necessary because Germany's finger appeared to be inching closer to the trigger. Its conclusion did not end the suspicions that existed between the two old rivals. The French were certain that their ally's appetite for the Ottomans' remaining territory was anything but satiated. After noticing where British officials like Sykes tended to take their holidays, at the end of 1912 they pressed the British government to confirm that it had no designs on Syria. The

---

* Muhammad Ahmad, a Sudanese Sufi shaykh, claimed that he was Mahdi, a messianic figure whose appearance is believed by many Muslims to herald the Day of Judgement.

British, who then thought Syria an empty, worthless place, were happy to oblige. Only later did they recognise the signal they had sent out by doing so. 'When we disclaimed any political aspirations for ourselves in Syria the French took it that they might have them,' the British ambassador to Paris later grumbled.[22]

On the outbreak of war in 1914 Britain joined forces with its erstwhile rivals, France and Russia, to fight the Germans and their Ottoman allies. But when the western front rapidly became dead-locked the two western powers began to argue about strategy, and recently buried jealousies quickly began to re-emerge. While the French favoured an immediate all-out attack on the western front, the British wanted to train the volunteers who were responding to Kitchener's call to arms before committing them to a great offensive. In the meantime 'Easterners' inside the British government pro-posed that they should deal with the weaker Ottomans instead, not least because the sultan had just used his authority as caliph to call upon Muslims across the world to join him in a holy war against his enemies. With a hundred million Muslim subjects spread across their empire, the British were the obvious target of the sultan's call.

The British had faced and crushed local uprisings inspired by Islam in India and the Sudan in the years before the war. They took the sultan's threat, which was of a different magnitude, extremely seriously. Within weeks of his declaration of jihad, the 'Easterners' came up with a plan to seize the Ottoman Empire by the throat and punch it in the guts by simultaneously landing troops at Gallipoli and Alexandretta. Gallipoli was not far from the Ottoman capital Constantinople; Alexandretta, in the crook of the Mediterranean where modern-day Turkey joins Syria, lay near the railway connect-ing Constantinople to Baghdad and Damascus, the main administrative centres in the Ottomans' Arab empire.

Sykes was certain that this plan had war-winning potential. In a typically energetic letter to Churchill, who had moved into politics and was by now First Lord of the Admiralty, Sykes argued that once the Ottomans surrendered the Germans would be far more vulnera-ble. Addressing his letter to 'the only man I know who will take risks', he wondered: 'Could you by June be fighting towards Vienna, you would have got your knife somewhere near the monster's vitals', enticing Churchill to throw his weight behind the plan.[23] But longer-term considerations drew others to this scheme. 'The only place from which a fleet can operate against Egypt is Alexandretta,' explained a junior intelligence officer based in Cairo at that time. 'It is a splendid natural naval base (which *we* don't want but which no one else can have without detriment to us).'[24] The name of this young strategist? It was T. E. Lawrence.

The Alexandretta scheme alarmed the French ambassador in Cairo. Suspecting that the British were reneging on their 1912 commitment about Syria, he warned his government of their ally's likely motives. On 8 February 1915 the French foreign minister, Théophile Delcassé, reminded Grey of their two-year-old agreement and force-fully asked him to stop his officials plotting.[25]

Tall, thin and tired, and perpetually torn between the lure of power in Westminster and the solitary pleasures of fly-fishing on the chalk streams of southern England, Grey was the man who had warned France not to trespass on the Nile two decades earlier. But in the intervening period his attitude towards the French had changed completely. By the time he became Britain's foreign secretary in 1905, he had reached the conclusion that the Germans were now the greater threat and that a pact with France was necessary to defeat them. That conviction, and exhaustion after ten years' trying to avert war through intricate and often rather secretive diplomacy, now shaped his decision to concede to Delcassé.

'I think it is important to let the French have what they want,' Grey wrote soon after Delcassé had complained. 'It will be fatal to cordial cooperation in the Mediterranean and perhaps everywhere if we arouse their suspicions as to anything in the region of Syria.'[26] He then ordered British officials in Egypt to stop pressing for the Alexandretta plan. 'It would mean a break with France,' he repeated a few days later, 'if we put forward any claims in Syria and Lebanon.'[27]

French pressure had forced the British to drop a brilliant plan. As the German field marshal, von Hindenburg, admitted after-wards, 'Perhaps not the whole course of the war, but certainly the fate of our Ottoman Ally, could have been settled out of hand, if England had secured a decision in that region, or even seriously attempted it. Possession of the country south of the Taurus [mountains] would have been lost to Turkey at a blow if the English had succeeded in landing in the Gulf of Alexandretta.'[28] Instead, as a consequence of French concerns, six weeks later an ill-fated, predominantly British force landed in the Dardanelles. It was 25 April 1915. Constantinople, and victory, were just one hundred and fifty miles away.

The French and British both anticipated the division of the spoils. In France a small but thick-skinned group of imperialists, the Comité de l'Asie Française, began to put pressure on Delcassé to lay claim to Syria and Palestine. Many of the Comité's supporters were diplomats working at the French foreign ministry on the Quai d'Orsay, who were concerned that the French government had not announced any formal 'war aims'. 'We may be certain that the others will not take the trouble to mark out our place for us,' the Comité argued in March 1915. 'Anyone who appears insufficiently determined to sit down risks seeing his chair removed.'[29]

This was a familiar argument from the Comité, which had traditionally relied heavily on the French public's Anglophobia to rouse support for its own agenda. Imperial expansion, it had always argued, denied the rapacious British gains at French expense. The wartime alliance with Britain now made such a line awkward, and so the Comité's secretary-general, an aristocratic diplomat named Robert de Caix, reached for the history books to make his case. He argued that France had a 'hereditary' right to Syria and Palestine because it was 'the land of the Crusades . . . where Western activity has been so French-dominated since the beginning of the Middle Ages that all the Europeans who live there are still called "Franks"'.[30] Disregarding the minor detail that the word 'Frank' was now used pejoratively to mean 'foreigner' by the Arabs, who had expelled the last of the crusaders six centuries before, de Caix brushed off the 'latent discord of race and religion' that his forebears had left behind and insisted that three centuries of sporadic bloodshed had in fact established 'a very special bond of union between the Franks of France and the world of Islam'.[31]

Such waffle bounced off Delcassé. Although he was willing to remind Grey to uphold the 1912 agreement, he did not want to strain the Entente any more than did the British foreign secretary over a relatively minor matter like Syria. In this he had the full support of two of his senior ambassadors, Maurice Bompard and Paul Cambon. Bompard, who had been envoy to Constantinople until the beginning of the war, dismissed Syria as 'a few uncultivated hectares'; Cambon, who had been appointed ambassador to London immediately after Fashoda to draw a line under the affair, saw no advantage in laying claim to a region that was, in his opinion, home only to 'a bunch of wild, thieving bandits'.[32]

The Comité, therefore, was obliged to try a different route. In May that year it arranged for its strongest ally in the French Senate, a corpulent lawyer named Etienne Flandin, to issue a report that it hoped would increase the pressure on Delcassé. Flandin's blustering effort makes entertaining reading. In it he needled the French foreign minister for the 'regrettable lethargy' of his diplomats in failing to defend French interests in Syria, and called on his government to 'save from death millions of fellow humans being hunted down by the Red Sultan's mercenaries'.[33] He listed the economic benefits of taking control of the country – everything from the healing powers of thermal springs to perfumes from flower oils and, in passing, petroleum. He promised renewed fertility once ancient Roman irrigation channels were rediscovered. He even drew attention to the fact that Syria could provide a base from where the French might blockade Suez. But he too failed to move Delcassé, although his accusation of inactivity did in due course sting.

Meanwhile in Britain the government formed a committee to decide which bits of Ottoman territory it wanted; Sykes found himself the youngest member of this taskforce. More familiar with the subject matter and less burdened with responsibility than the other members, he did most of its work. But his initial proposal, which was to divide the Ottoman Empire into northern Russian, central French and southern British sections, did not find favour with his colleagues. Together, they eventually agreed that the best way forward was to carve up the vanquished empire into provinces that Britain would seek to influence, rather than control directly. Sykes was dispatched to the Middle East and India to sell this idea to British officials there.

What Sykes heard when he arrived in Cairo persuaded him to resort to his original idea. At the beginning of the war the British government had sent an Indian Army force to seize the vital oil refineries at Abadan, on the southern coast of Persia and the nearest major port, Basra, in what is now Iraq. The officials whom Sykes met persuaded him to back a madcap scheme to link the Basra bridgehead with Egypt, establishing a permanent British cordon across a region he himself had once described as 'one great stretch of dead, forgotten desolation', a blunt if accurate depiction of what is now northern Saudi Arabia.[34]

Astonishingly, before Sykes set out for India he revealed this idea to French diplomats at a meeting on 28 July. After reassuring them that the British government had no designs on Syria, he then told his counterparts that his government was planning to build a railway between Basra and the Suez Canal once the war was over, and wanted control of the territory over which it ran. As the most direct route was not viable because drifting sand would clog the track, he explained that the railway would have to trace a huge arc through the stony desert further north, via Damascus, to reach the sea at Haifa. By way of consolation he offered the French Alexandretta and the nearby port of Adana as well as a share of Palmyra, the oasis in the Syrian desert that had once been a thriving Roman city. No doubt perturbed by Sykes's frugal definition of what constituted Syria, the French wired a full account of 'English designs' to the Quai d'Orsay in Paris the same day.[35]

Thanks to its members inside the Quai d'Orsay, the Comité de l'Asie Française found out immediately about Sykes's plan, which at last provided it with the ammunition that it needed. It reacted by issuing a counterproposal that placed Syria and Palestine entirely under French control. 'We should have to do no more in the Levant than reap the harvest of seven centuries of French endeavours,' it insisted, calling for negotiations with Britain.[36]

Delcassé, already under fire in the French parliament for failing to show more energetic action, now buckled under pressure. He told his ambassador in London, Cambon, that Sykes's ambitions could not be realised 'without the risk of one day posing a problem to Anglo-French relations'.[37] Cambon duly informed the British on 31

August 1915 that his government 'would not tolerate any infringe-
ment' of its 'rights' in Syria and Cilicia – the adjacent province, now
in southern Turkey.[38]

If that sounded uncharacteristic of Cambon, it was. The ambassador personally questioned the wisdom of claiming Syria, and his
forthright warning had in fact been drafted by a new attaché who
had arrived from Paris days earlier to join the French mission. Its
author, François Georges-Picot, had been France's consul in Beirut
immediately before the war, but it was his other affiliation that was
rather more important in the circumstances. He too was a member
of the Comité de l'Asie Française. Fair-haired, tall and angular – in
physique and character alike – Georges-Picot bore a long-standing
grudge against the British. His appearance in the British capital her-
alded a much more hard-nosed French approach.

2

MONSIEUR PICOT

FRANÇOIS GEORGES-PICOT'S BELIEF IN FRANCE'S IMPERIAL 'civilising mission' ran in his blood. Both he and his brother Charles were members of the Comité de l'Asie Française, which was pressing France's claim to Syria, and their late father Georges Picot had been a founder of another pressure group, the Comité de l'Afrique Française, which had been launched a quarter of a century earlier to spur the government to claim those parts of Africa that were 'still without a master'.[1]

Georges Picot had been an eminent lawyer, member of the Institut Français and author of a biography of Gladstone, the prime minister who had authorised the British seizure of Egypt. His son François Georges-Picot took his illustrious father's full name as his surname, as if to leave no one in any doubt about whose son he was. The British, in whom Georges-Picot's 'fluting voice' and condescending manner triggered an allergic reaction, pointedly ignored this affectation and called him plain old 'Monsieur Picot'.[2] But the French diplomat appears to have been unbothered. He was 'one of those rare Frenchmen', wrote a rattled British diplomat, 'who seemed never to have been young'.[3]

But the forty-three-year-old Georges-Picot had been young once. As a student he initially followed in his father's footsteps and read law at university. Then, at the age of twenty-eight, he suddenly changed career. The timing of his decision to become a diplomat is

crucial, for it took place in 1898: the same year as the Fashoda incident, a debacle that his father's pressure group had helped to cause.
'Fashoda' and its consequences dominated Georges-Picot's early
years at the Quai d'Orsay, and the humbling episode left its mark.
Having lost faith in the French government's determination to
defend the national interest, he and his contemporaries decided that
they would deal with Britain more forcefully in future. One British
politician later summed up their approach as 'to give nothing and to
claim everything'.[4]

Whereas Mark Sykes appeared oblivious to the political implications of the modernisation of the Arab world, Georges-Picot was
well aware of them. While serving as France's consul in the booming
port of Beirut immediately before the First World War he had
received letters from educated and ambitious young Arab army officers, lawyers and journalists who wanted France to help them
achieve their goal of autonomy within the Ottoman Empire. The
Arabs had even held a congress to discuss this aim in Paris in 1913,
but the French government was unwilling to help them because of its
financial stake in the Ottomans' endurance, and Georges-Picot could
only file the hopeful approaches carefully away.

In June 1914, Georges-Picot was sent an Arab leaflet demanding
complete independence for Syria that convinced him that his government's policy had to change. Believing that the flyer had 'more
chance than in the past of waking an echo in the souls of its readers',
he warned his masters that, if they did not help the Arabs, others –
by whom he meant the British – would.[5] His government, however,
did nothing. In desperation, when it looked likely that France and
the Ottomans were about to go to war that autumn, he secretly
arranged for the Greek government to supply Christians in the
Lebanon with fifteen thousand rifles and two million rounds of
ammunition. When war broke out, he was obliged to leave.

Georges-Picot wrongly expected that France would rapidly invade
to assist the Lebanese uprising that he hoped the arms and ammunition would start. On this assumption, rather than burn the letters he
had been sent by Arab correspondents, he naively entrusted the keys
to the consulate and its incriminating archives to the American
consul. As he hurried aboard a ship to leave Beirut, his parting shot

to the local employees he left behind was 'See you in a fortnight.'⁶

The invasion never happened, and the prospect of a revolt in the Lebanon evaporated when the Ottomans seized the French consulate's files and, because of Georges-Picot's carelessness, were able to round up and execute many of his former correspondents and their friends. Back in Paris and reunited with other similarly minded colleagues, the consul was left to orchestrate the Comité de l'Asie Française's efforts to oblige Delcassé to confront the 'Eastern question', both in parliament and among the businessmen of Lyon and Marseille who stood to profit from access to Syria's silk industry. Such was this lobby's growing power that, when Delcassé finally decided that he had no choice but to raise the matter with the British, it was Georges-Picot rather than the sceptical former ambassador to Constantinople, Bompard, whom he dispatched to London in August 1915.

Georges-Picot soon felt able to report an improvement in the situation to his allies in Paris and elsewhere. The British, he told his old friend the Cairo ambassador Albert Defrance, 'now have in their hands a text setting out our demands, and can no longer pretend to ignore them'.⁷ But although he was correct to say that he had forced the British government to address the matter that so exercised the Comité, what he did not know was that his British counterparts could no longer view France's demand in isolation either. For, unknown to him, but just as he had feared, they had been secretly making their own overtures to the Arabs. The upshot was another, overlapping territorial claim, this time from Sharif Husein of Mecca.

The British governor of Egypt, the high commissioner Sir Henry McMahon, had quietly approached Husein after it became clear that the Gallipoli landings had failed to achieve the knockout blow that Sykes and others had intended. A slight and cautious man with a reputation for being rather lazy, McMahon had served most of his career in India. He was posted to Egypt only as a stopgap after Kitchener, the previous incumbent, was recalled to London to head the War Office. McMahon felt uncomfortable with the responsibility he had been given, not least because he knew that as soon as British forces withdrew from the Dardanelles the Turks would counter-attack, and their target would probably be Egypt. This prospect raised another fear. Egypt's economy had been badly affected by the war, and its mostly Muslim Arab population was the closest and most susceptible audience of the sultan's call for jihad. By mid-1915 McMahon and his advisers were frightened that a Turkish attack on the canal might easily provide the spark that lit an Arab uprising against them in the Nile delta.

It was another self-confident young man, the devious, balding Ronald Storrs, who came up with the ingenious idea of using Sharif Husein to blunt the force of the jihad. Storrs, who was McMahon's Oriental Secretary, had worked in Britain's high commission in Cairo for several years. He knew that Husein's relations with the Ottomans were tense because just before the war the sharif's son, Abdullah, had directly asked him whether Britain might supply the family with arms to enable it to overthrow the Turks. Before the war, the British could not possibly help; now they could. At Storrs's instigation McMahon secretly made contact again with Husein, hinting that British aid would follow if he rose up against the enemy they now shared.

Storrs argued that the turbaned, white-bearded and austere Sharif Husein was ideally suited to undermine the sultan's resonant call for holy war. Not only was Husein ruler of the city that was the axis of the Muslim world – his telephone number was Mecca 1 – but as a 'sharif' he was recognised as a direct descendant of the Prophet Muhammad, an ancestry the sultan could not claim. Storrs also suggested that it was in Britain's imperial interest to encourage Husein's ambition to take the sultan's place as caliph. After the Ottoman Empire had collapsed, he wrote, Husein could be 'a hereditary spiritual Pope with no temporal power', dependent on the British for income and protection and a proxy to spread British influence in the Middle East.[8]

This unscrupulous attitude shaped McMahon's reaction when Husein responded to his overture in August 1915, just as Georges-Picot arrived in London to press the French claim to Syria. When the sharif unexpectedly demanded that Britain support his claim to a large empire encompassing not just the Arabian peninsula but Syria, Iraq and Palestine as well, McMahon initially refused to take him seriously. Storrs, who frequently haggled for antiques and carpets in the Cairo bazaar, regarded Husein as a salesman whose opening price he could in due course barter down. But when the British high commissioner tried to postpone discussion of the demand, Husein reacted sharply. 'The fact is,' the sharif retorted early in September, 'the proposed frontiers and boundaries represent not the suggestions of one individual whose claim might well await the conclusion of the War, but the demands of our people who believe that those frontiers form the minimum necessary to the establishment of the new order for which they are striving.'[9]

Husein's expansive claim to represent the Arab world would have sounded preposterous had it not been corroborated by another source. In an uncanny coincidence, just as his letter arrived in Cairo a young Arab officer in the Ottoman army named Muhammad al-Faruqi deserted to the British at Gallipoli. In a series of interviews with British officers in Cairo, including Sykes, who by now was on his way back home from India, al-Faruqi claimed that almost all his fellow Arab officers were members of an underground Arab nationalist movement. According to him the movement was at that very moment considering whether to throw its weight behind the Ottomans and the Germans, or to transfer allegiance to the British. Al-Faruqi was exaggerating wildly, but the British had no choice but to take him seriously when he disclosed that he knew they were secretly negotiating with Husein. Given the secrecy of that correspondence, it appeared that both al-Faruqi's far-reaching Arab network and Husein's dramatic claim to represent the wider Arab world were true.

Al-Faruqi's revelation forced McMahon to reassess the sharif's influence. On 18 October the British high commissioner tersely warned London in a telegram that 'the Arab party are at [a] parting of the ways' and that he therefore needed to raise his offer to Husein urgently.[10] He continued: 'unless we can give them immediate assurance of [a] nature to satisfy them they will throw themselves into the hands of Germany'. On his return to London Sykes backed up McMahon. He too felt that the Arabs would side with the Ottoman Turks 'in the event of our letting this opportunity go'.[11]

*

The developing situation in Cairo left Sir Edward Grey in an unen-
viable position. Unknown to one another, first Georges-Picot and
now Husein were asking him to recognise conflicting claims to overlapping tracts of the Middle East, obliging him to choose between
them. He was being advised by one of his officials that 'The position
must be clearly understood from both the French and the Arab side
from the outset, or we shall be heading straight for serious trouble,'
but he could also see that honesty held perils of its own.[12] To favour
the Arabs over the French could jeopardise the Entente; a spurned
Husein might throw the Arabs' weight behind the Ottoman sultan's
jihad.

Grey's diary, as well as rumours he had been hearing, made him
incline towards the French. He was due to meet Cambon to discuss
the French claim to Syria on 21 October, and in the meantime he was
receiving disturbing stories that public support in France for the war
was flagging. Both these factors convinced him that the need not to
annoy the French outweighed the danger of jihad. Having discussed
with his cabinet colleagues what instructions he should give
McMahon (his scribbled form of words was headed with the plain-
tive question, 'Will this do?'), on 20 October he sent a telegram to
Cairo telling the high commissioner to be as vague as possible in his
next letter to the sharif when discussing the north-western – Syrian –
corner of the territory Husein claimed.[13] But, given the speed at
which events were moving, crucially he also left McMahon with
'discretion in the matter as it is urgent and there is not time to discuss
an exact formula ... if something more precise than this is required
you can give it'.[14]

McMahon, unhappy at being passed the buck, closely followed
Grey's advice. Having used al-Faruqi as a sounding board to test
what the sharif might accept, in a letter dated 24 October he offered
Husein a woolly declaration that Britain would recognise his claim
to most of the area he wanted, excluding two of its most fertile
zones. One was the bridgehead at the head of the Persian Gulf which
the British army already occupied. The other was a coastal portion
of Syria coveted by the French which he only sketchily defined. 'I
had necessarily to be vague,' he explained later, 'as on the one hand
HMG disliked being committed to definite future action, and on the

other any detailed definition of our demands would have frightened off the Arab.'[15] The meaning of his wording has been debated ever since, which is not surprising, for it was never intended to be clear.

The evolution of the key sentence in this letter proves that McMahon was deliberately trying to mislead the sharif. Initially he intended to qualify his ability to recognise Husein's claim to the remaining area with the phrase 'in so far as England is free to act without detriment to the interests of her present Allies', but it occurred to him that this caveat might draw Husein's attention and so he toned it down. The final version of the letter stated that, subject to the modifications he had stipulated, 'we accept these limits of boundaries; and in regard to those portions of the territories therein in which Great Britain is free to act without detriment to the interests of her ally France' McMahon said he was 'empowered, in the name of the Government of Great Britain, to give the following assurances ...'

The proviso now sounded like a confirmation that nothing prevented Britain from recognising the Arabs' claim to the remainder of Syria, and had there been a comma between the words 'therein' and 'in which' it would have been, but McMahon quite deliberately omitted any punctuation because he wanted it to mean the opposite. He had, he told the foreign secretary, 'endeavoured to provide for possible French pretensions ... by a general modification to the effect that His Majesty's Government can only give assurances in regard to these territories "in which she can act without detriment to the interests of her ally France"'.[16] His decision to quote the exact phrase he had used suggests a certain smugness about its subtlety, but unfortunately for him the first person foxed by it was Storrs's secret agent and translator, Ruhi. Ruhi's Arabic translation, which was then sent to the sharif, entirely lost this second, qualifying, sense.[17] As a wistful Storrs reflected afterwards, Ruhi was 'a better agent than scholar'.[18]

By the time McMahon had sent this missive to Husein, Grey had seen the French ambassador, Cambon. When they met on 21 October the British foreign secretary proposed to Cambon that France appoint a representative to discuss the future borders of Syria because Britain wanted to back the creation of an independent Arab state, but he did not tell Cambon just how far discussions with Husein had already gone.[19] Cambon, who told Grey that he presumed the French government would be consulted over any dealings with the sharif, sent a report to Paris expressing his delight that Britain's foreign secretary had, by suggesting talks, effectively given 'formal and official recognition of our rights to Syria'.[20] He recommended his new adviser Georges-Picot as the negotiator, because Georges-Picot understood Syrian matters 'better than anyone'.[21]

From this point Georges-Picot became the ventriloquist for the French government's policy in the Middle East. He returned to Paris and anonymously drafted further instructions to Cambon, approving himself as Cambon's negotiator and ordering him to demand a Syria that encompassed Palestine by stretching south to the Egyptian frontier and east to Mosul. As he drily put it, writing his own orders was 'a good way of ensuring that my instructions are satisfactory'.[22] Then he returned to London to execute them.

As Georges-Picot prepared for his imminent confrontation with the British government, the French ambassador in Cairo, Defrance, managed to establish that Husein was in contact with the British by asking al-Faruqi. On 28 October (the very day that McMahon warned London that he had 'reason to suspect' that Defrance had 'wind of the recent interchange of messages between Mecca and ourselves') Defrance sent a report on the correspondence to Paris.[23] Misjudging the likely British response, he told the Quai d'Orsay that he thought McMahon would reject the sharif's demand, because if the French claim to Syria was not enough of a deterrent, Britain's desire to retain control of the area around Basra which they had occupied at the beginning of the war would be.

On 23 November an extraordinarily one-sided meeting took place in Whitehall. On one side of the table was the fair-haired Georges-Picot; arranged along the other were the seven British representatives of the three government departments which had an interest in the Middle East. When the leader of this British delegation, the head of the Foreign Office Sir Arthur Nicolson, told Georges-Picot exactly what the British government had already offered to the sharif, the Frenchman reacted with 'complete incredulity', according to one British witness.[24] Not only was Defrance's assumption that the

British would not concede territory to Husein wrong, but it was clear that the British had never intended to consult their ally before coming to an agreement with Husein.

'To promise the Arabs a large state is to throw dust in their eyes,' replied Georges-Picot, who rapidly regained his composure. 'Such a state will never materialise. You cannot transform a myriad of tribes into a viable whole.'[25] He showed little sympathy to British arguments about the threat of jihad, implying that the danger lay in the unpopularity of British rule in Egypt. In any case, he continued, the chauvinistic French public would never accept the British plan, nor would any government that agreed to it survive. 'Syria was very near the heart of the French,' he told his British counterparts, reminding them that, while they had been distracted by the Gallipoli expedition, France had borne the brunt of the fighting on the western front that year. 'Now, after the expenditure of so many lives, France would never consent to offer independence to the Arabs, though at the beginning of the war she might have done so.'

The meeting broke up with no agreement. Afterwards, the British representatives reconvened in smaller groups to share their frustration about Georges-Picot. They were left open-mouthed by the way in which the Frenchman talked 'as if Syria and even Palestine were as completely theirs as Normandy', and his hint that British rule in Egypt was illegitimate caused outright fury.[26] When the head of British military intelligence in Cairo, Bertie Clayton, received a copy of the minutes of the meeting, he was instantly reminded of Fashoda. He attacked Georges-Picot as 'one of the Anglophobe school of 1898' and dismissed his arguments as 'sentimental trash'.[27]

In London, however, the British quickly realised that they could not easily counter what Georges-Picot had said because he was cleverly playing on a significant vulnerability. The differences in strategy between the two allies meant that the French had sustained vastly greater casualties so far in the war, and the British government fretted constantly about the consequences. As recently as October, Britain's ambassador to Paris Lord Bertie had dismissed as 'travellers' tales' stories about the French 'not persisting and going on with the war *jusqu'au bout*'.[28] But days after Georges-Picot had met the British, Bertie was forced to admit that he had since detected 'an

inclination in *some* Society and Commercial quarters to think that
we are making use of France against Germany for our own sole
benefit and that much greater sacrifices are being made by France
than by England'.[29]

The danger, as the British rapidly appreciated, was that the furtive
nature of McMahon's overtures to Husein seemed only to corroborate the allegation that Britain was single-mindedly pursuing its
imperial ambitions while France sacrificed its soldiers for the
common cause on the western front. By linking the number of
French casualties to France's unwillingness to accept the British proposal Georges-Picot took advantage of this weakness, and the
Entente was too important and yet fragile for the British to dare to
call his bluff. As one general put it through clenched teeth, 'We have
got to keep in with our infernal Allies.'[30]

Alarmed by the reaction they had caused, the British tried to
play down the significance of the letter to Husein, arguing that the
sharif would never manage to claim the prize McMahon had
offered him. Nicolson, who had chaired the meeting with Georges-
Picot, began to echo the Frenchman's criticism of McMahon's offer.
The British diplomat now dismissed the promised Arab state as an
'absurdity' since the Arabs were 'a heap of scattered tribes with no
cohesion and no organisation'.[31] After Cambon complained bitterly
about being kept in the dark about how far the negotiations with
Husein had gone, another cabinet minister, Lord Crewe, directly
reassured him that Britain had 'no intention of arranging that a new
Arab state, if one could be formed, would include the Lebanon or
any part of the world to which the French could lay distinct
claim'.[32]

This speedy retreat left Georges-Picot under the impression that
'What the British want, is only to deceive the Arabs.'[33] On 2
December he reported to the French prime minister, Aristide Briand,
that 'They hope to accomplish this by offering them a lot while
admitting that the building they are constructing will probably not
last beyond the war.'

Briand was alarmed by Georges-Picot's success. Believing that the
acquisition of so much territory would place too great a burden on
the French state, when Georges-Picot next returned to Paris he told

the diplomat to scale back his demands. In particular, France did not need the region around Jerusalem, Briand argued, because it was 'a country of little value, which it is not desirable to acquire'.[34]

That was not how Georges-Picot put his revised negotiating position to the British on his return to London. When he met the British for a second time on 21 December he presented his willingness to accept a reduction in the size of the territory that France would control as a concession he had wrung from his reluctant superiors. Sensing that the British were 'panic-stricken' about the sharif, he demanded that they agree the French sphere of influence would still stretch past the city of Mosul to the river Tigris in the east.[35] Georges-Picot thought he would be able to force this bargain, but he met resistance. The British were willing to acknowledge the French demand for this eastward swathe of country, but in turn they had a request of their own. Contrary to what Lord Crewe had just told Cambon, the British delegation's leader Sir Arthur Nicolson told Georges-Picot that Britain wanted Lebanon to form part of a future Arab state. 'Take our proposition to your government: it won't rightly decline it,' Nicolson told him, tetchily. 'With this you will be in a significantly better position to the one we are in, in Egypt. What more could you want, exactly?'[36]

'You can sense the value of this place. That's exactly why you want it for the Sharif of Mecca,' Georges-Picot replied. He was not going to back down any further. 'You are wasting time that, you and I both know, is precious.' The second meeting, like the first, ended unresolved.

To break the impasse, Nicolson now turned to Sykes who, five days earlier, had impressed the cabinet with his apparent command of the subject and his sweeping division of the Middle East. The up-and-coming politician met Georges-Picot immediately, in private, on the afternoon of the 21st.

A deal along the lines that Sykes had just proposed to the British cabinet was quickly possible. Sykes had failed to see the stirrings of an Arab political consciousness on his travels in the Ottoman Empire before the war and, as one entry in the index of *The Caliphs' Last Heritage* – 'Arab character: *see also* Treachery' – light-heartedly makes clear, he saw no need whatsoever to acknowledge McMahon's earlier offer to Husein. Georges-Picot, who was well aware of the threat that Arab nationalism represented to his country's imperial ambitions, was happy to agree to a proposal that ignored it.[37]

In line with the strategic scheme he had been persuaded to champion earlier that summer in Cairo, Sykes saw his own task as 'to get [the] Arabs to concede as much as possible to [the] French, and to get our Haifa outlet and Palestine included in our sphere of enterprise in the form of a French concession to us'.[38] With this in mind he was happy to concede Mosul, a city that anyway he hated, and the Lebanon, to Georges-Picot.

On Palestine, however, the two men could not agree. Although Georges-Picot had been told by Briand not to pursue the claim, it was so central to the Parti Colonial's rhetoric that he refused to let it go. 'Any reference seems to excite memories of all grievances from Joan of Arc to Fashoda,' Sykes groaned after he had raised the subject.[39] Eventually the two men agreed that Palestine would come under international control. It was a compromise that neither of them liked – Georges-Picot because 'Nothing seems more likely to produce conflict in the future', Sykes because of the hole it left in his scheme of imperial defence – but it opened the way for the deal they reached on 3 January 1916.[40]

In the Sykes–Picot agreement, as the arrangement became known, the two men paid lip service to the promise of Arab independence that McMahon had made to Husein, but then used Sykes's line in the sand – from Acre on the Mediterranean coast to Kirkuk near the Persian frontier – to divide in two the region that the British high commissioner had offered to Husein. Territory north of the line would come under French protection; territory to the south, the British.

Within each of these two areas were zones where France and Britain could each establish full control if they so wished. The 'Blue', French, zone encompassed the Syrian and Lebanese coast, mushrooming into modern Turkey to the north. The 'Red', British, zone expanded the existing British bridgehead in southern Iraq up to Baghdad and, separately, covered the port of Haifa. Palestine was designated the colour brown. The two parties sought the approval of their ally Russia, and finalised the agreement in an exchange of letters in May 1916. For the time being the agreement was kept secret, a reflection of the fact that, even by the standards of the time, it was a shamelessly self-interested pact, reached well after the point when a growing number of people had started to blame empire-building for the present war.

The French were ecstatic about the concessions they had wrung from Britain. As soon as the draft deal had been reached the prime minister, Briand, urged Cambon to confirm the 'very important results already reached' because 'we risk seeing events change them'.[41] The challenge for France was now to hold its ally to the pact.

The British, on the other hand, were dismayed. 'It seems to me,' Britain's head of military intelligence complained, 'that we are rather in the position of the hunters who divided up the skin of the bear before they had killed it.'[42] His colleagues hoped that the terms of the agreement were not final. Resentful that they had been forced into the deal by Georges-Picot, they immediately began to look for ways to circumvent it, and in particular to plug the gap in their defences left by its unsatisfactory settlement of Palestine.

To do so, the British turned to an idea that had been circulating in government circles for a year. This was that support for Zionism – the as yet unsuccessful political campaign to create a Jewish state in Palestine – represented a better way for Britain to secure its position in the Middle East.

As soon as France had begun making noises about Syria in 1915, a cabinet minister, Herbert Samuel, who was both Jewish and a Zionist, spotted the opportunity to promote his long-held ambition to see a Jewish state in Palestine. He began to argue that, by supporting the creation of a Jewish colony immediately east of Suez, Britain could deny that territory to rival foreign powers who might then threaten its control of the Suez Canal. 'We cannot proceed on the supposition that our present happy relations with France will continue always,' he warned his colleagues. 'A common frontier with a European neighbour in the Lebanon is a far smaller risk to the vital interests of the British Empire than a common frontier at El Arish.'

Samuel also argued that such a move would generate goodwill for

Britain within the Jewish diaspora. Large numbers of Jews, who faced repression in Eastern Europe and especially in Russia, had migrated westwards in the years before the war. Yet, although the Jewish population in Britain quadrupled in the thirty years before the war, many Jews regarded their new home as tainted by its alliance with the oppressive Tsarist regime from which many of them had fled. Samuel was optimistic that this attitude could be reversed if Britain threw itself behind the Zionists' ambitions. 'Help given now towards the attainment of the idea which great numbers of Jews have never ceased to cherish through so many centuries of suffering cannot fail to secure, into a far-distant future, the gratitude of a whole race, whose goodwill, in time to come, may not be without its value,' Samuel declared.[43]

Samuel's argument played on the widespread prejudice that the Jews were an increasingly powerful political force. Sir Edward Grey now recognised its merit, both to trump the French and to improve relations with the Zionists, who in the United States successfully blocked the Tsarist government's attempt to raise money on Wall Street to fight the war. Soon after the Sykes–Picot agreement had been finalised he asked Britain's ambassador in Paris to find out how the French would react if Britain issued a declaration of support for the Zionists, 'to win the sympathies of Jewish forces in America, the East and elsewhere which at the present time are to a great extent if not preponderantly unfriendly to the Allies'.[44]

The French did not immediately appreciate what the British were trying to achieve and laughed off the idea. An announcement of support for a 'Kingdom of Israel' was 'laughable and would serve no purpose ... The less said about this the better,' a senior French diplomat declared.[45] By contrast the British could clearly see why it might be worthwhile courting the Zionists. When the Allies' great offensive on the Somme in July 1916 failed to deliver a decisive breakthrough, it became clear that American help was necessary to defeat the Germans. As Samuel pointed out, there were two million Jews in the United States, and his colleagues started to believe that winning their support might help draw the United States into the war.

So far the United States had been reluctant to join the Allies' side. As public opposition to imperialism grew stronger, late in 1916 the newly re-elected US president, Woodrow Wilson, urged all the belligerents to renounce the imperial ambitions that he believed were largely responsible for the war. His challenge elicited a disingenuous response from the British and French governments, in which they described themselves as 'fighting not for selfish interests but, above all, to safeguard the independence of peoples, right, and humanity'.[46] They even said that they were committed to 'the setting free of the populations subject to the bloody tyranny of the Turks'. The bespectacled, high-minded Wilson as yet knew nothing of the Sykes–Picot agreement, but all the same regarded this sudden conversion with the scepticism that it deserved. 'No nation should seek to extend its polity over any other nation or people,' he repeated in January 1917; 'every people should be left free to determine its own policy ... the little along with the great and the powerful.'[47] This was the doctrine that became known as 'self-determination'.

Wilson hoped to remain neutral but his hand was forced by Germany. In March 1917 three American ships were sunk following the Kaiser's decision to pursue unrestricted submarine warfare. He also learned from Britain that the Germans were trying to encourage Mexico to invade the United States. Wilson had no choice but to go to war, but he tried to make a distinction between the motives of his country and those of the other combatants. On 2 April he launched a general attack on the imperial foreign policies pursued by all the European powers. Singling out for criticism the 'little groups of ambitious men who were accustomed to use their fellow men as pawns and tools', he went on: 'We have no selfish ends to serve. We desire no conquest, no dominion. We seek no indemnities for ourselves, no material compensation for the sacrifices we shall freely make.'[48] The United States, the president concluded, would 'fight for the things which we have always carried nearest our hearts – for democracy, for the right of those who submit to authority to have a voice in their own governments, for the rights and liberties of small nations'.

President Wilson's attack made uncomfortable reading in London. Asquith and Grey had resigned in December 1916, and Asquith's successor as prime minister, David Lloyd George, had by now decided to launch the invasion of Palestine that he had long

favoured. Well aware that such a move would certainly spark accusations of imperialism, he decided that support for the stateless
Zionists' aspirations was a good way to thwart French ambitions in
the Middle East and silence Wilson simultaneously. Unlike the
Sykes–Picot agreement, sponsoring the Zionists looked high-minded,
but the prime minister's reasoning for doing so was unchanged. As
Asquith put it, sourly but accurately, 'Lloyd George … does not
care a damn for the Jews or their past or their future, but thinks it
would be an outrage to let the Christian Holy Places – Bethlehem,
Mount of Olives, Jerusalem &c – pass into the possession of
"Agnostic Atheistic France"!'[49]

The morning after President Wilson made his speech, Lloyd
George had breakfast with the leading British Zionist, Chaim
Weizmann, who assured him of the Zionists' support for Britain.
Later the same day he met Sykes, who was about to set off to Egypt
with Georges-Picot to deal with any questions that the invasion of
Palestine might raise. Explaining the new thrust of British policy, he
stressed the 'importance of not prejudicing the Zionist movement
and the possibility of its development under British auspices',
because the Jews 'might be able to render us more assistance than the
Arabs'.[50] Before Sykes left, Lloyd George repeated his initial warning. There should be no 'political pledges to the Arab, and
particularly none in regard to Palestine'. Sykes got the message.
When he next saw Georges-Picot he argued that it was 'the general
bias of Zionism in favour of British suzerainty' that now justified his
country's claim to Palestine.[51]

Although Georges-Picot immediately suspected that the British
were trying to render his deal with Sykes obsolete, his colleague
Robert de Caix was complacent. 'The question of an English protectorate over a Jewish Palestine scarcely arises … The British
government is certainly not dreaming of it,' he believed, presuming
that no one would be so stupid as to pursue a policy that was bound
to cause trouble between the Arabs and the Jews. 'It would, for a
very thin profit, provoke serious difficulties.'[52]

The United States' government finally found out about the
Sykes–Picot agreement a fortnight later when Lloyd George's foreign
secretary, Arthur Balfour, divulged its existence to Wilson's foreign

policy adviser, Edward House. In the light of Britain's commitment to 'the setting free of the populations subject to the bloody tyranny of the Turks', it is hardly surprising that the revelation made House furious. 'It is all bad and I told Balfour so. They are making it a breeding place for future war,' he wrote.[53] He grilled Balfour on exactly what the 'spheres of influence' that Sykes and Georges-Picot had agreed with one another involved. 'Balfour was hazy concerning this; whether it meant permanent occupation, or whether it meant that each nation had the exclusive right to develop the resources within their own sphere, he was not altogether clear.'

Balfour was uncertain because, as far as the British were concerned, the Sykes–Picot agreement had been an academic exercise to resolve an argument, not a blueprint for the future government of the region. As a hypothetical division of country that neither of its signatories yet controlled, it was extremely vulnerable to events, all the more so because it was a secret that was bound to cause controversy when finally it was exposed. As the British hoped, and the French feared, events in the Middle East might yet render the pact redundant.

It was this weakness that one man now did his utmost to exploit.

3

ENTER T. E. LAWRENCE

SHARIF HUSEIN'S REVOLT ERUPTED IN MECCA IN JUNE 1916, but it was not until May the following year that the young British officer who had become its organising genius discovered the details of the Sykes–Picot agreement from Mark Sykes himself and realised their profound implications. Although there is no contemporary record of the encounter between T. E. Lawrence and Sykes on the Red Sea coast of Arabia on 7 May bar the briefest note in Lawrence's own diary, there is plenty of other evidence that it did not go well.

'We thought you had been generous to the Arabs,' Lawrence wrote accusingly to Sykes afterwards, adding that until their meeting he had known only 'unofficially' that the British might concede Syria to the French.[1] Sykes, who had stopped off to meet Lawrence on his way back from a meeting with Sharif Husein, looked down at the short and scruffy Lawrence – eight years his junior, and just five feet six inches tall – and dismissed his support for Arab aspirations. 'Complete independence means ... Poverty and chaos,' he later scoffed. 'Let him consider this as he hopes for the people he is fighting for.'[2]

That the two men did not get on was unsurprising, for the twenty-eight-year-old Lawrence's experience of the Middle East could not have been more different from Mark Sykes's. Whereas Sykes's first visit to the region was as a tourist with his parents and a retinue of local guides and bag carriers, Lawrence first travelled there alone, to conduct first-hand research on the crusader castles of the Levant, while he was a student at Oxford University. Sykes could afford to be extravagant; the twenty-year-old Lawrence went on foot, armed with two maps, a water-bottle, a camera and a Mauser pistol, which he sold at the finish for a profit. He later caustically summarised Sykes's understanding of the region as 'of the outside'.[3]

Sykes left Cambridge without completing his degree, but found a job through contacts as an honorary attaché at the British embassy in Constantinople. The brilliantly clever Lawrence graduated with a First, partly on the strength of his crusader castles thesis, and went on to work on a series of archaeological digs in eastern Syria. There he spurred on the Arab labourers he was responsible for managing by firing his pistol in the air whenever they unearthed an interesting find. The experience left him with a good grasp of colloquial Arabic and a deep admiration for his workforce, which was evidently mutual, for it was reported that he 'gets on very well with natives'.[4] One visitor recalled drinking from freshly excavated Hittite cups with him, and practising their shooting at a matchbox from thirty yards. The writer Gertrude Bell, twenty years his senior, also came across Lawrence at this time. 'An interesting boy,' she pronounced, before predicting: 'he is going to make a traveller.'[5]

When war broke out in 1914 Lawrence volunteered and was swiftly posted to the British army's intelligence department in Cairo. But his job, of charting Ottoman army unit movements, bored him stiff and he became guilt-ridden when his brothers, Will and Frank, were killed in action on the western front in the course of 1915. 'They were both younger than I am,' he told a friend, 'and it doesn't seem right, somehow, that I should go on living peacefully in Cairo.'[6] His opportunity arose after Husein's long-awaited uprising broke out in June 1916 but quickly fizzled out after the capture of Mecca from the Turks. When, that October, Lawrence was sent on a short mission to Arabia to find out why the revolt was on the verge of failure, he seized the chance it represented to escape his desk job permanently.

If Lawrence could turn this adventure into a more permanent posting, it also represented a chance for him to fulfil a personal vendetta that he nursed. Like Sykes, he had noticed France's growing interest in the Ottoman Empire before the war – 'the French invasion', as he put it – and he was determined to thwart its further spread.[7] 'If only you had seen the ruination caused by the French influence you would never wish it to be extended,' he wrote to his mother from Syria before the war. 'Better a thousand times the Arab untouched.'[8]

Lawrence found himself surrounded by like-minded men on his arrival in Cairo. There, the Fashoda incident was a vivid memory for several of his superiors. His own chief, the head of the intelligence department Bertie Clayton, had served on Kitchener's expedition, as had Reginald Wingate, who replaced McMahon as high commissioner in 1917 and who, as Kitchener's chief intelligence officer, had exaggerated the threat posed by the Sudanese Mahdists so as to provide a reason to press south towards Fashoda. Both men regarded the Entente Cordiale as no more than an expedient pause in an ancient rivalry, a view that rapidly rubbed off on Lawrence, who wrote: 'One cannot go on betting that France will always be our friend.'[9]

That prejudice was only reinforced when the French vetoed the British plan to land at Alexandretta, and it gained a righteous tinge when the disaster at Gallipoli then unfolded. 'So far as Syria is concerned it is France and not Turkey that is the enemy,' Lawrence wrote home in February 1915 just as the Alexandretta plan was shelved after pressure from the French.[10] French presumption rankled; the spinelessness of British diplomats even more so: 'Curse and spit at and abominate the FO and all its desolations,' he wrote furiously to a friend.[11] A fortnight later he told his former university tutor, David Hogarth, of his hope of uniting the Bedu tribes of western Arabia; and that, with them, 'we can rush right up to Damascus, & biff the French out of all hope of Syria'.[12]

Lawrence expressed his dream to Hogarth in a private letter, but it did not take long for the French to recognise the threat posed by the Arab revolt after it broke out midway through 1916. What concerned them most was the influence that Sharif Husein might wield over their empire in Arab North Africa, if the rebellion was successful. At the Quai d'Orsay a senior official named Pierre de Margerie – another member of the Comité de l'Asie Française – warned the

French prime minister that what happened in Arabia 'could have the most serious repercussions in all our colonies'.[13] If the revolt succeeded, he predicted, France might find itself 'in the presence of an Arabised Islam that draws from its conquests new strength to expand and resist Christian power'. He advocated that the French 'discreetly associate ourselves with the Arabs' efforts to gain their freedom . . . to prevent their success turning against Christian powers with Muslim possessions'.

De Margerie's advice that France should carefully try to contain the uprising was quickly followed up. Colonel Edouard Brémond was dispatched to Arabia in September 1916 as head of the French military mission to the Arabs. 'If you can pull the Englishmen's legs, that's the best service you can do us,' Brémond was told at the Quai d'Orsay before his departure.[14] He proved adept at doing so, by offering the Arabs French assistance when the revolt's early momentum ebbed.

Although Brémond's offer was never actually fulfilled, it sparked a rancorous debate among the British about whether they should follow suit. While Husein had successfully expelled the Turks from Mecca, a substantial Ottoman force remained in Medina, two hundred miles to the north, where they received supplies by rail from Damascus. By October 1916 an Ottoman attempt to retake Mecca looked imminent. All that stood between the Turks and the epicentre of Islam was a chain of serrated mountains, the Hijaz, which were defended by the poorly armed Bedu tribesmen, wild men who wore woollen robes in brown and indigo, who decorated their eyes with kohl and washed their braided hair with camel urine to make it shine. Led by Husein's son Feisal, they fiercely opposed all foreign interference.

The Bedu in the mountains now urgently needed logistical support, but the British army was reluctant to provide it. Since Gallipoli the atmosphere at military headquarters in Egypt had been poisonous, and when the revolt began to falter through lack of materiel Clayton's rivals were quick to blame him, since he had been a leading advocate of encouraging the sharif to rebel. Were Britain now forced to bolster the Arabs with troops that it could ill afford to spare, Clayton knew that he would lose his job. But the intelligence chief, whom Lawrence described as working 'like water, or permeating oil, creeping silently and insistently through everything', hatched a plan to save himself. He would send his bright subordinate to Jeddah to report back from the spot that sending British troops to Arabia would make no difference.[15]

The trip was to be short because it was superfluous: it was designed only to give the argument against intervention the added weight of seeming to be based on first-hand knowledge. But, as Lawrence sailed down the Red Sea towards Jeddah with Storrs, it became rapidly apparent that his ambitions stretched far beyond completing the task that Clayton had entrusted to him. Rather than while away the boring journey talking to his colleague, he spent time practising his marksmanship, shooting at bottles balanced on the deck handrail.

'When at last we anchored in the outer harbour, off the white town hung between the blazing sky and its reflection in the mirage,' Lawrence later wrote of his arrival in Jeddah on 16 October, 'then the heat of Arabia came out like a drawn sword and struck us speechless.'[16] But before the day was out, despite the sapping temperature he had fulfilled his personal mission by extracting the most convincing evidence that French motives were not benign. Over dinner that evening Brémond, who liked Scotch whisky, confided to him that it was in neither of their interests for the uprising to succeed because 'the partisans for a great Arab kingdom seek afterwards to act in Syria, and in Iraq, from where we – French and English – must then expel them'.[17] This, of course, was not at all what either Lawrence or Clayton had in mind.

In a lengthy telephone conversation Storrs persuaded a reluctant Sharif Husein to allow Lawrence to go inland to assess the situation in the mountains for himself. Lawrence, who took great pleasure in being unorthodox and confrontational, readily donned the Arab robes his regular colleagues refused to wear on principle, and set off on camel-back into the ochre mountains that were Husein's last bulwark against Ottoman revenge.

'The Hijaz war is one of dervishes against regular troops and we are on the side of the dervishes,' Lawrence pronounced on his return to Cairo – deliberately provocative, since many of his colleagues were professional soldiers who had fought the dervishes in the Sudan a few years earlier.[18] He dismissed the prevalent view that the tribesmen were too ill-disciplined to halt an Ottoman counter-attack and therefore needed foreign reinforcements. Instead he argued, on the basis of a single day spent observing them in the mountains, that they were born guerrilla fighters who simply needed arms, ammunition, gold and advice from someone like himself. Quoting Brémond's views in his report, he added that the real reason why the French were so willing to send troops was to restrain the rebels rather than assist them. That cynical opinion struck a chord in London, the argument for sending troops rapidly disintegrated, and a grateful Clayton soon allowed Lawrence to return to the Hijaz, to channel materiel to the Arabs and reliable intelligence back to Cairo.

Lawrence was convinced that the revolt's failure so far owed much to the obstinate behaviour of its figurehead, Husein. The sixty-three-year-old sharif, who Storrs had assumed would be a pliable instrument of British interests, proved in reality to be truculent and reluctant to accept British help. Lawrence suggested that he should be bypassed altogether, and started to assess which of Sharif Husein's four sons it might be better to support.

The sharif's eldest son was too frail – he had tuberculosis – and the youngest too inexperienced. That left a choice between Feisal and his older brother, the round, jovial and independent-minded Abdullah, who had approached Storrs for arms before the war and was later nicely described as having a 'touch [of] Henry the Eighth' about him.[19] But Abdullah was suspicious of Lawrence, and Lawrence, though privately believing that Abdullah was in fact 'more businesslike' than his younger brother, reported hearsay evidence that the Arab practised his marksmanship by shooting at a teapot balanced on a servant's head, to portray him as utterly unreliable.[20]

Feisal, whom Lawrence had first met on his foray into the Hijaz mountains, looked much more promising. Two years older and at least four inches taller than Lawrence, he had a gaunt, strikingly regal face that lent credence to the family claim to be descendants of Muhammad. While Abdullah looked a little like Henry VIII, Feisal reminded Lawrence of the lion-hearted Richard I. In a report to

Clayton Lawrence transplanted Abdullah's competence to his younger brother. He described Feisal as 'A popular idol, and ambitious; full of dreams, and the capacity to realise them, with keen personal insight, and a very efficient man of business'.[21] Years later he would claim that he had known 'at first glance' that Feisal was the man who could 'set the desert on fire', but in truth, while Abdullah was an excellent shot and supremely self-assured, the better-looking and charismatic Feisal was nervy and prone to fluctuate rapidly between elation and despair.[22] 'He is not a strong character and much swayed by his surroundings,' wrote another British officer who worked closely with him.[23] But that, from Lawrence's point of view, made him the ideal recipient of British help.

There was a further, crucial, reason why Lawrence preferred Feisal. Whereas Abdullah's political horizons pointed southwards – he favoured uniting the arid Hijaz with the fertile Yemen to the south – Feisal knew members of the tiny Arab nationalist movement that had developed underground in the cities of Syria and Iraq. With these connections Feisal represented the best hope of expanding Husein's revolt far to the north, and turning Lawrence's dream of biffing the French out of all hope of Syria into a reality.

Lawrence encouraged Feisal's ambition to reach Damascus and quickly won his confidence by providing the gold that would help him tie his fractious army of tribesmen and Syrian and Iraqi nationalists together. In turn Feisal gave him a brilliant white Arab robe to wear, not as a disguise, but to make it clear that he fully supported the foreigner's presence in his camp. 'Such honesty, such faithfulness, such devotion to duty and such control,' the young shaykh later wrote of his deferential new adviser.[24] Lawrence saw it differently. 'Information had better come to me for him,' he whispered, 'since I like to make up my mind before he does.'[25]

With the help of Lawrence and a handful of other British advisers, aerial reconnaissance by a flight of British aeroplanes and the ambush of a Turkish column by the supposedly indolent Abdullah, the Arabs enjoyed a turnaround in their fortunes. In January 1917 they made a bold leap northwards, capturing the tiny Red Sea port of Wajh. Nondescript and otherwise unimportant, Wajh was the perfect base for the next, aggressive phase of the Arabs' revolt, for it was within striking distance of a two-hundred-mile stretch of the Hijaz Railway, on which the Turkish garrison in Medina depended for supplies. It was from Wajh, for the next two years, that Lawrence and his British colleagues led or organised a series of attacks against the trains, stations, track and water tanks along the railway, forcing the Turks on to the defensive.

Lawrence quickly fell out with the other British officers over tactics. While they wanted to concentrate their energies on forcing the capitulation of the Turks inside Medina by permanently severing the railway that linked them to Damascus, Lawrence knew that if their plan succeeded it would effectively bring the uprising to a premature end. British support would be withdrawn and his own hope of denying Damascus to the French would not be realised.

In this regard, the appearance in Wajh in April 1917 of an Arab shaykh named Auda abu Tayi gave Lawrence great encouragement, for Auda had come from far north to pledge his support for Feisal's cause. Auda was the leader of the Huwaytat, a small tribe who roamed the Sinai and the desert region now bisected by the Jordan-Saudi Arabian border, three hundred miles north of Wajh. He was a mesmerising character, who had been on the run from the Ottomans for several years after shooting dead two Turkish officials who had come to arrest him following his failure to pay tax. Married twenty-eight times, wounded on thirteen occasions and with a face like a hawk's, he had lost count of the number of men he had killed, whose raw hearts he was reputed to eat.

Auda convinced Lawrence that a remote inland valley called Wadi Sirhan, where his tribe frequently grazed their livestock, would be the perfect springboard for the expansion of the revolt into Syria. From the valley it would be possible to capture Aqaba, the port at the head of the Red Sea, which was currently in Turkish hands, and to win over the Rwala, the biggest clan of the powerful Aniza tribe, who roamed the desert further north. The Rwala's leader, Nuri Shaalan, who had murdered two of his brothers in order to seize control of the tribe years earlier, had previously argued that he could not afford to offer Feisal his support because he depended on the Turks for food. Once Feisal was in control of Aqaba, he could keep Nuri Shaalan and his tribesmen fed.

Lawrence added one last objective to this foray: the Jabal Druze, a high plateau south-east of Damascus. There he hoped to persuade the Druzes, the fractious people who lived there, to revolt against the Ottomans. They had done so twice in recent memory, and Lawrence was confident that he could make history repeat itself once more.

Lawrence's meeting with Mark Sykes took place three days before he set out with Auda and a small group of Bedu on this dangerous venture, and these circumstances explain why what Sykes told him angered him so much. Lawrence, who had repeatedly stressed that his government wanted to see the Arabs claim Damascus for themselves, now realised that Sykes's deal with Georges-Picot meant that he had inadvertently been lying. If the Sykes–Picot agreement survived the war, reaching Damascus would have no consequence at all: the Arabs 'might take – what we had already given'.[26]

There remained some grounds for optimism, however. The Sykes–Picot agreement was vulnerable because it was both hypothetical and secret. In a world that was increasingly anti-imperialist, it would be criticised as soon as it was exposed; and in the meantime Lawrence hoped that, if the Arabs could reach Damascus first, they could establish a far more plausible claim to the regions that Sykes and Georges-Picot had so arbitrarily carved up between them. Their 'title to them will be a fairly strong one – that of conquest by the means of the local inhabitants', he reasoned, 'and what are the two powers going to say about it?'[27]

Driven by this realisation, Lawrence set out with Auda and a small party of Bedu on the three-hundred-mile trek to Wadi Sirhan three days after meeting Sykes. The fortnight-long journey, which took them across an enormous gravel plain known even to the Bedu simply as Al Houl ('The Terror'), was agonising. Blinded by the sunlight and sand-blasted by hot winds by day, and unable to sleep because of hunger in the journey's final stages, Lawrence reached Wadi Sirhan to discover that Auda had misled him. Far from providing the grazing he had promised, the valley was 'pretty barren'.[28] Nor, after several days, was there any sign that his arrival there was having any gravitational effect on the Rwala. As Auda settled down for days of feasting with his fellow tribesmen, Lawrence, apparently suicidal with frustration at the failure of the plan, drafted a note to his chief: 'Clayton: I've decided to go off alone to Damascus hoping to get killed along the way. For all sakes try and clear this show up before it goes further. We are calling them to fight for us on a lie and I can't stand it.'[29]

On 5 June Lawrence impulsively set out alone, deep into enemy-controlled Syria to see whether he could redeem the situation. In an extraordinarily risky journey he ventured far into the zone Sykes had pledged to Georges-Picot, blowing up a railway bridge at Ras Baalbek, sixty miles north-east of Beirut. Although this sparked trouble among the volatile local people, the Metawala, he decided that it would not be possible to start a more general uprising imminently. Neither the Druze leader, Husein Atrash, nor Nuri Shaalan was willing to commit himself to Feisal at the moment, but Lawrence's meetings with both men gave him grounds for cautious optimism. Shaalan, whose eyes seemed to Lawrence to glint red in the sunlight, assured him that he would 'certainly be involved sooner or later'.[30]

Lawrence returned to Wadi Sirhan on 18 June to find that Auda had mustered a force of just 560 tribesmen, but they decided to attack Aqaba nonetheless. The port's garrison comprised three hundred Turkish soldiers, but its defences all faced out to sea. The Arabs' approach from the desert was unexpected and they were able to surround the main Turkish outpost at Abu al-Assal in the hills behind the port. After a day-long gunfight they overwhelmed the Turks with a final charge in which Lawrence accidentally shot the camel he was riding in the back of the head. Days later they surged down the narrow valley leading to Aqaba and the sea. The local Turkish commander surrendered and, on 6 July, Lawrence and the Huwaytat captured the strategically crucial port without a fight.

Lawrence was under no illusions about the depth of the Huwaytat's support. Short of food and money to repay the tribesmen, he set out the same afternoon by camel across the Sinai desert for Egypt, 150 miles away. His appearance in Bertie Clayton's office in Cairo four days later stunned his chief, who had only that morning finished a memorandum ruling out an attack on Aqaba because of the 'insuperable difficulties' it involved. Lawrence had – single-handedly, so far as the British were concerned – accounted for the deaths or capture of over 1,300 Turkish troops. One of those most impressed by this achievement was another member of the intelligence department in Cairo, who was, like Lawrence, itching to escape his desk job. 'I have just written to congratulate T. E. Lawrence[,] a little fair haired archaeologist ... do you remember him?' W. F. Stirling wrote to his sister, the words betraying his colleague's previous insignificance. 'He ought of course to have a VC,' he suggested; 'there is nothing they could give him which would be too great.'[31]

4

ALLENBY'S MAN

'LAWRENCE'S MOVE IS SPLENDID AND I WANT HIM KNIGHTED,' Sykes told Clayton – through gritted teeth, for he immediately appreciated that, from Aqaba, his young adversary might wreck his deal with Georges-Picot.[1] It was for this reason too, though with the opposite motivation, that the British high commissioner in Egypt, Reginald Wingate, wanted Lawrence's exploits covered up. 'For political reasons,' he told London, 'it is very important that nothing should be known publicly as to Lawrence's Syrian reconnaissance.'[2] As a consequence, the French never knew just how far north Lawrence had ventured, and it took five weeks for a French intelligence officer, Antonin Jaussen, to piece together some details of what Lawrence had achieved and their implications.

Jaussen had trained in Jerusalem as a priest but went on to make his name as an archaeologist. The two interests were closely connected, for, like Sykes, he believed in what Lawrence later derided as the 'unchanging East'.[3] Jaussen was convinced that by studying the nomadic Bedu he could gain an insight into the ancient scripture. Travelling east of the Jordan on this quest, he became fascinated by the remains of the ancient Nabataean and Sabaean civilisations which had controlled the frankincense trade between Yemen and Gaza hundreds of years earlier, and decided to find out more about them. In the years immediately before the war, while Sykes was registering his disappointment at the hotels of Damascus and Lawrence had been digging for Hittite remains in eastern Syria, Jaussen set out southwards on the Hijaz Railway with a colleague, a camera and a thirty-foot ladder to find and photograph the inscriptions these forgotten civilisations had left above the rock tombs they had carved into the sandstone cliffs of western Arabia.

Jaussen had made his way to Cairo after being expelled from Palmyra by the Turks when war broke out in 1914. There, like Lawrence, he was absorbed into the Allies' intelligence-gathering effort. The roly-poly priest had a comic air, for he resembled a pith-helmeted Friar Tuck, but he knew more about the area east of the Dead Sea than any of his British counterparts, with whom he got on well, at first. Early in 1915 Lawrence, who was twenty years his junior, described him as 'very amusing, and very clever: and very useful as interpreter'.[4]

The French veto of the Alexandretta plan and then the clear divergence of the two allies over the Arab revolt soured the collegiate atmosphere within the intelligence department. In March 1917 Jaussen visited Lawrence at Wajh and noted how his former colleague had built up a close rapport with Feisal and was 'a veritable influence' on the Arab leader. This was a problem, the French priest felt, because Lawrence 'shares and supports Feisal's and his followers' natural hostility to foreign intervention in Arabia. It would be better policy and more useful to Allied interests to tone down the instinctive repulsion of the nomad to those who are not of his tribe and race.'[5]

Five weeks after the capture of Aqaba, on 13 August 1917, Jaussen reported that his advice had not been followed. Bedu opposition to foreign interference was stronger than ever and, under Lawrence's direction, all the Bedu tribes in the region north of Aqaba were now being strongly encouraged to make common cause with Sharif Husein. The Frenchman instantly grasped the implication. The dividing line that Sykes and Georges-Picot had settled on, which he described as 'drawn in a fairly unclear way on paper without regard to the territory of the tribes or the lie of the land', might now 'conceivably undergo more than an adjustment under the pressure of events'.[6] The French ambassador in Cairo, Defrance, alerted the Quai d'Orsay to Jaussen's observation. He noted that the British appeared to have set no fixed limit to how far north towards Damascus and Syria the Arab movement might spread.

But another member of the French embassy in Cairo, a high-flying diplomat named René Doynel de St Quentin, felt that there was no need to worry. Doynel de St Quentin had been flattered by Lawrence as the 'one non-Englishman in Cairo to whom one could speak frankly about anything doing'.[7] As a consequence he did not realise that Lawrence now intended to encourage an uprising against the Turks in the heart of the zone France expected to rule after the war, because this was a strategy Lawrence had explicitly reassured him he would not follow. In an admiring profile of his British colleague – 'probably the most outstanding figure in the British army or administration in the East' – Doynel de St Quentin acknowledged Lawrence's identification with the Arabs but argued that the young British officer was 'too loyal not to defer to the orders of his chiefs if they clearly lay out a policy of Franco-British cooperation'.[8] It was several months before it became obvious to the French that Lawrence would not be reined in by official British policy because he was now significantly shaping it.

Lawrence's chance to do so had come when, days after he reached Cairo, he was summoned to see the new general in command of British forces in Egypt, Edmund Allenby. The encounter had the potential to be disastrous, for the dishevelled and contrary Lawrence – whom one angry regular soldier had described as a 'bumptious young ass' who 'wants kicking and kicking *hard* at that' – was about to meet a man with an infamously hot temper, known behind his back as 'The Bull'.[9] But although General Allenby may have had a fearsome reputation, he was also open-minded and aware of his own shortcomings: he later said that, having failed the Indian civil service examination twice, he had joined the army because he was 'too big a fool for anything else'.[10] He was also, as Lawrence shrewdly recognised, in a difficult predicament.

Allenby had just arrived in Egypt to take charge of a new effort to invade Palestine. Previously commander of Britain's Third Army, he had been sacked following criticism of his performance in France during the battle of Arras that spring, and given the command of the

Egyptian Expeditionary Force. Not only was this obviously a demotion but, before he set out for Cairo to take up the new appointment, he had received two conflicting messages. Lloyd George had told him to take 'Jerusalem by Christmas', but the government's chief military adviser, Sir William Robertson, who regarded the invasion of Palestine as a distraction from the western front, repeatedly warned him privately that he would spare no extra troops to help him fight the prime minister's crusade. Under similar pressures Allenby's hapless predecessor had twice tried and failed to capture Gaza from the Ottomans, and had paid for his failure with his job. Allenby was desperate to avoid falling into the same trap.

Lawrence realised that the general's greatest fear was that, as he pressed forward towards Jerusalem in pursuit of the prime minister's demand, the Turks would use the Hijaz Railway to concentrate their forces south-east of the Dead Sea and from there launch a counter-attack against his vulnerable supply lines stretching between Egypt and Gaza. So he used the meeting to propose a plan for a series of guerrilla raids by the Arabs against the Hijaz Railway near Aqaba that would make it impossible for the Turks to marshal enough troops to launch a counter-offensive. The motive beneath the plan was to make the Arabs seem indispensable to the general, undermining Sykes's deal.

Allenby was noncommittal in the meeting but he was evidently impressed because afterwards he recommended Lawrence's plan to London. Using Lawrence's proposal to reinforce his argument with Robertson that the invasion of Palestine should go ahead, he predicted that the combined effect of the two plans might cause 'a collapse of the Turkish campaigns in the Hijaz and in Syria and produce far-reaching results, both political as well as military'.[11] To coordinate activity on both sides of the Dead Sea he decided to bring Feisal and Lawrence under his command, formalising the Arabs' role in exactly the way that Lawrence had intended. Lawrence had brilliantly married his own political agenda to the tactical needs of Allenby's campaign.

To ensure the plan went ahead unimpeded, Allenby was willing to protect Lawrence from the French. He flatly rejected a French attempt to attach one of their men as a liaison officer to Lawrence.

If, in the course of his activities, Lawrence did enter the zone that the Sykes–Picot agreement had allocated to the French, the British general committed himself only to informing the French 'as fully as military exigencies permit'.[12] Military exigencies, of course, proved enormously restrictive, giving him the excuse to give the French no warning of any of Lawrence's operations because he knew that they would only object and try to veto them, as they had done with the Alexandretta plan.

In August 1917 Allenby received orders from London to take advantage of the capture of Aqaba and press ahead into Palestine, and Lawrence returned to the scene of his triumph to mastermind the hit-and-run campaign that he had outlined to his commanding officer. But he reached the port to find that, in his absence, fundamental divisions in the Arab army had begun to show. The Syrians and the Iraqis who had volunteered to fight for Husein were squabbling incessantly, and neither group had anything in common with the wild Bedu tribesmen who had originally rallied to the sharif. Far from demonstrating the characteristics of the nation he hoped would oust the French, the Arabs were perpetually feuding among themselves.

Riled by a letter from Sykes, who had written to tell him that it would take 'ten years' tutelage under the Entente' before the Arabs could be a nation, Lawrence drafted an aggressive reply. During his time in Cairo he had also heard about the British government's gravitation towards the Zionists, and he now asked Sykes to clarify the inconsistencies in Britain's promises to the Arabs, then to the French, and now to the Jews. 'We are in rather a hole,' he concluded; 'please tell me what, in your opinion, are the actual means by which we will find a way out.'[13]

Clayton, to whom Lawrence sent this letter, decided not to pass it on to Sykes. He did not want to challenge Sykes, he explained, at a time when the Sykes–Picot agreement – 'never a very workable instrument' – was 'now almost a lifeless monument'.[14] Georges-Picot was also deeply unpopular, he claimed, because by now it was widely known that his negligence had led directly to the deaths of several Arab nationalists who were betrayed when their correspondence with him was exposed.

Contrary to Clayton's expectation the Sykes–Picot agreement did survive the war, but at this point Sykes certainly felt vulnerable to the consequences of Lawrence's coup and the increasingly hostile public attitude towards imperialism. A fortnight after the capture of Aqaba the British MP conceded that his deal with Georges-Picot was now 'quite contrary to the spirit of the time'.[15] 'I am going to slam into Paris to make the French play up to the Arab cause as their only hope,' he wrote soon afterwards, adding very optimistically: 'Colonialism is madness and I believe Picot and I can prove it to them.'[16]

No longer worried about British interest drying up if the Arabs' guerrilla war succeeded, Lawrence set out to try to wreck the Hijaz Railway permanently – the very operation he had once advised against. The steam engines that plied the railway needed regular refuelling with water, and he decided to try to destroy the vital wells at the station of Mudawwarah, today on the Jordan-Saudi Arabian border, in a bid to create a waterless stretch of line that was so long that the locomotives could not pass it. But his attempt to do so was handicapped by feuding between the tribesmen who made up his raiding party. Reconciling them was like trying to mend a 'broken necklace', he complained, adding that during this expedition he was more concerned by 'questions of supply, transport, tribal pay, disputes, division of spoil, feuds, march order, and the like, than with the explosive work'.[17] Having reached Mudawwarah and reconnoitred it at night, Lawrence decided his own force was not sufficiently cohesive to take on the Turks, who outnumbered them by two to one. Disappointed, he had turned to the two regular soldiers he had brought with him – Yells and Brook – to organise the ambush of a train.

While Yells and Brook set up a mortar and a machine-gun on a nearby hill from where they had a commanding view of the line, down by the track Lawrence spent two hours burying a sandbag filled with fifty pounds of blasting gelatine beneath the rails at the point where they crossed a bridge. Since Turkish patrols by now regularly scoured the railway for mines he had to spend another four hours concealing the command wire, and then attaching it to an electric detonator, which he entrusted to a tribesman. A long and

anxious wait ensued. When, the following afternoon, a train pulled
by two locomotives was finally spotted, Lawrence gave the order to
press the plunger just as the first engine reached the mine.

'There followed a terrific roar,' he recollected afterwards, 'and the
line vanished from sight behind a spouting column of black dust and
smoke a hundred feet high and wide. Out of the darkness came
shattering crashes and long, loud metallic clangings of ripped steel,
with many lumps of iron and plate; while one entire wheel of a
locomotive whirled up suddenly black out of the cloud against the
sky, and sailed musically over our heads to fall slowly and heavily
into the desert behind.'[18] After a moment's silence a vicious gunfight
ensued between the Arabs and the surviving Turks. The mortar and
the machine-gun proved decisive.

This was the first time that Lawrence had seen fighting at close
quarters, and he was shocked by it. The bridge had been ruined by
the blast, and in the aftermath he found the second engine 'a
blanched pile of smoking iron' in the bottom of the wadi that it
crossed, together with the dead and dying of the first carriage who
were mixed together in a mangled heap. 'I'm not going to last out
this game much longer,' he confided to a friend, describing how the
experience of finding the Turks 'all over the place in bits' had been
'horrible'.[19]

This searing experience and his fraying patience with the Bedu
encouraged Lawrence to look for other suitable British officers and
men to help him. He needed men who were reliable, particularly in
the later stages of the campaign when close coordination of his operations with Allenby's advance into Palestine would be crucial. One of
them was his former colleague W. F. Stirling, whose letter of con-
gratulation he received on his return to Aqaba. In a bid to persuade
Stirling, who spoke Arabic, to come to join him he swallowed his
horror at what he had seen, and in an airy account of the 'last stunt'
described how 'two beautiful shots' from the mortar and a hail of
machine-gun fire had resulted in seventy Turkish deaths, thirty
wounded and eighty prisoners, in the space of just ten minutes. 'I
hope this sounds the fun it is,' he finished. 'It's the most amateurish,
Buffalo Billy sort of performance. Only you will think it heaven
because there aren't any returns, or orders, or superiors, or inferiors;

no doctors, no accounts, no meals, and no drinks.'[20] Stirling eagerly
joined him for the campaign's climax the following year. He was 'just
the fellow', agreed a colleague, 'to send off stunting with the
circus'.[21]

When Lawrence returned to Aqaba early in October 1917 he
found a summons from Allenby waiting for him. Allenby had
decided to launch his offensive against Gaza at the end of the same
month, but information he had received led him to believe that the
number of enemy divisions facing him had doubled. Keen to stop the
Ottomans moving further reinforcements to oppose him, he proposed that Lawrence attack the branch line of the Hijaz Railway
connecting Damascus with Palestine. When they met, the point the
two men settled on was where the railway criss-crossed the steep-
sided Yarmuk valley as it descended towards Palestine.

Deep in Ottoman-occupied territory, the Yarmuk expedition was
to be Lawrence's most dangerous mission yet, but he had no choice
but to agree since he had originally come up with the idea because
the valley formed part of the dividing line Sykes and Georges-Picot
had defined. He decided to take a Royal Engineer with him who
could carry out the demolition if he himself was killed, and a party
of Gurkha soldiers to provide extra firepower. His guide was Abdul
Qadir al Jazairi, a member of a prominent Damascene family whose
grandfather had led resistance to the French in Algeria in the 1840s.
Abdul Qadir told Lawrence that he could command the support of
the Algerian community who lived on the north side of the Yarmuk
valley.

Allenby's attack was a success. Rather than attempt a head-on
assault on Gaza yet again, on 31 October his forces attacked
Beersheba, to the east. It was a misty, moonlit night, and the Turks
were taken by surprise. The following night, the British began a
five-hour bombardment of Gaza itself. By dawn, British forces had
captured a crucial position overlooking Gaza's harbour, but sand-
storms and a water shortage meant that the British in Beersheba
were unable to surround Gaza. The Turks avoided the British pincer
movement from Gaza and Beersheba and withdrew with most of
their force intact. The British restored the momentum of their offensive with a cavalry advance.

To ward off the inevitable French pressure for an international administration once Palestine had been conquered, the British government now made its support for Zionism public. On 7 November *The Times* published a letter from the foreign secretary Arthur Balfour to Lord Rothschild, a prominent British Zionist. Deeply sceptical about the wisdom of taking over Palestine when Sykes had proposed the idea two years earlier, Balfour had now changed his mind. 'I have much pleasure in conveying to you,' he announced theatrically to Rothschild, 'the following declaration of sympathy with Jewish Zionist aspirations which has been submitted to, and approved by, the Cabinet.' The Balfour Declaration read:

> His Majesty's Government view with favour the establishment in Palestine of a national home for the Jewish people, and will use their best endeavours to facilitate the achievement of this object, it being clearly understood that nothing shall be done which may prejudice the civil and religious rights of existing non-Jewish communities in Palestine, or the rights and political status enjoyed by Jews in any other country.[22]

Lawrence was as yet unaware of this world-changing development. Deep behind enemy lines, he had hoped to attack the railway in the Yarmuk valley on 5 November, but his difficulty recruiting sympathetic tribesmen to his cause and the mysterious desertion of his guide, Abdul Qadir al Jazairi, both delayed him. It was only after nightfall on 7 November that he finally reached the Yarmuk gorge.

Across the valley the glimmer of a fire identified the location of the Turkish guard tent on the nearest railway bridge. Lawrence left the Gurkhas at the top of the scarp to machine-gun the tent if the sentry on the bridge raised the alarm, and crept forward with the tribesmen, who were carrying bags of explosive, down towards the metal bridge which spanned the black chasm. Discovering that he could not reach its vulnerable lower girders, Lawrence had just turned to tell the tribesmen to follow him when, far above, there was a clatter as someone dropped a rifle.

Alerted by this unmistakable noise, the Turkish sentry on the bridge now spotted the Gurkhas. He shouted a challenge, started shooting and yelled for help. 'Instantly all was confusion,' Lawrence later recollected.[23] The tribesmen behind him, who had been invisible, immediately returned fire, giving their position away in the process. Before the Gurkhas had time to riddle the guard tent with bullets, the Turkish guards rushed out and began shooting back at the tribesmen, who panicked because they had been told that, if hit by a bullet, the explosives they were carrying would explode. Awoken by the gunfire, the local villagers turned out to defend their property. With volleys of shots blasting into the night sky, Lawrence decided the time had come to leave. His attempt to destroy the main supply line to Palestine had degenerated into a fiasco.

Lawrence nearly killed himself in an attempt days later to mine a train: a shortage of electric cable at Aqaba meant that he had made do with an inadequate length of wire. Too close to the track when he detonated the mine beneath a train carrying Turkish reinforcements to Palestine, 'The explosion was terrific,' he recalled afterwards. 'The ground spouted blackly into my face, and I was sent spinning, to sit up with the shirt torn to my shoulder and the blood dripping from long, ragged scratches on my left arm. Between my knees lay the exploder, crushed under a twisted sheet of sooty iron. When I peered through the dust and steam of the explosion, the whole boiler of the first engine seemed missing. Just in front of me was the scalded and smoking upper half of a man.'[24] The train was carrying a senior Turkish general, and his soldiers fought back fiercely.

Lawrence was lucky to escape with five bullet holes through his clothing and a broken toe caused by a shrapnel wound. Aware that 'we must try and enlist on our side a favourable press', he sent the engineer and the Gurkhas back to Aqaba with a report of the train attack for the newspapers. He now turned east to seek sanctuary at Azraq, a ruined castle at a desert oasis east of Amman where he had met Nuri Shaalan earlier that year.[25] There he stayed for several days before returning to Aqaba. He reached the port on 26 November and almost immediately flew to southern Palestine to discuss tactics with Allenby.

Allenby's army had by then made further progress into Palestine.

While Lawrence was at Azraq, on 13 November British forces had captured Junction Station, where the branch lines to Gaza and Jerusalem joined the main line north, which passed through the Yarmuk valley to Damascus. Three days later, British troops entered Jaffa. At a cost of over six thousand casualties, they were now within striking distance of Jerusalem. By the time Lawrence met Allenby the Holy City was cut off but, due to his failure to sever the railway in the Yarmuk valley, the Turks could still supply their troops in northern Palestine by rail.

Early in December the Turks withdrew northwards from Jerusalem and, to Allenby's relief, British forces took the Holy City without a fight. Anticipating that the French would try to muscle in on the administration for the city, the British government told Allenby to ignore any such request while Palestine was still a war zone, but to 'avoid any impression ... that a British annexation is being contemplated'.[26] On 11 December 1917, the British general made a formal entrance on foot through the Jaffa Gate. It was 'a brilliant day; hoar frost here ... and then iced sunshine, with no wind', he told his wife.[27] Behind him walked Georges-Picot, as well as Clayton and Lawrence. Newsreel footage from the day briefly shows Lawrence grinning broadly.

Allenby's pledge that he would uphold religious freedom in the city was read out, and afterwards there was a buffet lunch for Allied officers. There, as predicted, Georges-Picot raised the matter of the future government of the city. 'Tomorrow, my dear General, I will take the necessary steps to set up civil government in this town,' the French diplomat announced. According to Lawrence he was met with silence. 'Salad and chicken mayonnaise and foie gras sandwiches hung in our mouths unmunched,' Lawrence remembered, 'while we turned our round eyes on Allenby and waited.'

Allenby went red. 'In the military zone the only authority is that of the Commander-in-Chief, myself.'

'But Sir Grey, Sir Edward Grey —'

'Sir Edward Grey referred to the civil government which will be established when I judge that the military situation permits,' snapped Allenby, cutting Georges-Picot dead in his tracks.[28]

*

The military situation did not change for many months. Although Allenby now had wholehearted support from London, where Lloyd George had persuaded the French to approve further operations in Palestine and sacked his military adviser Sir William Robertson, events on the western front intervened before Allenby could resume his advance. In March 1918 the Germans launched a massive spring offensive, and Allenby was ordered by the War Office to send sixty thousand of his best troops home to reinforce the Allied line.

As his force shrank dramatically in size, Allenby grew increasingly concerned about the security of his exposed eastern flank. Despite Lawrence's optimism, the Arabs had failed to wreck the Hijaz Railway, which led the general to try twice to seize the east bank of the Jordan himself. Both attempts were failures, and following the onset of summer, he had to accept that no further progress would be possible until the autumn. Itching to make rapid headway once the temperature subsided he reorganised his forces, disbanding the camel corps within his force so as to increase the number of mounted divisions under his command from three to four.

Lawrence, who spent much of May 1918 at Allenby's headquarters, heard about this move and one evening over dinner asked for two thousand camels.

'What do you want them for?' asked Allenby.

'To put a thousand men into Dara any day you please,' Lawrence boldly told 'The Bull', who rapidly agreed.[29]

A small and dusty town eighty miles south of Damascus, Dara was the hub of the Syrian railway network, connecting Palestine, southern Syria and the Hijaz to Damascus. Through an attack on the town Lawrence hoped to have paralysed the Turkish railway system by the time Allenby finally launched a new offensive. But there was a second, less obvious reason for the plan. Dara lay just inside the zone that Sykes had promised to Georges-Picot. An Arab attack there that enabled Allenby to press northwards would seal the Arabs' claim to be liberating their own territory and to have been instrumental in Allenby's eventual triumph.

The idea reflected Lawrence's acute awareness of the temper of the times. Despite spending months deep in the desert, he was well aware of the groundswell against imperialism that was forcing Lloyd

George to support self-determination. After the Bolsheviks seized power in Russia and published all the secret treaties – including the Sykes–Picot agreement – to which the Tsarist government had been privy, Lloyd George had been forced by the Labour Party in Britain to hint that the government's policy might change.

At the start of 1918 the prime minister assured the Trades Union Congress that 'Arabia, Armenia, Mesopotamia, Syria and Palestine' would be 'entitled to a recognition of their separate national conditions', though in his typically slippery fashion he avoided defining precisely what that meant.[30] Days later, President Wilson set out his own views more clearly in his celebrated Fourteen Points about the shape of the postwar world. Point Twelve declared that the Turks should be 'assured a secure sovereignty' and that the other nationalities they currently ruled should also be 'assured an undoubted security of life and an absolutely unmolested opportunity of autonomous development'.

In London, Sykes could see the danger of being caught on the wrong side of this trend. He admitted that the world had 'marched so far' since 1915 that his agreement with Georges-Picot could 'now only be considered as a reactionary measure'.[31] It was 'dead and gone, and the sooner scrapped the better'. In August 1918 he began drafting a new declaration to the Arabs that would substantially revise the 1916 deal. But he was discouraged from discussing it with Georges-Picot by the Foreign Office minister Lord Robert Cecil who thought that it would be better to open negotiations only after British troops had entered the French zone. 'We must never forget that, internationally, the French are a grasping people,' said Cecil, 'and we shall have a much better chance of getting reasonable terms out of them if they come to us in the first instance to get something which they want.'[32] Cecil's aim, with which Lawrence would have wholeheartedly agreed, was to create 'facts on the ground' that would render the Sykes–Picot agreement irrelevant.

Lawrence's attack on Dara, which fitted with this goal, started on 16 September 1918, three days before Allenby's own advance began. It formed the tactical climax of the Arabs' campaign. With a thousand tribesmen on camels, led by him and Stirling, and a handful of other British colleagues in Rolls-Royce armoured cars, he cut the railway to the west and south of the town by destroying railway bridges. By placing explosives ingeniously beneath the line's metal sleepers, Lawrence's force twisted hundreds of yards of railway track beyond repair. Lawrence himself also cut the telegraph wires connecting the German general in command of Turkish forces in Palestine, Liman von Sanders, to Damascus and Constantinople. The general's loss of contact with the outside world was reflected several days later when, after his communications were at last restored, he received a wildly irrelevant request from the Ottoman capital. 'The telegram,' he recalled afterwards, 'inquired whether I was willing to offer a prize for a sack race in a competition in Constantinople on October 8th.'[33]

At 4.30 a.m. on 19 September Allenby launched his main offensive. Convinced that the assault on Dara revealed Allenby's true intentions, Liman von Sanders dismissed accurate intelligence he had received that the thrust would be up the coast as a clever attempt to deceive him. When, after a short and brutal bombardment, the British did just that, the Ottoman army was taken completely by surprise and collapsed. Allenby's forces rapidly overran the Turkish headquarters in Tulkarm, and almost captured Liman von Sanders when they entered Nazareth. By the time they reached Dara, the Arab flag was already flying over the town, just as Lawrence had intended.

The day after Allenby's advance began the French intelligence officer Antonin Jaussen reported to Paris the 'very important news' that a force led by Lawrence had destroyed the railway around Dara.[34] Suddenly aware of what Lawrence was trying to do, the Quai d'Orsay ordered its ambassador in London, Cambon, to remind Balfour that the Sykes–Picot agreement 'should not be lost sight of'.[35] Although powerless to stop Lawrence, French diplomats also moved to puncture the impression that the Arabs had achieved their success alone. They did so by exposing to the wider world the role that the British officer had played. On 24 September the conservative, nationalist French newspaper the *Echo de Paris* made the first public reference to Lawrence's role in the campaign, which until now had been kept completely secret. 'We must mention Colonel Lawrence,' the paper added, as it reported Allenby's triumph.[36]

Attributing Lawrence's success to his 'experience of the country and his talent for organisation', it explained how, 'At the head of the cavalry force, which he had formed with Bedouins and Druzes, he cut the railway at Dara, thus severing enemy communications between Damascus and Haifa', a 'part of the greatest importance in the Palestine victory'. The implication was obvious. Without Lawrence to lead them, the Arabs would not have been capable of such a feat.

Hard on the heels of the retreating Ottoman army, early on 1 October 1918 Lawrence drove into Damascus with Stirling in a commandeered Rolls-Royce, just after the Turks had evacuated the city. Mounted Australian troops had already passed through Damascus in pursuit of the Turks, but Allenby had ordered most of his troops to hold back so that the Arabs could enter the city first. Years later Stirling could still vividly recall the day. 'Dervishes danced around us. The horses of the Bedouin, curvetting and prancing, gradually cleared a way for us through the dense crowds, while from the balconies and rooftops veiled women pelted us with flowers and – far worse – with attar of roses,' he remembered. 'It was weeks before I could get the smell of the essence out of my clothing.'[37]

But the euphoria did not last long. 'The Arab cause has been successful beyond the wildest dreams of anybody. That is just the trouble,' Stirling complained afterwards.[38] The situation that the British had smugly thought inconceivable had come to pass. With the Arabs laying claim to Damascus by right of conquest, the British would now be forced to admit that they had promised the city not just to them but also to the French. Arthur Balfour, the British foreign secretary, did not agree with the confrontational approach preferred by his junior minister Cecil, and decreed that Britain would respect the Sykes–Picot agreement as it stood.

Balfour's decision caused outrage in Damascus. When, in an awkward meeting with Feisal, Allenby announced that France was to be the protecting power in Syria, Feisal flatly rejected the proposal. Stirling received delegations of 'frenzied and almost despairing Arabs who could not believe that we had signed an agreement which would hand them over to the French'.[39]

To delay more serious trouble, Allenby did his best to mollify the Arabs by offering them a generous interpretation of Sykes's deal.

When he finalised interim arrangements for the occupation of enemy territory, he left the Arabs in control in Damascus and the territory to the east. To the French he gave a shallow strip of coastal Lebanon that did not even encompass the area Sykes had promised them. But he realised that this was a short-term palliative. 'The future, when martial law no longer prevails, is not so cloudless,' he wrote to the chief of the imperial general staff in London. 'If the Arabs have no access to the sea, there will be endless trouble.'[40]

Having witnessed Allenby's encounter with Feisal, Lawrence left for London on 4 October to continue his campaign in Whitehall. He rightly suspected that the British government, faced with the exposure of the contradictory promises it had made to both the Arabs and the French, might yet betray its Arab allies. As he had conceded a year earlier to Sykes, 'I quite recognise that we may have to sell our small friends to pay for our big friends, or sell our future security in the Near East to pay for our present victory in Flanders.'[41] But he was determined to do his utmost to stop that happening. He raced home to argue that the Sykes–Picot agreement had been overtaken by events, that Feisal and his brothers should take control of the Arab territories of the Ottoman Empire, and to insist that the Arabs, as British allies, should be represented at the coming Paris Peace Conference, which would start in January 1919. But it took him three weeks to reach the capital, and in that time another, deciding, factor intervened.

5

I WANT MOSUL

As THE SCALE OF THE OTTOMAN COLLAPSE IN SYRIA BECAME apparent, after dinner on 6 October 1918 David Lloyd George began to mull over how he would go about 'the cutting up of Turkey'.[1] The British prime minister was in Paris, and had spent the day with the French agreeing the terms of the armistice that they would offer to their enemy. Lloyd George viscerally disliked the Turks – so obviously that one of his ministers wondered whether he dreamed in Greek – and he had long wished for the destruction of the Ottoman Empire. It had turned 'the cradle of civilisation' into 'a blighted desert', he had told his cabinet the year before. 'The Turks must never be allowed to misgovern these great lands in future.'[2]

But if not the Ottomans, then who? The Sykes–Picot agreement provided a blueprint for a postwar settlement, but it was not one that Lloyd George liked. In the meeting with his cabinet at which he discovered that Balfour had told Allenby to respect the controversial deal, he described it as 'quite unapplicable to the present circumstances, and ... altogether a most undesirable agreement from the British point of view'.[3] So far as he was concerned, Britain had defeated the Ottomans single-handedly – 'The other Governments had only put in a few nigger policemen to see that we did not steal the Holy Sepulchre!' he later wrote – and Britain should therefore take the lion's share of the spoils.[4] But regardless of this fact Cambon, the French ambassador, had insisted that the treaty must be honoured. By the time Lawrence reached Damascus it was already clear that the French government was not going to relinquish without a fight the concessions that Georges-Picot had squeezed from Britain three years earlier.

Over dinner that night in Paris with two colleagues Lloyd George 'took a very intransigent attitude', according to his cabinet secretary Maurice Hankey, who was also present.[5] He 'wanted to go back on the Sykes–Picot agreement, so as to get Palestine for us and to bring Mosul into the British zone, and even to keep the French out of Syria'. Hankey added that although the prime minister was 'very contemptuous' of President Wilson, he could see how the sanctimonious American might have his uses in the bargaining that was to follow. According to Hankey, in the course of the subsequent discussion Lloyd George had raised 'some subtle dodge for asking America to take Palestine and Syria, in order to render the French more anxious to give us Palestine, so that they might have an excuse of keeping Syria'.

The prime minister's sudden interest in Mosul was down to Hankey. It was he who had alerted Lloyd George to the importance of the city eight weeks earlier, after he had read a memorandum written by a senior admiral on Britain's need for oil. The admiral explained that, as oil was four times more efficient than coal, it would eventually take over as the major marine fuel. This would leave Britain vulnerable because whereas it had coal reserves of its own, it depended on the United States for its supply of oil. Against the backdrop of President Wilson's hostility to imperialism, if the British Empire were to remain the dominant maritime power, it was therefore vital 'to obtain the undisputed control of the greatest amount of Petroleum that we can'.[6]

The admiral had timed his intervention quite deliberately, because the British government was at that moment considering its strategy in the months ahead. The Allies had only narrowly fended off the German spring offensive, and expected the war to last at least another year. The general staff, which was planning imminent attacks in northern France and Palestine, had told the cabinet that they did not plan to advance further north in Mesopotamia. There British troops had advanced from Basra to Baghdad, and then

Kirkuk – the end point of the line Sykes had suggested at his meeting in Number 10 three years before.

As the admiral went on to observe, this British force was within
tantalising reach of the oilfields believed to lie further north, beneath
the stony steppe around Mosul, which was then still in Ottoman
hands. Reports from German geologists who had explored that
region before the war led him to believe that these were 'the largest
undeveloped resources at present known in the world'. He then predicted: 'the Power that controls the oil lands of Persia and
Mesopotamia will control the source of supply of the majority of the
liquid fuel of the future'. On one further point he was emphatic.
'This control must be absolute and there must be no foreign interests
involved in it of any sort.'

Hankey, a former naval intelligence officer, was instantly convinced and felt that the prime minister should consider the admiral's
advice as well. Knowing that Lloyd George loathed reading memoranda, he topped it with a covering note, which he marked 'Very
Secret and Important'.[7] In this he observed that, while there was no
military basis for a British advance into northern Iraq, 'there may be
reasons other than purely military for pushing on in Mesopotamia
where the British have an enormous preponderance of force. Would
it not be an advantage, before the end of the war, to secure the valuable oil wells in Mesopotamia?'

The advantage was obvious, but there were two significant obsta-
cles. Not only had Sykes readily promised Mosul to the French three
years before, but the seizure of the city would defy the principles that
President Wilson had declared must guide the new world order.
Balfour, who had been grilled by Wilson's irate adviser Colonel
House the year before, fretted that such a move would look 'purely
Imperialist', but Hankey argued that securing an independent oil
supply before 'the next war' was a 'first class British War Aim', and
Lloyd George, who regarded his foreign secretary as weak-willed,
agreed.[8] When that October it became obvious that the Ottomans
were collapsing but that the French remained wedded to
Sykes–Picot, Lloyd George ordered British troops to take Mosul so
that he could present his allies with a fait accompli. Just over a
month after Lawrence and the Arabs reached Damascus, and four

days *after* the armistice with Turkey, on 3 November British troops occupied the city.

Lloyd George had built his career on opportunism of this sort. 'My supreme idea is to get on,' he had admitted to his future wife Margaret long before he even entered parliament.[9] 'To this idea, I shall sacrifice everything – except, I trust, honesty. I am prepared to thrust even love itself under the wheels of my Juggernaut if it obstructs the way.' In the end he offered up both love and honesty in his quest for power. An affair with his secretary and adviser Frances Stevenson was one of several that earned him the soubriquet 'the Goat', while his integrity never quite recovered from his embroilment in an insider-trading scandal, the infamous Marconi affair. Women and wealth fascinated him, and a civil servant told an anecdote that summed up his other guiding priority. Delivering him a note in a dull meeting one day, he found that the politician 'had spent the last hour in writing the word VOTES in enormous block letters, and then embellishing them with all sorts of scrolls and borders in blue, green, red pencil'.[10]

'For veracity, Ananias, for friendship Brutus, for his other qualities I refer you to Signor Marconi,' the politician and writer Lord Morley reputedly remarked about Lloyd George.[11] But after Kitchener's volunteer army met disaster on the Somme and Asquith's Liberal government split over conscription, such reservations about Lloyd George were grimly swallowed. Now, it was the dogged, belligerent qualities that he had shown as minister of munitions and then secretary of state for war that recommended him to run the country. But when Lloyd George took power at the end of 1916, the kingmakers were not his fellow Liberals but the Conservatives, who shared his belief that conscription was now necessary, his enthusiasm for imperial expansion and his thirst for power. He was 'the one public man here who has an undoubted touch of genius', the American ambassador to London reported home.[12] 'There is something very remarkable about him,' wrote a young British diplomat after meeting him for the first time. 'He creates the impression of a great man and he does it without seeming theatrical and without seeming insincere ... He is a great contrast to Mr Asquith who prefers to talk of nothing nearer home than Thucydides.'[13]

Before the term became a toxic one, Lloyd George described himself as a 'Nationalist Socialist'.[14] He appointed a new five-man cabinet that included the prominent imperialists Lords Curzon and Milner to run the war. He chose Hankey to run its business, made his lover Stevenson his private secretary and largely seized control of foreign policy himself. His concentration of power was controversial and made him enemies, but it worked. With victory in sight, he was on the verge of being lionised as the man who had won the war. Before the elation died away he was determined to seize the opportunities that triumph brought. On that October night in Paris, he thought 'it would attract less attention to our enormous gains in this war, if we swallowed our share of Turkey now, and the German colonies later.'[15]

This order reflected Lloyd George's desire to avoid President Wilson's disapproving gaze. He was calculating that, because the United States had not declared war on the Ottomans, Wilson had less excuse to interfere in the Middle East. But it rapidly became obvious that Lloyd George had been over-optimistic. After Wilson briefed the Washington foreign press corps about the approach he intended to take at the peace conference, news reached London that he was 'strongly opposed to Britain profiting by [the] peace terms' and specifically 'opposed to [a] British Protectorate over Palestine and Mesopotamia'.[16] That jeopardised Lloyd George's hope of gaining 'absolute' control over Mosul's oil.

As a consequence Lawrence generated substantial interest when he reached London on 28 October. But whereas he had come to establish what the British government might do for the Arabs, it quickly became apparent that the officials whom he met were wondering what Lawrence might be able to make the Arabs do for them. As one of those he met put it, 'the rise of the Arab movement has been a fortunate development for the British Empire at a crucial point of its history'.[17]

At a meeting the same day the Foreign Office minister Lord Robert Cecil raised the government of Mesopotamia with him, and recorded afterwards that Lawrence had 'urged that it should be put under an Arab Government of as little practical activity as possible. He suggested that one of King Husein's sons should be Governor.

Abdullah would do very well.'[18] The following day the Eastern Committee also asked Lawrence about Arab leaders' attitudes towards the settlement of the region. Lawrence answered that Feisal was pro-British, but that his supporters' willingness to accept Britain's rights to Palestine and Mesopotamia by conquest would depend on whether Britain opposed France's claims. By the end of the week the effect of Lawrence's arrival was obvious to his former mentor, David Hogarth. 'Our whole attitude towards the French is hardening here,' wrote Hogarth. 'TEL has put the wind up everybody and done much good.'[19]

Although Lawrence's approach raised fears at the India Office, where one senior official worried that backing an Arab government in northern Iraq would 'incur the ill-will of France' and deter the investment needed to finance oil exploration, such concerns were, for the time being, ignored.[20] Lawrence's 'violently anti-French' message fitted with the times. The chairman of the Eastern Committee, Lord Curzon, declared that he was 'seriously afraid that the great Power from whom we may have most to fear in the future is France', and that attitude was widely shared.[21] With Germany and the Ottomans defeated, from London, Britain's wartime ally looked like a rival once again.

The impression was reinforced by the combative approach the French government was taking. Stiffened by intense lobbying from the Comité de l'Asie Française and from parliament, at the beginning of November it successfully blunted a British attempt to make it endorse Arab self-rule so as to avoid Wilson's likely criticism. The resulting 'Anglo-French Declaration', which was issued on 9 November, prematurely triggered wild Arab celebrations because it pledged both governments' support for 'the setting up of national governments and administrations deriving their authority from the free exercise of the initiative and choice of the indigenous populations'. But in the next breath it gave both powers carte blanche for endless interference by declaring their intention to 'ensure by their support and adequate assistance' that the new governments performed well. And so, when the French foreign minister, Stephen Pichon, addressed the French parliament at the end of December, he was able to assure the assembly that 'the accords established with

England continue to bind England and us'.[22] He also promised that France would press for the recognition of its right to Syria at the peace conference.

Nevertheless the Eastern Committee and the Foreign Office continued to believe that unilateral support for self-determination represented the best way to achieve the British goal of dominance in the Middle East obliquely. In a second appearance before the Eastern Committee, Lawrence argued that the British government should support the Arabs' presence at the peace conference. That certainly appealed to Cecil, the junior foreign minister. Worried that 'we should undoubtedly have a very difficult case from the international point of view, particularly with regard to the presentation of it to the Americans', he argued that it would be 'very important if we could produce an Arab who would back up our claims'.[23] The committee's chairman, Curzon, was similarly convinced. 'We ought to play self-determination for all it is worth,' he felt, 'knowing in the bottom of our hearts we are more likely to benefit from it than anybody else.'[24] Lawrence was sent to France to fetch Feisal for talks in London.

Once the British government had decided to support self-determination for those who could be trusted to ask for British help, on 12 December Balfour brought together the two men on whom it was now relying. Feisal and the British Zionist Chaim Weizmann had already met once before that year, in May, near Aqaba. Balfour now encouraged both to sign a deal that would defer one foreseeable cause of acrimony until after the peace conference was over. In a pact on 3 January 1919 the two men agreed to set a definite boundary between the Hijaz and Palestine, after the peace conference had ended.[25] Today, this pact is sometimes cited as a freely given Arab acknowledgement of the legitimate existence of the state of Israel, but Feisal depended on a British subsidy of £150,000 a month and that was why he signed. He also made his support conditional on the Arabs achieving their independence.

At the same time, with substantial help from Lawrence, Feisal completed a memorandum that set out Arab hopes at the conference. He insisted on full independence for Syria, but in Mesopotamia and Palestine he accepted the need for outside help. Acknowledging that there was a desire 'to exploit Mesopotamia rapidly', he accepted that the government there would 'have to be buttressed by the men and material resources of a great foreign Power'.[26] In Palestine he declared his reluctance to take responsibility for 'holding level the scales in the clash of races and religions that have, in this one province, so often involved the world in difficulties', and called for 'the effective super-position of a great trustee'. In both cases, it was obvious which power he had in mind.

In the meantime, however, the restless Lloyd George had tried a different, and more aggressive, tack. Anxious to resolve the question of the status of Mosul and Palestine before the matter was subjected to American scrutiny at the peace conference, he decided to tie the issue to France's core objective – the recovery of Alsace-Lorraine, the province it had lost to Germany in 1871. He knew that the French prime minister, Georges Clemenceau, would need British support to be certain of regaining this disputed former territory because it was not clear how the local population might vote if they were asked to settle the matter themselves. He also knew that his French counterpart, unlike many of his officials in the Quai d'Orsay, took no interest whatsoever in the Middle East. A year earlier, soon after taking power, Clemenceau had told him that 'He did not want Syria for France' but that if Lloyd George could 'get him a protectorate over Syria for France he would not refuse it "as it would please some reactionaries", but he attached no importance to it'.[27] It was a conversation that the British prime minister had not forgotten.

Accordingly, shortly before Clemenceau was due to come to London to discuss tactics ahead of the peace conference, Lloyd George had Balfour warn the French ambassador that British support over Alsace-Lorraine was not guaranteed. Complaining about French intransigence over the Sykes–Picot agreement, Balfour icily informed the French: 'His Majesty's Government can only hope that the French Government may not on their part experience the embarrassment which an equally unaccommodating attitude on the part of their Allies would be likely to cause.'[28] It did not require great skill for the French ambassador to appreciate that this message was 'a sort of menace'.[29]

On 1 December Clemenceau arrived in London, where he was

met by cheering crowds. 'Well,' he began when he met Lloyd George for private talks, 'what are we to discuss?'

Lloyd George seized the moment. 'Mesopotamia and Palestine,' he answered.

'Tell me what you want,' said Clemenceau.

'I want Mosul.'

'You shall have it', responded Clemenceau. 'Anything else?'

'Yes, I want Jerusalem too.'

'You shall have it,' Clemenceau said again, although he warned Lloyd George that his imperialist foreign minister Stephen Pichon would 'make difficulties about Mosul'.[30] The French commitment seemed clear enough, but the conversation generated new tensions. For it left Clemenceau wishing that he had been less generous and Lloyd George under the impression that he should have pushed for more.

The supreme council of the five victorious powers first met on 12 January 1919 in the office of the foreign minister at the Quai d'Orsay. As the oldest leader and the host, Clemenceau chaired the proceedings. From an armchair before the open fire he could survey his four counterparts – President Wilson, Lloyd George, and the prime ministers of Italy and Japan – as they sat opposite him in the panelled room, with their foreign ministers and advisers behind them.

On home soil Clemenceau showed none of the weakness that Lloyd George had so deftly exploited six weeks earlier. His nickname was 'the Tiger', but the seventy-seven-year-old French premier was a stout, bald man whose snow-white moustache gave him a closer resemblance to a walrus. Watching him, the British diplomat Harold Nicolson observed 'the half-smile of an irritated, sceptical and neurasthenic gorilla'.[31] Whichever animal comparison the French premier evoked, there was unanimous agreement that he was ponderous and autocratic. The council's meetings elongated as a consequence.

In the cold, outside the palace, the world's press hung around waiting for developments. Inside, the early hopes of clear and swift results dissolved. 'Nobody who has not had experience of committee work in actual practice can conceive of the difficulty of inducing a Frenchman, an Italian, an American and an Englishman to agree on anything,' Nicolson wrote in his diary. 'A majority agreement is easy enough: an unanimous agreement is an impossibility; or, if possible, then possible only in the form of some paralytic compromise.'[32] That was good news only for the fashionable portrait painter Augustus John, who had seen the business possibilities in such an unprecedented conglomeration of vanity, and come to Paris to set up shop.

Clemenceau was unapologetic about the time the preliminary negotiations were taking. 'The art of arranging how men are to live is even more complex than that of massacring them,' he later wrote.[33] Like Lloyd George, he was a radical supported by his country's right who owed his premiership to a widespread belief that he had the tenacity to win the war. A qualified doctor who had been jailed in his youth for duelling, he held the dubious honour of being the longest-serving prime minister during the unstable Third Republic, having held on in office for thirty-three months between 1906 and 1909. Early in the war he ran a newspaper, *L'Homme enchaîné*, which he used to eviscerate a war minister and his leading general, and then the interior minister when the Germans were discovered to be subsidising an anti-war French newspaper called *Le Bonnet Rouge*. 'No more pacifist campaigns, no more German intrigues,' he declared when asked to form a government following this scandal in November 1917. 'Neither treason nor taint of treason; the war, nothing but the war.'[34]

Clemenceau's abrasiveness was part of his allure: unlike Lloyd George, 'the Tiger' had not used charm to reach the top. His speciality was belittling his ministers. He complained loudly that Klotz, his finance minister, was the only Jew who could not count. 'Who is Pichon?' he once demanded, when his infamously lazy foreign minister was mentioned. 'So he is,' he said, when he was reminded; 'I had forgotten it.'[35] The British ambassador in Paris put it well: 'The Tiger did not invite individuals to be members of his cabinet in order to hear what they might have to say but to carry out his views.'[36] That strategy had worked. Having crushed the defeatism of 1917, Clemenceau finished the war as 'Père la Victoire'. Now, he had to demonstrate that he could win the peace.

The cost of the victory was enormous. One million four hundred thousand Frenchmen were dead. Three million more were wounded. A swathe of northern France was ruined. Six hundred and seventy thousand women were now widows, and France was seven billion dollars in debt. Yet, at the armistice Clemenceau predicted: 'France, formerly the warrior of God, now the saviour of humanity, always the warrior of the ideal, will recover her place in the world and continue her magnificent, unending race in pursuit of human progress.'[37] The first part of that revival required an advantageous settlement at the peace conference.

The colonialists in France claimed, predictably, that imperial expansion at the enemy's expense would help France to recover. 'The colonial development of France is one of the essential conditions for the re-establishment of her strength in the face of a Germany that will remain ... her implacable enemy,' ran the argument in one paper put before Clemenceau.[38] But it rapidly became clear when the peace conference began that their aim would be difficult to achieve.

The stumbling block was the attitudes of both Wilson and Lloyd George. Complaining that he was caught between 'Jesus Christ on the one hand, and Napoleon Bonaparte on the other', Clemenceau was forced to accept that the enemies' colonies would be turned into 'mandates' that one or other of them would rule as 'mandatories' of the League of Nations, the embryonic international organisation championed by President Wilson.[39] In the former Ottoman Empire there would be three – Mesopotamia, Syria and Palestine – and the wording that was hammered out to define the mandatories' responsibilities in all three implied that independence for all of them was not far off. Their independence was to be 'provisionally recognised subject to the rendering of administrative advice and assistance by a Mandatory until such time as they are able to stand alone'. The 'wishes of these communities must be a principal consideration in the selection of the Mandatory'.

Anticipating this outcome, while these negotiations were going on, behind the scenes French officials tried to exclude Feisal from the peace conference's proceedings. The 'magnificent welcome' the British had accorded the Arab leader the previous month raised

French suspicions that Feisal was key to a plan 'to create in Asia Minor, to the detriment of our influence, a vast organisation in the pay of Great Britain'.[40] When Feisal found his name was missing from the official list of delegates and complained, the head of the Asian department at the Quai d'Orsay, Jean Goût, tried to detach him from his British sponsors by claiming that it was they who had deliberately excluded him. If Feisal transferred his allegiance to the French, said Goût, 'we can arrange things for you'.[41]

The British reacted furiously when Feisal reported what Goût had said, and insisted on their Arab ally's inclusion. Feisal eventually addressed the conference on 6 February, with Lawrence as his interpreter. Lawrence had already briefed a series of American correspondents on Feisal's aims and, in line with this, Feisal based his argument for the recognition of the Arabs on Wilson's call for self-determination, and not on Britain's woolly wartime promise to his father. Acknowledging that Palestine and Lebanon would need to be treated differently, he called for Arab independence elsewhere. He evidently impressed the American delegation. According to the secretary of state, Robert Lansing, he 'seemed to breathe the perfume of frankincense'.[42] In Wilson's adviser Colonel House he inspired 'a kindly feeling for the Arabs', while another United States official reported that he was 'the most winning figure, so everyone says, at the whole Peace Conference'.[43]

When, during his speech, Feisal praised the British for the help that they had given him to oust the Turks, the French foreign minister interrupted. Had not the French also provided the Arabs with assistance? Pichon asked. Feisal, who was seemingly ready for this intervention, thanked the French for sending 'a small contingent with four antiquated guns and two new ones to join his forces'.[44] In the words of the British observer who gleefully recorded the exchange, 'Pichon was sorry he had spoken and looked a fool.' When Clemenceau, following his Quai d'Orsay brief, claimed that in Syria France had 'a centuries-old Protectorate, the origins of which date back to the Crusades', Lawrence tartly reminded the premier, who was more or less an atheist, that 'the Crusaders had been defeated and the Crusades had failed'.[45]

Having failed to exclude and belittle Feisal, the French now tried

to demonise him. The following morning the French newspapers
launched a headlong attack on the Arab leader and his translator,
whom one French general described as 'British imperialism with
Arab headgear'.[46] *Paris Midi* alleged that his true ambitions were
pan-Islamic – and so a threat to Britain's other Muslim possessions
including India – and remarked that Lawrence 'appeared to have
become more pan-Arab than English'.[47] Harking back to the
Fashoda era, the newspaper compared Lawrence to Gordon of
Khartoum, describing both as 'men who have contributed both
greatness and misfortune to their country; mystics who are at the
same time adventurers. Once they are possessed by their dream,
nothing can stop them, not even the recognised interests of their
own country.' The *Echo de Paris*, which had unmasked Lawrence
the previous September, pursued a similar line, arguing that
Lawrence was seeking to present Whitehall officials with a fait
accompli, in the belief that 'England never abandons a buccaneer
who succeeds'.[48] In the background, French officials briefed the press
that the only reason Britain had been able to spare the troops to con-
quer Syria was because France had done most of the fighting on the
western front.[49] France as well, therefore, deserved a share of the
Middle Eastern spoils.

The results of this press campaign alarmed the British. By late
February the Foreign Office's Political Intelligence Department reck-
oned that Syria had become one of the two 'difficult questions'
facing the peace conference (the other was the question of whether
France would occupy the Rhineland), because 'practically all
Frenchmen except the Socialists' were insisting that the former
Ottoman province should now become a French colony.[50] The
French ambassador in London reinforced this impression. He
warned his British counterparts that although the French interest in
Syria was 'possibly rather sentimental than material ... the feeling
that existed was very strong indeed'.[51]

Lloyd George kicked himself for allowing Paris to be the venue for
the conference. 'We knew beforehand that the French Bureaucracy
would resort to these underhand methods of influencing our
deliberations, bullying, cajoling, lying, sowing dissension and resort-
ing to all their well-known methods for achieving their ends by

devious means,' he wrote. 'Their articles on Syria have been perfectly intolerable.'[52]

The French put up an Arab named Shukri Ganem to argue that Feisal should be ignored because he was not a Syrian, but this tactic backfired. Ganem had lived in Paris for over thirty years and admitted that he had forgotten how to speak Arabic. He further undermined his case for French control of Syria by speaking for two and a half hours. The fidgety President Wilson, who was due to sail for the United States for a brief visit the following day, got out of his chair to look out of the window. Clemenceau turned round and glared at Pichon. 'What did you get this fellow here for anyway?' he asked. Pichon spread his hands and pouted. 'Well I didn't know he was going to carry on this way.'[53]

A French effort to lay a counter-claim to Palestine went similarly wrong. After Chaim Weizmann spoke briefly and forcefully in favour of a British mandate, the Jew the Quai d'Orsay had found to press its case droned on for half an hour. Clemenceau's spokesman, André Tardieu, told the press that day that his government renounced its claim to Palestine and would accept a British mandate. Alarmed by the course of events, the Comité de l'Asie Française submitted its own memorandum to the French government, pressing Clemenceau to take a stand against Lloyd George. Having noted that Britain had emerged 'unquestionably very aggrandised' from the conflict, it insisted: 'We will no longer accept any diminution of our general situation in the world.'[54] In Syria, it claimed, France had 'an incontestable right, as yet unsatisfied, to impose our culture'.

The French government did not follow the Comité's advice. On 15 February the Quai d'Orsay sent a memorandum to the British which confirmed Clemenceau's offer of Mosul and the abandonment of the Sykes–Picot agreement, so long as Britain supported France's claim to the mandate for both coastal and inland Syria. Having recognised the significance of oil more slowly than their British rivals, French diplomats also demanded an equal share of Mesopotamian oil.

The British had also seen a copy of the Comité's memorandum, and dismissed it. 'Wounded pride drowns its misgivings as to its own strength by setting itself an extravagant programme to accomplish,' wrote one official, who believed that French energies were better spent accepting that 'if France is in the future to lead the world her leadership can only be intellectual not political'.[55] Aware that the French government had ignored the Comité as well, the British sensed they had the upper hand. They replied aggressively to the French government's proposal. Having been advised by its own oil experts that the oasis of Palmyra, which lay halfway between Damascus and the Euphrates, would be a vital station for an oil pipeline running from Mosul to the Mediterranean, they insisted that Palmyra should be part of Mesopotamia – thereby dramatically reducing the area which the French were counting on as being part of Syria.

By doing so, the British overstepped the mark. 'Too many Englishmen have failed to recognise that France, bleeding and plundered, is entitled to something better than daily advice to renounce her rights,' André Tardieu complained.[56] His chief, Clemenceau, also felt betrayed by Lloyd George. He claimed that in their private meeting the previous December the British prime minister had said that he accepted France's claim to Syria. Lloyd George initially denied that he had ever made such a promise, although later he said that he had. 'Lloyd George was a most difficult man to deal with,' one French diplomat later said, 'as one never could tell from day to day what his position might be.'[57]

'From the very day after the Armistice I found you an enemy of France,' the French prime minister accused Lloyd George. 'Well,' his British counterpart volleyed, 'was it not always our traditional policy?'[58] With good reason, Clemenceau did not see the joke, for it was all too obvious that the wartime allies were now rivals once again. Feeling pressured by the vengeful attitude of the French public, he decided he would entertain Lloyd George's exorbitant demands no more. 'I won't budge,' he told the French president, Raymond Poincaré, the following month. 'I won't give way on anything any more. We'll see if they can do without me. Lloyd George is a cheat. He has managed to turn me into a "Syrian".'[59]

6

DEADLOCK

AFTER PRESIDENT WILSON HAD RETURNED FROM WASHINGTON to Paris, on 20 March 1919 he met Lloyd George and Balfour, Clemenceau and Pichon at Lloyd George's elegant apartment on the Rue Nitot.

Pichon opened the discussion by describing the intricate negotiations that had taken place so far. He briefly described the Sykes–Picot agreement, the Anglo-French Declaration of 9 November 1918 by which Britain had tried to blunt it, and the Tiger's meeting with Lloyd George in London in December. Then there were the more recent proposals made in Paris: his own government's of 15 February, and the British counter-proposal limiting the size of Syria, which the French had instantly rejected.

Known as Clemenceau's 'faithful shadow', Pichon was, like the prime minister, a doctor turned journalist. But unlike Clemenceau, the foreign minister was a paid-up member of the Comité de l'Asie Française and a committed, if laid-back, supporter of France's claim to the Levant, which he had promised to advance when he addressed the French parliament at the end of the previous year. He was as aware as Clemenceau of the strength of parliamentary and public feeling about Syria, and he told Wilson and Lloyd George that the 15 February proposal was the most the French government could offer. Echoing the argument that Georges-Picot had used in Whitehall more than three years earlier, he insisted that 'French opinion would

not admit that France could be even partly excluded after the sacrifices she had made in the war, even if she had not been able to play
a great part in the Syrian campaign'.[1]

Pichon then launched into a wide-ranging justification of France's
claim to Syria. 'France,' he pointed out, 'had a great number of hos-
pitals in Syria ... some 50,000 children were educated in French
primary schools ... the railway system of Syria was French ... Beirut
was entirely a French port. The gas and electricity works were
French, and the same applied to the lighting along the coast.' France
must have the mandate for Syria.

Lloyd George said no. To give France the mandate for inland
Syria would contravene 'the Treaty with the Arabs', he replied,
referring to the vague promise that McMahon had made to Husein
in October 1915.[2] Clearly exasperated, Pichon said that the first
time he had seen McMahon's letter was when Lloyd George's
adviser, Hankey, had handed him a copy a few weeks earlier. 'How
could France be bound by an agreement the very existence of which
was unknown to her at the time when the 1916 agreement was
signed?'

Official minutes rarely betray raised voices, but those for this
meeting unmistakably do. Lloyd George said that 'the agreement
might have been made by England alone, but it was England who
had organised the whole of the Syrian campaign. There would have
been no question of Syria but for England.'[3] Riled by the French
efforts to stoke public anger through the newspapers, he reminded
Pichon that 'if there was a French public opinion there was also a
British public opinion'. The British knew, he said, that the 'whole
burden of the Syrian campaign had fallen upon Great Britain. The
number of French troops taking part ... had been so small as to
make no difference.' Up to a million British troops had been
involved, there had been 125,000 casualties and the campaign had
cost 'hundreds of millions of pounds'. He added that 'Arab help
had been essential'.

Until now President Wilson had been silent while the British and
French argued with each other. He interrupted to suggest an idea
that had been circulating in Paris for several weeks. 'One of the fundamental principles to which the United States of America adhered

was the consent of the governed,' he declared.[4] For that reason, from his point of view 'the only idea … was as to whether France would be agreeable to the Syrians' and 'whether Great Britain would be agreeable to the inhabitants of Mesopotamia'. The only way to find out was to send a commission 'to discover the desires of the population in these regions'. Clemenceau sensed an opportunity to embarrass Lloyd George, and agreed to this proposal. He stressed that, if the commission was to seek to establish opinion in Syria, then it must visit Palestine and Mesopotamia as well.

Lawrence was ecstatic at this plan; the other members of the British delegation, on the other hand, were not. Independent scrutiny of Britain's claim to be the power that the people of Mesopotamia and Palestine wanted to rule them was the last thing that British officials wanted. 'The weak point of our position,' Balfour had already warned Lloyd George, 'is that in the case of Palestine we deliberately and rightly decline to accept the principle of self-determination. If the present inhabitants were consulted they would unquestionably give an anti-Jewish verdict.'[5] The commission was certain to expose this. Who knew what it might find out in Mesopotamia, where Lawrence had identified the presence of some 'very vivid Arab nationalists'?[6]

The British knew that the commission would find in favour of Arab independence in Syria. But even if it did also accept the case for British rule in Mesopotamia and Palestine, the Syrian example was bound to be infectious. As Gertrude Bell – who had spent much of the war in Mesopotamia as a political officer with British forces – pointed out, 'We have got an embryo Nationalist party in Baghdad and if they make an independent Arab state in Syria they will be forever looking in that direction and complaining that they haven't got the same.' Bell, who had been dismissive of the French claim to Syria, now concluded: 'I would gladly see the French installed there, still more gladly the Americans. Anything rather than creating an Arab state in one place[,] effective British control in another.'[7]

The British delegation's tacit support for Arab independence in Syria ebbed as they realised that the unrest it would generate had implications for Britain's ability to exploit the oil beneath Mosul. In a further memorandum on petroleum the Admiralty's intelligence

department stressed that the experience of oil exploration in neighbouring Persia, where the drilling company's operations had
depended heavily on its relations with the local tribes, showed that
it was 'essential' that a 'strong and stable' government be set up in
Mesopotamia.[8] As Lawrence later acknowledged, 'Lloyd George
couldn't dare to promise any wide measure of self-government
there.'[9]

Seeking to undermine Lawrence further, the India Office sent both
Gertrude Bell and her immediate superior, Arnold Wilson, from
Baghdad to Paris to counterbalance Lawrence's views. Wilson met
Lawrence and reported: 'He seems to me to have done immense
harm and our difficulties with the French in Syria seem to me to be
mainly due to his action and advice.'[10] Lawrence found himself
increasingly sidelined. The man for whom the American president
had made space in his diary in February now had the time to visit the
circus in the evening. When one day at the hotel where the British
delegation was based he looked over the balustrade to see Lloyd
George, Arthur Balfour and the British ambassador to Paris sitting at
the bottom of the stairwell, he went and found two packs of lavatory
paper and emptied their contents into the air above them. At the end
of May he left suddenly for Cairo, ostensibly to retrieve some notes
that would help him as he wrote his book about the campaign, in
truth to try to sway the situation in the region.

There was a further reason why the British appetite for a row with
France was waning, which was a growing disillusionment that a
lasting peace could be achieved. 'We are losing the peace rapidly and
all the hard work done is being wasted,' wrote Harold Nicolson
towards the end of March.[11] When Cecil, the British foreign minister, saw the draft treaty with Germany in May, he warned Lloyd
George that he believed that it was 'neither generous nor just'.[12] If
the peace was to be short-lived, then it would pay Britain not to
aggravate its wartime ally further. Balfour summed up the mood
perfectly. Declaring himself 'very distressed by the Syrian muddle, all
the more so as he perhaps was personally responsible for it', he
admitted that, although 'We had not been honest with either French
or Arab ... it was now preferable to quarrel with the Arab rather
than the French, if there was to be a quarrel at all.'[13]

In an attempt to avert the conflict that the imposition of a French mandate was bound to cause in Syria, the British tried to broker a deal between Feisal and Clemenceau. Clemenceau was willing to meet Feisal because he was keen to reach an agreement that would render President Wilson's commission unnecessary, but when the two men met on 13 April Feisal would not accept Clemenceau's demand that French troops occupy Damascus. As the Arab leader was delighted by the prospect of the commission, soon afterwards he set out for Syria, to French alarm.

As Feisal was still receiving a substantial British subsidy, Clemenceau's advisers urged the French leader to do everything he could to persuade the British to cut off their financial support and to withdraw their troops from Syria. Lloyd George, however, was unwilling to do either. He doubted that the French had the resources to fill the vacuum as quickly as the Arab nationalists, who, if they took control of Damascus, would create an unstoppable momentum for Arab independence in Mesopotamia and Palestine. Nor would he concede Palmyra, because of its strategic importance. The French interpreted his reluctance as proof that Britain did nurse ambitions to rule Syria as well. Such was the atmosphere of suspicion that, when eventually Lloyd George changed his mind and offered to pull back British troops, Clemenceau refused to trust his guarantee. 'You are the very baddest boy,' he told his British counterpart, who was twenty-two years his junior.[14]

A final effort to settle the Syrian question in Paris collapsed during a further meeting at Lloyd George's flat on 22 May that involved 'more explosions and shouting', according to one witness.[15] When Lloyd George reneged on an oil-sharing deal that the British and French delegations had inconveniently negotiated on their own initiative, Clemenceau retaliated by withdrawing his offer of Mosul. The British prime minister launched a tirade against France's obstructive approach to operations against the Ottomans during the war. Clemenceau in turn said that France would not participate in Wilson's commission unless British troops first withdrew from Syria. But, as the two men could not agree on where the Syrian border lay – each still wanted Palmyra – Lloyd George refused to pull back his troops until Wilson's commission had reported. And he said he would send commissioners only if Clemenceau did – and by now, the Frenchman had no intention of giving the commission greater clout by doing so. The meeting closed with no agreement. Although the French prime minister 'does not really care much about Syria', the British ambassador in Paris observed, 'it has now become a question of amour propre and nothing will induce Clemenceau to give way'.[16]

As a consequence of the British and French boycott, when Wilson's commission reached Palestine on 10 June it comprised just two Americans, Henry King and Charles Crane. King was a theologian, Crane a Chicago businessman with an interest in foreign policy whom Wilson had described as a 'very experienced and cosmopolitan man'.[17] Their mission was to decide how best to divide the Ottomans' Arab territory and allocate the three Middle Eastern mandates in order to promote 'order, peace and development', by asking the people themselves what they wanted; their northward progress took them from Jaffa to Jerusalem, Damascus, Beirut and Aleppo, sparking what one British general described as a 'political orgy' as they went.[18]

Although the British and French governments had tried to undermine the commission's clout by refusing to participate, both knew well that its conclusions were bound to carry weight. As a consequence the British and French officials on the spot did their utmost to influence the result. After registering that one of the commissioners' advisers, William Yale, had been the local representative of the American petroleum company Standard Oil before the war, the British managed to dissuade the two commissioners from visiting Mesopotamia at all, and instead supplied them with a summary of Iraqi opinion which was, predictably, pro-British. 'There are the Sunnis and the Shiahs, the townsfolk and the tribes. There must be some outside authority to keep the peace between them,' said one man quoted in the report, which was laughably entitled 'Self-Determination in Iraq'.[19] 'The British must govern the country themselves,' declared another, supplying the answer to the uncertainty left by the first.

In Palestine the two commissioners noticed that 'Two or three military governors seemed to have taken some action to procure votes for Britain', but otherwise felt that the British officials whom they met had been 'courteous, obliging and helpful'.[20] Yale, however, later claimed that Lawrence's old chief, Clayton, who was now the chief political officer in Palestine, had tried to limit the commission's investigations by warning him not to provoke the growing tensions in the country: 'If you show any partiality or commit any indiscretion, Yale, there will be bloodshed.'[21]

In Syria the British let Feisal, to whom they were still paying a monthly subsidy, do the dirty work himself. On his return to Damascus Feisal had set up a parliament called the General Syrian Congress. Just as Crane and King arrived in the city the Congress voted for 'full and absolute independence for Syria' and issued a total rejection of the French.[22] When Yale confronted another British officer with his suspicion that Britain had condoned a 'wide-spread, highly organized, and effective anti-French propaganda campaign', he was told: 'You are correct, Yale, there has been an anti-French propaganda campaign. But we had nothing to do with it.'[23]

Whereas British efforts were relatively discreet, French attempts to sway public opinion in their zone in the Lebanon were 'so bad as to be insulting', the commissioners complained. In a confidential annexe to their report, King and Crane accused the French of using 'inspired articles in the newspapers, attempts at browbeating and espionage', 'threats and bribes, and even imprisonment and banishment' to stop the inhabitants of their zone giving the commissioners their true opinions. Despite these strenuous efforts, 60 per cent of the petitions that King and Crane received were anti-French. As a result of the lobbying and their own experience, the two commissioners finally reported that they were 'reluctantly compelled to believe' that it was 'impossible to recommend a single French mandate for all Syria'.[24]

Instead, on the basis of the petitions they had received, they proposed that the United States should take on the mandate for a united Syria and Palestine, of which Feisal, whom they described as a 'unique outstanding figure capable of rendering [the] greatest service for world peace', should be head of state.[25] Just as the British wanted, they recommended that Great Britain should be the mandatory in Mesopotamia. And, in notable contrast to later American support for Zionism, they argued that the 'extreme Zionist program' in Palestine would require 'serious modification' to prevent war between the Arabs and the Jews.[26]

Even before the two Americans had submitted their report on 28 August, the French guessed the likely outcome of their deliberations and launched a vitriolic press campaign accusing the British of devious work behind the scenes. The leader of the Comité de l'Asie Française, the diplomat Robert de Caix, wrote an article for his organisation's *Bulletin* which accused renegade British officials of a range of underhand tactics designed to undermine French rule.[27] He alleged that the British had denied visas to pro-French Arabs returning to lobby the commissioners, had banned the teaching of French in some schools, and were spreading rumours that the French were interested in the welfare of the Christian population only.

Much of what de Caix alleged is now very hard to validate. But his claims that British officials had also commandeered all the motor transport and had effectively blocked the export of wheat from Syria to Lebanon were true. In all this de Caix saw 'systematic sabotage', but in reality the British were trying to grapple with the chaos left by the Ottoman defeat.[28] De Caix ignored this context. By his own admission, his outlook was Manichaean. 'For me there are only two things in the world, those which serve my country, and those which harm it. I don't look at political questions in any other light,' he wrote.[29]

The *Bulletin* was obscure, but de Caix was influential – 'where he leads other leader-writers follow,' wrote a British diplomat in Paris.[30] When *Le Temps*, a newspaper known for its closeness to the French government, reprinted de Caix's article at the end of July, it endorsed its analysis and, like its author, tried to persuade London to act by drawing a distinction between the honourable British government and its wayward men on the spot in Syria. This was to become a familiar French refrain in the thirty years that followed.

The press campaign alarmed the British government, which increasingly worried more about the abrupt deterioration in its relations with the French than about pressing for a just solution for its wartime Arab allies. A British diplomat went to see Pichon to ask him to put 'the soft pedal down upon this loud anti-British campaign', but the French foreign minister refused to do so. Menacingly, he told his British visitor that it would be 'the greatest mistake' to underestimate 'the almost passionate interest' that the French took in Syria.[31] Le Temps published a further article days later accusing Britain of shipping large quantities of arms to Feisal through Beirut.[32] There was some basis to this allegation, for Britain was trying to reduce the number of its troops in Syria by creating an Arab gendarmerie that could keep the peace instead, but Lloyd George denied that the government had supplied the gendarmes with any weapons.[33]

One man was certainly still doing his utmost to thwart the French efforts to expand their influence beyond their bridgehead in the Lebanon. Lawrence had left Paris in May to return to Egypt to collect his wartime notes so that he could finish writing his long-planned memoir of the campaign. But when he reached Cairo in June he wrote an astonishing, now infamous, letter to W. F. Stirling, his wartime comrade and currently deputy chief political officer with British forces. In it he claimed that in November 1917 he had been betrayed by his Arab guide, Abdul Qadir al Jazairi, and arrested by the Turks during an attempt to reconnoitre the railway junction at Dara.

> I went into Daraa in disguise to spy out the defences, was caught, and identified by Hajim Bey, the governor, by virtue of Abdul Qadir's descriptions of me. (I learned all about his treachery from Hajim's conversation, and from my guards.) Hajim was an ardent pederast and took a fancy to me. So he kept me under guard till night, and then tried to have me. I was unwilling, and prevailed after some difficulty. Hajim sent me to the hospital, and I escaped before dawn, being not as hurt as he thought.[34]

There is good evidence that Lawrence invented this story, and certainly his decision to accuse Abdul Qadir al Jazairi of treachery now was quite deliberate. The Jazairis were a rich, influential and ambitious Damascene family who were determined to usurp Feisal. In October 1918 Lawrence had summarily dismissed Abdul Qadir's brother, Mohammed Said al Jazairi, whom the Turks had left behind as governor of Damascus when they fled. When the two brothers mounted a coup days later in retaliation, Lawrence crushed it. Abdul Qadir was killed during a further effort to overthrow Feisal, and soon afterwards Mohammed Said was interned by the British.

Lawrence's motive in trying to implicate Mohammed Said by association was quite simple. To his alarm, the troublesome former governor had recently been released and it was widely known that, to undermine Feisal, he was backing the French as future rulers of Syria in the hope that the French might reward him in return.[35] The French did exactly that, promoting Mohammed Said as an alternative to Feisal whom they were willing to support. It looked from Mohammed Said's release as if the British authorities might acquiesce to this arrangement, as a means of reconciling the French and the Arabs.

Stirling evidently trusted Lawrence's word, for on 15 August 1919 the British re-arrested Mohammed Said in Beirut; and *The Times*, justifying the decision a few days later, repeated many of the accusations Lawrence had made privately to Stirling almost word for word.[36] The French were furious at Britain's interference inside the zone Allenby had allocated to them. Pichon ordered his ambassador in London to complain to the British that their seizure of a man he described as France's 'protégé' was 'intolerable'.[37]

Lawrence made one further, unsuccessful, effort to derail French ambitions in Syria. When on 1 September he was demobilised, following further criticism of his role in stoking tensions with the French, he decided to reveal the secret wartime agreements that Britain had entered into in a letter to *The Times*, for although they were now common knowledge within government circles, in general they remained unknown. He did so because he knew that the British and French governments were due to reopen discussions on the Middle East that month, and he wanted to increase the pressure on them to involve Feisal in that process.[38]

But Lawrence was too late, again. On 9 September, two days before his letter was published in *The Times*, Lloyd George held a further meeting of five of his closest advisers to discuss his forth-coming negotiations with Clemenceau. Uppermost in all their minds was the pressing need to save money. The press barons, the Harmsworth brothers, had recently launched an 'anti-waste' cam-paign to curb record state expenditure, and amid the calls for austerity Lloyd George and his colleagues knew that the cost of maintaining over three hundred thousand British soldiers in the former Ottoman Empire was unjustifiable. Curzon, who foresaw that trouble in the Middle East might make a rapid British exit even harder, advised leaving both Syria and Palestine 'while we yet can'.[39]

Lloyd George would not, however, concede Palestine. Having fought so hard with Clemenceau over the territory, he said that it could not be given up 'without great loss of prestige', by which he truly meant his own.[40] He therefore instructed his new secretary of state for war, Churchill, to slash the cost of Britain's presence in Mesopotamia. He proposed to wash his hands of Syria, by with-drawing British troops there to Palestine and leaving the French and Feisal to work out an accommodation between them.

At the 9 September Lloyd George set out his plan. 'We could keep faith both with the French and with the Arabs,' he argued, 'if we were to clear out of Syria, handing our military posts there to the French, and at the same time, clear out of Damascus, Homs, Hama and Aleppo, handing them over to Feisal. If the French then got into trouble with Feisal it would not be our fault.'[41] The next day the prime minister and his advisers debated where the frontier between Syria and Palestine lay. Lloyd George had previously talked airily of a Palestine stretching from 'Dan to Beersheba', but the weakness of this biblical formula lay in the fact that no one knew where Dan was.[42] Eventually, after a long and inconclusive discussion, a frus-trated Lloyd George told Hankey to telephone London to find out from two Christian publishers how the authorities on the Bible defined Palestine.

'The truth is that any division of the Arab country between Aleppo and Mecca is unnatural,' one British adviser admitted, 'there-fore whatever division is made should be decided by practical requirements. Strategy forms the best guide.'[43] In line with this, more contemporary concerns than the scripture determined the location of the line to which British troops would pull back. The rapid development of air power during the war was making the War Office think about the defence of the Suez Canal against air attack, and Allenby declared that the northern border of Palestine probably lay just south of the ancient port of Tyre – a suspiciously round two hundred miles from the mouth of the canal. When, finally, an authority on the region joined the meeting the following day to finish sketching out the frontier, this was not an expert on the scripture but the managing director of the Anglo-Persian Oil Company.

Once the British had traced the perfect frontier on the map, one that gave British troops access to water sources that would also support a railway from northern Mesopotamia to the Mediterranean, Lloyd George contacted Clemenceau asking him for a meeting. 'For us,' he now told his French counterpart, 'the friendship of France is worth ten Syrias.'[44] He suggested that Feisal join their discussion of the arrangements, but the French prime minister, who saw Feisal as a British puppet, vetoed that idea. On 13 September in Paris Lloyd George formally told Clemenceau that British forces would pull back from Syria, from 1 November.

Two days later Lawrence submitted one last memorandum to the Foreign Office, in which he predicted that premature French interference in the Arab zone would 'only unite the Arabs against them'.[45] Anticipating that the British government would not regard this as their problem, he also warned his former colleagues, with equal prescience, that if they did not involve the Arabs more in the government of Mesopotamia he expected an uprising to erupt there 'about March next'. Then he left London for Oxford, where he took up a fellowship offered to him by All Souls College. He intended to complete his memoir of the war, but he was exhausted and depressed and the period was not fruitful. His mother later recalled that he could 'sometimes sit the entire morning between breakfast and lunch in the same position, without moving, and with the same expression on his face'.[46]

As a consequence of Clemenceau's refusal to include Feisal in their conversation, Lloyd George only told the Arab leader of his plan to withdraw from Syria six days later, at a meeting in 10 Downing

Street. According to one witness, the prime minister 'gave his usual display of verbal acrobatics, speaking much and saying little', and Feisal was not impressed.[47] Expressing his fear that the French would fill the void that the British were about to leave, he told Lloyd George how, in the Middle Ages, a slave 'had had the right to demand to be sold to another master. He hoped that in the twentieth century at least that right would be preserved.'[48] But in a further meeting Lloyd George told Feisal bluntly that the British people were no longer willing to tolerate extensive troop deployments abroad: the withdrawal from Syria would go ahead regardless.

Lloyd George had not only an angry Feisal to contend with; Clemenceau was just as furious when he realised that his British counterpart was going to cede inland Syria to the Arabs rather than to him. The French prime minister was in the midst of an election campaign in which his rivals, the Parti Colonial, were gaining ground. In a bid to limit the damage that the news from Syria was bound to do him, Clemenceau hurriedly announced that he was sending a very popular general, Henri Gouraud, to be the new high commissioner to the Levant. Gouraud had made his name crushing opposition to French rule in North Africa before the war. To mollify the colonial lobby further, de Caix, the head of the Comité de l'Asie Française, was to be Gouraud's chief secretary.

When Lloyd George then suggested that Gouraud might meet Feisal to coordinate arrangements, Clemenceau exploded. Convinced that the precipitate British withdrawal was a deliberate attempt to handicap France, on 14 October he sent a fiery telegram to the prime minister in which he argued that the British move broke the commitment in the Sykes–Picot agreement that Britain and France would 'protect' an Arab state. He also attacked Britain's support for Feisal. 'How can an entente be possible with the Emir,' he raged, 'if that man, who claims sovereignty over all Syria, remains the protégé of the English?'[49]

Clemenceau's telegram enraged Lloyd George, who took issue with his claim that under the Sykes–Picot agreement France would 'protect' an Arab state. 'The word used in the Agreement is "soutenir" (uphold) which bears an entirely different significance,' Lloyd George pointed out, before accusing Clemenceau of 'an attitude of suspicion and opposition wholly unwarranted by the facts', which was liable to lead to 'serious and long-continued disturbances throughout the Arab territories'.[50] This worried him, because the worse the trouble was, the more troops Britain would need to maintain in Palestine and Mesopotamia.

Clemenceau relented a little. After the British withdrawal had begun, he allowed Gouraud to meet Feisal in Paris. Over lunch, according to Feisal, the general acknowledged that the Arabs would not tolerate the division of their country, but warned that, if blood had to be shed to impose order within Syria, he would not hesitate to shed it. On 16 November he set out to take charge of the French administration in Syria.

'Your mission,' Clemenceau airily told Gouraud before he left, 'is to establish a centre of French influence in the heart of the Mediterranean ... Put a *poilu** of ours everywhere that there is a British Tommy. I know that you have not chosen to go there, but there are two types of men: those who put themselves before their country and the others. I know you are one of the latter. *Allez!*'[51]

---

* A familiar term for a French soldier, equivalent to 'Tommy', and literally meaning 'hairy'.

PART TWO

INTERWAR TENSIONS:
1920–1939

Stop and search, Palestine, 1938. Death was the penalty for the unauthorised possession of a firearm. But the Arabs thwarted Britain's counter-insurgency in Palestine by using neighbouring Syria and Lebanon as a sanctuary.

7

THE CRUSADER

THE NEW HIGH COMMISSIONER IN SYRIA, GENERAL HENRI Gouraud, arrived in Beirut on 21 November 1919 to deal with Feisal and stamp French authority on Syria. He was met by cheering crowds, but this apparently spontaneous display of loyalty owed itself to prior work behind the scenes by French political officers.[1] Aged fifty-two, Gouraud was a slight, wiry, blue-eyed man. One British diplomat neatly summed him up as 'fiery, bearded, one-armed and heavy handed'.[2]

The story of how Gouraud had lost his arm was legendary. While leading French forces at Gallipoli four years earlier, he had been badly injured by an exploding Turkish shell, and one of his wounds became infected. 'It's a sure sign of gangrene, General: you'll have to agree to us amputating it, or you could die this evening,' he was told in the field hospital. 'What an odd request,' Gouraud answered, managing a smile. 'I know no one who wants to die this evening. You neither, I don't doubt.'[3]

As a result of his injuries Gouraud lost his arm and gained a limp, but neither stopped him from returning to the front. In July 1918, in command of the French Fourth Army, he successfully repelled a last-ditch effort by the Germans to break through the Champagne region to Paris. In a sign of just how much that victory meant, when he was met by Clemenceau shortly afterwards the prime minister, who generally preferred shaking hands, greeted him with uncharacteristic passion – perhaps because Gouraud had no right hand to shake. 'He kissed me twenty times, on the cheeks, on the eyes, on the forehead,' Gouraud later recalled.[4] Now, when the Parti Colonial won a landslide victory in the November 1919 elections, the prime minister looked to 'the lion of Champagne' to rescue him again.

Unmarried, militantly pious and monastically austere, Gouraud saw himself as a crusader. In his mind's eye, when he disembarked at Beirut he was following in the footsteps of the predominantly French warrior monks who had responded to the papal call eight centuries earlier, and whose castles still crowned the olive-dotted Lebanese and Syrian hills. One of his best officers, Georges Catroux, revealingly commented how 'as a Christian, as a soldier and a romantic' the general had set his sights on Damascus as soon as he set foot in Beirut.[5] From a Spartan bedroom decorated only with a picture of his mother, Gouraud plotted France's acquisition of the city his crusading forebears had never reached. For, as Catroux put it, Damascus was not just 'the town of St Paul's revelation' but also that 'unconquered fortress which defied the assaults of the Franks, the capital and burial place of the great Saladin, chivalrous victor over Lusignan at Hattin'.* In the words of de Caix, Gouraud was, 'too much of a soldier'.[6]

On his arrival in Beirut, Gouraud declared that victory in Europe had freed French troops to come to Syria, but in truth he simply did not have the manpower to fulfil Clemenceau's directive to place a French soldier everywhere there had been a British one. At his disposal he had barely thirty thousand men.[7] As the British army pulled out, the smallness of the French force that replaced it became embarrassingly obvious because, as one French officer recalled, 'we could not put a battalion where they had had a regiment'.[8] According to Gouraud's officials, 'Instead of giving the East a demonstration of force, we showed our weakness.'[9]

That mattered, because Gouraud faced trouble on the northern and eastern borders of the coastal zone that was now in French

---

* Guy de Lusignan, from Poitou in France, was briefly king of Jerusalem until his defeat by Saladin at the battle of Hattin, near the Sea of Galilee, on 4 July 1187. Saladin went on to seize Jerusalem that October; the city did not return to Christian hands until its capture by Allenby in 1917.

hands. To the north, his forces in Cilicia – now south-east Turkey – were being attacked by Turkish nationalists led by the brilliant general Mustapha Kemal. To the east, the British had left the Beqaa valley in Arab hands, although under the terms of the Sykes–Picot agreement it was part of the 'Blue', French, zone.[10] As the fertile valley was key to the viability of both the French and Arab zones, tensions between French and Arab forces in the vicinity were mounting.

Gouraud was itching to take control of the Beqaa, but Clemenceau initially vetoed any move, saying that he wanted to prove 'the moderation of our policy', while he tried to reach agreement with Feisal who had come to Paris after his disappointing meetings with Lloyd George in London.[11] Although Feisal turned down his opening offer that France take complete control of Syria, Clemenceau remained optimistic that a deal was possible. On 9 December he told Gouraud that once he had reached a deal with Feisal it would be 'in our interest to build up his importance and put our trust in him'.[12]

France's faith in Feisal was short-lived. On 14 December Arab forces clashed with the French in the Beqaa valley, giving Gouraud the excuse he needed to disregard the orders from Paris. Claiming that the incident showed that Feisal could not keep order, next day he sent his troops into the Beqaa in force, and there was fighting when they then seized Baalbek, the valley's major town.

Alarmed by the news, Feisal, who was still in Paris, told the French that he was willing to accept the offer that Clemenceau had made him to buy himself some time. He raced back to Damascus, ostensibly to canvass the nationalist factions on the deal, but really because he recognised the dangerous precedent France's move into the Beqaa had set.[13] Well aware that 'Many of the officers in Gouraud's entourage have no other goal than the conquest of the country,' he predicted that 'local military disturbances or incidents will give them an excuse to occupy Damascus': which was exactly what eventually happened.[14]

Earlier that year a British official had described Feisal's attempts to control the increasingly unhappy nationalists as like 'a novice trying to drive a team of colts'.[15] When the Arab shaykh reached Damascus he was unable to persuade the nationalists to accept the deal that Clemenceau had offered him. Accused of a betrayal by his own supporters, he felt obliged to harden his own position towards the French. He refused to allow Gouraud to use the railway line between Damascus and Aleppo, which the French general needed to supply his hard-pressed troops on the northern, Turkish front. French resupply convoys that had previously taken four days by rail now spent a fortnight at sea.[16] Arab nationalists made French logistics harder still by using the expertise taught to them by Lawrence to blow up the railway between Alexandretta and Aleppo.

In Paris, Clemenceau resigned so that he could fight the presidential election. His successor as prime minister, Alexandre Millerand, was unwilling to give Feisal the benefit of the doubt for any longer. He could feel confident that the Americans would not interfere: in September 1919 President Wilson had been incapacitated by a stroke and the Senate had rejected U.S. membership of the League of Nations soon afterwards. On 10 February 1920 Millerand told Gouraud that Feisal had to offer 'more complete proof of his ability to impose his authority'.[17] If the Arab leader could not do so, Millerand authorised his general 'to take any measures necessary for the maintenance of order, the defence of the people, and the safety of our troops. ... you certainly possess the means of imposing respect for our rights'.

Here, Millerand was being just as unrealistic as Clemenceau had been, for Gouraud simply did not have enough troops to enforce order. This shortfall left Gouraud with one option: before he could crush Arab opposition, he would need to reach a deal with Mustapha Kemal, the Turkish leader, and he needed the backing of the British. After the General Syrian Congress proclaimed Feisal king of Syria and Palestine, and Abdullah, his ambitious older brother, emir of Mesopotamia on 8 March, the French ambassador Cambon asked to see the British foreign secretary Lord Curzon, to agree concerted action.

Even though the Congress's announcements had profound implications for the British, Curzon was initially unwilling to help Cambon, to the latter's surprise. Although the British foreign secretary agreed that the Congress's step was 'unwarranted and intolerable', he blamed it on the French government for forcing themselves into areas where they were unwelcome.[18] 'I felt it neces-sary,' the infamously superior Curzon wrote afterwards, 'to place on record that the responsibility was not ours, but belonged in the main, if not exclusively, to the French.' Millerand reacted sharply. Ahead of a conference at San Remo on the Italian Riviera, at which the allocation of the mandates was to be decided, he threatened to insist on an international administration in Palestine, as the Sykes–Picot agreement had set out.

This threat caused deep anxiety within the British government. Its relations with the Zionists were deteriorating rapidly and British officials were no longer certain that the Zionists would necessarily support a British mandate for Palestine. The friendship had soured because, while the British had committed themselves to supporting a Jewish national home so long as it did not impinge on the existing, mostly Arab, population's rights, the Zionists were determined to establish a Jewish state as fast as possible, regardless. A British car-dinal who visited Palestine early in 1919 described them, with a mixture of surprise and distaste, as 'already asserting themselves in every way, claiming official posts for their nominees and generally interfering'.[19]

Worried that the Zionists would destabilise Palestine, the British tried to restrain them. 'We should go slow about the Zionist aspira-tions and the Zionist State,' the British general in command in Palestine advised, because 'a Jewish Government in any form would mean an Arab rising, and the nine-tenths of the population who are not Jews would make short shrift with the Hebrews'.[20] In London, Curzon agreed. He felt that 'the pretensions of Weizmann and Company' were 'extravagant and ought to be checked'.[21]

The Zionists complained about the sluggish progress towards self-government, accusing the British of anti-Semitism. Unwilling to accept that their own activity was causing Arab anger, they also alleged that the French were behind the Arab protests. Weizmann claimed that Arab hostility towards the Jews in Palestine was 'artifi-cial, brought about by agencies working in the dark, operating against Great Britain's position in the East'.[22] It was an explanation that suited British prejudices. When demonstrations took place in Jerusalem in February 1920 in favour of the unification of Syria and Palestine, and against Zionism, Britain's chief political officer in Palestine, Richard Meinertzhagen, wrote that they were 'undoubtedly' the result of French efforts to destabilise British rule in Palestine.[23] Lawrence's colleague W. F. Stirling, who was by now governor of Jaffa, was also convinced that the trouble he had to deal with 'was invariably instigated by the French Consulate'.[24]

Amid these suspicions, and days after Millerand's threat to call for an international administration for Palestine, riots broke out in Jerusalem on 4 April at the Muslim festival of Nebi Musa. The festival, which drew large numbers of Muslims into the Holy City, was traditionally a flashpoint and had been heavily policed in Ottoman times. Storrs, now the British governor of Jerusalem, failed to foresee how the Syrian Congress's proclamation would fuel trouble, and sent only a small number of policemen to the spot, perhaps because Meinertzhagen had just reassured him that he did 'not anticipate any immediate trouble in Palestine'.[25] As a consequence, there were fewer than two hundred police available that day to marshal an Arab crowd that grew to nearly seventy thousand. From the balcony of the Arab Club under which the crowd had gathered, a series of speakers denounced Zionism. One of them, the younger brother of the Grand Mufti of the city, held up a portrait of Feisal and proclaimed, 'This is your King.'[26] 'God save the King!' the crowd roared back at him.

As the day went on, the crowd grew angrier. Chants of 'Independence! Independence!' gave way to 'Palestine is our land, the Jews are our dogs!'[27] Inevitably, at some point there was a push, jostling; possibly someone spat at someone else's flag. It is not clear who or what exactly started the rioting that followed. What was crucial was that it took the British four days to quell the violence, by which time five Jews and four Arabs had been killed and over 250, mostly Jews, had been injured.

The Zionists believed that Storrs's slow reaction to the rioting was further evidence of anti-Zionism and even anti-Semitism within his administration, and said so to his face. Aware that the Zionists' allegations contained some truth, Lloyd George promised to replace the military government of Palestine with a civilian administration headed by Herbert Samuel, the Jewish cabinet minister who, five years earlier, had suggested that Britain back the Zionist cause. 'At any rate they won't be able to accuse him of anti-Semitism,' observed one British official, cynically but accurately.[28]

The British realised, however, that they had burdened themselves with an insoluble problem. 'The problem of Palestine,' wrote Britain's most senior general, '[was] the same as the problem of Ireland, namely, two peoples living in a small country hating each other like hell.'[29] Nor were the Jews showing the gratitude the British expected of them. When the director of military intelligence visited Palestine soon after the riots, it dawned on him that there was no reason to suppose that the Zionists and British would ever be 'really friendly'. The friendship would 'only last as long as the Zionist State were dependent on Great Britain for military protection', he realised. This was an insight that would prove acute.[30]

With their relations with the Zionists in trouble, and convinced that the French were stirring the troubled situation in Palestine, the British did not feel secure enough to confront Millerand at the San Remo conference that April. Although they knew that agreeing to a French mandate for Syria was certain to cause Arab uproar, they also knew that if they objected the French prime minister would retaliate by calling for an international administration in Palestine – a step that in current circumstances the Zionists might support. So at San Remo Britain did not object to the French claim to Syria and Millerand did not follow through with his threat. The French mandate for Syria and Lebanon, and the British mandates for Palestine and Mesopotamia were confirmed. At the resort the two powers also finalised an agreement that gave the French a quarter share in the company set up to explore for oil around Mosul. When, soon afterwards, Curzon finally conceded that the French were now 'the best judges of the military measures necessary to control the local situation', Millerand saw his opportunity.[31] The following day his officials decided to draw up plans for the invasion of Syria while Feisal's government was still disorganised. Three days later, they told Gouraud that action against Feisal was 'indispensable and urgent' and that he would receive two further divisions for the purpose of occupying Damascus and Aleppo.[32] By now the number of troops at

Gouraud's disposal had grown substantially, from thirty-four to fifty battalions, in the space of just twelve weeks.

In the meantime his adviser, Robert de Caix, had cleared the way for action against Feisal by agreeing an armistice and an arms deal with the Turks. It was only after the armistice came into force that the French told the British of its existence and of their plans to use military force to impose their will on Feisal. The British took this revelation very badly, for in their eyes the French negotiation of a separate peace was a betrayal of their alliance. For years afterwards they suspected that the French were quietly encouraging the Turks to try to seize the Mosul region, in return for an increased share of the oil.[33]

The abrupt and unilateral French move reinforced British suspicions that their late ally was doing its utmost to destabilise their rule in Palestine. Churchill, in particular, was convinced that the French invasion of Syria would lead to wider trouble. He urged his colleagues not to withdraw troops from Palestine, reminding them of its importance as a buffer. To do so would 'merely ... transfer the scene of future trouble from Palestine to Egypt and the Suez Canal where it would be more difficult to deal with and more dangerous in its effect.'[34] With Churchill's support, Allenby also moved to buttress Feisal. His aim, which both Churchill and Herbert Samuel shared, was to keep the Arab leader independent if possible, to try to stop unrest spreading into Arab Palestine. Defying an order from Curzon not to pay Feisal any more money, he released two months' subsidy after Feisal's supporters told him that they needed funds to restore order – and deny Gouraud any excuse for further intervention – but Allenby must have known that the money would be used against the French, as it had been previously. He also told Feisal that Britain was ready to recognise him as the head of an independent Syrian state, and urged him to come to Europe to make his case.[35] Feisal, however, would not make the journey unless he was recognised first.

On Bastille Day 1920 Gouraud moved decisively against Feisal, by issuing an ultimatum telling him that he had two days to accept the French mandate and the franc, and to end hostile activity against the French. But he agreed when Feisal asked for a forty-eight-hour extension, a concession that enraged Millerand in Paris. As a result of Millerand's reaction, Gouraud pressed on regardless when Feisal belatedly telegraphed his acceptance of the conditions, demanding that the Arabs now accept complete French control of the Syrian state.

Feisal, under pressure from his own nationalist supporters, could not accept this additional demand. On 24 July French troops overwhelmed a much smaller Arab force at Maysalun, outside Damascus, using tanks and aircraft against the Arabs' artillery and machine-guns. French troops entered the Syrian capital the next day, and Gouraud soon afterwards, on the 26th. While Feisal fled southwards into British-controlled Palestine, the French general headed straight to the centre of the ancient city, to the austere tomb of the Muslim world's most famous warrior, who had been buried there over seven hundred years before. 'Saladin,' he announced when he arrived, 'we're back.'[36]

Gouraud's decision to expel Feisal surprised the British, who had expected the French general would retain him as a puppet. Feisal's appearance soon afterwards in Palestine presented them with a dilemma. As one British official put it, 'We have either got to let him down or have a row with the French.'[37] His bosses quickly solved the quandary. After allowing Feisal a short stay in Palestine, they escorted him to the Egyptian border. There the man who had been briefly king of Syria was left to await a train, 'sitting on his luggage'.[38]

Yet, if the British hoped that by spiriting Feisal through their territory they might avoid the ramifications of his sudden ejection from Syria, they were only misleading themselves. The French, reviewing the situation later, pointed out that pressure had been building on the British since November 1918 when they had promised with the French, in the Anglo-French Declaration, to support freely chosen national governments. As the French observed, with more than a hint of schadenfreude, within days of that commitment 'there was no other question in Mesopotamia but the choice of an Emir. The example of Damascus was contagious.'[39] The brief autonomy the Arabs had enjoyed in Syria after the collapse of the Ottoman Empire inspired them to seize independence for themselves. By the time Gouraud ousted Feisal, they had begun to do so in Mesopotamia.

8

REVOLT IN IRAQ

'GET UP; DEMAND YOUR RIGHTS, DEMAND YOUR COMPLETE independence,' the Syrian Arab nationalists urged their fellow countrymen in Mesopotamia as it became clear that Gouraud was about to suffocate their own ambitions.[1] The timing of the uprising that then broke out across Mesopotamia in June 1920 was intimately connected with events in Syria, but it drew its strength from the anger that three years of British military rule in Iraq had by then caused. For although the British had promised to act not 'as conquerors or enemies but as liberators' when they marched into Baghdad in 1917, they had failed to live up to this promise. Partly out of military necessity, they then sacked the mostly Arab officials who had previously run the country for the Ottomans and replaced them with their own political officers, whose tasks were to secure adequate food supplies for British forces in the country and ensure the security of their lines of communication between Baghdad and the Persian Gulf, which ran down the Euphrates valley.

These were ad hoc arrangements that could be justified during wartime, but they remained in place long after the armistice. By then the popular proconsul, Sir Percy Cox, had been moved to a posting in Tehran, and responsibility for the government of Mesopotamia had passed to his brilliantly clever but overconfident thirty-five-year-old deputy, Arnold Wilson, who believed that the country's destiny was as a colony of India. Under Wilson, British political officers continued to rule arbitrarily, using the promise of gold and the threat of military reprisal as carrot and stick. By mid-1919 stories of rough justice were reaching Syria, angering the Baghdadi supporters of Feisal in particular. British officials were reputed to settle the guilt of a defendant on the toss of a coin. In another incident a British officer allegedly announced that he was going to sing a song in Arabic, and whichever of the suspects brought before him laughed first at his appalling accent would be pronounced guilty.[2]

What made matters worse was Britain's failure to honour the commitment it had made in the Anglo-French Declaration to support 'the free choice of the indigenous populations' in establishing national governments across the former Ottoman Empire. For when in May 1919 Feisal's Iraqi supporters pointed to the declaration and asked the British if they could return home and set up their own administration in Baghdad, they received a derisory reply from Arnold Wilson. Provocatively, he dismissed the Iraqis' hopes as 'moonshine' to their faces when he met them in Damascus.[3] His colleague Gertrude Bell later identified this encounter as the turning point – the moment when the Iraqis realised that they would get no further help from the British, and that it was therefore time to try to oust their former allies.

Bell had previously agreed with Wilson that the Arabs were neither capable of, nor interested in, governing themselves. Both of them had been summoned to the peace conference by the British India Office to say so, in an effort to undermine Lawrence. But Bell then changed her mind when she experienced what was, quite literally, a Damascene conversion on her way back from Paris to Baghdad. When she too met the nationalist leaders in Damascus, she was astonished by the power the Baghdadi faction wielded and the extent of their ambitions. She warned London that there was 'no way of keeping the people of Mesopotamia in the path of peace but by giving them something which they won't willingly abandon. Good government, by someone else, e.g. by us, isn't enough.'[4]

Bell was being alarmist, said Wilson. Dismissing her opinion as 'erroneous', he stressed the deep sectarian divisions within Mesopotamia between Sunni and Shia, Arab and Kurd, and argued that the Shia would not support a government imposed by the Sunni Baghdadi faction in Damascus.[5] An 'amateur Arab government' would bring 'the rapid decay of authority, law and order', he boomed. His working relationship with Bell collapsed soon after-wards. 'There are days when I would knife him if I could,' she hissed.[6]

The contradictory views emanating from Baghdad, together with the fact that the vestigial Ottoman government had still not signed the peace treaty that would formally acknowledge the break-up of their empire, gave officials in London an excuse to dither.[7] Even though they could clearly see that the political situa-tion in Mesopotamia was deteriorating they worried that if they gave the Arabs a degree of autonomy in Baghdad, the French would accuse them of trying to destabilise Syria and retaliate by vetoing the British claim to the Mosul oilfields and Palestine at the League of Nations. Inertia, therefore, was the order of the day. That suited Arnold Wilson, but the delay was to have terrible con-sequences. 'Think,' wrote Gertrude Bell in 1921, 'if we had begun establishing native institutions two years ago! By now we should have got Arab govt. and an Army going; we should have had no tribal revolt; all the money and lives wasted this year would have been saved.'[8]

With Whitehall unable to agree on what policy to pursue in Mesopotamia, in Baghdad Arnold Wilson was free to do as he pleased. He began 1920 in buoyant mood, reporting to Cox that 'The Shaykhs and tribes of the outlying districts are everywhere settling down. The political atmosphere in Basrah is good, in Baghdad fair and improving, and I think even in Mosul things are getting better.'[9] Even a fancy dress party on New Year's Eve had been a roaring success. 'The dresses of the men who were dressed up as women were, on the whole, better than those of the real ladies.' His New Year message the following day was unapolo-getic. In it he patronisingly asked 'those of you who are impatient to see a Civil Government re-established and commercial inter-course become more normal, to remember that this is one of the few corners of the world where anarchy has not yet raised its ugly head'.[10]

As a consequence, when in March 1920 the General Syrian Congress declared Feisal and Abdullah the heads of Syria and Mesopotamia respectively, there was no Arab government in place in Baghdad, nor was there any sign that one was imminent. 'Well we are in for it,' Bell wrote when she heard the news from Damascus. 'We shall need every scrap of personal influence ... to keep this country from falling into chaos.'[11] Her optimism that her own influence might still work was utterly misplaced because, by then, the British had run out of credit with the Iraqis. As she later admitted, 'We didn't show any signs of an intention to fulfil our promises; as far as the local administration was concerned we didn't intend to fulfil them if we could possibly help it.'[12]

Wilson at last recognised the seriousness of the situation. When Britain's mandate for Mesopotamia was finally confirmed at the San Remo conference, he hurried out an announcement hinting that he was going to make concessions in a bid to placate the nationalists. But all that he achieved by doing so was to make himself look weak, an impression reinforced by Britain's troop withdrawals. Encouraged by these signs of weakness, the nationalists managed to unite both Sunni and Shia factions in Baghdad during Ramadan, which was always a time, especially in the summer, when political tensions flared. 'There's a lot of semi-religious, semi-political preaching and reciting of poems,' Bell reported, unnerved both by the unprecedented consensus and the fact that 'the underlying thought is out with the infidel'.[13]

Just as it became obvious that trouble in Mesopotamia was unavoidable, a row erupted about the expense of the administration of the mandate. On 1 June The Times alleged that the mandate might cost as much as £50 million a year and demanded greater transparency from the government. Days later it returned to the subject, drawing attention to discrepancies between the figures Churchill had published eight weeks earlier in his budget estimates and the numbers that he had since been obliged to publish, under pressure. These showed that, far from shrinking as the War Office claimed it would, the garrison had actually grown over the previous two months – by more than eight thousand men, to over seventy thousand.[14]

Despite the vast size of the British garrison in Mesopotamia, the as yet undefined frontiers of the country were held by skeleton units which were isolated and vulnerable. On the morning of 4 June one such outpost in the north-western town of Tall Afar was attacked by armed Arab nationalists, led by Feisal's military commander in Damascus. 'What occurred in the town will probably never be exactly known,' wrote General Aylmer Haldane, the commander of British forces in Mesopotamia, in his very defensive memoir of the uprising.[15] From the bodies that the British later found there it appeared that their colleagues had taken a last stand on the flat roof of their office before being overwhelmed. The corpse of the local political officer, who had been kidnapped days earlier, was discovered two miles away. A column of armoured cars, sent to relieve the town, badly underestimated the opposition and never made it into Tall Afar. It was ambushed, and every single British soldier in the force was killed.

The British dispatched a further, punitive expedition to raze Tall Afar to the ground and drive its population into the desert, but the incident revealed that they were not invincible. It was 'the knowledge of this military weakness', said Arnold Wilson, 'which encourages every tribesman to turn his hand against us'.[16] In desperation he now sanctioned a series of pre-emptive arrests of the potential ringleaders of the revolt, but the move only inflamed the situation further by driving undecided tribesmen into the hands of the extremists.

Panicking, Wilson warned London that the alternatives were 'either govern or go'.[17] The British government decided on the former, but the price was Wilson's effective resignation. On 20 June he announced that Sir Percy Cox was being recalled to Baghdad to take over from him and start work on the creation of 'an organic law' – in other words a constitution supported by the local population – that would form the basis for the government of the country 'until such time as it can stand by itself, when the mandate will come to an end'.[18] The British government only admitted what Wilson had done in a debate on the War Office's budget for Mesopotamia three days later, on 23 June.

Until that point the government had justified the cost of its presence in Mesopotamia by pointing towards the financial rewards of future oil production. However, by now the terms of the oil-sharing arrangement that Britain had reached with France on the sidelines of the San Remo conference had become public and were attracting controversy, particularly in the United States, which had been excluded from the deal. During the 23 June debate Lloyd George's predecessor Asquith systematically tore into Churchill's figures to demonstrate that the costs of Britain's presence were still unclear, and questioned the assumption that Britain would ulti-mately reap a dividend from its mandate. He attacked Lloyd George's root interest in the country, for its oil, as a 'fundamental violation' of the League of Nations covenant signed by Britain, and warned his colleagues that until the League of Nations confirmed the mandate, Britain had 'no legal footing in Mesopotamia what-soever'.[19]

Lloyd George's reply fed press suspicion that the money being spent in Mesopotamia was irredeemable. *The Times* commented the following day that the prime minister's 'windy generalities' would 'not appease a nation whose business is developing creeping paraly-sis as a consequence of over-taxation and enormously wasteful expenditure'.[20] The paper, which was widely regarded as having helped oust Asquith in 1916, concluded threateningly: 'Any British Government, however large its majority, which proposes to con-tinue to force the British public to provide £40,000,000 a year for Mesopotamian semi-nomads will overtax the patience of the country.'

The costs were about to increase further. At the beginning of July the small British garrison in the town of Rumaythah on the railway 150 miles south of Baghdad was attacked by thousands of well-armed and disciplined insurgents, who also sprang from jail a lead-ing shaykh arrested on Wilson's orders. Led by the nationalists and backed by the Shia's powerful religious leaders, the rebellion quickly spread among the tribes of the fertile Euphrates flood plain, who were as fed up as *The Times*'s leader-writers with paying taxes to the British government. The tribesmen cut the railway in several places, and within days much of the area between Rumaythah and Diwaniyah, fifty miles to the north, was in revolt.

The British government tried to hide the scale of the uprising, but like all cover-ups this only made the problem worse. On 16 July Churchill was obliged to reveal more details to parliament. His statement was a shock, one witness wrote, because 'Most people had assumed the troubles ... to be purely local, but it now appears that ... we have what may be a very serious war on our hands.'[21] In a bleak memorandum to his cabinet colleagues the next day, Churchill privately blamed the situation on the French, who had 'practically declared war on Feisal'.[22] Predicting that Feisal would now inevitably turn his attentions to Mesopotamia, he told the cabinet that an additional division 'costing millions' was being sent to Basra to crush the insurgency.

Most damagingly for the government, T. E. Lawrence joined the attack. By now he was a household name. During his exile in Oxford he had become a celebrity after an American journalist, Lowell Thomas, who had briefly met him in the war, put on a London show about his exploits. Consequently, when Lawrence decided to criticise the government's policy, publication of his opinions was guaranteed.

The previous September Lawrence had predicted that a revolt would break out in Mesopotamia 'if we do not mend our ways'.[23] The agreeable sensation of being proved correct now shook him from the torpor that had overcome him in Oxford. In a series of articles he took his revenge on Arnold Wilson, whose last-minute concessions to the Arabs he dismissed as 'belated, insincere, incomplete'.[24] In a letter to The Times on 23 July he blamed the uprising on the failure of Wilson's administration in Baghdad to honour the promise of self-government Britain had made in its November 1918 declaration.[25] He predicted that the cost of quelling the insurgency might reach £50 million that year – adding more than 5 per cent to the government's already unsustainable expenditure.[26] To cut that bill, his answer was to 'make the Arabs do the work'. From Baghdad Gertrude Bell angrily accused him of making the situation worse by writing 'tosh' but, as she acknowledged, 'the fact that we are really guilty of an initial mistake makes it very difficult to answer letters like those of T. E. Lawrence'.[27]

In Mesopotamia, the situation continued to deteriorate. On the same day that Lawrence's letter was published, a British force set out from their base at Hillah, on the railway, to relieve Kufah, a small town on the Euphrates where a tiny British garrison had been cut off by tribesmen three days earlier. What had been conceived as an awe-inspiring show of British force turned into a vivid demonstration of weakness when the expedition went horribly wrong. The members of the eight-hundred-strong force misjudged the severity of the withering summer sun and took far too little water with them for the thirty-mile march to Kufah. By the time exhaustion forced them to make camp beside a canal in the early afternoon, men were collapsing with heatstroke, and it was at this point that as many as a thousand Arabs were spotted converging on their camp.

The British decided they had no choice but to withdraw, but that move was one the tribesmen had already anticipated. When the column wearily began to retreat back up the road to Hillah, it was ambushed by more Arabs. The attack was swift and savage. According to one officer, 'the gun-teams were attacked by the knives of Arabs who rose up from the ditches alongside to slit the bellies of the horses from below'.[28] As night descended, the soldiers were easily picked off as they lost their way in the scrubby semi-desert: over three hundred were killed or taken prisoner. On the same day that the Arabs had been routed by the French at Maysalun, they had inflicted a stunning defeat on the British.

When news of disaster reached Wilson he was forced to consider the previously unthinkable. Worried that British forces might have to abandon the Euphrates valley altogether, four days after Feisal's expulsion from Damascus, he contacted London to ask whether it might consider the possibility of offering the deposed Arab leader the Amirate of Mesopotamia.[29] If the government wanted to reduce the cost of governing the territory in future, he thought 'there would be a better prospect of it being done with Feisal ... than by any other possible arrangement'.[30] By doing so, he argued, 'not only might we re-establish our position in the eyes of the Arab world but we might go far to wipe out the accusation which would otherwise be made against us of bad faith both with Feisal and with the people of this country'.

In London the government agreed. The idea rapidly leaked out: on 5 August, the newspapers reported that Feisal might become the 'possible ruler of Mesopotamia'.[31] The instructions for Wilson's replacement, Sir Percy Cox, which were put before the cabinet for approval the same day were rather more explicit. They included the installation of Feisal as ruler in Baghdad, so long as there was 'spontaneous demand ... from a sufficiently representative body of public opinion in Mesopotamia'.[32]

Lawrence seized the opportunity to promote Feisal. In the *Observer* he argued that his wartime comrade deserved sympathy because the treatment he had received at Gouraud's hands was a 'poor return' for his support for Britain during the war.[33] He finished by advocating the 'tearing up of what we have done' and the institution of an Arab government backed by British advisers that would 'save us a million pounds a week'. In two anonymous articles for *The Times* he paid tribute to 'the greatest Arab leader since Saladin'.[34] In the first – rather hilariously, given that he was bylined 'A Correspondent' – he tried to dispel the idea that Feisal was 'set up and secretly supported by Great Britain, as part of an insidious scheme to spread British influence beyond the sphere of British political control', and argued that his own role in the Arab revolt had been overstated.[35] In the second he described the difficulties Feisal had in setting up an administration in Syria after the armistice. 'In the circumstances,' he suggested, 'it is wonderful he lasted so long.' Describing Feisal as '33, vigorous, and not yet at the height of his powers', Lawrence ended by archly wondering what he might do next.

The French government had already been told. On 8 August, Curzon plucked up the courage to inform Millerand that Feisal might take charge in Mesopotamia. A few days later, France's senior diplomat in London registered his objection to the proposal. He said it would be a 'severe test' of the Anglo-French alliance, because Feisal would inevitably start intriguing in Damascus.[36]

The British were not inclined to pay any attention. After Gouraud's arrival in Damascus the British ambassador in Paris warned Curzon that the French general intended to extend French influence southwards from the city, driving a wedge between

British-controlled Palestine and Mesopotamia that threatened to destroy the idea of a defensive cordon across the Middle East that the British had nurtured since 1915. In London, officials at the Foreign Office dug out the original map used to illustrate the Sykes–Picot agreement, in an attempt to establish where exactly the dividing line between British and French territory ran. On about 20 August Sir Herbert Samuel left Jerusalem for the town of Salt, on the east bank of the Jordan, where local shaykhs had been invited to meet him. When he announced that he was going to pardon one of the ringleaders of the Nebi Musa disturbances who had fled across the Jordan, the shaykhs applauded, and Samuel, according to one onlooker, 'very cleverly caught them on the top of the wave, and said "all those who want the British Government come forward and give in their names" and they all trooped forward'.[37]

Through this intervention the British effectively stopped French encroachment into an area they regarded as part of their Palestine mandate, but they still had not crushed the uprising in Mesopotamia. On 20 August *The Times* asked why it was taking Churchill so long to organise the relief of Kufah, when he had promised almost a month earlier that a column would set out 'shortly'. Churchill had no instant answer. It was only after the cabinet had sanctioned even more expenditure that he was able to inform Haldane that 'by the middle or end of October you should be possessed of effective striking forces, and a vigorous use of these to put down and punish disaffection combined with the policy of setting up an Arab state should bring about a better situation'.[38] Infamously, Churchill even authorised the Royal Air Force to investigate the use of mustard gas against 'recalcitrant natives'.[39] Although the Air Force wisely did not, by the end of the revolt over 8,400 Arabs would be dead.[40] So too were almost 2,300 British soldiers.

Most of the British casualties were Indian troops, and it was the financial, rather than the human, cost that caused Churchill more alarm. At the end of August he complained to Lloyd George that it seemed 'so gratuitous that after all the struggles of war, just when we want to get together our slender military resources and re-establish our finances and have a little in hand in case of danger here or there, we should be compelled to go on pouring armies and treasure into these thankless deserts'.[41] He complained that 'the military expense of this year alone will probably amount to something like fifty millions, thus by capital expenditure knocking all the bloom off any commercial possibilities which may have existed'.

The reason why Churchill was so fixated on expense was because he dreamed of being chancellor of the exchequer and then prime minister, and believed that he must 'win a reputation for economy' to attain that ambition.[42] He desperately wanted to outdo his father, Lord Randolph, who had run the Treasury thirty years before. Distant and disapproving, Lord Randolph had once attacked his son for leading an 'idle useless unprofitable life', and then died two years later at the age of only forty-five before Churchill could prove him wrong.[43] Driven by the fear that his family's genes might not give him long to do so, Churchill – now aged forty-six – was determined to outshine his father, at almost any cost. 'He would make a drum out of the skin of his own mother in order to sound his own praises,' jibed Lloyd George.[44]

Churchill knew the precariousness of politics too well. A born risk-taker – as a correspondent with British forces on the Indian North-West Frontier he had written how 'Nothing in life is so exhilarating as to be shot at without result' – he had entered parliament for the Conservatives, switched sides to the Liberals, and become the youngest cabinet minister by the age of thirty-three.[45] Indeed, as First Lord of the Admiralty in 1912 he had taken the decision to switch the fleet from coal to oil: the decision that now embroiled Britain in Iraq. But then, with Sykes's encouragement, he made the fateful decision to back the Gallipoli landings, and was made the scapegoat by his many enemies when the venture failed. When in 1916 Lloyd George replaced Asquith and invited the Conservatives to join a coalition government, the Tories' price included Churchill's resignation.

For a man who lived for politics and for power, who enjoyed gossiping drunkenly late into the night about who was up and who was down, this was an awful blow – not least because he considered Lloyd George his friend. After serving briefly on the western front he returned to Britain and, still in the doldrums, took up painting to counter his depression. Describing his approach as 'a joy ride in a paint box', he acknowledged that he could not 'pretend to feel impartial about the colours, I rejoice with the brilliant ones, and am genuinely sorry for the poor browns'.[46] Critics sniffed at the results, but when Churchill first exhibited his work he sold four out of five paintings. He signed them with a pseudonym so that the critics would not be swayed, and could not resist going along to admire the exhibition himself. As he admitted to his wife Clementine, 'I am so devoured by egoism.'[47]

Churchill owed his subsequent return to the cabinet to Lloyd George, who at the end of 1918 made him secretary of state for war. For the prime minister, the rehabilitation of a man widely regarded as responsible for one of the war's great military disasters was a significant risk. The *Morning Post* described the reappearance of its 'brilliant and erratic' former correspondent as 'an appointment which makes us tremble for the future'.[48] Strange though hindsight makes that doubt seem today, it was a common feeling at the time. 'He might do anything stupid and his military judgement is almost always at fault,' Britain's most senior general quietly warned: 'He thinks he's the Duke of Marlborough.'[49]

On his return to government he found that his relationship with Lloyd George had changed irreversibly. The two men argued frequently, particularly over the need for a settlement with the Turks. Churchill, driven by the savings that would follow from it, was all in favour; Lloyd George, blinkered by his hatred of the Turks, was not, and Churchill, now dependent on his former friend for his survival, had no choice but to agree.

The two men maintained a spiky correspondence. Lloyd George accused Churchill of failing to devote his 'great abilities, energy and courage' to 'the reduction of expense'.[50] Churchill was angry that he was expected to maintain British control of Mesopotamia in the face of both Arab and Turkish hostility, with dwindling resources and against a hostile press. 'We have not got a single friend in the press upon the subject and there is no point of which they make more effective use to injure the Government. Week after week and month after month for a long time we shall have a continuance of this miserable, wasteful, sporadic warfare,' he complained to the prime minister in August.[51] But, as he contemplated the danger of being inextricably associated with yet another military disaster, he had a brainwave: to buy the silence of the government's most potent critic by hiring him as his adviser.

9

THE BEST AND CHEAPEST SOLUTION

ON 4 DECEMBER 1920 CHURCHILL'S PRIVATE SECRETARY invited T. E. Lawrence to a meeting with his boss. Churchill had first met Lawrence soon after the armistice, and the encounter remained vivid. When, back then, Lawrence had explained that he had just turned down a knighthood from the king, Churchill had rebuked him. 'I said at once that his conduct was most wrong, not fair to the King as a gentleman and grossly disrespectful to him as a sovereign,' he later wrote.[1] Lawrence took the criticism in good part. He explained it was the only way he could make the king realise that 'the honour of Great Britain was at stake in the faithful treatment of the Arabs and that their betrayal to the Syrian demands of France would be an indelible blot on our history'. Churchill would not forget the man whose 'flashing eyes loaded with fire' had confronted him across the table.[2] In December 1920, he invited Lawrence to work for him.

In a reshuffle at the beginning of 1921 Lloyd George moved Churchill from the War Office to take charge of the Colonial Office. With typical vanity, Churchill was pleased to find that his new office was twice the size of his old one, but the increase in square footage was scant compensation for the headaches that came with it. For, to Churchill's dismay, the prime minister made him fully responsible for Palestine and, worse, for Mesopotamia where, after the end of the uprising, his task was to establish a form of government that would

satisfy both Arab aspirations and Britain's strategic interests.
Churchill could not afford to snub Lloyd George, but he had 'some
misgivings about the political consequence to myself' of taking on
the job of looking after Mesopotamia and Palestine – 'twin babies in
his care', as he described them, of which he was emphatically 'not
the father'.[3]

It was for this reason that Churchill was so anxious to neutralise
Lawrence, because the young ex-officer's celebrity meant that he
had the greatest power to damage him. He later claimed that
Lawrence had immediately accepted his invitation, but Lawrence
said that it was only on Churchill's third attempt that he had finally
been persuaded to return to what he termed 'the shallow grave of
public duty', probably because he was running short of money by
this time.[4] Lawrence's account is the more plausible, for it was only
on 16 February 1921 that Churchill could express his delight to his
wife Clementine that he had finally 'got Lawrence to put on a bridle
and collar'.[5] Within days, Lawrence was working late into the night
in the Colonial Office, now choreographer of the abrupt change of
policy the British government was about to make. Churchill was
delighted that he had persuaded his most dangerous critic to become
a government servant once again – effectively silencing him in the
process. But the deal looked promising to Lawrence, too. For him it
was a 'very great chance given me' to reverse the failure that had
depressed him throughout 1920.[6]

Lawrence's optimism related to the fact that, in the period since
Churchill offered him the job, the idea of inserting Feisal as a figurehead had become government policy. The turning point came at
a meeting in Whitehall in December 1920 at which the English and
Arabic texts of McMahon's correspondence with Sharif Husein were
compared. In his crucial letter of 24 October 1915 McMahon had
used an ambiguous phrase that hinged on the absence of a comma to
make it look as if he accepted Husein's exorbitant demands, when in
fact he was preserving Britain's room for manoeuvre with the
French. For five years the British believed that he had successfully
done so, until, to the horror of those present at the December 1920
meeting, it was revealed that this sleight of hand had then been lost
in the Arabic translation. As one official, who was present, put it:

In the Arabic version sent to King Husain this is so translated as to make it appear that Gt Britain is free to act without detriment to France in the whole of the limits mentioned. This passage of course had been our sheet anchor: it enabled us to tell the French that we had reserved their rights, and the Arabs that there were regions in which they wd have eventually to come to terms with the French. It is extremely awkward to have this piece of solid ground cut from under our feet. I think that HMG will probably jump at the opportunity of making a sort of *amende* by sending Feisal to Mesopotamia.[7]

This prediction was absolutely right. Two days later the cabinet authorised Curzon to approach Feisal to see whether he would be interested in ruling Mesopotamia. Soon afterwards Feisal came to London.

The secret talks that followed were encouraging. The Arab leader indicated that he was 'not indisposed' to the idea, providing that his brother Abdullah did not want the throne.[8] Feisal also met Lawrence at this time, and said that he was willing to give up any claim to Syria and Palestine, although he wanted to see an Arab state set up in the territory across the Jordan. His attitude left Lawrence very optimistic. 'All question of pledges and promises, fulfilled or broken, are set aside,' he told Churchill's private secretary. 'Feisal can help very much towards a rapid settlement of these countries, if he wants to.'[9]

Those two words, 'rapid settlement', appealed enormously to Churchill, and so did Feisal's illustrious ancestry. Although he had passed out of Sandhurst as a cavalry officer, he made his name as a war correspondent reporting the small wars of the last days of the nineteenth century, participating enthusiastically in battles he then reported. Having witnessed the havoc caused by the mad Mullah's call to jihad on the North-West Frontier*, and the fanaticism the

---

* The Mad Mullah achieved notoriety in July 1897 when he led Pashtun tribesmen in an attack on the British camp at Malakand on the North-West Frontier. Churchill participated in its relief.

Mahdi aroused in the Sudan, Churchill liked the idea that Feisal might use his authority as a descendant of the Prophet Muhammad to achieve stability. Having conjured up an image of the Arab in his mind, he was disappointed when Feisal appeared at their first meeting wearing a top hat and tails. 'Tell the Emir I am so sorry to see he has lost his nice clothes,' Churchill asked Lawrence to translate. 'Yes,' replied Feisal, 'and my nice kingdom too!'[10]

Dusting off a tactic by which the British had kept the peace along the North-West Frontier, Churchill advocated paying subsidies to Feisal in Baghdad, Abdullah in Transjordan, and their elderly father in Mecca. 'If Feisal knew that not only his father's subsidy … but also the position of his brother in Transjordan was dependent on his own good behaviour,' ran Churchill's thinking, 'he would be much easier to deal with.'[11] The ambitious Abdullah and his truculent father, Sharif Husein, would be similarly constrained.

By 12 January Churchill had made up his mind, telling Curzon that he had 'a strong feeling' that Feisal was 'the best man' for the job.[12] Just in case the people of Mesopotamia did not agree with him, the same day he informed Sir Percy Cox that in the forthcoming plebiscite, in which the people of Mesopotamia were to be asked whether they wanted Feisal as their ruler, 'Western political methods are not necessarily applicable … and [the] basis of election should be framed.'[13]

Churchill's determination that Feisal should receive some sort of local endorsement was designed to stop the French blaming the British for his return to Baghdad, for the French remained the major sticking point in the success of the British plan. Until that point the British had deflected French complaints by claiming that they were scrupulously neutral in the question of who would front an Arab government in Baghdad. By early 1921, however, that charade was looking threadbare. A gaffe by a senior British diplomat alerted the French to the fact that Feisal was in London talking to the British, and the manner of this discovery, together with Lawrence's reappointment, led them to suspect the worst. The French ambassador warned the Foreign Office that the appointment of Feisal would strain relations between both countries, not least because Gouraud completely distrusted the Arab leader.

Relying on Feisal, the French emphasised, would be like 'leaning on a broken reed'.[14]

Churchill had already decided to organise a conference of officials in Cairo during March to rubber-stamp the choice of Feisal, but before it could take place he realised he needed a 'definite and clear understanding' with the French.[15] On 24 February he met Gouraud and Philippe Berthelot, the head of the Quai d'Orsay, who immediately launched a head-on attack on British policy. Describing Feisal as 'most treacherous, principally out of weakness of character', Berthelot said that France's rule in Syria would be undermined if he were installed in Baghdad.[16] Gouraud backed him up, saying that earlier that year Feisal had completely gone back on promises he had previously made.

Churchill tried to let the French down gently. Although he misleadingly claimed that he still had a 'completely open mind on the subject' of whom the British government might parachute in to head the government of Mesopotamia, he told his French counterparts 'how difficult it would be for him … to return to the House of Commons and state that all British local advisers were in favour of the instalment of the Emir Feisal and that nevertheless he had to recommend evacuation of all save a bridgehead because of the French point of view'.[17]

Britain's experts on the Middle East met in Cairo on 13 March, and were instantly dubbed the 'forty thieves', to Churchill's great amusement. There were senior British military officers, Churchill's London-based advisers, and the officials from the region including Gertrude Bell and Sir Percy Cox. But it was the British agent in Somaliland, Sir Geoffrey Archer, who stole the show when he arrived with two young lions. Allenby – now Britain's high commissioner in Egypt – hosted a party at the start, and described the moment when the lions spotted one of his own pets across the Residency garden. 'They broke loose,' he wrote, 'and went full gallop for my Marabou stork. He fled for his life. They nearly got him; but Archer and his black servant raced after them and just stopped them in time. They are bound for London Zoo.'[18]

The presence of these advisers was purely theatrical, for the outcome of the conference had already been decided. 'Talk of leaving things to the man on the spot. We left nothing,' Lawrence later wrote.[19]

Churchill opened the conference the following day by flourishing a draft telegram to the prime minister. 'I think we shall reach a unanimous conclusion ... that Feisal offers hope of best and cheapest solution,' he announced, adding that he was confident Lawrence would be able to persuade Feisal to take the role as head of the country that would now be called 'Iraq'.[20] In the discussion of the options that followed, Lawrence championed Feisal against his elder brother, just as he had four years earlier in Arabia. While Feisal was 'an active and inspiring personality', Abdullah was 'lazy and by no means dominating', he maintained. As no one else present could claim to know the brothers so well, they all agreed. Churchill set out for the Pyramids with his painting kit. 'We did not see him again till dark,' his aide-de-camp reported.[21]

The following day Churchill headed off to paint again, while his officials – divided into two committees, one covering political and military aspects, the other finance – began to address the detail of the plans to insert Feisal and cut the cost of Britain's presence in Mesopotamia. It was 'one of the longest fortnights I ever lived,' said Lawrence, and Gertrude Bell agreed.[22] On 15 March she and Cox argued in favour of an Iraqi state that included the northern Kurdish hinterland, and by the time Churchill had returned from the Pyramids once again this had been agreed, although it was not his personal preference. After another day's painting on the 16th, this time at a monastery on the east side of the city, Churchill telegraphed Lloyd George to tell him that his main advisers had reached 'complete agreement on all the points, both political and military', and that savings of £20 million a year were possible from the defence scheme he had proposed, in which the Royal Air Force would primarily keep the peace via threat of aerial bombardment. 'Do please realise,' Churchill liked to remind his officials, 'that everything that happens in the Middle East is secondary to the reduction of expense.'[23]

Discussions now moved on to Palestine and Transjordan, the hinterland where the British feared the French wanted to extend their influence. Matters had been complicated there by the arrival of

Feisal's brother Abdullah the previous November, and when Sir Herbert Samuel came from Jerusalem to join the discussions he lobbied Churchill for a formal takeover of this territory. In the following days he argued that the 'probability of controversy in Palestine for some years on the question of Zionism' made the enlargement of the province to defuse neighbourly tensions between Jews and Arabs desirable.[24]

Both Churchill and Lawrence disagreed with Samuel's idea. Churchill was keen not to antagonise Abdullah, and Lawrence argued that it would be better to use Transjordan as a safety valve, appointing a ruler whom the British could influence to restrain Arab opposition to the Zionists. His ideal candidate would be 'not too powerful, and who was not an inhabitant of Transjordania, but who relied upon His Majesty's Government for the retention of his office'.[25] Abdullah was the man he had in mind. This proposal found the support of the cabinet in London, which did not like Samuel's alternative because of the additional cost it would involve. As one imperially minded official complained, 'They have thought *solely* of £sd.'[26]

By 20 March all was done. Churchill and his colleagues took a camel ride to the Pyramids, where along the way Churchill's mount reacted to his determination to force the pace and threw him off. Churchill posed with Bell and Lawrence for a photograph before the Sphinx. A more formal photograph taken back at the hotel with all the participants at the conference shows him at the centre of the group, with Lawrence close behind him. What is most noticeable is that there are just two Arabs in the picture, and only one of them was an Iraqi – Jafar Pasha, one of Feisal's wartime generals. An awkward-looking Bell was obliged to stand beside Arnold Wilson, who had moved seamlessly from government service to the payroll of the Anglo-Persian Oil Company. And in the front row on a large Persian carpet the two lions are fighting playfully. Lawrence telegraphed Feisal with good news. 'Things have gone exactly as hoped,' he told him. 'Please start at once for Mecca ... on no account put anything in the press.'[27]

Churchill left for Jerusalem on the 23rd, receiving a noisy reception at the Gaza border from protesters chanting 'Down with the

Jews!' and 'Cut their throats!'[28] Later in his visit he accepted an invitation to visit a Jewish settlement – 'We were invited to sample the excellent wines which the establishment produced, and to inspect the many beauties of the groves,' he wrote, impressed – but the pressing matter was the settlement of whom to place in Transjordan.[29] Lawrence went ahead to meet Abdullah and persuaded him to return with him to Jerusalem to meet Churchill. Abdullah agreed to Churchill's suggestion that he might rule Transjordan and promised in return to stop trying to unseat the French from Damascus. To make him keep his word, the British restricted his initial 'contract' to six months.

Churchill had originally been keen to make an outright declaration in favour of Feisal that would enable Cox to sideline Feisal's two possible local rivals, the Naqib of Baghdad, the elderly religious leader of the Sunni community in that city, and Sayyid Talib, a younger, ambitious nationalist from Basra. In London, however, Lloyd George worried that the news that Britain was planning to install Feisal and Abdullah simultaneously in two new neighbouring states could only be interpreted by the French as 'a menace to their position in Syria, deliberately plotted by ourselves'.[30] He insisted that the initiative must be seen to come from Iraq.

As a consequence, when Churchill met Gouraud's adviser de Caix, he was obliged to claim implausibly that British policy would be 'guided by the wishes of the people both in Iraq and elsewhere', though he admitted that it was 'leading to a Sherifian solution'.[31] The reality was that while Feisal travelled out to Mecca to seek the approval of his father, Churchill sent Cox and Bell back to Baghdad in March 1921 with instructions to stir up what he entertainingly described as 'a spontaneous movement for Feisal in Mesopotamia as a prelude to his being countenanced by us'.[32]

The task of Bell and Cox was complicated by the fact that both the Naqib and Sayyid Talib had been busy in their absence. Talib had now thrown his weight behind the elderly Naqib, hoping to inherit the title from him when he died. The time available to Cox to deal with these two pretenders was short, since Feisal had been told that he could announce on 23 April that he was willing to rule Iraq. Cox therefore invited Talib to tea, and unsportingly had him arrested as he left afterwards. Talib was spirited to Basra and ultimately, Ceylon. The British proconsul then tackled the Naqib. It must have been a touching scene when he told the venerable religious leader that, as a friend, he felt obliged to let him know that 'at his great age and with his failing health he would hardly be expected to command [the] support of [the] principal people'.[33]

The French tried one final time to poison British minds against their chosen candidate. Towards the end of April, the French ambassador met Curzon and revealed Feisal's willingness, the previous year, to work with Gouraud to wrestle Mosul from the British. The revelation did not have quite the punch the French had hoped it would, for when Churchill looked to Lawrence for reassurance, Lawrence told him that it was quite possible he had authorised Feisal to make exactly that suggestion in a bid to win French agreement during the tortuous 1919 negotiations. When the French prime minister heard that Feisal had landed at Basra anyway, he called the British ambassador in to see him and told him that the news that Britain had thrown its weight behind the man Gouraud had so recently deposed was 'very hard to swallow'.[34]

Feisal landed at Basra on 21 June and embarked on a journey up the Euphrates that bore a close resemblance to a royal progress. But Cox, who accompanied him up-country and was described in one report as Feisal's electioneering agent, was disappointed by the lukewarm reception given to him in the Shia heartland where the uprising had been most intense, because he had been led to believe that the Shia were willing to accept a sharif in Baghdad.[35] In Baghdad, meanwhile, Bell concentrated on the easier task of winning round the Sunni population. 'You know where you are with them,' she wrote, 'they are guided, according to their lights, by reason; whereas with the Shias, however well intentioned they may be, at any moment some ignorant fanatic of an alim* may tell them that by the order of God and himself they are to think differently.'[36] The difficulty the British had throughout this time – as the Ottomans had before them – in engaging with the Shia population ensured that

---

* An expert on Islam.

most Iraqis would feel marginalised by the predominantly Sunni
government that they now set up.

Having returned to London, Churchill grew increasingly impatient.
During his Middle Eastern trip, the chancellor of the exchequer
Austen Chamberlain had taken over from Bonar Law as the
Conservative Party leader and Lloyd George's right-hand man, leaving the job that Churchill coveted vacant. Churchill, naturally, hoped
that he might finally be offered the chancellorship: when he was
not, he was, in Chamberlain's words, 'as cross as a bear with a sore
head'.[37] Sick of how long the process in Iraq was taking, he now
wired Cox telling him to hurry up. The policy, he reminded the high
commissioner, was 'to get another large wave of troops out of the
country and so to reduce expenditure to the British taxpayer' and 'to
get Feisal on the throne as soon as possible'.[38]

The plebiscite took place early in August. Soon afterwards Cox,
the election agent turned returning officer, was able to tell Churchill
that the poll had revealed that an 'overwhelming majority representing 96 per cent of the electorate have declared their assent to the
election of Amir Feisal as King of Iraq', a result that was then published on 15 August.[39]

When, however, Feisal was declared king at an early-morning ceremony in the centre of Baghdad eight days later, there could be no
doubt that it was the British, and not the Iraqis, who were the kingmakers. Feisal was flanked by Cox and General Haldane. The red,
white, black and green flags that decorated the arena were of British
design; in the absence of an Iraqi national anthem, the British military band played 'God Save the King'. Feisal, though, successfully
held out against acknowledging in his acceptance speech that Cox
retained ultimate authority. His words were 'very fine and simple
and heartfelt', reported Gertrude Bell, who was watching in the
front row of the audience. It was, she said with evident relief, 'an
amazing thing to see all Iraq, from north to south gathered together'
to endorse him.[40]

As the choreography suggested, the enthronement of the Arab
Feisal was initially of mainly symbolic importance. But in the Middle
East it was an important departure, and it poisoned relations

between Britain and France. As the French had feared it would, Britain's decision to promote a man whom they had just kicked out of Syria quickly raised Arab hopes of self-government elsewhere. As an angry former secretary-general of the Comité de l'Asie Française put it, 'Traitor and perjurer, assassin of French soldiers: this is the man whom our British allies have just raised to the throne!'[41]

10

THE DRUZE REVOLT

'GET GOING, MAN! PUT YOUR FOOT DOWN!' GENERAL Gouraud bellowed at his driver, as bullets cracked through the air around them.[1] It was 23 June 1921, and they had just been ambushed by assassins dressed as Syrian gendarmes on the narrow, winding road from Damascus to Qunaytirah in the Golan Heights. Gouraud's interpreter was already lying dead in the road behind them, flung from the vehicle by the shot that had struck him in the head. The governor of Damascus, Hakki Bey al-Azm, was also wounded, but only slightly. Three rounds passed through the one-armed Gouraud's empty sleeve but none of them hit him, or Georges Catroux, his able young representative in Damascus, who was sitting on the back seat beside him. Their visit to Qunaytirah had, ironically, been designed to demonstrate that the French writ now ran all the way to the frontier with Palestine.

Two days earlier Feisal had landed at Basra to begin his journey to Baghdad, and in Gouraud's mind the timing of the attack vindicated the concerns he had put to Churchill in February – that by their support of Feisal the British were 'building up, like Frankenstein, a monster which would eventually devour us'.[2] When Catroux, who felt responsible for the breach of security, offered Gouraud his resignation, the general refused to accept it. Instead, he said, he wanted his representative to find the killers. The ultimate consequences of that hunt would be profound.

Catroux's investigation quickly focused on a man named Ahmed Merawed, who had announced Gouraud's death early on the day that the ambush later took place, and then fled southwards into Transjordan when he found that his prediction was somewhat premature. Safely out of French reach, Merawed – Catroux claimed – was living 'under the indulgent eye' of the British political officer responsible for the border area.[3] After Gouraud protested to Sir Herbert Samuel about Merawed's flight to territory nominally under British control, the British were stung into taking action. In September they made a bid to seize the would-be murderer of the French high commissioner, which failed when Abdullah got wind of what was going on.[4] As one frustrated political officer concluded, there was no point attempting to arrest the suspects while they were being protected by any of Abdullah's followers, unless the British government was 'prepared to reach a good deal of trouble'.[5]

The British government was not. When Lawrence was sent to Transjordan later in the year by Churchill to assess the situation, he suggested that the French should be told that 'although the catching of assassins is no doubt desirable, and one of the functions of government ... we in Trans-Jordan have first to make the government, and then to make public opinion disapprove of political assassination'.[6] In his view, succumbing to French pressure to pursue the killers was 'silly' when the French were so unpopular themselves. There was nothing to be gained from being seen to be supporting a French regime that was barely distinguishable from the despotic Ottoman regime it had replaced.

In 1915 Etienne Flandin, the lawyer who had argued for French rule of Syria, had wisely warned his countrymen not to treat the Syrians as primitive, and predicted that they would need to 'demonstrate regularity in administration, incorruptibility and impartiality in justice and probity in financial matters' to win their support.[7] However, six years on, in practice French rule in Syria and Lebanon appeared increasingly arbitrary, confessional, exploitative and corrupt.

After Gouraud had seized Damascus in 1920, his secretary de Caix bluntly set out the options open to the general. France could

either 'build a Syrian nation which does not yet exist ... by smooth-
ing out the deep rifts which still divide it', he suggested, or 'cultivate
and maintain all the phenomena, requiring our arbitration, that
these divisions give [us]. I must say that only the second option
interests me.'[8] Gouraud agreed. In August 1920 he hived off
Lebanon in a bid to curry favour with the significant Christian population there, and carved up Syria into four separate provinces that
divided Damascus and Aleppo and recognised the minority Alawite
and Druze sects.

Gouraud cast the move as an acknowledgement of the country's
religious and ethnic differences, but it was immediately recognised
for what it truly was: a cynical attempt to split the nationalists that
was also directly contradictory to the mandate, which required
France to prepare Syria and Lebanon for self-government. A French
commentator accused him of dealing with 'an evolved and civilized
country like Syria ... as if they were dealing with the Atlas tribes or
the Blacks in the Sudan' – which was true, for Gouraud was using
tactics he had learned from his mentor Hubert Lyautey in North
Africa.[9] Partly because of the anger that this division caused, partly
because of its crippling expense, in 1922 the French were forced to
reintegrate three of the four states into a federation. Only the Jabal
Druze remained separate.

At first glance, the French did appear to have learned one lesson
from Britain's experience in Iraq, however. Unlike in neighbouring
Mesopotamia, from the outset the government in Syria had an Arab
veneer, for in each province Gouraud appointed an Arab governor,
like Hakki Bey al Azm. But the British described Hakki Bey as 'wise,
old ... spineless', and that reflected the fact that the general vested
real power with each governor's French adviser, the délégué, to
whom he gave carte blanche to deal bluntly with his enemies, much
as the political officers had done in Mesopotamia.[10] As a result, a
culture in which the ends justified the means rapidly took root. Once
the British had solved their own problems in Mesopotamia they
were deeply critical of the way in which French officials deliberately
overtaxed their opponents and settled court cases against them, and
the speed with which they were willing to resort to violence if this
'administrative penalisation' failed.[11] 'They still seem to have a

completely 18th or 19th century attitude to "Natives",' one British officer jeered as late as 1945: 'The pernicious Napoleonic maxim of a "whiff of grapeshot" still seems to be a standard doctrine.'[12]

Although Catroux denied that Gouraud was a 'prisoner of his faith' and claimed that he was 'animated by a spirit of sympathy and respect for Islam and for the Arab civilisation which derived from it', a legal system in which, in practice, no Muslim's word was taken against a Christian's in court revealed the ingrained bias of the French regime.[13] The heavy French reliance on Lebanese translators – summed up by one British officer as government by 'French sergeants and Christian interpreters' – reinforced the impression of partiality and quickly alienated the Muslim majority.[14]

'Syria was milked of its more profitable resources,' believed Lawrence's wartime comrade W. F. Stirling, who noted that the country's profitable utilities and monopolies were all French-owned and that what infrastructure existed was built 'for strategic purposes and not for public benefit'.[15] And corruption was pervasive: it was not long before one British diplomat reported that French officials were 'expecting liberal presents for services rendered by them'.[16] As even Catroux commented, 'we were in the Orient where nothing comes for free'.[17]

As Lawrence had argued during his visit to Transjordan, there was absolutely no advantage to the British in being seen to be propping up the French. But whereas he had never wanted the French to take control of Syria, his contemporaries realised that there was actually an advantage in their unpopular rivals' presence in Syria and Lebanon next door. Not only did the French presence attract the brunt of Arab anger; it also made the British look positively enlightened by comparison. Samuel, the high commissioner in Palestine, put it cynically: 'Whatever may be the criticism in Palestine of the British administration, there is probably not one among the Arab critics who would wish it replaced by a French.'[18] He liked to remind the Palestinian Arabs that, were Britain to pull out of Palestine, the French would almost certainly take over. It was, he said, 'one of the most cogent reasons that led them to offer no serious opposition to the exercise of the British mandate'.

As the British refused to help the French track down Gouraud's assailants, the French were obliged to confine their efforts to the territory that they controlled. During 1922, they received a new lead from the governor whom Gouraud had installed in the Jabal Druze, Salim Atrash, who told them that another of Gouraud's attackers was staying with his cousin and rival, Sultan Atrash. The French raided Sultan's home and arrested the suspect, but the convoy of armoured cars they sent to escort the prisoner back to Damascus was ambushed by Sultan and a French officer was killed. Following considerable embroidery, the story ran that the thirty-one-year-old Sultan had personally decapitated the unfortunate Frenchman with one blow of his sword.[19] This was France's bloody introduction to Sultan Atrash, the man who would harass them for the next five years.

Sultan cut a menacing figure, even twenty years later. When the British explorer and soldier Wilfred Thesiger met the man he called his 'boyhood hero' in 1941, he was delighted to see that even in middle age Sultan surpassed his expectations. 'His face, framed in a white headcloth, was austere and authoritative; his body, wrapped in a black cloth of finest weave, was lean and upright,' Thesiger recalled.[20] A photograph from the 1920s shows Sultan, then a wary outlaw, staring alertly at the camera. He sports a debonair moustache and, befitting his then status as a fugitive, several days' stubble.

Sultan Atrash's father had been executed by the Turks when the Druzes last revolted in 1909, and at the climax of the Arab revolt he had joined Feisal and Lawrence to oust the Ottomans from Damascus. But the Druzes and the Bedu had never been natural allies, and after Sultan had entered Damascus with the Arabs on 1 October 1918 he immediately picked a fight with Feisal's main Bedu supporter, Auda abu Tayi; it had been Lawrence who had pulled the two men apart, but not before Sultan had struck Auda across the face. Lawrence had Sultan spirited out of the city and back to the Jabal Druze before he could do more damage.

Three years on, the Atrash family remained the largest and most powerful in the Jabal Druze, the high and fertile plateau south-east of Damascus named after the stubbornly independent people who had lived there for over sixty years. Deceptively unimpressive from a distance, the 'Druze Mountain' was in fact a natural fortress.

Volcanic in origin, it owed its security on its northern flank to a chaotic lava field called the Laja, a maze of clefts and caves that provided innumerable opportunities to ambush unwelcome interlopers, as well as hideaways for wanted men. To the south it was now protected by the hazy frontier with Transjordan, which the French could not approach without crossing into British territory and sparking a diplomatic incident with their neighbour. Ferociously high temperatures in summer and cruel wet winters provided additional protection against intruders. The Druzes took full advantage of the sanctuary that the harsh, dark and stony landscape of the Jabal gave them. There was no one, believed one French officer, who was better than a Druze 'at hiding among the rocks, in the bushes, and using the ground to surprise his enemy and deal him a fatal blow'.[21]

The Druzes were named after a man called Durazi, a missionary who had come to Lebanon nearly a thousand years earlier to spread the word that the Shia Fatimid caliph at the time, al-Hakim, was God. Regarded as heretics by other Muslims, the Druzes had led an isolated existence in mountain Lebanon until the 1860s, when they fled inland to the Jabal after their massacre of neighbouring Christian Maronites triggered the threat of French retaliation. Although they in turn had approached the British for protection, they had a fierce reputation as born warriors and excellent shots. Over a millennium they had accumulated a range of esoteric beliefs, the most eye-catching of which, at least as far as outsiders were concerned, was a belief in reincarnation that gave them a cavalier disregard for death. One survivor of a Druze charge described it as like 'the very earth moving in landslide, five thousand of them on horse and foot ... They brandished their weapons and howled as they came, and at their head were four great black banners flanking the emir.'[22] The Druzes' religion and geographical isolation reinforced each other. Society on the Jabal was feudal, and one Druze emir still went into battle in chain mail, although his followers were more conventionally armed with modern rifles and grenades.

The Ottomans had respected the fearsome reputation of the Druzes, exempting them from taxation and military service, and the French had initially followed suit. But when Salim Atrash died in September 1923, the French could not resist trying to bring the Jabal under tighter control, not least because they knew that the Druzes maintained close contact with the British. When the Atrash family failed to agree on a successor to Salim, the French inserted their own governor, a tough-looking young officer named Gabriel Carbillet who had previously served in French West Africa.

Described as a 'Robespierre without a guillotine', Carbillet zealously set about undermining the Atrash family's grip on the Jabal by building roads, schools, irrigation systems, and an appeal court in the Jabal's principal town, Suwayda. To do so he used forced labour – he sentenced one member of the Atrash family to break stones.[23] After a year-long construction spree, and by now deeply unpopular, he took extended leave early in 1925. Sultan Atrash chose this moment to complain vehemently about the hyperactive Frenchman's conduct to the new high commissioner in Beirut.

The high commissioner, the sixty-nine-year-old former general Maurice Sarrail, was a man with a face the colour of brick and a temper to match. He had arrived in Beirut at the start of January 1925, at a time when French domestic politics was in turmoil. The doubling of the French government's debt in the five years since the end of the war had led finally to a run on the franc in 1924. That financial crisis helped topple the tough-talking government of Raymond Poincaré, which had occupied the Ruhr when Germany proved unable to meet the reparations payments demanded of it at the Paris Peace Conference. Edouard Herriot's Cartel des Gauches won the election in May that year with slogans including 'For Peace' and 'Against the Power of Money', but the former university lecturer had failed to stop the franc's descent.

Unusually for a senior army officer, Sarrail had openly backed the left-wing Herriot, and his many enemies claimed that his posting to Beirut was a reward for his support. But this is not entirely fair. Sarrail had long been a fierce critic of the nationalist government's policy in Syria because it had benefited only 'a handful of financiers and merchants' and depended on the support of the Catholic Church, an institution that, like many French socialists, he despised.[24] 'I do not give a damn about you or your Mass,' he told the head of a leading monastic order on his arrival, when he was invited to a service giving him the Church's blessing.[25]

Herriot sent Sarrail to Beirut to reverse the policy the general had condemned, and to seek a rapprochement with the Muslim majority. The problem was that it was an about-turn fraught with risk. 'To abandon the solid Christian support which they have taken years to build up in favour of a very uncertain and in fact extremely improbable Moslem support, hardly seems a wise move,' wrote Britain's liaison officer with the French army, Guy Salisbury-Jones.[26] Sarrail's abrasive arrival made the task an even taller order. Salisbury-Jones believed that Sarrail lost the confidence of most of his fellow countrymen and of all the Christians 'before he had been in the country 24 hours'.[27]

Sarrail quickly floundered when he tried to block the appointment of a conservative Catholic general as governor of Lebanon. Having grandly proposed that the Lebanese Representative Council, a toothless body set up by Gouraud, should pick three other candidates instead, he took exception to the shortlist that they then proposed. When he vetoed one of the three, a clever Beirut lawyer named Emile Eddé who he felt was too closely connected to the Church, the council stopped cooperating with him and he was obliged to impose a French governor instead. His plan to placate the nationalists by offering them direct elections then collapsed when, back in Paris, Herriot refused to sanction it, and by the time he visited Damascus in February he was met with stony silence. There was 'not a greeting, not a smile, not a cheer from the crowd' that witnessed his arrival, according to one onlooker.[28] When the Herriot government then imploded, he was suddenly exposed. Not only did he now lack support in Paris, but he was in the invidious position of being hated by both the Christians and the Muslims, and most importantly by his own officials, whose views were very different from his own; and it was this that would ultimately undo him.

Sultan Atrash, believing that Sarrail was on the ropes, reckoned that this was the right moment to complain about Carbillet's behaviour. But when a Druze delegation arrived in Beirut, the high commissioner refused to meet it. With his authority ebbing, the general may have believed he had picked an easy fight that would help restore his status. After all, the outgoing chief secretary, de Caix, had described the Jabal as 'of small importance' and home to 'only about

50,000 inhabitants'.[29] What the French did not yet know was that as many as ten thousand of them might be armed.[30]

When, early in July 1925, shots were fired at a Druze ceremony in Suwayda in the Jabal, Sarrail ordered the head of intelligence in Damascus, Tommy Martin, to take charge. When Martin confirmed that a rebellion looked imminent, Sarrail ordered him to invite the four main Druze leaders to Damascus. Three of the four accepted the invitation, and found themselves imprisoned on arrival in the capital. The only man who did not fall for Sarrail's trick was Sultan Atrash: his father had succumbed to exactly the same ruse, and it had cost him his life.

In Salisbury-Jones's opinion, Sarrail's deceit 'only served to heap coals onto the fire'.[31] Nine days later, in retaliation, Sultan Atrash seized the village of Salkhad in the south of the Jabal Druze. Again, Sarrail underestimated his opponents. Against Carbillet's advice he ordered a junior officer named Normand to set out from Suwayda, with just 160 men, to take back Salkhad. But Normand never got there. Having ignored a warning from a friendly shaykh that an attack was imminent, he was ambushed halfway to Salkhad by Sultan. The French were particularly shocked that among the dead was a French doctor well known to the Druzes, whom he had regularly treated.[32] Another was the unfortunate Normand. Fewer than half his men survived. Sultan capitalised on his victory, pressing northwards to Suwayda, which he surrounded on 28 July.

Worse was to come for France. Five days later a second French force, under General Roger Michaud, set out from the railway south of Damascus to break the siege. Comprising over three thousand men, this force was much larger than the first, but it had been thrown together: one of its units had only just disembarked in Beirut. Its size also proved to be a weakness. As that year had been extremely dry, the soldiers were forced to take their water with them by lorry, up the only motorable road into the Jabal. As a consequence the convoy was not only slow; its route was entirely predictable. The Druzes, tipped off by sympathetic railway workers, ambushed and shot up the water lorries.

Michaud later said that he had never, in his entire career, seen troops suffer so much from heat. He panicked when he saw his men being shot dead as they thirstily drank from the water lorries' spouting bullet holes, rather than fight back. Less than six miles from Suwayda he decided to turn back, but his force was then ambushed again and an orderly retreat quickly degenerated into a rout. Over six hundred French were killed. Just as importantly, the Druzes gained about two thousand rifles, machine-guns and ammunition. It was only later in the year that the French were able to reach the site. 'It was a vision of disaster,' one officer reflected. 'Everywhere there were bones and corpses mummified by the dry soil of the Levant. Here crumpled cars with punctured wheels, there burned-out trucks reduced to their carcasses, further off, wrecked armoured cars and, beside them, the bodies of their crews.'[33]

It took a third attempt, led by Michaud's level-headed replacement General Maurice Gamelin, to relieve Suwayda. Gamelin, a retiring, modest man who exuded an air of competence, had made his name at the battle of the Marne in 1914 at which the French had stopped the German advance towards Paris. He arrived in mid-September, and set up his headquarters near the railway west of the Jabal Druze on the 22nd. A day later he set out with a seven-thousand-strong force, including a significant contingent of the Foreign Legion, into the Jabal. They freed the French garrison at Suwayda without difficulty the following afternoon. Short of food and water, however, Gamelin had no choice but to withdraw after he had razed the village. The descent of a bitter winter soon afterwards made it impossible to re-establish a French presence at the heart of the mountain. The French would not return to the Jabal until the following spring.

France's transparent weakness encouraged other separatists. Trouble now broke out in Hama, a market town on the river Orontes one hundred and seventy miles to the north. Its leader was Fawzi al-Qawukji, a flamboyant, fair-haired Syrian gendarme who had fought in the Arab army defeated by the French at Maysalun outside Damascus in 1920. Now inspired by the Arab insurgents who had invaded the French zone of Morocco and were now putting up stiff resistance to the French in the Rif mountains, al-Qawukji made contact with Sultan Atrash, and on 4 October 1925 began a mutiny within the Hama gendarmerie. Although this uprising quickly fizzled out under a French artillery and aerial bombardment that killed four hundred civilians, he lived to fight another day, and the example that he set would prove contagious.

Al-Qawukji was not the only nationalist who drew strength from the Druzes' example: so too did Abdul Rahman Shahbandar. A star student at the American College in Beirut, Shahbandar had graduated top of his class in medicine, but it was as an orator and rhetorician that he then made his mark. Having escaped from Syria and spent much of the First World War in Egypt where he was courted by the British, he had returned to Syria following the armistice; he served as interpreter to the American commissioner Charles Crane, and then briefly as Feisal's foreign minister. When Crane returned to Syria in 1922 and made a speech in Damascus, Shahbandar simultaneously translated, turning the American's inoffensive words into a powerful critique of French rule. Convicted for his demagoguery, Shahbandar was imprisoned and sent into exile before being pardoned in 1924. But he had lost none of his determination to see the French ousted from his homeland, and when the Druze revolt broke out he saw his chance. Having made contact with the Druzes he declared Sultan Atrash king of Syria and then took the nationalists who had escaped the French purge that summer into the Ghouta, a vast thicket of densely planted orchards south-east of Damascus in which it was easy to hide and live by banditry.

After these outlaws started to make travel to and from Damascus hazardous, the French tried to dislodge them by burning and bombing the villages in the orchards. In an astonishingly misjudged attempt to demonstrate that they were succeeding, and to discourage other potential rebels in Damascus, they brought the corpses of those they had killed back to the city and exhibited them in the main square. A French expatriate living there, Alice Poulleau, was appalled at the spectacle of the neat line of bodies surrounded by soldiers, gendarmes, and the chief of police with his whip. Temporarily lost for words, she eventually dubbed what she had seen 'the regime of the boot'.[34]

The stunt backfired, increasing sympathy in the city for the opponents of the French. There was, Poulleau reported, a disconcerting increase in the number of Syrians who believed that 'If you're going to die anyway, you might as well die fighting.'[35]

Attacks on French soldiers increased. A few days later twelve soldiers' bodies were dumped outside the city's eastern gate. On 18 October the Druzes appeared again in the Maydan, the straggling suburb that ran south from the city next to the Hijaz Railway. This down-at-heel quarter was already tense: earlier that day two soldiers had killed a Damascene Muslim after a quarrel, and there had been a separate demonstration after a child was run over by a tram. News of the Druzes' appearance caused hysteria. The cry, 'Shut the shops, the Druzes are coming', spread across the city.[36] Helped by nationalist sympathisers including a former city nightwatchman, Hassan Kharrat, the Druzes hoped to kidnap Sarrail at his grand Damascus residence, the Azm Palace, but the high commissioner had left earlier that day. By nightfall the palace was ablaze, the French had dispatched tanks into the bazaars, and the chatter of intensifying gunfire was competing with the call to prayer across the city.

Unwilling to risk his troops in a 'murderous' street-by-street fight, the following day Gamelin resorted to his artillery to wrench the old city back from the insurgents.[37] In the next twenty-four hours intense French shellfire destroyed much of the old commercial quarter, and inflicted havoc in the Maydan south of the city wall. Officially, the French put the death toll at 150, but a French communist newspaper reckoned it was closer to 1,400. The French claimed that most of the damage had been done by the insurgents, but their version of events was quickly contradicted by *The Times*'s correspondent, who had ventured into what had been the city's heart soon afterwards.[38] The damage to 'house upon house and shop after shop', he then reported, had been 'unmistakably made by shell'.[39] Soon afterwards cartoons began to circulate in Damascus depicting a giant Sarrail killing women and children in his bid to flush out Kharrat, the gamekeeper-turned-poacher who had helped the rebels infiltrate the city.

France's relationship with the Syrians, which Sarrail had sought to improve, was irreparably damaged. As Britain's vice-consul in Damascus John Vaughan-Russell put it, 'It is difficult to see how the Mandatory authorities, after all the hatred and bitterness which they have stirred up, can for many years find any responsible Syrians to collaborate whole-heartedly with them in the task of governing the country.'[40]

Having so obviously failed, Sarrail was by now in an extremely precarious position. Intelligence officers on his staff leaked documents to Henri de Kerillis, an aristocratic reporter on the nationalist *Echo de Paris* who was in Syria at the time. On 21 October de Kerillis reported that the high commissioner had ignored warnings that trouble was brewing in the Jabal Druze. He blamed France's problems on '1. Sarrail 2. Sarrail 3. Sarrail'.[41]

After the leaks the beleaguered high commissioner dismissed most of his intelligence staff, but his paranoid attempt to prevent further bad news reaching Europe was predictably ineffective. When *The Times* broke the story of the bombardment on 27 October, days after the new French government had signed the Locarno Treaty – 'designed to ensure the maintenance of peace' – Sarrail was finished.[42] On the 30th he was recalled to Paris in disgrace.

Sarrail was a useful scapegoat for French woes, but his conduct could not answer several fundamental questions. How were the Druzes so organised? From where were they getting the intelligence and the arms that enabled them to ambush the French, and the food that kept them in the field? And how come *The Times* was so well informed about what was happening? To the Frenchmen who mulled over these conundrums, the finger of suspicion pointed in a single direction: south, towards the British.

11

THE CRUSHING OF THE DRUZES

DARK RUMOURS THAT THERE WAS A HIDDEN HAND BEHIND THE Druze revolt began circulating in Syria as soon as the uprising began in July 1925. By August talk was rife that that hand belonged to Britain. 'It is openly said,' reported Alice Poulleau, the French expatriate living in Damascus, 'that the English are resupplying the Druzes, and giving them, for a gold pound, a rifle, a hundred rounds, and a sack of flour.'[1]

The French somehow acquired a memorandum by Gertrude Bell, in which she commented: 'it is the Druze who will enable his brother Syrians to evict the French'.[2] Since they were convinced that Britain's priority was to oust them, it followed from Bell's assessment that the British would logically be providing the Druzes with help.

'Britain' provided an easy explanation for the drubbing that the well-organised Druzes were giving the French forces in the Jabal. The increasingly paranoid high commissioner, Maurice Sarrail, was convinced that Sultan Atrash had gone to meet the British resident in Amman soon after the beginning of the revolt. He told a friend he had proof of British involvement and, having thus made up his mind, interpreted the friendliness of the British liaison officer, Guy Salisbury-Jones, as evidence of a guilty conscience.[3] Even a level-headed French officer like Colonel Andréa, Gamelin's right-hand man in Damascus, believed that Britain was funding the rebellion he had been sent to crush. 'The insurrection wasn't short of money,'

Andréa noted archly in his memoir of the uprising. 'It came in large sums from across the borders, with the encouragement and advice of those who always hoped France would leave Syria.'[4]

Britain's consul in Damascus, Walter Smart, was well aware of 'a considerable intensification of anti-British feeling' at this time.[5] A tall, thin man with longish hair, a diffident manner and avant-garde opinions, Smart was an unlikely-looking diplomat, but these cultivated attributes disguised an altogether harder edge. He had, in the wonderful phrase of one of his friends, 'the extreme elegance of a praying mantis'.[6] Another described a man with 'total realism and iron determination' who would ultimately become the 'last High Priest of British power in the Middle East'.[7] Smart shrugged off the ill-will that he felt, blaming it on the way that France's political and economic instability had generated 'a vague, general perception of France's helplessness in the world to-day and ... an exasperated realisation of the inevitable progress of Anglo-Saxon predominance'.

Partly because of the breakdown of his relations with the French, Smart relied increasingly on the Druzes for information, and was secretly in touch with the nationalists who were organising the revolt. Making contact with the rebels was not a particularly difficult task, as one of the leading Arab nationalists lived next door to the consulate, but Salisbury-Jones was nonetheless surprised when Smart showed him 'a most interesting document which had come into his possession, giving the Druze order of battle'.[8] Smart's deputy Vaughan-Russell did not even try to hide his sympathy for the insurgents, describing their 'hard and gallant struggle against hopeless odds'.[9] Another, Francophile, British officer accused both British diplomats of being united in their 'hatred of the French'.[10]

Not surprisingly, the French believed that Smart was in league with the Druzes, and although this was untrue the British consul did certainly try to make trouble for the French in Syria. As his priority was to stop the unrest spreading southwards into Palestine and Transjordan, he was determined to portray the Druze revolt as a backlash against bad French government. Vaughan-Russell explained the thinking within the consulate neatly. His great fear was that 'if too much prominence be given to the phrase "Anglo-French cooperation in the Near East" – which the French press loves to repeat at every opportunity – this anti-French odium may spread and eventually communicate itself to the Moslems under our Mandated zones, and develop into an anti-colonisation (and hence anti-British) feeling'.[11] It was therefore vital that relations between the British and the French did not appear too cosy.

Smart was probably the origin of stories reported by *The Times*'s correspondent Arthur Merton that were designed to show that a rift had opened up between the British and the French authorities. Merton, who had arrived from Cairo to see the aftermath of the bombardment of Damascus for himself, duly reported that Smart had filed a claim for damages with the French authorities following the shelling, which made it implicitly clear that the consul rejected the French claim that the Druzes were to blame for the damage. Three days later he produced a glowing tribute to the 'fearless way' in which Smart had ensured the safety of the Christian population of the city by negotiations with 'certain influential Moslem gentlemen', after the French soldiers guarding the Christian quarter had run for their lives.[12] Three days later, the paper published a photograph that Merton had taken from a minaret on the edge of the old city showing the scale of the damage that the French bombardment had done.

The French hated the 'insolent publicity' that *The Times* was giving them, and became increasingly obsessed by Smart.[13] The British diplomat had been expelled from Tehran in 1921, which convinced the French that he had been involved in the coup that had brought Reza Shah to power and was probably still involved in clandestine work. In Syria they believed he was behind the creation of the nationalist Iron Hand Society. Such was their paranoia about his influence that they believed the society's aim was to expel 'all foreign influences', and yet at the same time enable 'the British seizure of the Military, Financial and Administrative gearwheels of the State'.[14]

On 19 November 1925, the new French high commissioner arrived in London to raise Smart's activities with the British government. Bertrand Henri Léon Robert de Jouvenel des Ursins, to give Henri de Jouvenel his full name, was a politician, unlike his military predecessors. Born in 1876, the forty-nine-year-old senator had originally studied law, but then opted for a career in journalism on *Le Matin*. Now defunct, the newspaper was renowned for its brave reporting: de Jouvenel, with his idealistic, mordant style, fitted in and ended up as editor. In the meantime he divorced his wife, and took off with the scandalous writer Colette. He then fought in the war, but his ability to speak in language that reporters understood made him more useful back in Paris. The transport minister hired him as an adviser and later encouraged him to go into politics.

After being elected senator for the Corrèze in rural central France in 1921, de Jouvenel was chosen to represent his country as delegate to the League of Nations. Experienced at defending French colonial policy, and having won the confidence of other delegates at the League, he was the obvious choice to replace the discredited Sarrail at the end of 1925, at a time when French conduct in Syria was attracting international scrutiny. Although de Jouvenel was probably happy to take on a foreign posting – he had just divorced Colette, after her affair with his son from his first marriage was exposed – he saw the Syrian job as a potential cul-de-sac. Rather than permanently replace Sarrail, he agreed only to conduct an 'exploratory mission' to Syria to review the situation, and to act as high commissioner while he was there.

De Jouvenel well knew that British help was key to dealing with the Druzes, because the Druzes' supplies came from Transjordan. Before he could set out for Beirut, therefore, he needed to clear the air with his British counterparts. When he arrived in London, however, it quickly became apparent that British support had a price: French assistance in their long-running dispute with the Turks over the ownership of Mosul. Britain had recently referred the 'Mosul question' to the League of Nations for arbitration, following several years of intermittent trouble in northern Iraq, where the Turks were backing Kurdish separatists who wished to establish an independent state. To complicate matters further the French were siding with the Turks, in an attempt to gain a greater share of Mosul's oil than Clemenceau had won after the end of the war. Now, when de Jouvenel made allegations about Smart's activities, the British government confronted him about the fact that the French had allowed the Turks to use the railway that formed the frontier between Syria and Turkey to ferry soldiers east towards the Iraqi frontier.[15]

De Jouvenel immediately grasped the connection that the British were making. He agreed to stop further Turkish troop movements towards Mosul, knowing that, if he did not do so, he could expect no help from the British to deal with the Druze supply lines which ran through Transjordan. As Salisbury-Jones commented, once the British had tied the Mosul and Druze problems together, the Druze revolt was extremely useful, since it had 'momentarily put an end to any thought which they [the French] may have had of working against the British'.[16] The Mosul question was resolved, in Britain's favour, in March 1926. Until it was, Britain left France to deal with the uprising alone.

De Jouvenel arrived in Syria early in December 1925 and immediately made a better impression than his predecessor. While Sarrail had dropped bombs, he served up ice-cream *bombes*, ran a limp joke at the time. As his first task was to stem the flow of hostile reporting, he invited all the foreign correspondents to his residence for Sunday lunch, using the opportunity to draw attention to his appeal 'to all Syrians of goodwill, to all patriots of good faith' to work with him to create a constitution for the Lebanon and hold elections in those parts of Syria unaffected by the violence in the south.[17] A little pointedly, he went to see the British correspondent who could not attend, apparently because of illness, soon afterwards. And, behind the scenes, he also told the Druzes that he was willing to negotiate.

While de Jouvenel started to give the French mandate in Syria a more liberal front, Gamelin's commander in Damascus, Charles Andréa, set about restoring complete control of the city using rather more familiar methods. Four days after de Jouvenel met the journalists, Andréa – 'the coolest Frenchman I have ever met,' said Salisbury-Jones – gathered the city's leaders together and announced that he intended to restart work on a new boulevard encircling the old city, a project that had been put on hold when the French administration ran out of money a few years earlier.[18] The Syrians were sceptical, but Andréa was insistent. He would find compensation to pay those whose houses were destroyed, and wages for up to 1,500 workers, he said. The Syrians relented, and the work began immediately.

It was only once the boulevard was completed early in 1926 that its true purpose became clear, when French engineers arrived to lay barbed-wire defences along its length. Andréa wanted to create a ring of steel around the old city that would separate its commercial centre from the warren of suburbs that offered the rebels numerous hiding places and routes into its heart. He was under pressure from both the British and the American consuls in the city who were threatening to tell their nationals, publicly, to leave.[19]

With the centre of Damascus now more secure, Andréa could turn his attention to the undergrowth of the lawless Ghouta orchards. He began by sending in flying columns of irregular Circassian, Armenian and Kurdish soldiers, led by a junior intelligence officer named Alessandri, who fought the rebels using guerrilla tactics themselves. Their methods were criminal, violent and arbitrary: they looted 'anything portable or capable of walking' and burned down the houses of any they believed were harbouring the rebels; suspects they captured tended to be 'shot while trying to escape'.[20]

As the two sides vied for control of the outskirts of Damascus the fighting worsened. 'Scarcely a day or night passes but Damascus reverberates with the crack and roar of artillery and with the explosions of bombs and shells in the vicinity or outside the city,' Vice-consul Vaughan-Russell wrote.[21] On 12 February his colleague Smart reported that the gunfire overnight had been the worst he could remember since the bombardment the previous October, but nobody had been killed. These vicious exchanges achieved little. The following month Vaughan-Russell observed that although French control of the city centre was now indisputable, their grip on the surrounding countryside did not extend beyond the range of their artillery. As a consequence, the Druzes were still under no great pressure to give up their struggle, and when de Jouvenel made a direct appeal to them Sultan Atrash rebuffed his overture. In reply, Sultan demanded an independent Syria: he had an eye on developments in Paris, where a series of short-lived governments was perpetuating the sense of political chaos, and there was now a possibility that the socialists, who were traditionally anti-imperialist, might take over. De Jouvenel rejected Sultan's demand out of hand.

The warmer weather of spring offered Andréa an opportunity to return permanently to the Jabal Druze. Over the winter he had formed a plan to recapture Suwayda, and then branch out north-wards to seek a deal with the Amer clan, rivals of the Atrash. Finally he intended to concentrate his full military might against the Atrash's stronghold in the southern Jabal.

In April Andréa put that plan into action. Although Sultan again got wind of the forthcoming French offensive and made a series of attempts to cut the railway south of Damascus, he failed to stop the build-up of French troops. Andréa's advance force set out on 22 April, and after a stiff battle with the Druzes outside Suwayda, the French retook the town three days later. Andréa soon started to receive letters of submission from Druzes in the villages to the north. His engineers set about fortifying Suwayda so that it could serve as a base for the next stage of operations.

In the meantime Alessandri's guerrilla operations in the Ghouta delivered a significant scalp – Ahmed Merawed, the man wanted since 1921 for Gouraud's attempted murder. A letter from Fawzi al-Qawukji found on Merawed's body, complaining about the 'prolonged silence and current inertia' of the rebels, corroborated intelligence that there were by now serious divisions between the Druzes, who wanted to negotiate a truce, and the nationalists, who did not.[22] In an attempt to deepen that split further de Jouvenel prematurely offered a major political concession. Two days after the capture of Suwayda he suddenly announced that he was replacing the French délégué in Damascus with a new prime minister, Damad Ahmed Nami Bey, an aristocrat who had married a daughter of the Ottoman sultan and who was not obviously in France's pocket.

Although this experiment in self-government initially looked promising, Ahmed Nami Bey was rapidly hamstrung by the same pressures that had undone Feisal six years earlier. The three nation-alists he appointed to his cabinet quickly began to make demands – specifically, for a general amnesty and the reunification of Syria and Lebanon – that de Jouvenel would not accept. In a reshuffle in June Ahmed Nami Bey brought in moderates to replace the nationalists (who were exiled to inner Syria), but he could not persuade the rebels to give up nor the French to moderate their approach. De

Jouvenel returned to France to publicise his achievement regardless, but in truth his plan had backfired. As Gamelin ruefully reported in July, 'far from obtaining the desired result, this policy has been seen as a sign of our profound weakness'.[23] Meanwhile, the attacks on French forces operating outside Damascus continued unabated.

It was France's victory over the rebels in Morocco, however, that gave the French in Syria a major boost. Until that point France had been fighting on two fronts, and Morocco had been the priority. After the rebel leader Abd al-Krim was forced to surrender in May 1926, the cash-strapped government was able to move large numbers of battle-hardened troops and their equipment eastwards to reconquer Syria. With 95,000 men at his disposal – up from 15,000 when the revolt broke out – Gamelin finally had enough manpower to fight on several fronts in Syria simultaneously. In the Ghouta on 20 July he launched a massive ten-hour artillery bombardment that killed four hundred rebels and left the French undisputed masters of the lawless green zone: when they next swept the orchards only a single shot was fired at them. The army built a narrow-gauge railway into the Jabal Druze, which enabled them to supply a much expanded military operation on the mountain, including an expedition into the tangled Laja lava field. Ahead of a further League of Nations meeting at which the situation in Syria would be scrutinised, Gamelin sent an upbeat report to Paris saying that the situation had 'completely changed' during the preceding month.[24] The reason for the turnaround, he explained, was that there was no longer significant local support for the rebellion.

That was true, but it did not reflect the situation fully. The problem, as Charles Andréa, the general in command of operations in the Jabal, explained, was that even if the Druzes were growing weary of the uprising, the rebels still had plenty of support nearby. 'The rebellion would have been long finished if the leaders of the revolt had not found the money, arms and ammunition in Transjordan to continue it, and had not had complete freedom to plot and support the unrest in the Druze country and the Hauran,'* he later wrote.[25]

---

* The Hauran was a fertile zone west of the Jabal Druze where much of Syria's wheat was grown.

Gamelin had already met the British high commissioner in Palestine, Lord Plumer, in June to press him to stop the rebels from playing a game of cat and mouse across the frontier. Although an embarrassed Plumer had promised that he would do what he could to help, and even hinted that the French could discreetly cross the border to chase the rebels, the meeting did not result in any real improvement in the situation. In French eyes, the British seemed to be making no effort to help them. Plumer's officials said that they did not have the manpower to police the border properly and, to French exasperation, insisted on treating Druzes who had crossed the border into Transjordan as political refugees.

France's earlier tendency to side with the Turks still meant that the British viewed their neighbour's problems unsympathetically.[26] Salisbury-Jones's successor as British liaison officer with the French army, John Codrington, described how, 'From the High Commissioner, Lord Plumer, downwards to the pilot officers at Amman, there was antipathy to the French. The French were considered cads; they did not (as His Excellency once remarked to me) play cricket.'[27] British officials, he claimed, savoured the news of French reversals. '"Damned good show," they said, "fancy a few tough Arabs taking on France – they must be real sportsmen."'

Suspicions that the British were actively assisting the rebels grew when, in July 1926, the French captured a leading rebel who made some startling allegations. Under interrogation their prisoner claimed that the British had supplied the Druzes with the information that enabled them to inflict the terrible defeat on Michaud the previous year, and then sent an intelligence officer disguised as a journalist into the Jabal to photograph the bodies of dead French soldiers. He also said that supplies for the Druzes were transported up the railway from Amman to Mafraq, where, under British supervision, they were loaded on to camels and mules and escorted to the border into the Jabal and to Azraq, the desert hideout used by Lawrence during the war, where 1,500 Druzes were now camped. 'You say that if the English wanted to stop the traffic, they could?' the French officer conducting the questioning repeated. 'Absolutely,' the Druze replied.[28]

In fact, the Druze prisoner was only reporting rumours cooked up by Sultan and Shahbandar to hearten their own supporters and spark tensions between the British and the French. But what mattered was that the French believed him. In September French intelligence officers put the allegations directly to a British officer, who dismissed them. Gouraud's former aide, Georges Catroux, who had been brought back to Syria to run the French intelligence service there, set out for Jerusalem days later to raise the matter with Plumer's chief secretary, Stewart Symes. Invoking 'the spirit of European solidarity', he asked the British to demonstrate that they were not supporting the revolt by expelling the Druzes from Azraq.[29] Symes refused to do so. 'This country is too troubled ... for me to make the mistake of irritating it,' he told Catroux. 'I cannot anger these people by taking action against Druze women and children.'[30] Back in Beirut Catroux submitted a downbeat report on his encounter. 'Unless this base camp is seized from the rebels,' he warned Paris, 'we risk seeing Sultan Atrash retake the Druze country over the winter which will prevent us reacting.'[31]

Catroux's prediction did not come true, however. Although Azraq remained in Druze hands throughout the winter of 1926–27, Sultan failed to regain control of the Jabal. The rebels grew short of money and medical supplies, and their flyblown camp at Azraq, though beyond French reach, proved a thoroughly unwholesome place to live. By the end of November, the British consul in Damascus reported that the revolt was on the verge of collapse. 'All the nationalists with whom I have come into contact are thoroughly disheartened,' he told London; 'their hopes that England or the League of Nations would espouse their cause have been disappointed.'[32]

When, in January 1927, the British decided that it was finally time to clear the camp at Azraq, there were two reasons for their change of heart. To the south the rising power in the Arabian peninsula, Ibn Saud, had by now expelled Sharif Husein from the Hijaz, and the British worried that he aspired to add Transjordan to his kingdom too. They were also increasingly concerned that the French might give up the mandate, having failed to reach agreement with the Syrians on the outline of an 'organic law' within the three-year period set by the League of Nations. This possibility had gained plausibility when a French diplomat, the Comte de Fels, publicly suggested handing Syria over to the British. What was the point, he asked, after totting up the cost of France's mandate, of being 'indef-initely condemned ... to police the Syrian borders expensively and dangerously, for the benefit of other countries'?[33]

The possibility of French withdrawal from Syria left the British in a bind. So far they had wanted to avoid abetting the brutal French response to the Syrian revolt. But if, as a consequence, the French were forced to leave, they would be obliged to take on the costly Syrian mandate themselves or accept a government of Arab nation-alists that would undoubtedly trigger Arab demands for self-government across the frontier in the neighbouring mandates they ruled. Walter Smart perfectly encapsulated the dilemma: 'It would be most inconvenient for us to appear as the supporters of a modern crusade. Yet it is obviously in our interest that somehow or other France should remain in Syria.'[34]

As a consequence, when in April 1927 Plumer finally confirmed that he intended to deal with the Druze camp at Azraq, he was very keen for the plan to be presented 'not as the outcome of an Anglo-French plan for military cooperation – which would provoke plenty of critics – but as a local policing measure made necessary by the repeated failure of the Druze chiefs to keep the promises they had made to the British authorities'.[35] The British operation to expel the Druzes from Azraq finally began in the middle of June. At the end of the month Paul Beynet, the French intelligence officer attached to the British for this period, reported with satisfaction that of the fifteen hundred Druzes originally at Azraq only forty-eight men, who had just sixteen rifles between them, remained. The others had either submitted, so that they could return to the Jabal, or been driven suf-ficiently far southwards into the waterless desert that they no longer posed a threat. Despite this good news, Beynet continued to suspect the true loyalties of the British, who, he noticed, 'never stopped looking after the great Druze chiefs'.[36]

Although military operations in Syria were to continue through-out the following year, one month after the clearance of Azraq, on

26 July 1927, Georges Catroux called a press conference that effectively marked the end of the revolt. Having announced that France would absorb the Jabal Druze into the state of Syria, he also took the opportunity to deny the rumours that France might give up the mandate. 'Having received the mission to facilitate the progressive development of Syria and Lebanon as independent states and to guarantee protection and rights to every citizen, the Mandatory Power will not fail in its task,' he insisted, warning that impatience and violence would only slow the process.[37]

That August, Maurice Gamelin, the French commander-in-chief, praised the 'combined action of the French and British authorities' for bringing the uprising to a close.[38] But there was deep anger among his officers, particularly those who worked in France's sizeable intelligence operation in Syria, who were convinced that the British had done their utmost to prolong the revolt in a bid to force France out of Syria. With hindsight, Britain's liaison officer to the French forces saw the damage that had been done. When, towards the end of the revolt, he tentatively suggested to Catroux that the relationship between their countries was improving, Catroux pursed his lips and gave him a look that reminded him of a 'cold and venomous Richelieu'. No, the French officer replied, emphatically, 'things are certainly not going better'.[39]

THE PIPELINE

WHEN OIL WAS AT LAST STRUCK IN NORTHERN IRAQ ON 14 October 1927 at Baba Gurgur, two drillers were killed by the black fountain they unleashed, which spewed ninety thousand barrels into the air in the following twenty-four hours. Baba Gurgur, on the steppe ten miles north-west of Kirkuk, had seemed a good place to start when exploration began six months earlier, for it had been famous for thousands of years as the site of an eternal flame, a flare of natural gas licking up from a shallow crater in the ground. But it was only some time after the Baba Gurgur strike that the chairman of the Turkish Petroleum Company, which had exclusive exploration rights, felt he could report with certainty that the presence of commercially viable quantities of oil had been 'definitely established, and there has been opened up the promise of one field, or possibly several fields, of great richness'.[1] This discovery would trigger another row between two of the company's major shareholders, the British and French governments, over the route by which the oil should be transported to the market.

There was nothing Turkish about the Turkish Petroleum Company, as the name and nationality of its chairman revealed. Sir John Cadman, a British academic turned businessman, was the ideal person to run the company at a time when exploration and extraction were its immediate focus. Born in a mining village, a mining engineer by training – just as his father had been before him –

Cadman might have spent his life in and around the collieries of the Midlands had he not found time to pursue his interest in the extraction of petroleum from shale while professor of mining at Birmingham University.

Dismissed as a blind alley by other academics, Cadman's apparently eccentric enthusiasm was to change his life. In 1913 he was invited to join the Admiralty Fuel Oil Commission, the body ordered by Winston Churchill to 'find the oil' that would enable Britain to convert its fleet.[2] Cadman went to Persia to investigate, and the Commission's conclusion, that the Persian supply was reliable enough, formed the basis for the government's momentous decision to switch to oil and take a controlling stake in the Anglo-Persian Oil Company. It was a move that led the British army to occupy Basra and its nearby refineries when war broke out a year later, then Baghdad, and ultimately Mosul.

By the end of the war Cadman was directing the Petroleum Executive, which was responsible for the sourcing and supply of oil to power the war effort. Like other government departments, in December 1918 it set out its views ahead of the peace conference. Describing Britain's 'most disquieting' dependence on the Americans for oil, it urged the government to take control of the provinces of Baghdad and Mosul and insisted that in 'any territorial adjustments in Syria or elsewhere wayleaves for pipelines etc from Mesopotamia and from Persia to the Mediterranean should be secured for British interests'.[3]

The British negotiators in Paris broadly followed that advice. Determined to run a pipeline from northern Iraq's oilfields to the Mediterranean coast over territory under British control, they demanded the oasis of Palmyra, sparking an argument with the French. The impasse was resolved in 1919 when tribesmen loyal to Feisal (and possibly encouraged by the French) then captured the Euphrates towns of Dayr az Zor and Abu Kamal from the British, who had occupied them at the end of the First World War. The tribesmen's action left Syria with a convex eastern border that meant that the most direct route from northern Iraq to the sea ran through French-controlled territory. This was to have significant implications when, following the Baba Gurgur discovery of 1927, the question of the route of the pipeline from the oilfields to the Mediterranean arose.

The British had initially also hoped that any oil found beneath the arid steppe of northern Iraq would be theirs alone, but the price of France's willingness to forfeit Mosul was a share in any oil discovered. To placate the French, on the sidelines of the San Remo conference in 1920 Cadman negotiated a deal with Philippe Berthelot of the Quai d'Orsay to divide between them the enemy's stake in the company that had oil exploration rights in northern Iraq. This was the Turkish Petroleum Company, a multinational vehicle involving both British and German firms, which before the war had secured a letter from the Ottoman sultan's chief minister, the Grand Vizier, that gave it drilling rights near Mosul. The British government already had a substantial interest in the company through its stake in Anglo-Persian, which was one of the TPC's founders. As a result of Cadman's San Remo agreement, so now did the French.

Shortly afterwards, the Americans – then the world's largest oil producers – muscled in. Convinced that their own stocks were dwindling, they feared that Iraqi oil might threaten their dominant position in the market. The American ambassador in London reminded the British that his government expected Britain's new mandates to 'be held and governed in such a way as to assure equal treatment in law and in fact to the commerce of all nations'.[4] The Americans also began publicly to question the validity of the Grand Vizier's letter.

The British initially stood up to American pressure, but the ongoing dispute over the ownership of Mosul that lasted through the early 1920s forced them to change tack. On the strength of intelligence reports that both the French and Americans were secretly encouraging the Turks to retake Mosul by force, Churchill concluded early in 1922 that 'so long as the Americans are excluded from participation in Iraq oil, we shall never see the end of our difficulties in the Middle East'.[5]

Once the British government had decided that control of northern Iraq mattered more than the question of who was allowed to join the Turkish Petroleum Company, Cadman went to the United States later in 1922 to hammer out a provisional agreement that offered the Americans participation in the company. That done, American criticism magically evaporated, the Mosul dispute was eventually resolved in 1926 and the deal was signed in July 1928. By its terms, four companies – Anglo-Persian, Royal Dutch Shell, the French state-owned Compagnie Française des Pétroles and the Near East Development Corporation (which represented the various US companies' interests) – each had an equal stake of 23.75 per cent in the TPC. 'Mr Five Percent', Calouste Gulbenkian, who had set up the company, retained the remainder.

Cadman, already chairman of Anglo-Persian, became chairman of the Turkish Petroleum Company, which had struck an advantageous deal with the Iraqi government in 1925. Under its terms the TPC had to select twenty-four sites where it would drill, and construct a pipeline across the desert to the Mediterranean, by November 1928. The Iraqis could then invite other companies to bid to choose further plots of their own.

The problem was that the Turkish Petroleum Company was a concession-hunting vehicle for four competing interests, and not an independent business with a strategy of its own. Differences between the shareholders rapidly appeared. While the Compagnie Française des Pétroles wanted the TPC to start pumping oil as soon as possible to make up for France's lack of fuel, the three other companies on the board did not. Anglo-Persian's situation was representative of all three dissidents. It already had drilling rights in neighbouring Persia, and exported oil from there by sea to Europe – incurring shipping costs and Suez Canal levies by doing so. Oil pumped down a pipeline from northern Iraq to the Mediterranean would be eleven shillings a ton cheaper, destroying the European market for its Persian oil.[6] Nor did it want a glut of Iraqi oil to depress the global price. As chairman of both Anglo-Persian and the TPC, Cadman had a significant conflict of interest.

The exploratory drilling carried out for the TPC convinced the three dissident companies that there was also a flaw in the 1925 deal the TPC had agreed with the Iraqi government. Their geologists believed that the Iraqi oilfield was probably a single whole, so that any other companies offered later concessions by the Iraqis would be drilling into the same reservoir and competing for the same, finite supply. The race would be on to extract the lion's share, and the consequent flood of oil on to the market would cause the oil price, and their profits, to plummet. This was probably the real reason why, in March 1928, Cadman described the construction of a pipeline as 'premature'.[7]

Cadman wanted to delay the decision over the pipeline's route by eighteen months, but once oil was struck in viable quantities the issue became impossible to avoid. The facts strongly favoured the French. Of the four possible terminal ports, three, Beirut, Tripoli and Alexandretta, were under French control. All of them were closer to the northern Iraqi oilfields and thus cheaper options than Haifa, the sole British contender.

The French argued the economy of their route, the British the security of theirs. But fundamentally both nations' motives were entirely strategic. Early in 1928 officials at the French ministry of war privately argued that control of 'le pipeline' and its terminus was almost as good as control of the oilfields themselves. 'If ... England declared war on us, we could, for a while at least, block their supply of Iraqi petroleum, and in the last resort, render the terminus and a significant length of the pipeline running through Syria unserviceable.'[8] When in March they warned the French prime minister that a decision on the pipeline's route was imminent, they reminded him that, if the route to Haifa was chosen, it would deprive the country of 'the only source of oil to which France has ownership rights'.[9]

British officials' concerns about the route of the pipeline mirrored their French counterparts'. Asked by the prime minister at the end of February to investigate the matter, they reported in June that, in the view of the chiefs of staff, it was 'of the greatest strategical importance' that the Haifa route be chosen, since this would bring oil a thousand miles closer to Britain and give the nation 'virtual control over the output of what may well prove to be one of the richest oilfields in the world'. If, on the other hand, they warned, the pipeline was routed to a Syrian port, Great Britain would be placing herself 'at the mercy of the French'.[10] In view of the economic advantages of the French-sponsored alternatives, the officials concluded that the only way of ensuring that the pipeline was laid through British-controlled territory was to subsidise the construction of a railway across the desert that would bring down the cost of the construction of the pipeline, in collaboration with the TPC.

To avoid torpedoing the deal over the ownership of the Turkish Petroleum Company, which was in the process of being finalised, the British and the French both kept quiet about the pipeline. As a consequence, when the French diplomat Philippe Berthelot visited London in July 1928, he left under the erroneous impression that the British had ruled out the Haifa route because it raised 'more drawbacks than advantages'.[11] Similarly, Cadman mistakenly believed that the French were reconciled to the likelihood that Haifa would be the terminus, but simply wanted to keep the ultimate decision as quiet as possible. The misunderstanding only became clear that October, when the Turkish Petroleum Company asked for another extension of the deadline it had been given to choose where it wished to drill for oil. Feisal's government reluctantly agreed a two-year extension, on the condition that the TPC undertook a survey of its preferred route for the pipeline – which was to Haifa. The Iraqis supported this more expensive option to counter the threat coming from the rival Saudis to the south. They felt that the pipeline, and the railway that was supposed to accompany it, would be a good way to create strong political and commercial ties with Palestine and Transjordan.

Cadman quickly realised that the Iraqi government's quid pro quo would be incendiary to the French. When he met the British colonial secretary Leo Amery to discuss his answer to the Iraqis, he explained that in deference to French sensitivities he had acknowledged the Iraqi government's requirement only in an annexe to the main agreement, which stated merely that an assessment of the Iraqis' preferred route was 'among the surveys to be made'.[12] Amery, though, disliked the vagueness of this formula. He told Cadman to revise the letter so that it only made reference to the survey of the Haifa route; Cadman eventually agreed.

When Cadman passed the revised draft to the French at the beginning of November, explaining that the change had been necessary to obtain Britain's support as the mandatory power, unsurprisingly they were furious. He was only able to force the revision through by a majority vote: he was supported by the Americans and Dutch, for whom any debate over the pipeline was useful if it delayed the export of oil.

Cadman's counterpart in the San Remo negotiations eight years earlier, Philippe Berthelot, who was by now the head of the Quai d'Orsay, went to see the British ambassador in Paris. In a stormy meeting he accused the British of 'grave interference', and hinted that the French were forging an alliance with the Americans over the issue of the company's freedom of action, which he said Cadman had guaranteed at San Remo.[13]

The possibility that the French and Americans might gang up caused deep concern within the Foreign Office. In February 1929 its top official warned the Colonial Office that a serious dispute with the French might cut Britain's chances of securing the Haifa route. That drew a swift rebuke from the Colonial Office, which accused its diplomatic cousins of contemplating 'a definite surrender' to the French.[14] Pointing out that British and French interests were 'diametrically opposed', it believed that a dispute was not only inevitable but best had now, before the French-American alliance strengthened any further. When the cabinet discussed the matter weeks later, it showed no great appetite for the confrontation the Colonial Office desired. Instead, it preferred to distance itself as far as possible from the matter, instructing the ambassador in Paris to do what he could to dispel the impression that the British government had leant heavily on the Iraqis. So, at the end of April the ambassador implausibly told the French that there was nothing the British could do to change either the TPC's decision or the Iraqis' minds.

Over the next few months the British seemed to be losing the battle. With a general election due in May, the Conservative government was reluctant to plough public money into a railway along the Haifa route even though it would make the construction of a pipeline considerably less expensive. But the French showed no such reticence. In February 1929 the French high commissioner told the British that, to make the Syrian route more attractive, his government was planning to build a railway across Syria to the Euphrates. It would be financed by a bond issue from the Syrian and Lebanese governments guaranteed by France. The British were disturbed to learn that he had also assured the TPC that France would build a 'first rate' harbour at Tripoli – 'whatever might be the cost, and whatever might be its natural disadvantages'.[15] Meanwhile, the British claim that a pipeline running through 'peaceful' Palestine would be safer was wrecked when, in August 1929, riots in Jerusalem set off an Arab massacre of Jews in Hebron and revenge attacks across the mandate that left 271 dead and a further 580 wounded. Less than three weeks later the British liaison officer at the French headquarters in Beirut reported that the Iraq Petroleum Company – as the TPC had belatedly renamed itself – had requested permission to survey the route the French proposed.

When the Conservatives lost the general election at the end of May, the Labour government that replaced them soon revisited the issue. The key concern of the era, even before the Wall Street Crash, was unemployment, and the new colonial secretary Lord Passfield argued that the cabinet should back a railway to Haifa because its £1.5 million cost was outweighed by the £3 million of business that its construction could be expected to generate in Britain. Others in the cabinet were less sure. One of Passfield's colleagues felt that nothing should be done until it was clear that the French had actually started spending money. Another signalled his refusal to support 'a gamble in which no authority can assure us a commercial return'.[16] As a whole, the cabinet shared his scepticism, and a decision was again postponed.

The matter resurfaced when the British government received a letter from Cadman on 20 March 1930. In it Cadman warned the government that unless it could offer 'financial and other facilities', the Iraq Petroleum Company would choose the northern, Syrian, route, which would be cheaper to build and to run. He proposed that the British government should immediately open negotiations with the French to achieve the best possible terms and act as a guarantor of a new international company that would build the railway and pipeline through French territory. Secret intelligence revealed to the cabinet days later suggested that Cadman was not bluffing: the French were definitely considering building the railway in an effort to sway the IPC's board.

The British cabinet initially felt there was no choice but to follow Cadman's advice. On 1 May it was advised that the French would take a 'generous attitude' in any negotiation on British access to the railway and the oil terminal because the British government's help would be needed to persuade the Iraqis.[17] When the Admiralty declared that it would be disastrous to follow Cadman's suggestion, however, there was a change of heart. The cabinet agreed to take no decision until it had sought the opinion of the Iraqi government.

The British government had steered clear of the question of the pipeline in its dealings with the Iraqi government for almost a year when, on 13 May, the British high commissioner in Baghdad met Feisal, his prime minister Nuri Said and war minister Jafar Pasha, and revealed what had been going on. Sweetened by a British offer to support Iraqi independence, their response was entirely predictable, and just what the British wanted. All three were utterly opposed to the Syrian route, and were on the point of halting negotiations over the changes to the concession that the IPC so badly needed. Nothing the French government could offer would induce them to agree to the Tripoli proposal, they said.

Baghdad's uncompromising response laid the basis for a deal. When Cadman met the British government that summer for talks, it became clear that his priority was to amend the 1925 agreement so that the IPC would not face competition from other companies that were concession-hunting in northern Iraq. He also privately admitted that he personally favoured the southern, Haifa, route, probably because, as the Iraqis' own preferred route, support for it in the face of the compelling French economic argument represented the best way to persuade the Iraqis to amend the original concession. If the Iraqis offered to renegotiate the earlier deal in exchange for IPC support for the Haifa route, he predicted, the IPC's board would agree.

This compromise formed the basis for talks with Feisal, who arrived in London soon afterwards to negotiate with Cadman. After the surreptitious mediation of the British high commissioner in Baghdad, who had conveniently also come to London, Cadman put the deal to the IPC board at a meeting on 13 August. Debate was delayed, however, when the representative of the American Near East Development Corporation announced that he would need to take instructions from New York.

Furious at the reversal of their fortunes, the French realised that the Americans had not yet decided whether they would support Cadman's initiative. Primed by the Quai d'Orsay, on 16 August a senior French banker named Horace Finaly invited the president of Standard Oil New Jersey for lunch. Walter Teagle, who was passing through Paris at the time, was the mainstay of the Near East Development Corporation – he had conceived the company as a way to gain the backing of the State Department nine years earlier. Finaly's bank, Paribas, had provided Jersey Standard with financial and political backing when it set up a French subsidiary a few years earlier, but he overestimated his influence when he remarked menacingly to Teagle 'how useful it could be for Standard to avoid adopting an unfriendly attitude toward France in this pipeline business'.[18]

In the previous two years the French government had introduced import quotas and created a new refining company that foreign oil companies already doing business on French soil were forced to use. Its aim was to protect the embryonic French oil industry and create a certain domestic market for their share of Iraqi oil, but they succeeded in irritating the American oil companies operating in France. Teagle's response to Finaly was therefore blunt. France could not expect the large American companies 'to furnish friendly support in London if she harasses them at home'.[19]

Teagle went from Paris to London, where he met Cadman to discuss the pipeline. Both men knew the depth of French feeling on the subject – the prime minister André Tardieu had claimed of the pipeline that 'no French government could give away this card and survive' – so they had to find a compromise.[20] In discussions in Whitehall weeks earlier the possibility of a bifurcated pipeline terminating at both Haifa and Tripoli had been raised, and the two men agreed to pursue this further now. Teagle contacted the American surveyor who had assessed the Syrian route earlier that year to cost this option, and Cadman cancelled his meeting with the British government to give Teagle time to go back to France to speak to

Tardieu. Teagle told Tardieu that support for this new solution depended on the relaxation of the restrictions he now faced in France. Tardieu had little option but to agree.

The French were annoyed to have been outmanoeuvred. At a meeting at the Quai d'Orsay Philippe Berthelot complained at the way in which Cadman had successfully joined the need to revise the concession with the question of the pipeline's route. The French threatened legal action, and their old favourite, hostile press coverage. They even quietly made overtures to Feisal, to see if he would be interested in becoming king of Syria. But they failed to stop the bifurcated pipeline from going ahead. The principle was agreed that October. A revised convention was thrashed out and finally agreed in March 1931. The Americans were mollified: when France announced new import quotas that year, Teagle's company received three times that allocated to Anglo-Persian. The pipeline finally came into service in 1934. It was, said one oil geologist, 'one of the most spectacular engineering achievements of recent years'.[21]

Britain's determination to maintain control of Iraq's oil had reached a successful conclusion, but the cost had been the further aggravation of relations with the French. As the colonial secretary Lord Passfield noted, 'our professions of non-intervention and complete neutrality have left the French Government entirely unconvinced and unimpressed. They do not believe that the Iraq Government's insistence upon the Haifa alignment was other than directly inspired by His Majesty's Government.'[22] But they were 'much too polite to say so on paper'.

The altercation was certainly worthwhile, for by 1940 the Iraqi fields produced four million tons of oil a year; Britain's share of overall production supplied 5 per cent of domestic needs, but the full requirements of its Mediterranean fleet. Small wonder, then, that *Time* magazine dubbed the pipeline 'the carotid artery of the British Empire'.[23] Acquired by Britain in 1920 as an eastern bulwark to the Suez Canal, Palestine now gained a new strategic importance as the outlet for Iraq's oil. That made the British determined to cling on there – amid mounting opposition to their presence – seemingly at almost any cost.

13

REVENGE! REVENGE!

On Monday 3 August 1936, readers of the British news-papers learned of a weekend of renewed violence in the north of Palestine. Four British soldiers had been wounded during attacks by an Arab gang in the neighbourhood of Afula, a village in the hills just south of Nazareth. In the port of Haifa, to the west, an Arab detective in the Palestine Police had been shot dead, and another Arab constable wounded. Two Jewish watchmen in the village of Rihania, close to the Lebanese border, had been murdered, and another Jew in Haifa wounded. And just across the border in Transjordan, the brand-new pipeline linking northern Iraq with Haifa had been punctured twice and the oil ignited. *The Times* said that the flames were visible up to twenty miles away, and blamed the action on another Arab gang.[1] The situation that developed in the next three years would mirror what had happened in the Jabal Druze a decade earlier. This time, however, Arab opponents of foreign rule would use Syria as a safe haven to launch attacks on neighbouring Palestine. France's reluctance to help the British would profoundly shape the way the British tried to deal with terror.

What is now known as the Arab revolt had started four months earlier when, on 15 April 1936, on the road between Tulkarm and Nablus, Arab bandits ambushed a bus to rob its Arab and Jewish passengers. They murdered one of the Jews and seriously injured two more, one of whom then died. Two Jews decided to take revenge the following day, going to an isolated Arab farmer's hut near Petah Tiqwa and murdering its two occupants. News of this reprisal sparked a riot in Jaffa, the main port in Palestine. 'Soon the approaches were strewn with overturned cars and burning buses amid a welter of blood, stones and broken glass,' reported a British officer who was present at the time.[2] The Arabs organised themselves with unprecedented speed, forming the Arab Higher Committee to coordinate strikes across the mandate, in protest at the British administration's continuing support for Jewish immigration.

Jewish immigration into Palestine had not, until recently, been a political issue. The work that colonising the country involved – like breaking stones and draining malarial swamps – was unattractive, and in the early 1920s few Jews chose to move to Palestine. In 1927, there was actually net Jewish emigration from the mandate; unemployment among the Jewish population had reached six thousand that year: roughly 10 per cent of the working population.[3]

Tougher immigration policies brought in by the United States and other western countries in the 1920s began to change this situation by narrowing Jewish migrants' options. The arrival of Jews from Eastern Europe with ambitions to create an independent state led to growing tensions with the Arabs, particularly in Jerusalem at the western – 'Wailing' – Wall which was the only remnant of the Temple. Today, there is a large piazza before the Wall, but in the 1920s that did not exist. The area was crowded with Muslim housing, and the Wall itself simply formed one side of a narrow passage. Jewish access to the Wall became a source of friction. In 1928 the Muslims complained when the Jews erected a screen across the passageway to segregate male and female worshippers. A protest at the Wall in August 1929 by young radical Jews resulted in a riot which spread to the nearby towns of Hebron and Safad. Two hundred and seventy-one Jews and Arabs were killed, and a further 580 injured. More Jews would have died in Hebron had they not been hidden by sympathetic Arabs.

The British, who had started out so confident that they could successfully resolve Arab–Jewish tensions, could not contain the violence and started to be sapped by a weary cynicism. 'That the Noble Race will ever lie down with the Peculiar People for any length of time I very much doubt,' wrote one general.[4] It began to dawn on them that not only could they not mend that rift, but also their policy was exacerbating it.

In May 1930 the British high commissioner in Palestine, Sir John Chancellor, bluntly told the British government that its policy of supporting Zionist aspirations was a 'colossal blunder'.[5] Believing that the underlying causes of the riots were continued Jewish immigration and land purchase from poor and heavily indebted Arab farmers, he argued that the government should intervene to limit both. If they did not, he foresaw more unrest in Palestine. 'Should there be a recurrence of the disturbances,' he warned presciently, 'they will on the next occasion be more formidable than those of last August; for both parties are now smuggling arms into the country, the outbreaks will be organised, and the Palestine-Arabs will almost inevitably have the material support of Arabs from the neighbouring territories and certainly the moral support of the whole Moslem world.'[6]

Back in London, the Labour government initially followed Chancellor's advice, but then hurriedly backtracked. Having published a White Paper that proposed limiting Jewish immigration, it found itself under attack from supporters of the Zionist movement who accused the government of breaking the terms of the mandate. Stones were thrown at Lord Passfield, the colonial secretary, when he visited Tel Aviv in October 1930. The government, which did not have a parliamentary majority, panicked. The prime minister, Ramsay MacDonald, wrote to Weizmann to reassure him that the government did not now intend to turn the White Paper into law. Read out to parliament in February 1931, this 'Black Letter' (as the Arabs dubbed it) ensured that immigration would continue to be determined by Palestine's 'economic absorptive capacity', a scientific-sounding but meaningless formula that Churchill had invented when he was responsible for Palestine a decade earlier.

Britain therefore hesitantly maintained its support for Jewish immigration – a major cause of the Arab revolt that followed in 1936 – into the era when, following Hitler's seizure of power in 1933, the numbers seeking refuge in Palestine suddenly jumped. Whereas in 1932 just 9,500 Jews arrived in Palestine, three times as many came the next year. There was a further 50 per cent increase in immigrants in 1934, and another similarly sized leap the following year, when the anti-Semitic Nuremberg Laws came into force in Germany. The arrival of over 61,000 Jews in Palestine that year brought the Jewish population in the mandate to 355,000 – a total reached at a speed that the British had never envisaged. Jews now made up more than a quarter of the population of Palestine, up from 9 per cent fifteen years earlier.

Jewish immigration created a demand for land that the growing but poor Arab population was under mounting pressure to sell off. Whereas, in the early years of the mandate, Jews bought land from rich Arab landowners living in Syria and Lebanon who wanted to dispense with swathes of their estates in Palestine that had been cut off by the frontier, by the late 1920s they were buying from the Arab fellahin, the peasants. 'Distressingly poor and ... heavily in debt to usurious money lenders', according to High Commissioner Chancellor, they had 'no alternative but to sell their land in order to clear themselves of their liabilities'.[7] The Arab sellers, or their tenants, were usually evicted by the Jewish purchasers. 'Unfortunately it was part of our job to make sure they did leave,' said a policeman, Reubin Kitson, who had joined the force on the strength of an advertisement he had seen in Britain. He had thought that 'it would be a nice thing to go to Palestine, not knowing any better'.[8]

The construction of the oil pipeline across northern Palestine aggravated an already tense situation. Under the convention negotiated with the British government, the Iraq Petroleum Company was able to draw freely on local water supplies for its own requirements, putting it into competition with local farmers. Nor, astonishingly, were landowners compensated for the disruption caused by the pipeline running through their land. One analyst of the deal the British government had struck was highly critical. 'The Power most concerned in the Iraq Petroleum Company has allowed that Company the very important right of transit through Palestine without demanding any adequate compensation in return, without taking the interests of the inhabitants sufficiently into consideration, and while limiting many of the prior rights of these inhabitants,' he wrote in 1932.[9]

The man who now exploited the anger caused by Jewish immigration was Hajj Mohammed Amin al-Husayni, the Grand Mufti of Jerusalem. A short, cautious and rather delicate-looking man with red hair, blue eyes and a lisp, Amin owed his position as chief interpreter of the Sharia law to his birth into one of Palestine's two most powerful families. After an education at Al-Azhar University in Cairo where he had set up a club for opponents of Jewish immigration into Palestine, he had served in the Ottoman army in the war, deserted to the British following the capture of Jerusalem in 1917, and then backed Feisal as king of a united Syria and Palestine through the turbulent postwar era of the King–Crane commission and the General Syrian Congress. On 4 April 1920, when the riots erupted in Jerusalem at the festival of Nebi Musa, it had been he who, standing on the balcony of the Arab Club, held up a portrait of Feisal and provocatively shouted at the seething crowd below: 'This is your King.'

Amin never served the ten-year jail sentence for incitement that this declaration earned him because he fled across the Jordan and was soon pardoned by the then British high commissioner for Palestine, Sir Herbert Samuel. At the time, the gesture, which was supposed to cement British influence in Transjordan, had seemed a small price to pay.[10]

Not long after Amin returned to Jerusalem following the pardon, it became clear that his brother Kemal, the then Mufti, was dying. Although their father had held the title before Kemal, the role was not hereditary. Anticipating a contest for the succession with the rival Nashashibi family, Amin decided that a change of headgear was in order to demonstrate his pro-Arab allegiance. Having swapped his traditional Turkish tarboosh for a turban, he had time to grow a convincing-looking beard before his brother died in March the next year.

The British tried to balance the Husaynis and the Nashashibis by dividing up the major public roles in Palestine between them. Following the Nebi Musa riots they had sacked the Husayni mayor of Jerusalem and replaced him with a Nashashibi. Partly because it was now the Husaynis' turn again, partly because the British hoped that the added responsibility might sober Amin up, they approved the former rabble-rouser as Grand Mufti of the Holy City in May 1921. The following year they helped him secure the presidency of a new Supreme Muslim Council, which was to take charge of the expenditure of the tithe-like *awqaf* religious revenues and the Sharia courts.

The presidency gave Amin significant financial power. He now controlled a budget of £50,000, which he carefully spent in ways that reinforced his own position relative to the Nashashibis. He raised a further £80,000 through a shrewd appeal to the Muslim world for funds to restore the Dome of the Rock and the al-Aqsa Mosque atop the Temple Mount, both of which badly needed repair. In this his timing was superb. Just as the Caliphate was being abolished by the Turks and Sharif Husein was being expelled by the Saudis from Mecca, Amin al-Husayni was effectively staking a claim to the leadership of the Muslim world. When the Druzes revolted against the French, he set up a relief committee to collect donations and organise the dispatch of food and medical equipment across the border to the rebels; the French believed that money from the mosque appeal was diverted to buy weapons for their opponents in Syria.

The role of organising resistance to the French brought the Mufti closer to the nationalists, but it also placed him in the invidious position of having to serve two masters. On the one hand there were the British, who were paying him to steer the Arab population; on the other the nationalists, who would support him in exchange for money. An event in 1935 forced him to choose between them, precipitating the trouble that followed.

In November 1935 a fiery Syrian preacher named Shaykh Izzadin al-Qassam was shot dead in a skirmish with British forces in the hills of Galilee. As al-Qassam had attracted a large following of young and disenchanted Arabs in Haifa, the news of his killing caused uproar in the town. An Arab journalist who witnessed the return of al-Qassam's and his followers' bodies reported how, as the corpses were carried through the streets, 'a voice cried out: Revenge! Revenge!' The crowd which had gathered for the funeral 'responded with one voice like a roar of thunder'.

'Revenge! Revenge!' they chanted back.[11]

Al-Qassam's death was a turning point because it forced the Mufti to choose which of his two masters he would serve. As his own status within the Arab movement was being threatened by the Nashashibis, he decided it was wisest to take a tougher line with the British. When, after the April 1936 bus shootings, the leaders of the various nationalist factions asked him whether he would be president of the newly constituted Arab Higher Committee, he accepted.

Under the Mufti's leadership the Arab Higher Committee called a general strike that brought Palestine to a halt that summer. It also sanctioned violence. Fawzi al-Qawukji, the man who had caused the French so much trouble in Hama ten years earlier, appeared in Palestine with a force of about two hundred Syrian, Iraqi and Transjordanian Arabs to attack Jewish and British targets. They threw up barricades, cut telegraph wires, threw bombs into crowded markets and attacked the Iraq Petroleum Company's brand-new pipeline. The lawlessness that resulted encouraged a range of other local men to take advantage of the situation. These were bandits, not ideologues – opportunists who saw the potential in the circumstances for self-aggrandisement. One of them, Shaykh Yusuf Abu Dorreh, had previously been a lemonade hawker in the Haifa souq. 'His family had no tradition of leadership, and the title of Shaykh was undoubtedly self-bestowed,' said one British police-man.[12]

Underestimating their Arab opponents, the British initially took a complacent attitude towards the violence, partly because its protag-onists looked so amateurish, partly because it was aimed primarily at the Jews. 'It was all good clean fun,' recalled another, senior, police-man. 'We chased them and they did their best to get out of the way ... You were chasing an enemy you could see, who stopped and fired at you, and you fired at him. It wasn't a case of a concealed land mine or killing from an ambush. That came later.'[13]

It did not take long for the gangs to turn an 'unusual anxiety for the safety of their own skins' (as the British put it) to their advan-tage.[14] Knowing they could not win head-on encounters with well armed British troops in daylight, they resorted to guerrilla tactics, laying landmines at night to disrupt British efforts to track them down. 'They would leave a mine on the inner side of a mountain bend in the road,' recalled one soldier, 'so that when a vehicle tripped a wire that went across the road the driver's instinctive action was to turn his wheel away from the bang and over the edge of the road ... and the vehicle would fall over.'[15] When another truck was blasted over the edge in similar circumstances, all a soldier following in the vehicle behind could find of its unfortunate driver was a foot inside a boot.[16] 'Lawrence of Arabia certainly taught the Arabs how to make bombs,' he mused.

What T. E. Lawrence had also demonstrated was that it was most unwise to underestimate guerrillas, no matter how 'Billy Buffalo' they looked, and this was a truth that the British were now forced to learn from the receiving end. Containing an insurgency demands large numbers of mobile troops, but the British had neither the manpower nor the mobility needed to succeed. In their heavy blue serge uniforms, the police could be seen a mile off. They would arrive at the scene of a crime 'soaked in perspiration and considerably plastered in mud'.[17] The soldiers, weighed down by weapons such as mortars, and Bren guns that jammed with sand, were slower still. By the time they caught up, one army intelligence officer observed, 'the men who had been firing upon them an hour before were now peacefully sitting in coffee shops or attending to the fields, while the villagers to a man – and woman – were fully prepared to cover up'.[18]

Some Arabs certainly supported the rebels, but another reason why they refused to cooperate with the British was because they were terrified of what would happen to them if they did. When the gang leader and former lemonade salesman Abu Dorreh had a narrow escape from British forces, which he suspected resulted from a tip-off, he returned to the village where he had almost been captured, found the mukhtar* and shot him dead before his family. The gangs forced local Arabs to demonstrate their loyalties in other insidious ways. They banned men from wearing tarbooshes and from shaving, and warned women against 'the uncovering of their breasts and arms – their dress should be extremely modest and should cover their knees'.[19]

---

* The village headman.

Poorly informed, under-strength, ill-equipped and frightened by the threat of landmines, the British were forced on to the defensive. Patrolling ceased at nightfall and, once the rebels owned the night, the police abandoned their remote outposts because these had become death traps. Visiting police barracks, British officials found that an 'excessive amount of time and energy' was now being 'wasted on "spit and polish", office work etc' by policemen who no longer dared to venture beyond the walls.[20] And this retrenchment had a vital consequence: it allowed the rebels to move back and forth across the frontier with Syria and Lebanon with impunity.

By the end of 1936, the British were arguing among themselves about how to deal with the trouble. The new commander of British forces in Palestine, Sir John Dill, who had arrived in September to lead an expanded British force of twenty thousand men, wanted to impose martial law. The high commissioner, Sir Arthur Wauchope, resisted him, because he did not want to admit failure. Wauchope, who gave the impression of believing that 'he alone was destined . . . to restore peace in the Holy Land', instead approached the Mufti, offering him a Royal Commission to investigate the Arabs' grievances if he would call off the strike and the violence.[21] Since the strike had proved self-defeating because it only made the Arabs' economic situation worse, and as the citrus harvest was now imminent, on 9 October the Mufti agreed. In a measure of how far Britain had lost control in Palestine, the high commissioner proposed a seven-day ceasefire to allow the message to be passed around the country. Such was the Mufti's control over the situation, however, that the violence ended instantly.

In a year that had already seen Hitler remilitarise the Rhineland and Mussolini's troops reach Addis Ababa, the truce bought the British welcome breathing space. But General Dill recognised that the speed with which it had come about was ominous. 'It may sound odd to you,' he wrote to a colleague back in London, 'but I regard the most disturbing side of the situation as being the demonstration of power which the Higher Arab Committee has given in calling off the rebellion so completely and so quickly – by a word.'[22]

The promised Royal Commission reached Jerusalem on 11 November 1936. Led by Lord Peel, its members swiftly decided that the conflict between Jews and Arabs was 'irrepressible'.[23] At the end of their exhaustive four-hundred-page report, published in July the following year, they gingerly recommended the partition of the mandate into separate Jewish and Arab areas. This proposal would be unappealing, they readily admitted, since 'neither will get all it wants'. But they hoped that, on reflection, both parties would recognise that it was the answer. For partition was the only option that offered 'a prospect ... of obtaining the inestimable boon of peace'.[24]

'We counted – perhaps rather optimistically – on the Commission solving our political difficulties. It looked as though it might only have made them worse,' wrote a British diplomat in London afterwards.[25] For the Commission not only proposed partition, but tentatively recommended how it might be implemented, in a map appended to the very end of its report. The map destroyed the painstaking nuance of the report, because it clearly allocated much of northern and coastal Palestine, along with its Arab population, to the Jews. And with that single page, the Peel Commission immediately made a quarter of a million enemies for Britain.

The British army's poor performance in 1936 gave the Arabs no incentive to accept the Peel Commission's verdict, and the gangs resumed their violent campaign. The experience of the previous year made them confident – overconfident, as it transpired – of success. As Dill observed, six months' fighting had left them 'better organised to resist than they have ever been before' and their leaders, especially the Mufti, enjoying 'a strengthened position and ... an enhanced prestige'.[26]

Nor was it just the Arabs who admired the Mufti. Back in Britain, amid mounting concerns about the German threat, the chief of the general staff detected a growing empathy for the Arabs, who were 'only fighting to keep the land which they consider is theirs'.[27] At the end of July, the *Daily Telegraph* introduced the mastermind of the Arab revolt to its readers in unmistakably sympathetic terms. 'With light eyes, which periodically break into a merry twinkle, the Mufti, in appearance, suggests nothing of the political agitator or even of the militant ecclesiastic,' it reported.[28] 'Yet he is the custodian of huge funds, director of all Islamic institutions, and nominator of all religious judges, and has become the motive force of the Arabs' political movement. He is the real power of Arab Palestine.'

The benevolent attitude towards the Mufti did not last long, however. On Sunday 26 September Arab assassins shot dead the assistant district commissioner in northern Palestine, Lewis Andrews, and his bodyguard as they walked to church in Nazareth. This was the turning point in the British government's approach in Palestine. Previously unwilling to sanction the use of overwhelming force, it was obliged to take a tougher line following the murders. Three days later it outlawed the Arab Higher Committee, so that its members could be arrested. Most of them were detained the following morning but the Mufti, dressed as a woman, got away.

The Mufti's reappearance in Lebanon three weeks later provided conclusive proof that the Arabs were now using Syria and Lebanon as a base that was out of Britain's reach. After the truce the previous year, both Fawzi al-Qawukji and another notorious insurgent, Muhammad al-Ashmar, received a rapturous reception on their arrival in Damascus. In that city the man who had taken over al-Qassam's crown, Shaykh Khalil Muhammad Eissa, masterminded the business of raising money and buying weapons. Eissa was not short of funds, a British official complained, adding that the sale of arms and arrangements for their transport to the Palestine frontier were 'undertaken openly'.[29]

The British now approached the French for help, but were rebuffed. When the British consul in Damascus, Gilbert MacKereth, pressed the French *délégué* in the city to arrest al-Ashmar, the Frenchman refused to do so. He told MacKereth he was worried that the seizure of such a popular figure might cause an uproar.[30] A similar overture by the British ambassador in Paris to René Doynel de St Quentin at the Quai d'Orsay was just as unsuccessful. At the end of 1936 the French government had been obliged to sign a treaty that gave the Syrians more autonomy, following a similar British move in Egypt. Although the French parliament had not yet ratified the pact – in fact it never would – Doynel de St Quentin pointed to it, shrugged, and said that there was not much that France could do. Two decades earlier, it was he who had been hoodwinked by T. E. Lawrence over Britain's ambitions in the Middle East. He was not inclined to help the British now.

MacKereth understood this. He realised that such memories, and not the treaty, explained French indifference to Britain's problems. He recalled that when al-Ashmar had been convicted *in absentia* of killing five French soldiers in 1925 the British had refused to hand him over, on the grounds that he was a political refugee. 'We failed in 1925 and 1926 to show adequate sympathy with the difficulties the French had themselves in Syria at that time,' he wrote. 'British authorities in Palestine and particularly in Trans-Jordan showed a hospitality to Syrian bandits and rebels which now we must ruefully regret.'[31] This policy had now come back to bite the British, he concluded, for 'most of those who then benefited from British asylum are now planning to go, or have already gone, to Palestine, to continue their acts of terrorism, this time directed against the British administration.'

Just as the French had been during the Druzes' revolt ten years earlier, the British were convinced that the reason the rebels were so strong was because they enjoyed support and sanctuary across the frontier. At the end of 1937, a frustrated British official in Palestine assessed the problem: 'If Damascus and Beirut continue to provide a safe base for terrorist activity and if reports are true that the exiled leaders have considerable financial resources it is difficult to see how terrorism in Palestine is to be completely eliminated.'[32] In the absence of French help, he felt that it was time his colleagues took matters into their own hands. For, as he put it, 'Until some means of carrying the war into the rebel camp can be found I can see no hope of peace being fully restored.'

14

FIGHTING TERROR WITH TERROR

'SHORT, BALD, AND VERY UNIMPRESSIVE IN LOOKS' WAS HOW one contemporary mockingly described the man who, in the absence of French help, was about to launch a private war against the Arab rebels operating from inside Syria.[1] But Gilbert MacKereth, Britain's consul in Damascus, was proof that appearances can be deceptive, for he was an extraordinarily brave and resourceful man. As a young battalion commander in the Great War, he was reputed to have told a general that he was unwilling to carry out his proposed attack because it would be disastrous. Such insubordination could have led to a court martial and the firing squad, but MacKereth was no coward. In the space of eighteen months he had risen from sub-altern to lieutenant-colonel and he had won a Military Cross – the citation describes how he went a hundred yards over open ground under heavy fire to help a patrol that had become isolated. As he apparently told the general, his low opinion of the latter's battle plan was based on his personal reconnaissance of no-man's-land at night.[2]

Like many war heroes, MacKereth was confronted by the troubling question of what to do with himself once the war was over. Having decided to join the consular service, he worked widely across the French empire in the Arab world before being posted to Damascus in 1933. There he quickly came to dislike the 'utter and callous hypocrisy' of the mandatory system and, to let off steam, he ridiculed the officials the French government sent to run it in a series of drily entertaining reports to London.[3] In one dispatch he memorably depicted the arrival of a new French high commissioner, Damien de Martel, in a uniform he described as like a lion tamer's, 'which it is hinted is to his own design'.[4] Deliciously, he summed up two other French officials as 'combining inexperience with dynamism; a dangerous combination'.[5]

Such incisive mockery did not go down well in Whitehall. MacKereth was quickly accused of being anti-French, but he volleyed the accusation that he held the French administration in contempt. 'I know well and play Bridge with many members of it,' he replied, failing to resist the urge to add, 'and like most of them.'[6]

Shortly before the Peel Commission revealed its unpopular proposal of partition, MacKereth went to see the Syrian prime minister Jamil Mardam, to find out what Mardam's government might do to help stop the gangs operating across the frontier. The chief negotiator of the 1936 treaty with the French, Mardam was by far the most impressive of the Syrian nationalists. Bland in appearance, he was a man with a brain like a scimitar, whom the French accurately described as 'a liar who has no scruples'.[7] MacKereth quickly realised that it would not be easy to persuade him to provide help, not least because he had spent a year in prison after the British extradited him from Jaffa during the Druze revolt. When MacKereth called the gangs' activities 'brigandage', Mardam replied slyly that he preferred to call it 'Arab patriotism'.[8]

As the French proved similarly unwilling to give assistance, MacKereth decided to take the task of dealing with the rebels upon himself. From then on, as he later put it with considerable understatement, 'Much of my work was of an unusual nature.'[9]

MacKereth's belief that he could personally make a difference arose from the fact that he was receiving accurate intelligence about the rebels. In September 1937, a spy he had employed attended a congress of Arab nationalists at the Grand Hotel in Bludan, near Damascus. The three-day get-together was the Mufti's idea: he wanted to organise a demonstration of pan-Arab anger at the Peel Commission's conclusions, and he paid the travel and living expenses of the delegates who met in the resort. MacKereth sent an account of the turgid proceedings back to London, lightening it with a description of the moment when the departing activists were obliged to settle their accounts. 'There were some painful scenes when a number of the visitors, having already spent their allowances, were unable to meet their hotel bills.'[10]

MacKereth's informant discovered that about a hundred of the Bludan delegates, who were disgruntled by the congress's proceedings, had agreed to meet in Damascus afterwards to discuss taking violent action against the British. MacKereth dispatched another spy to infiltrate their late-night meeting. As refreshment for the delegates arrived, this agent saw his opportunity to adopt 'the disguise of a purveyor of ice'.[11] MacKereth, who had a keen eye for the absurd, reported how, by 'the subterfuge of helping to carry in the block of ice for cooling the sherbet', his man had managed to witness the discussion that finally started at one o'clock the following morning. The spy discovered that weapons were being stockpiled in the Nablus and Tulkarm area and that it had been agreed that Arabs who were in contact with the British should be the targets of a new wave of 'systematic personal attacks'. The gist of this intelligence was correct, though the crucial detail about the targets was not. A fortnight after MacKereth reported this information to London, District Commissioner Andrews was shot dead in Nazareth.

Soon after Andrews's murder, MacKereth reported that a full-scale resumption of hostilities was imminent. He told London that he had established 'beyond reasonable doubt' that 'small bands of Syrians had been formed under group leaders, had received earnest money in amounts varying between two and four Palestinian pounds, a rifle, a few rounds of ammunition, a warm jalabieh,* and a water-bottle'.[12] They were waiting for a signal to set out for a rendezvous in the hills of the West Bank.

MacKereth now hired an Arab hit man to intercept these bands in the border area. One of his operations killed three gunrunners and captured nearly forty weapons and two boxes of dynamite.[13]

* A wool cloak.

MacKereth also arranged the burglaries at the Damascus homes of two of the Arab rebel ringleaders, the fundraiser and arms-buyer Khalil Eissa and the organiser of the Bludan congress, Nebih al-Asmah, whose brother was the Syrian minister of the interior.[14] Al-Asmah's house yielded a diary, which was removed, photographed and replaced. Eissa's – broken into while its owner was out at prayers – provided a list of codes that linked the gunrunner with Andrews's murder by showing that he had sanctioned the killing of an Arab Palestine policeman who had been shot with the same weapon that was then used to kill Andrews.[15]

MacKereth hoped that he might shame Mardam into action if he could produce evidence linking the nationalists with murders taking place in Palestine, but although the Syrian prime minister did eventually sanction the arrest of the insurgent leader Muhammad al-Ashmar, it became clear that the support for the rebels went to the highest levels of the Syrian government. When MacKereth acted on a tip-off supplied by an informant about a lorry-load of weapons that had just been dispatched towards the border, his informant was arrested, interrogated by the interior minister personally, and severely beaten up at a Damascus police station.

Even this did not put MacKereth off. Although he had only £45 of Secret Service money to spend each year, he seems to have directed some of it to the French officer attached to the Syrian gendarmerie. He was soon able to report that the financial incentive had had a marked effect on the security of the frontier. At the end of October 1937, he told London that 'a remarkable feature' of the previous week had been 'the comparative ease with which the Syrian gendarmerie has been able to arrest ... about thirty young men attempting to enter Palestine to join the rebels there when, during the previous month, not a single one had been caught'.[16]

By then it was clear to MacKereth that the Syrians had an inkling of what he was up to. The same month he wrote to the Foreign Office enclosing the third death threat he had received that year, signed off this time by someone who called himself the 'Black Hand tinged with Blood'.[17] MacKereth may have been fearless, but stupid he was not. A few days later he wrote again to his superiors asking them to dispatch him a 'bullet-proof waistcoat'.[18]

MacKereth was not popular with the head of the Eastern Department at the Foreign Office in London, George Rendel, who sharply disagreed with his view that the revolt was the work of a small band of terrorists. Rendel, who was sympathetic to the Arabs and concerned about Britain's relations with the Arab world, saw the violence as 'part of a very widespread and deep-seated national movement spreading through all the Arabic-speaking countries against our policy in Palestine'.[19] He recognised that the death threat that MacKereth had received presented a golden opportunity to argue for his recall, rather than to send out some armour-plated tailoring. Even if MacKereth 'were to secure the arrest and execution of every Palestinian terrorist and were to lose his life in doing so – which he is all too likely to do in any case', he wrote, he was 'convinced that the trouble would go on undiminished and indeed probably with increased vigour'. In his view MacKereth was 'not touching the source of the trouble', which was Britain's policy on Jewish immigration.

MacKereth, however, successfully parried Rendel's unsubtle attempt to silence him. Bypassing Rendel, he wrote directly to the permanent secretary at the Foreign Office, breezily reassuring him that the death threats were 'not made against me personally' and that his successor would be at exactly the same risk, less able to protect himself, and lacking the contacts he himself had acquired over the years. British officials in Palestine backed him up. 'MacKereth has collected a great deal of information in Damascus and has obviously got good lines of communication,' wrote Sir Charles Tegart, a senior police officer who had been brought in to assess the situation in Palestine. 'He has also unquestionably done everything he can, on his own initiative, to bring pressure on the French, the Syrian Government, the Foreign Office, and the Palestine Government to remedy the situation.'[20] MacKereth stayed put.

Two major gang attacks in the north of Palestine, in December 1937 and January 1938, convinced Tegart to approach the French again to ask for help in arresting the ringleader, a man named Shaykh Muhammad Attiyeh, who was based in Syria. Every five or six weeks Attiyeh would assemble a gang, cross the border, start a battle designed to bring down British retribution upon Arab villages that did not yet support him, then speedily withdraw to the safety of Damascus. After MacKereth failed to persuade the French to act, Tegart, who described the situation as 'intolerable', decided it was time to visit Beirut in the hope that he might be able to persuade his counterparts there to place Attiyeh in 'preventative detention'.[21] It was to be a disappointing trip.

In his mid-fifties, Tegart had recently retired as commissioner of police in Calcutta, to widespread praise. Originally from Londonderry, he had been sent to the Indian city after it was beset by a series of politically motivated assassinations on the assumption that his Irishness endowed him with some special insight into the terrorist's mind. In fact, Tegart had turned the situation around by a mixture of instinct, imperturbability, luck and a readiness to break the rules. Although tall and muscular, with dark-blue eyes and a Celt's reddish skin, he proved remarkably adept at disguise, passing himself off as a Sikh taxi driver, a Kabuli or a Pashtun, in night-time intelligence-gathering missions. Despite the threat to his own life from bomb-throwers, by day he drove around the city in an open car; his dog, a Staffordshire bull terrier, skulked behind him in the hood.

Tegart's devil-may-care attitude inspired his colleagues, who became convinced that 'somehow or other he could not fail', a feeling reinforced by his survival of several unsuccessful attempts on his life – and another close shave that was self-inflicted.[22] Having for a while used a small iron bomb as a paperweight, believing it was inert, one day as a joke he had hurled it at a map across his office. 'Instantly,' according to a contemporary, 'there was a shattering explosion, part of the wall blew out, dust and debris littered the room, and members of the staff came running in convinced that yet another assassination had taken place.'[23] Tegart survived to accept a knighthood in 1926, after his force crushed the revolutionaries' campaign and halved non-violent crime across Calcutta. In a lecture in 1932 he defined his philosophy. 'When you scratch a monster like terrorism instead of killing it, your weapon acts merely as a spur.'[24]

In his quest to kill the monster, Tegart had some experience of working successfully with the French. In a celebrated episode during his Indian career, in 1930 he had asked the French authorities if he could attack rebels who had taken sanctuary in the French enclave of Chandannagar, believing that there they were out of Tegart's reach. After the French had given him permission to enter this remnant of their Indian empire, Tegart personally led the subsequent assault: his constables, armed with sawn-off shotguns, killed one Indian and wounded and arrested four others after a gun battle in the dead of night. So when he arrived in Beirut he was probably hopeful of securing French support for action against the Arab rebels, who were similarly flitting to and fro across the border.

But Tegart's meetings with French officials in the Levant demonstrated that any such expectations were misplaced. In Beirut the head of the Sûreté Générale, a shady Corsican named Colombani, said he was unable to help and pointed him in the direction of a colleague named Perissé in Damascus. The Sûreté was responsible for covert police work, and yet Perissé, whom Tegart found 'extraordinarily laconic and uncommunicative', said that he had no files on any of the Palestinian rebels wanted by the British.[25]

In Damascus only the head of the Services Spéciaux, which dealt with counter-espionage and national security, offered him a glimmer of hope. He volunteered to try to keep the leading rebel under surveillance, and explained why his colleagues in the Sûreté were so reticent. He told Tegart that it was too dangerous for them to enter the Maydan, the poor suburb of Damascus where many of the rebels lived, and which had been a no-go area since the French bombardments during the Druze revolt a decade earlier. When Tegart asked whether any attempt to search the rebels' houses could be made, the French spy chief was candid. 'No,' he answered. 'It would be quite useless to do so', because the job would have to be delegated to the Syrian police, whose sympathies lay with the rebels.[26] The high commissioner Damien de Martel was similarly reluctant. 'If we attempted to touch these people in the Maydan Quarter there would be a revolution,' he explained when Tegart pressed him to arrest the leading agitators.[27] For similar reasons he was also unwilling to clamp down on the Mufti, who was living under Sûreté surveillance in the Lebanese seaside resort of Joûnié, because the Arab leader was, as one Frenchman nicely put it, 'no longer a man but a flag'.[28]

To allay tensions that threatened the *Entente Cordiale*, Sir Mark
Sykes proposed dividing the Middle East with France along a line
that ran 'from the "e" in Acre to the last "k" in Kirkuk'.

François Georges-Picot,
the French negotiator
of the deal with Sykes.
The British complained
that his tactic was 'to
give nothing and to
claim everything'.
By kind permission of Mme
Anne Parent

Lawrence in Damascus, October 1918. Lawrence hoped that
the Arabs could render the Sykes–Picot agreement irrelevant by
reaching Damascus before the war's end. © Rolls-Royce Heritage Trust

Clemenceau and Lloyd George at the Peace Conference, 1919. The two leaders fell out spectacularly over the settlement of the Middle East. © Getty Images

Churchill with his wife Clementine (left) and advisers Gertrude Bell
and T. E. Lawrence (right). Churchill convened the Cairo conference in
March 1921 to rubber stamp Feisal as the new ruler of Iraq.

Sultan Atrash, leader of the Druze revolt against the French,
October 1925. The French always suspected that Atrash
owed his success to clandestine British support.

Syrian rebels are executed in Damascus, 1925. Britain tried to distance itself from France's methods during the Druze revolt. © Bettmann/CORBIS

The Mufti, August 1937. Having helped organise opposition to the French in Syria the mufti turned his attentions against British rule in Palestine in the 1930s.
© Bettmann/CORBIS

Orde Wingate. After Britain failed to engage French assistance to defeat the Arab rebels Wingate proposed 'Special Night Squads', comprising local Jews, and using aggressive tactics. © Imperial War Museum, IND 2085

Spears and Catroux. Spears was despatched to the Levant in 1942 to hold the Free French to the promise of independence they had made to the Syrians and Lebanese.

Egged on by his hard-line advisers, Jean Helleu had the newly elected Lebanese government arrested in November 1943, precipitating a far-reaching political crisis. © Time & Life Pictures/Getty Images

Elected prime minister of Lebanon in 1943, Riad as-Sulh worked closely with the British to expel the French from the Levant.

For his part, the Mufti played brilliantly upon French suspicions of their neighbour. He told the French that the British had approached him with a suggestion that the Arabs form a united 'Greater Syria', comprising Arab Palestine, Transjordan and the whole of Syria.

'Greater Syria' was in fact originally the idea of the Young Arabs who began agitating for Arab independence before the First World War; but it is easy to see why the French thought otherwise, for many British officials from Lawrence onwards had subsequently given it their backing. After the death of Feisal in 1933, his brother Abdullah and his one-time prime minister, Nuri Said, separately began to press for Arab unity, though each on his own terms. Abdullah wanted to unite – and rule – Palestine, Transjordan and Syria. Nuri, meanwhile, wanted to join Palestine with Transjordan and Iraq. Although the British government repeatedly denied it, both men's links with London, and the fact that their schemes would be detrimental to the French, immediately suggested British inspiration. The French feared that the Peel Commission's partition plan would result in the unification of the Arab areas of Palestine with Transjordan, which would generate momentum for an Arab union that included Syria. If partition went ahead, they might be left with just a bridgehead in the Lebanon.

At their meeting, de Martel raised this fear with Tegart. Explaining that he had heard of Nuri Said's ideas, he asked the British policeman what Britain's solution to the Palestine question was. Tegart, of course, had no answer. He left Damascus empty-handed.

Following his disappointing trip to Lebanon and Syria, on 19 February 1938 Tegart wrote to the chief secretary of the government of Palestine to set out two new measures designed to stop the gang attacks from Syria. One was a fifty-mile fence along Palestine's border with Lebanon and Syria, to be scoured by searchlights and patrolled by the police, which would become known as Tegart's Wall. The other was the lowering of the standards that governed police recruitment. 'Gangs of banditry, armed with rifles, cannot be dealt with by policemen with notebooks,' he argued.[29] He wanted permission to enlist 'the tough type of man, not necessarily literate',

who was 'capable of fighting rural lawlessness by its own methods'.[30] By these and other controversial means the British would
now seek to deal ruthlessly with the rebels where diplomacy – even
of MacKereth's maverick brand – had failed.

Tegart had been toying with both ideas since his arrival in
Palestine in November 1937, but it was his meetings in Beirut and
Damascus that convinced him it was time to act on them. Alec
Kirkbride, the new district commissioner who had just stepped into
the shoes of the murdered Lewis Andrews, was unsurprisingly enthusiastic about the fence. 'Several Jewish contractors who were
practically on the rocks would hail such an order as a God-send and
would, he thought, be likely to quote rock-bottom prices', Tegart
recorded.[31] Kirkbride then got on the telephone to Haifa and found
Tegart a company that was interested, Solel Boneh.

A strange outdoor meeting soon followed. Besides Tegart and
Kirkbride, the inspector general of police and the local British military commander were present. So too was the director of Solel
Boneh, David Hacohen. Before them stood a squad of Royal
Engineers and three sample sections of fence, which Hacohen's company had erected. The engineers were challenged to break through
each section as fast as possible. It was the last of these – comprising
two parallel six-foot-high fences, sandwiching a three-foot-high
fence and a thicket of barbed wire – that proved the most resilient,
but even so it took only two minutes and twenty seconds for the
sappers to cut through. Nevertheless, it formed the basis for the
design that Solel Boneh would ultimately build, and for the way it
was patrolled by cars with mounted searchlights. Under this scheme
no part of the fence was in darkness for more than the time it had
taken the engineers to breach it in broad daylight. Like many security measures, the fence was primarily a theatrical device, as useful
for its 'moral effect', as Tegart put it, as for its ability to keep the
gangs at bay, and the veteran policeman did not for a minute think
it would solve the problem.[32] Rather, as he had already argued at
the beginning of the year, 'The real remedy must lie in attack.'[33] And
it was with this in mind that he now turned his attentions to the
police.

Tegart proposed a complete revolution in the police approach,

designed to wrench the initiative from the bandits. Recruiting standards were relaxed, so that illiterate agricultural workers who knew
the territory and 'as much of the game as the other side' could be
brought into the ranks.[34] Ex-servicemen from Britain were also
encouraged to join up. The conspicuous blue serge uniforms were
swapped for 'rough, rat-catching kit of nondescript character'. Night
patrols were issued with shotguns. Doberman dogs, at £500 apiece,
were brought in from South Africa to compensate for the unwillingness of the villagers to talk. The combination of all these tactics
rang a bell with officers who had served in Ireland earlier in their
careers. There was 'definitely a certain degree of black and tan methods about the Police,' wrote one.[35] When the police played a Brigade
of Guards team at rugby they thrashed them, fifty points to nil.[36]

'It got to the stage where the so-called terrorism became critical
and in order to fight terrorism, we became terrorists more or less,'
the policeman Reubin Kitson admitted, years later.[37] Frightened
British troops dealt with the threat of roadside bombs by taking
Arabs hostage and making them sit on the front of the leading vehicle, a policy that was sanctioned from the top.[38] In an interview fifty
years on, a former soldier with the Manchester Regiment, Arthur
Lane, could vividly recall what had happened to these 'mascots' or
'minesweepers', as they were called, once they had served their purpose. 'The driver would switch his wheel back and to, to make the
truck waver, and the poor wog on the front would roll off onto the
deck. Well if he was lucky he'd get away with a broken leg, but if he
was unlucky the truck coming up behind would hit him. But nobody
bothered to go and pick the bits up.'[39] Lane's commanding officer
eventually put a stop to the practice, but only because otherwise,
'before long they'd be running out of bloody rebels to sit on the
bonnet'.

As both the Peel Commission and the League of Nations had criticised the British government for *failing* to introduce martial law in
1936, there was little criticism of Britain's brutal tactics. Moreover,
after Hitler reoccupied the Rhineland and annexed Austria, international attention was focused elsewhere. In 1938 the British
government toughened Palestine's laws further. The possession of
firearms, damage to the fence and wearing military or police uniform

without authorisation were added to a list of capital offences that already included arson, sabotage and intimidation. The chances of successful prosecution increased, for verbal statements made outside court were now deemed acceptable as evidence.

Now that death was the punishment for being caught in possession of a gun, 'cordon and search' operations restarted in earnest when the British army surged into northern Palestine in May 1938. While one force surrounded a village, another would go in to hunt for suspects and their weapons. This task was 'thoroughly nauseating, both physically and mentally', wrote one soldier, during a search in which five Arabs were killed.[40] 'The smell, dust and heat were perfectly frightful and one could not help feeling the whole time that one was rather bullying a lot of comparatively innocent people on account of a few blackguards who had probably forcibly thrust themselves upon them.'

British soldiers arrested those suspected of assisting the insurgents, and dynamited or bulldozed their homes. Collective punishments were imposed on villages where individual culprits could not be singled out. Arthur Lane went to one village suspected of assisting the rebellion with another soldier to demand a fine from the mukhtar. After the headman slammed his front door in Lane's face, and then his irate wife emerged brandishing a wooden spoon to chase Lane's colleague away, Lane tersely remembered what happened next: 'We burned her house down.'[41]

'We did certainly mess villages up and of course that created a tremendous lot of antagonism amongst the people in the countryside,' said Kitson, who was one of many who recognised that the British approach was making matters worse.[42] Born out of the frustration and fear generated by the insurgents, this brutal and indiscriminate approach led the British into a vicious circle. Collective punishment generated support for the rebels where previously it had not existed, and turned what had been disjointed banditry into a general insurgency. The approach also made it harder to gain accurate intelligence and alienated the Arab constables in the Palestine Police, encouraging them to tip off the rebels or even moonlight with the gangs. A lack of intelligence led the British to be less discriminating still.

The British soon appreciated that the Arab police were 'in a very embarrassing position', and decided to remove as many of them as possible from armed frontline duties, but not discharge them altogether because they realised that to do so would encourage them to join with the insurgents full-time.[43] However, as the Arabs made up almost 60 per cent of the overall police strength, the decision carried one big implication. The British would need to recruit more British and Jewish policemen to make up the shortfall. The Jews could be relied upon, Britain's colonial secretary believed. The only problem, he said, was that in a fight they were 'too apt to shoot off their ammunition in a great hurry'.[44]

One young, well-connected and faintly unhinged army officer was convinced he had the answer. The nephew of a former high commissioner of Egypt, Orde Wingate had arrived in Palestine in 1936 at a time when the British administration, in a forlorn effort to avoid fuelling the Arab insurgency, was hardening its policy towards Jewish immigration. After German Jews were stripped of their citizenship in 1935 the British squeezed Jewish immigration to Palestine, citing the 'general disturbance of the country and the interruption of industry, commerce and communications' to justify their move.[45] Stiff financial conditions were attached to entry permits and, as a consequence, the number of Jews who entered Palestine in 1936 was half the record number of the previous year.

'For pity's sake, let us do something just and honourable,' wrote Wingate. 'Let us redeem our promises to Jewry and shame the devil of Nazism, Fascism and our own prejudices.'[46] He admired the Jews' industry (a Jew was 'worth twenty, thirty or even a hundred' Arabs, he believed) and he instinctively sympathised with their predicament because he had been an outsider all his life.[47] The son of Plymouth Brethren, he had been ostracised at boarding school where, as a day-boy who disliked team sports, he acquired the nickname 'Stinker'. It was only after he scraped into officer training that he realised he could turn his unsettling, cadaverous looks to his advantage – when he was challenged to run the gauntlet of his fellow cadets naked, Wingate walked up to each in turn and dared them to strike him, and thus made it through untouched. 'He had fiery, searching, unsmiling eyes – extraordinary deep-set eyes that penetrated into your inner being in such a way that you could not conceal the slightest of your facial movements or say a single superfluous word,' said David Hacohen, the man who had built Tegart's fence.[48] 'He was fanatical,' recalled the man who had shared an office with him in Jerusalem. 'I liked him very much. I got on very well with him. But I must admit he was a fanatic.'[49]

Wingate argued that, to turn the tables on the insurgents, the British should set up 'Special Night Squads' comprising British soldiers and Jewish supernumeraries who knew Arabic and the local country, who could wrench back the initiative from the Arab rebels.[50] Fit, working in silence and trained in ambush tactics, they would try 'to persuade the gangs that, in their predatory raids, there is every chance of their running into a Government gang which is determined to destroy them, not by an exchange of shots at a distance, but by bodily assault with bayonet and bomb'.[51]

Wingate did not think it would take long to persuade the Arab gang-leaders to stay in at night. 'In person they are feeble and their whole theory of war is to cut and run. Like all ignorant and primitive people they are especially liable to panic.'[52] Once the threat of the gangs had gone, the villagers would have no excuse for silence. At that point, Wingate argued, the British could more reasonably put the villages under pressure, because non-cooperation could only imply complicity with the gangs.

Events helped Wingate. The uncertain situation in Europe, where Germany's annexation of Austria had sparked similar demands for integration among the German population of Czechoslovakia, meant that troops could not be spared for Palestine for much of 1938, while the Czech crisis looked as if it could trigger another war. In these circumstances, the economy of Wingate's plan appealed to the authorities, and he received permission to set up three squads to take on the bandits and defend the oil pipeline in the Jezreel valley in northern Palestine. To minimise the chances of leaks about their whereabouts, Wingate chose three Jewish settlements on the south side of the valley for bases, setting up headquarters at Ein Harod. It was a deliberately resonant choice, for according to the Bible Ein Harod was the place where Gideon had picked the three hundred men who would scatter the Midianites. Wingate, who was by then teaching himself Hebrew using the Bible, originally wanted to name his outfit 'Gideon Force', but higher authority intervened.

One of the men whom Wingate recruited was Moshe Dayan, the future Israeli general. Dayan, then in his early twenties, was already a member of the Haganah, an illicit Jewish self-defence organisation, and a supernumerary policeman licensed by the British to carry a rifle, but even he admitted surprise at what Wingate now proposed. 'We had always set our ambushes near the approaches to the Jewish settlement to be defended and not near the exit from an Arab village serving as a terrorist base,' he later wrote.[53] He was both inspired and intimidated by Wingate, who initially addressed his recruits in broken Hebrew, revolver in one hand, Bible in the other. 'After a while we asked him to switch to English,' said Dayan, 'since we had difficulty in following his strange Hebrew accent and could understand only the recognisable biblical quotations in our language.'

When the Special Night Squads began their raids in June 1938, Wingate proved a demanding and savage leader. He struck one member of his squad across the face with a stick when the man failed to shoot an Arab horseman silhouetted against the skyline. On another occasion he interrogated one of four captured Arabs by choking him with a handful of grit and sand he had scooped up from the ground. When his prisoner still refused to talk, he turned to one of the Jewish recruits. 'Shoot this man,' he ordered, but the recruit hesitated. 'Did you hear? Shoot him.' The recruit did as he was told. Wingate turned to the three surviving detainees. 'Now speak!' he bellowed.[54] Back at camp, Wingate's men were bemused by his behaviour. He would sit in his tent naked, reading the Bible and scrubbing himself with a brush, or eating a raw onion as if it were an apple.

The number of attacks on the pipeline fell, but the Special Night Squads experiment did not last long. Early in July, Wingate overreached himself when he decided to attack an Arab gang, which had occupied Nazareth, with a force of over eighty men from all three squads. The operation started to go wrong when Wingate set up ambushes around the wrong village. Having realised his mistake, he led an assault on the settlement where the gang was resting, but in a chaotic night attack was hit by friendly fire. It was 'a cock-up of the first water', said a colleague.[55] Wingate wrote up his report of the operation from hospital. 'More deliberation and care is called for,' he admitted.[56]

Although Wingate recovered and returned to lead the night squads on further raids, the squads were wound up later in the year. By then, Wingate's refusal to share the details of his plans – on the grounds of operational security – had annoyed other British officers. Wingate was an easy scapegoat for the more general failings of British policy. A senior policeman described him as a 'definite hindrance'.[57] He said that Wingate made 'no attempt to co-ordinate what he did with the government force for law and order, the police force, at all.' Another official believed that the night squads' tactics had 'forfeited our general reputation for fair fighting'.[58] In truth, the British had sacrificed that long before.

In August 1938 the high commissioner in Palestine, Sir Harold MacMichael, tersely observed how Britain's heavy-handed approach in the mandate had been entirely counterproductive. Two years previously, he noted, the disorder had been 'chiefly kept alive by foreign volunteers assisted by Palestinians. Position is now reversed.'[59] Belatedly, the British realised that, if war broke out in Europe, they needed Palestine to be stable. And the only way to ensure that outcome was through political, not military, means.

15

PLACATING THE ARABS

BRITAIN'S INEFFECTIVE APPROACH TO COUNTER-INSURGENCY
in Palestine not only alienated the Arab population but also failed to
stop a far more general escalation in the violence, which was caused
by the Jews' increasing willingness to take matters into their own
hands. Up to early 1938 the Jewish community, the Yishuv, had followed a policy of self-restraint they called *havlagah*. But, as it
became clear that the British were unable to protect them, that
approach became contentious. The future Israeli prime minister
Yitzhak Shamir later described *havlagah* as 'disastrous'. It was
'short-sighted, self-deceiving and based on an inexplicable ... and
unjustified belief that, sooner or later, if we refrained from angering
them, the British would keep the promises they had made to us',
Shamir believed, describing why he had taken up arms against the
British.[1]

The first sign that the consensus that had maintained *havlagah*
was crumbling came on 12 April 1938, when two British constables
died in a brave but inept attempt to defuse a bomb that had been
found on a train used by Arab workers at the oil terminal in Haifa.
Havlagah collapsed in June that year after two Jewish youths were
sentenced to death by a British military court for shooting at an
Arab bus, although they caused no casualties. One death sentence
was commuted, but the other was carried out. The hanging of the
twenty-three-year-old Schlomo Yousef on 29 June led to outrage

because he was the first Jew to be executed by the British in Palestine, and because, until that point, the British had condoned Jewish efforts to defend themselves using their defence organisation, the Haganah.[2] The execution triggered a wave of revenge attacks by the Irgun Zvai Leumi,* a right-wing faction of the Haganah, of which Yousef had been a member.

On 6 July two bombs were thrown in Haifa market, killing twenty-one Arabs and six Jews, and wounding 106. On 15 July another bomb, on David Street in Jerusalem, killed ten Arabs and wounded thirty more. Further carnage was averted when a Jew was spotted leaving a basket containing a fifteen-pound bomb covered with vegetables, which was timed to detonate at eight o'clock that morning. Another bomb exploded in Haifa market on the 25th. Fifty-three Arabs were killed, and thirty-seven wounded. The police and army quickly cordoned off the area, but, according to a British report, they were 'unable to prevent a wave of Arab reprisals in which 4 Jews were killed and 13 wounded by stoning, beating and stabbing and considerable destruction of Jewish property by arson, sabotage and looting'.[3] Another bombing in the Haifa market at the end of August killed twenty-four Arabs and wounded thirty-five. The same report described how, as a result, sudden noises like 'a back-firing car or the fall of a book in a crowded cinema' were now liable to cause panic. 'Any parcel left lying about is an object of suspicion and to throw an empty cigarette tin out of a car is to invite pursuit.'

This escalating tit-for-tat between the Arabs and the Jews left the British in an impossible position. *The Times*, which on Allenby's entry to Jerusalem two decades earlier had predicted that Britain would establish 'a new order' in Palestine, 'founded on the ideals of righteousness and justice', now described a nightmare in which the police 'must protect themselves against assassins, moderate Arabs from extremists, Jews against Arabs, and now, innocent Arabs from well-planned attacks which almost everyone considers to be Jewish reprisals'.[4] By the beginning of September 1938 the high commissioner felt it necessary to warn London that the situation was

---

* 'The National Military Organisation'.

deteriorating rapidly and had reached the point at which the rebel leaders were 'more feared and respected than we are'.[5]

In London the colonial secretary, Malcolm MacDonald, faced two difficulties. The first was that while the Czech crisis over the Sudetenland made war in Europe look imminent, the British government could spare no troops to reinforce the garrison in Palestine. The second was that even if the Sudeten crisis passed, and extra troops could then be sent, reinforcements alone would not solve the problem. As he put it later in the year, 'the real problem in Palestine is not a military problem but a political problem. Our troops can restore order; they cannot restore peace.'[6]

The 'political problem' had been created by the Balfour Declaration and, in trying to fix it, the Peel Commission had only made matters worse. As long as Peel's proposal for partition was on the table, even moderate Arabs refused to negotiate with the British. MacDonald experienced this at first hand when he made a secret flying visit to Jerusalem in August 1938. He had hoped, on his arrival, to meet both Jewish and Arab leaders, but the high commissioner told him that there was no question of him doing so. While Britain supported partition, no Arab would willingly talk to him for fear of being murdered as a traitor, the high commissioner explained.[7] The high commissioner also wanted to stave off the unwelcome impression of weakness that talks in the current climate were bound to generate.

The government dispatched a second commission of inquiry, led by a distinguished civil servant, Sir John Woodhead, to extricate it from the mess created by the Peel Commission. Charged with assessing whether Peel's proposals were achievable, its members spent three months touring Palestine, while all around them the violence grew steadily worse. Woodhead himself gave an Arab boy a piece of chocolate when he visited a school in Beersheba. The child threw it on the ground, saying that he would never take anything from a man who had come to divide Palestine and give its best land to the Jews. The truth was that, in many cases, the Jews had turned rocky hills and malarial swamps into the best land by sheer hard work. But, as the British had come to realise, this transformation had not made the Arabs any more sympathetic to the Jews. Not surprisingly, when

Woodhead did finally submit his report to the government in October, he ruled out the Peel Commission's proposal for partition but he revealed that his colleagues could not agree on which of two possible alternatives might be better. This gave the British government the excuse it needed to ditch the Peel report. But it did not reveal that decision immediately. In a futile bid to avoid giving the Arabs the impression that the gangs' campaign of violence had forced their hand, they decided to delay the announcement that partition had been abandoned 'until the military situation indicates that we have the upper hand of the rebels'.[8]

The Munich Agreement at the end of September, after which Chamberlain infamously proclaimed 'peace in our time', gave the British government the breathing space it needed. In October the cabinet decided to send more troops to Palestine and to announce the Woodhead Commission's findings early in November. The reinforcements' first task was to re-establish British control over Jerusalem, where Arab rebels were in complete control over the old city, before moving on to Jaffa.

In command of this operation was an as yet little-known major-general named Bernard Montgomery. He took the view, as MacKereth, Tegart and Wingate had done before him, that a relatively small group of troublemakers was responsible for the violence. The British army's 'first and primary task', he believed, was 'to hunt down and destroy these armed gangs. They must be hunted relentlessly; when engaged in battle with them we must shoot to kill.'[9] Over the next three months, resistance was brutally stamped out. The most recent estimate is that between 1936 and 1939 about five thousand Arab men were killed and ten thousand more wounded. By the end of the uprising, 10 per cent of the adult male Palestinian Arab population had been killed or wounded, imprisoned or sent into exile.[10] Senior British officers remarked with satisfaction that the tarboosh – banned by the rebels – had started to reappear.

The threat of war in Europe now obliged the French to repair their relations with the British. In Paris the government made overtures to London, seeking high-level military talks in anticipation of a conflict. The French government had by then shelved the parliamentary ratification of their 1936 treaty with the Syrians, which would have given Syria more autonomy, on the grounds that 'if the emancipation of Syria was allowed to take place too suddenly that country might fall under German influence'.[11] To deal with one other potential source of conflict, the French had also secretly begun negotiations that would end in the transfer of the northern Syrian port of Alexandretta to the Turks. When the British foreign secretary, Lord Halifax, raised the question of the Mufti at a meeting in Paris in November, he was reassured by the French that the Mufti was 'now under very close supervision' and 'seeing no one of any importance'.[12] The British were sceptical that these words would be translated into action, but in Damascus MacKereth noticed a great improvement in the French willingness to take action against the rebels' operations in Syria.[13]

The Syrian nationalists' fury at France's refusal to give them greater autonomy and its willingness to surrender Alexandretta to the Turks also helped the British. Convinced that British pressure was responsible for France's stiffer attitude towards them, and believing that, with British help, they could win independence from the French, the nationalists now withdrew their support from the Palestinian rebels. Exactly why they thought the British might ultimately assist them is explained by the note in the British archives that makes it clear that, for some time, MacKereth had been paying a secret monthly subsidy to the Syrian prime minister, Jamil Mardam.[14] These payments only ceased when war began to loom and London decided that it was important to end 'all those extraconsular activities which might arouse suspicion in the minds of the French'.

Meanwhile, the British cabinet thrashed out a new policy for Palestine, well aware that the likelihood of war made strategic considerations paramount. Previously it had worried that a policy that prejudiced the Jews might lead to the estrangement of the United States government because of the possibility that the Jewish population in America could stir up public opinion there. Such was the urgency of the situation, however, that the fear about the Arabs' numerical strength outweighed concerns about the Jews' political influence. 'If another crisis should find us with a hostile Arab world behind us in the Middle East,' one cabinet minister warned his colleagues, 'then our military position would be quite untenable.'[15] The Suez Canal and the uninterrupted flow of oil from Iraq to Haifa were now both far more important than a twenty-two-year-old commitment to the Zionists given by a man who was nearly ten years dead. So too was the need to extricate the twenty thousand frontline troops that it had taken to hammer the Palestine insurgents.

On 20 April 1939 the cabinet therefore discussed a White Paper making changes to the government's policy on Palestine. Introducing the proposals, MacDonald admitted that the document included 'certain features which would not have been there if we had been allowed to give our undivided attention to devising the best plan for the future good government of Palestine'.[16] The paper proposed limiting Jewish immigration to fifteen thousand a year for the next five years and restricting Jews' ability to buy Arab land. In the relative secrecy of a cabinet meeting MacDonald could be blunt about why both measures were required. It was, he admitted, 'to placate the Arabs'.

The prime minister, Neville Chamberlain, weighed in behind MacDonald, urging his colleagues to 'consider the Palestine problem mainly from the view of its effects on the international situation', and in particular the 'immense importance' of keeping the Muslim world on side.[17] Echoing his predecessor Arthur Balfour, who had declared two decades earlier that, if a quarrel were inevitable, it was 'preferable to quarrel with the Arab rather than the French', Chamberlain now offered his colleagues a similarly stark choice. 'If we must offend one side,' he finished, 'let us offend the Jews rather than the Arabs.'

Following a fruitless effort to reconcile both Jewish and Arab representatives at a conference in London, the White Paper was eventually published on 17 May. In July, MacDonald announced a six-month suspension of immigration altogether. When, three months later, the Permanent Council of the League of Nations put Britain's change of policy to the vote, it decided by four votes to three that the White Paper's provisions contravened the mandate. The White Paper was thus unlawful, but by then the League of Nations had long since ceased to matter. Fifteen days later, Hitler invaded Poland.

Implicit in Britain's decision to back the Arabs was a simple calculation. Whereas – as in the previous world war – the Arabs were dangerously unaligned, Hitler's clear hatred left the Jews without a choice. 'The Jews?' the British ambassador to Egypt asked rhetorically. 'Let us be practical. They are anybody's game these days. But we need not desert them. They have waited 2,000 years for their "home". They can well afford to wait a bit until we are better able to help them get their last pound of flesh ... We have not done badly by them so far and they should be made to realise that crying for the moon won't get them anywhere – especially if we are the only friends they have left in the world.'[18]

The outbreak of war in September 1939 left the Jews with no alternative but to wait. In the meantime they would make new friends, and digest the most important lesson from the last three years: that when dealing with the British, violence worked.

PART THREE

THE SECRET WAR: 1940–1945

British soldiers at Palymra, 1941. The British waged a short but bloody war in 1941 to wrest Syria and Lebanon from the Vichy French.

16

A KING IN EXILE

ON THE EVENING OF 18 JUNE 1940 – THE DAY AFTER THE French government said that it was seeking an armistice with the invading German army – the BBC broadcast a defiant message from a French brigadier-general who had narrowly escaped to London. 'Is the last word said? Must hope disappear? Is defeat final?' he asked rhetorically, in the ponderous tones for which he would later become famous. 'No! ... For France is not alone! She is not alone! She has a vast empire behind her. She can make common cause with the British empire which commands the seas and is continuing the struggle ... This war has not been decided by the battle of France. This war is a world war ... The fate of the world is at stake ... Whatever happens the flame of French resistance must not and shall not be quenched.'[1] With two-thirds of France now occupied by Germany and the other third ruled by Pétain's Vichy government, which had indicated its willingness to collaborate with Hitler in return for some autonomy, the vast French empire would be central to the fight-back envisaged by the speaker, Charles de Gaulle. At the heart of this strategy lay the Levant.

Tall and aloof, Charles André Joseph Marie de Gaulle had been born forty-nine years earlier into a family that was at pains to distinguish itself from the ordinary bourgeoisie. The de Gaulles were minor aristocracy: his parents, Henri and Jeanne, were first cousins, and they lived a threadbare but proud existence. Devout Catholics and ardent monarchists, they would not sing the Marseillaise, nor celebrate Bastille Day.

Henri de Gaulle had fought in the Franco-Prussian war but had not had the means to be an officer. For a time he worked in the interior ministry, until the trend of government policy against religion alienated him. Thereafter he became headmaster of two Jesuit schools in Paris, which had escaped the purge of clerical institutions by going private. An avid reader of the new right-wing daily newspaper *Action Française*, which called for the restoration of the monarchy and campaigned against the influence of foreigners, Jews, protestants and freemasons in French life, he was proud of his aristocratic forebears' walk-on parts at various stages in his country's history, and vocal about the signs of national decline he saw about him. As a consequence, one of Charles's first political memories was of 'the surrender of Fashoda'.[2] De Gaulle was born into a family in which suspicion of France's old enemy ran deep. 'Perfidious?' Henri de Gaulle is reputed to have said, about the British. 'The adjective hardly seems strong enough.'[3]

Given this upbringing, it was not surprising that Charles de Gaulle would join the army. In 1912 he signed up with the 33rd Regiment, an infantry unit led by a sarcastic and blunt-talking colonel, Philippe Pétain. Similarly, it was not surprising that, when he was wounded soon after war broke out in 1914, he blamed his injury on the British government's failure to join the battle faster. Described on his graduation from the military academy at St Cyr as 'a very highly gifted cadet', de Gaulle had limited opportunity to demonstrate his ability during the war. He spent much of it in captivity after he was again wounded and taken prisoner at Verdun in 1916.[4] All five of the attempts he made to escape failed.

After the armistice de Gaulle fought briefly with the Poles against Soviet Russia before returning to St Cyr to teach history, and continuing his own training at staff college. From there he emerged with a report that summed up the two sides of his character. He was 'an intelligent, well-read officer' with 'brilliant and resourceful qualities', but who spoiled these talents 'by his excessive assurance, his contempt for other people's point of view, and his attitude of a king in exile'.[5] He was uncannily suited for the role in which he cast himself in 1940.

Backed by Pétain, now a marshal, who described him as the most intelligent officer in the French army, de Gaulle ignored his critics. 'The man of action invariably has a strong dose of egoism, pride, hardness and guile,' he wrote in a book published in 1932.[6] 'Those under his command quietly complain about his arrogance and demands. But, once in action, the whisperers shut up. Their will, their hopes, are drawn to him like iron to a magnet.'

In a second book de Gaulle proposed that the French army should transform itself into a mechanised and mobile armoured force, an argument that gained him the nickname 'Colonel Motors'. The French government did not follow his advice, but instead invested heavily in static defence: the Maginot Line. But, just as de Gaulle had predicted, this supposedly impregnable chain of forts in eastern France failed either to deter or to repel the Germans, and when he went into action in May 1940 in command of France's Fourth Armoured Division his greatest handicap was a lack of fuel. The deep bitterness that he felt at France's eventual defeat was mitigated slightly by a profound sense of vindication.

On 6 June de Gaulle was pulled from the front line by the French prime minister, Paul Reynaud, made a junior minister, then sent to London three days later to ask for more help from Winston Churchill, whose own premiership was not yet one month old. After years in the political wilderness in the 1930s, Churchill had finally disproved his father's prediction that he would never make good, but in the least auspicious circumstances. The Dunkirk evacuation had been completed, and having grimly told the nation to be ready to 'fight on the beaches' he was now thinking ahead to the battle over Britain for air supremacy that would precede a seaborne invasion by the German Wehrmacht.

It was de Gaulle's first ever visit to Britain, and when he asked Churchill for further precious aeroplanes he got short shrift. But he understood the reason why, and calmly told the prime minister that he had made the right decision – an acknowledgement that Churchill did not forget. After he returned to France, Reynaud resigned, and when it became clear that nothing would stop Reynaud's successor, his former mentor Marshal Pétain, from surrendering and setting up what would become the infamous 'Vichy' government, Churchill organised his escape. When de Gaulle accompanied a friend of Churchill's, a member of parliament named Edward Louis Spears, on to the tarmac at Bordeaux airport ostensibly to say goodbye, he was hauled aboard the aircraft by Spears as it began to taxi off. 'I felt stripped naked, like a man on a beach planning to swim an ocean,' de Gaulle admitted later, in a rare admission of vulnerability.[7]

Spears recalled de Gaulle as 'straight, direct, even rather brutal ... a strange-looking man' who 'dominated everybody else by his height' and who, he realised, was 'very shrewd'.[8] He bolstered de Gaulle in those unsettling early days in London, while his friend Churchill argued that the Frenchman should be turned into a symbol of resistance. The prime minister later suggested that he had picked de Gaulle for his personal qualities – 'He was young and energetic and had made a very favourable impression on me,' he wrote – but the reality was that, at the time, he did not have the luxury of choice: there was no one better-known available.[9] Following the nauseatingly swift collapse of France Churchill needed a Frenchman who could reassure the British that they were not as isolated as they felt. It was primarily for this reason that he insisted – against opposition from members of his cabinet – that de Gaulle be allowed to broadcast a message on the radio on 18 June. Churchill's strategy succeeded. A survey in Britain that September rated de Gaulle as the most popular foreign personality, though the competition was hardly stiff. He was still relatively unknown in his own country.

De Gaulle followed up his radio broadcast by telegraphing the high officials in each of France's colonies, inviting them to join him. But these cold calls almost entirely failed. De Gaulle was trying to persuade men who were, many of them, close to retirement and with families back home in France. Spears observed that such men were 'unwilling to sacrifice the fruits of a lifetime of service to what appeared to be an adventure, however honourable it might be'.[10]

Joining the Free French represented an enormous risk, even for more junior officers. 'Have you thought what it means for me to do so?' one asked when a British counterpart suggested it. 'I shall be condemned to death and shot if captured; my estates in France will be forfeited and I shall have broken the oath, which I took on becoming an officer, to serve the Government of France faithfully. I do not approve of the present French Government, but that fact is beside the point, I did not swear to obey the government which I approved.'[11] Finally, he added, two of his sons were serving in the French army; his desertion would ruin their careers.

When de Gaulle wired Beirut, telling the high commissioner and the general commanding the 37,000-strong Armée du Levant that it was their 'duty to defend the honour and integrity of the Empire and of France', he was rebuffed.[12] The commander of the Armée did not like being told the obvious by 'a comparatively junior officer' who appeared to be in Britain's pocket, and he and the high commissioner quickly fell in behind the Vichy government when they were accused of treachery by Pétain.[13] They felt justified when, days later, Churchill took the drastic step of ordering the sinking of the French fleet anchored off Mers el Kébir in French Algeria, in order to deny it to the Germans. The bombardment, which killed thirteen hundred French sailors, revived and validated the traditional suspicions among the Levantine French of their British rival's true ambitions.[14] It also made de Gaulle's task much harder. Only Georges Catroux, the former aide to the one-armed General Gouraud and now high commissioner of French Indo-China, responded enthusiastically. Catroux also knew de Gaulle personally from their time together in prison camp during the previous war.

Churchill was caught off guard when de Gaulle reported the disappointing outcome of his call to arms. 'You are all alone?' he queried, before recovering: 'Well, then I recognise you all alone.'[15] This abrupt decision caused consternation among some of his colleagues, who wanted to avoid antagonising the Vichy government in the mistaken belief that it might yet be won over. So, when the British government confirmed its support for de Gaulle the following day, it chose its words with care. It recognised General de Gaulle (the 'Brigadier' prefix had by now vanished) not as head of a French government in exile, but as 'leader of all free Frenchmen, wherever they may be, who rally to him in support of the Allied cause'.[16]

The British had admired de Gaulle's pig-headedness when it manifested itself in his refusal to admit defeat, but they were less enamoured when the Frenchman exhibited the same trait towards them. As Catroux succinctly put it, while the British conceived of Free France as 'an instrument in the service of its policy', the Free French saw themselves quite differently as 'the emanation of France'.[17] De Gaulle believed he had assumed power of attorney over a country whose leader, Pétain, had gone 'gaga'.[18] 'I, General de Gaulle, French soldier and leader, am aware that I speak in the name of France,' he declared on 19 June, a day after his first broadcast.[19] Yet infuriatingly, when he was later asked by Churchill to grant Syria and Lebanon independence, the general was just as ready to quote the British definition of his limited powers to argue that he had no authority to do so.

The collapse of France was humiliating enough, but just as bad so far as de Gaulle was concerned was his sudden dependence on the nation that he had been taught from boyhood to distrust. He decided that the best way to hide his insecurity was to pretend that France, though currently indisposed, was as great a power as ever, and to be obstinate and aggressive towards anyone who dared to disagree. Only if he posed as 'the inflexible champion of the nation and the state' could he win 'support among the French and respect from foreigners', he later wrote.[20]

When most of his British counterparts failed to stand up to these intimidating tactics, de Gaulle was encouraged to try them all the time. 'You have to bang the table,' he surmised, of dealing with the British; 'they back down.'[21] Even Spears, his most loyal supporter, observed how he 'soon developed a dislike of being liked as if it were a weakness'.[22] In his memoirs de Gaulle recalled with relish how Britain's foreign secretary, Anthony Eden, had once asked him if he realised that he had caused more trouble than 'all our other European allies put together'. 'I don't doubt it,' de Gaulle replied. 'France is a great power.'[23]

As a child de Gaulle had dreamed of commanding an army of two hundred thousand men, and late in the summer of 1940 he set out to turn that ambition into reality. The auspices looked good. The highly regarded black governor of Chad had announced his support for de Gaulle, precipitating similar declarations in the French Congo and

Gabon. De Gaulle grew overconfident. Ahead of an expedition to Dakar on the west African coast he was seen buying a tropical uniform in a London department store, one of a number of breaches of security that were identified after the exploit turned into a fiasco. Although, when this happened, he briefly thought of blowing his own brains out, he did not lose the confidence of the British. Bouncing swiftly back, he turned his attention to Syria once more. If he could win over the Armée du Levant, he would become a serious force whom the British could not ignore.

The British supported de Gaulle's ambition. As soon as the French in the Levant had sided with the Vichy government, they knew they had a problem. At the least the Levant would provide a bridgehead for German espionage and subversion in Palestine, so recently racked by three years of revolt. It might also provide a base for an Axis air attack on Suez or on the oil installations of Iraq. A secret memorandum prepared in Whitehall that summer warned that Britain's position in the Middle East would 'probably be untenable' unless Syria and the Lebanon were brought under friendly, or direct British, control.[24] Before long British newspapers were reporting that the Lebanon was seeing a sudden surge in tourists, who were travelling on Hungarian or Bulgarian passports but spoke faultless German.[25]

The British also recognised that the Levant situation would be hard for them to solve, for they were well aware that if they tried to take control of Lebanon and Syria directly they would only stoke the old fear that their true ambition was to oust France from the region. This political calculation was reinforced by a military fact. After the Italians began advancing from Libya towards Egypt in mid-September, the British could not spare the troops to take control of Syria and Lebanon by force. For a time they maintained discreet relations with the Vichy French in Lebanon and Syria in a bid to win them over, but the failure of this approach to deliver any tangible result gave ammunition to those within the British government who were pressing for a tougher line. Towards the end of August 1940 the British government decided to let the Free French mount a coup that would remove the Vichy government in the Levant. It chose Georges Catroux, because of his long career in the Levant, as the man to front the attempt.

From his own experience of British–French antagonism in the region, Catroux shared the British view that it was important that the Free French should be seen to win Syria and Lebanon without recourse to British help. Unfortunately, though, this determination coloured his assessment of his chances. When he arrived in Cairo in the autumn he thought it would be only a matter of time before the coup happened. 'I shall not hesitate to take power in Syria as soon as I am certain of having with me two-thirds of the Army and the majority of the Air Force,' he told de Gaulle, reassuring him that the operation would be 'carried out without the support of the British forces which is to be avoided for psychological reasons'.[26]

Catroux's optimism was misplaced. Having made what Britain's consul in Beirut described as a 'mountainous overestimate' of the level of support for the Free French in the Levant, he did not antici-pate the repressive steps that the Vichy French in Syria would take against his allies.[27] Colombani, the head of the Sûreté who had unsuccessfully rummaged through his files for details on Arab insur-gents when Tegart visited him in 1938, knew rather more about his fellow countrymen. When a Free French agent offered him a bribe to overthrow the government, Colombani went to his superiors and betrayed the plot in return for a higher offer.[28] French officers sus-pected of Gaullist sympathies were swiftly repatriated to France, and the Free French spy network that had offered him the money was rounded up soon afterwards. Both the high commissioner and the general in command of the Armée du Levant were recalled and replaced by Henri Dentz, who had previously served in the Levant during the Druze revolt as chief of intelligence under Sarrail. Dentz, who was recalled to Paris with Sarrail, made his own opinion starkly clear. 'The British,' he believed, 'represent those things that almost destroyed us: democratic-masonic politics and Judeo-Saxon finance. They represent the past, nothing constructive.'[29]

By December, Catroux accepted that there was no longer any chance of a coup taking place in the Levant. In a telegram to de Gaulle he described Syria as 'a bitter fruit that continues unwilling to ripen', and admitted that, as a consequence, 'we may only be able to get it by force'.[30] The problem, as both men knew, was that they did not have sufficient men to do that job alone.

Nor, at that point, were the British prepared to make up the short-fall. In Egypt the commander-in-chief of British forces was the hard-pressed Archibald Wavell. 'Short of everything but courage', Wavell would not consider opening a new front while he was fighting the Italians, who were threatening Egypt from Libya and Abyssinia.[31] And yet, even after he had beaten the Italians on both fronts, he still opposed taking action in Syria. Indeed, he even argued that his defeat of the Italians might encourage 'a steady growth of the Free French Movement amongst the junior ranks' in Syria, to justify procrastination.[32]

De Gaulle, who was beginning to worry that Catroux might usurp him, arrived in Cairo on 1 April 1941 to assess the situation and assert himself. With him was his British liaison officer and arch-supporter, Spears. Spears quickly decided that Wavell was 'living in a fool's paradise' because he took the Vichy government in Syria at its word when it said that it would not help the Germans.[33] He and de Gaulle correctly feared that the Vichy French would quickly cave in to any German demand to allow the Luftwaffe to use French air-fields in the Levant.

By the time Spears had telegraphed his cutting assessment of Wavell to London, a series of events had taken place that made his call for action compelling. In Iraq on 2 April a nationalist army officer named Rashid Ali al-Gaylani seized power in Baghdad, after months of German propaganda in the country. The following day Hitler's brilliant general Erwin Rommel captured Benghazi on the Libyan coast, and on the 6th German troops invaded Greece and Yugoslavia. Yugoslavia surrendered within a week, and when Greece capitulated on the 24th almost a quarter of the 55,000-strong British force that had been sent to reinforce the country was taken prisoner.

Spears hoped that a conference convened in Cairo on 15 April to discuss the Syrian situation might lead to a tougher blockade of the Levant coast, but it went badly wrong when, to his horror, Catroux proposed that two British divisions be dispatched to seize control of Beirut and Damascus. With the British at full stretch elsewhere, this demand for 'the unobtainable to achieve the unattainable', as another of the attendees put it, made the Free French look utterly out of touch. And that gave Wavell's headquarters a reason to ignore Syria for a little longer.[34]

Besides, events in Iraq were more immediately alarming. Following al-Gaylani's coup, the British embassy in Baghdad was now effectively besieged and the Royal Air Force base at Habbaniyah, which stood between the Iraqi capital and the vital oil pipeline to Haifa, had been surrounded by hostile Iraqi forces. Wavell wanted the government to reach a deal with al-Gaylani so that he would not have to send troops, but when fighting broke out around the airbase he was overruled. 'We can make no concessions,' London told him on 4 May, ordering him to send reinforcements.[35] 'Habforce' was hurriedly scratched together to break the siege of Habbaniyah – its transport included buses requisitioned from the streets of Jerusalem and Haifa – and it set out across the desert soon afterwards. Uppermost in Churchill's mind was the need 'to do all in our power to save Habbaniyah and to control the pipe-line to the Mediterranean'.[36]

The Germans recognised the importance of Iraq to Britain, too. After al-Gaylani appealed to them for assistance, Berlin forced the Vichy government to allow the Luftwaffe to land and refuel in Syria en route for Iraq. When British intelligence intercepted the Vichy government's order to Dentz telling him to allow the German aeroplanes to land, alarm bells began jangling in London. Churchill, who so far had put no pressure on Wavell to address the situation, began to worry that the Germans might seize Syria and Iraq via 'petty air forces, tourists and local revolts'.[37] Envisaging that this outcome could be avoided by what he described as 'an armed political inroad' into Syria, he told Wavell on 9 May to provide Catroux with transport to launch such an operation, and to order the RAF to bomb Syria's aerodromes.[38] Wavell's own staff, however, correctly believed that the Germans were far more likely to launch an overwhelming attack on Crete before they took over Syria, and concentrated on the more immediate threat. They were also anxious not to drive the Vichy French into the arms of the Axis by the preemptive bombing desired by Churchill. It was only on 12 May, when the British consul in Beirut reported that he had heard German bombers droning eastwards overhead that morning, that they finally accepted that a confrontation with the Vichy French could no longer be postponed. On 15 May the British bombed Syria's main airstrips, destroying several German aircraft on the ground.

By 20 May – the day the Germans dropped parachutists into Crete – there was overwhelming pressure to take action. Spears telegraphed London with the rumour that Dentz was pulling back his forces from Syria into Lebanon, leaving a vacuum that the Arab nationalists and the Germans might fill. 'If the only troops available are the Free French, why not use them?' he suggested.[39] He believed that, faced with a choice between their own countrymen or a German occupation, the Vichy French would hardly fight.

Time was of the essence, said a French naval officer who had escaped from Beirut. He urged the British to take advantage of the chaos that their bombing had caused. 'In two weeks,' he argued, 'it will be too late.'[40] The chiefs of staff in London caught this contagious sense of urgency. Thinking the opportunity 'too good to miss', they told Wavell that he should give the Free French the authority to move into Syria if the situation there was favourable. 'The advance must be regarded as a political coup, in which time is all important, rather than as a military operation.'[41] But as the Free French lacked the necessary manpower, they came up with the idea of offering a manifesto for radical change instead.

17

A SQUALID EPISODE

IT WAS GEORGES CATROUX WHO CAME UP WITH THE IDEA THAT the Free French might offer independence to Syria and Lebanon to make the invasion of the Levant much easier. Just as in the First World War, when the British had turned the Arabs against the Turks with a grandiose commitment, he hoped that the promise could turn the Arabs of Syria and Lebanon against Vichy. But he recognised that it was a risky offer. It would 'certainly provoke irritation, and perhaps troubles in the Levant, troubles which we should not be in a position to appease', he warned de Gaulle.[1] He was quite right: his idea was to haunt French relations with the British for the next five years.

De Gaulle's liaison officer, Spears, thought that Catroux's idea of a 'most solemn guarantee of absolute Syrian independence without any reservation whatever' was an excellent one, because he worried that the Free French might encounter fierce Syrian opposition when they crossed the border.[2] With his backing Catroux told de Gaulle on 19 May that, on his entry into Syria, he would 'proclaim the end of the mandate and the coming of independence'.[3]

It was only in the draft declaration that Catroux worked up the same evening that he admitted the quid pro quo he and de Gaulle intended to attach to this plan. In it he also stated that the Free French would 'shoulder the responsibilities which France had assumed' in the Levant and that he expected Syria and Lebanon would be 'bound' to France by a treaty of alliance.[4] Spears evidently disliked the draft, because after reading it he feverishly cooked up a version of his own which he dispatched to London at 12.45 a.m. on 20 May, thirty minutes behind Catroux's.

As had happened to McMahon at the crucial moment in his correspondence with Sharif Husein twenty-five years earlier, various pieces of information now emerged that convinced the British and the French that they would need to raise their offer to the Arabs. Late on 20 May Catroux went up to the Syrian frontier for a secret meeting with a sympathetic French officer who was planning to defect from Vichy to the Free French. But Captain Philibert Collet, who looked as if he was 'straight out of Beau Geste', brought him disappointing news.[5] Contrary to Catroux's expectation, Collet was certain that the Vichy French would put up a stiff fight. Catroux warned de Gaulle that propaganda alone was insufficient and that help from British forces would now certainly be necessary.[6]

Spears did not initially trust Collet's information, but when he met the veteran French officer, who defected with two hundred men soon afterwards, he changed his mind. He learned from Collet that the Free French were 'anything but popular' in Syria and that the British were likely to receive a warmer welcome.[7] Collet also told him that Catroux had little standing among French soldiers and officials. Spears reached the conclusion that Catroux's word would not be sufficient in itself.

A nightmarish situation began to crystallise in Spears's mind. The British needed to allow the Free French to lead a takeover of Syria to avoid the impression that they were trying to usurp the French. But it looked from the intelligence that the involvement of the Free French would antagonise both the Syrians, who wanted the British to liberate them, and the Vichy French, who saw the Free French as a British front. Also, rumours were circulating about the 'imminent danger' that the Syrians might unite with the Iraqis to form an Arab confederation under German sponsorship. And it looked as if Catroux's word alone might not be enough to stop it.

When this welter of disturbing information reached London, Churchill asked his debonair foreign secretary Anthony Eden for an urgent review of British policy towards the Arab world. On 27 May

Eden circulated a short but crucial memorandum to his cabinet colleagues. In it he admitted that the root cause of Arab dissatisfaction
was 'the Palestine problem', but argued that it might most easily be
assuaged by a British promise that the Syrians and Lebanese would
have their independence, if the Free French refused to offer such a
guarantee, or, having offered it, it failed to work.[8] 'We should hold
ourselves free to turn from the Free French towards the Syrian
Arabs,' suggested Eden. He also backed the idea that the British
government should publicly support Arabs' calls for unity, even
though he personally did not think that Arab union was a possibility. After the cabinet agreed, two days later he announced the
government's support for Arab aspirations, in a speech at Mansion
House.[9]

The British government had just committed itself to pursuing a
policy of support for Lebanese and Syrian independence designed to
defuse Arab anger caused by their rule in Palestine.

De Gaulle immediately appreciated that the British government
was willing to promote Arab unity at French expense, and he did not
like it one bit. But he realised that he had no choice but to accept the
declaration that Catroux proposed, because the British would promise the Levant independence, causing the Arabs to gravitate to them,
if he did not offer the same carrot first. He did, though, try to put his
own gloss upon the declaration before it was made public. On 31
May he wrote to his Free French supporters, arguing that, because
Syria might become a battleground and they did not have the legal
power to 'declare the mandate purely and simply abolished', there
should be a 'transitional stage in the transmission of powers' in the
Levant instead.[10] 'We shall merely say that we are coming to put an
end to the mandate regime and to conclude a treaty guaranteeing
independence and sovereignty.' When it came to honouring the
promise of independence, it was already clear that de Gaulle was
thinking of a rather longer timescale than the British. A year earlier,
the French general had said that he believed 'the greatest and most
immediate danger may come from the Muslim band which goes
from Tangiers to India'.[11]

Spears had already anticipated that de Gaulle would start back-
sliding, and proposed that Britain guarantee the Free French

declaration so as to stop this tactic working. He even managed to slip the idea past de Gaulle by presenting it to him as an endorsement of his leadership of the Free French. Having suggested that a French offer of independence would enhance de Gaulle's own prestige, when de Gaulle then wondered whether such a promise would seem rather insubstantial, Spears swiftly answered: 'If this were so ... would not a British guarantee of his undertaking meet the case?' Churchill then wrote to de Gaulle to reassure him that he had 'no intention of exploiting the tragic position of France for our own gain', and seeking to bind the general to his promise of independence. 'I agree that we must not in any settlement of the Syrian question endanger the stability of the Middle East. But subject to this we must both do everything possible to meet Arab aspirations and susceptibilities.'[12]

And so on 8 June, as British and Free French forces crossed the border and Catroux declared that he was 'coming to put an end to the mandate' and to proclaim Lebanon and Syria 'free and independent', the British government also issued a statement saying that it supported and associated itself with the assurance of independence given by General Catroux.[13] The word 'guarantee' was not used, but that implication was absolutely clear – indeed, that was how the statement was reported in the newspapers. By making this announcement, the British government put itself in an invidious position. Once the campaign was over, it would have to ensure that the Free French kept their word.

Just after dawn on 9 June three parties of well-armed British commandos – five hundred men, their faces blackened with burnt cork – landed on the coast of southern Lebanon, near the mouth of the river Litani. The steep-sided river ran about twenty miles north of the arbitrary border between Palestine and Lebanon that Britain and France had agreed two decades earlier. It was a natural frontier, which the Vichy French had further fortified.

Codenamed Z Force, the commandos had the task of capturing the main Qasimiye bridge that crossed the Litani near the coast, and holding it until the advancing Australian Seventh Division arrived. Their original plan was to land north of the river so that they could attack the Vichy French defences from behind. But the operation was hastily planned, and their aerial photographs of their targets did not include the coastline. As a consequence, the south-ernmost of the three parties landed on the wrong side of the Litani – in front of, not behind, the French positions – and came under heavy fire.

The central party, under Z Force's commander Colonel Richard Pedder, also met fierce opposition. De Gaulle's arrival in Haifa days earlier had given away what was about to happen, so that the com-mandos landed on the beach with bullets cracking overhead. After capturing several Frenchmen who were still in their pyjamas, they started inland for the local French barracks and its artillery battery. They seized the first gun and turned it on the others, but as they were making their escape southwards Pedder was shot dead and another officer fatally wounded by snipers hidden in the trees. Ultimately it was the most northerly party which managed to make its way south-wards to force the surrender of the French redoubt over the Litani. In all, the commandos lost a quarter of their number, killed and wounded. The survivors were relieved by the Australians the fol-lowing day.

The Australians were part of 'Operation Exporter', a two-pronged advance devised by Wavell to seize Beirut and Damascus simultan-eously, bypassing the mountain backbone that forms the spine of the Levant. In the previous weeks Wavell had cobbled together an inva-sion force of Australian, British, Indian and Free French troops, placing them under the overall command of Maitland 'Jumbo' Wilson, a popular general whose bulk was seemingly contained only by a Sam Browne belt straining at its outer settings. 'More trouble, gentlemen, I am afraid!' Jumbo had enthusiastically declared when he arrived in Jerusalem to take command, smiling like the Cheshire Cat.[14] Such imperturbability recommended him to lead this shoe-string operation.

Beirut, capital of the Vichy regime in the French Middle East, was the objective of the left-hand, Australian, prong of Wilson's ramshackle army, while Damascus was the more resonant objective of the right-hand force, comprising two Indian Army brigades, part of the First Cavalry Division, and six battalions of Free French under the aptly named General Legentilhomme. His second-in-command, Pierre Koenig, was known for his catchphrase, 'Bloody English' – the only two words of the language that he spoke.[15] Koenig did not mean it entirely seriously, but the fact remained that the Free French were only able to use half the troops they wanted to because of a shortage of British transport.

The British did not expect resistance. They had been told by de Gaulle to expect minimal opposition from the Vichy French, whose 'will to fight would very soon crumble'.[16] To ensure the goodwill of the population, the British had not only guaranteed Catroux's dec- laration of independence but had also secretly underwritten it with £200,000 of payments to Druze and Bedu leaders inside Syria. So, when the two prongs of this Allied force set out northward into French territory on 8 June, they did so 'with about as much attempt at disguising their intentions as a postman distributing letters down a street'.[17] The Australians were ordered to swap their steel helmets for their felt slouch hats.

The initial experiences of the invading force suggested that de Gaulle's claim was correct. When the Australians crossed the border the first Frenchman they met, at the police post on the frontier, was still in bed. On the right, the British reached the town of Dara by lunchtime on the first day of their advance. Just as they had hoped, the Druzes quickly offered their support and the French officer in charge of the dusty railway junction equally quickly defected. The Frenchman explained how, when he had been trying to escape north- wards and the front wheel of his car had parted company from its axle, the choice had been very simple. 'We became Free French at once!'[18]

In his memoirs the author Roald Dahl, who took part in the inva- sion as a Hurricane pilot, confirmed the impression that the Vichy French were unprepared. Sent to strafe the Vichy aerodrome at Rayak, he recalled, on his first low pass over the landing strip, being astonished to see 'a bunch of girls in brightly coloured cotton dresses standing out by the planes with glasses in their hands having drinks with the French pilots, and I remember bottles of wine standing on the wing of one of the planes as we went swooshing over'.[19] It was a Sunday morning and 'the Frenchmen were evidently entertaining their girlfriends and showing off their aircraft to them, which was a very French thing to do in the middle of a war at a front-line aerodrome. Every one of us held our fire on that first pass over the flying field and it was wonderfully comical to see the girls all dropping their wine glasses and galloping in their high heels for the door of the nearest building ... we destroyed five of their planes on the ground.'

But the hope that the invasion would be a walkover evaporated when both prongs of Wilson's invading force started to meet stiff resistance. As the left-hand Australian force made its way up the broad valley leading to Marjayoun – the largest inland town south of the Litani – they met withering machine-gun fire. Their effort to secure the valley involved desperate fighting. In one village grenades were 'thrown and thrown back again'.[20] On the right, the British encountered similarly determined resistance along the road towards Damascus. 'Vichy armoured cars contested every yard of our advance,' reported a senior British officer.[21]

This came as an unpleasant surprise. While Spears had expected that the Vichy French would passively allow the Germans to use their airfields, it never dawned on him that they might fiercely resist the British and Free French advance. But the Vichy government had ordered its soldiers to resist, and its press had urged their fellow countrymen to fight 'the hereditary enemy' and salvage their country's tattered military reputation.[22] 'Every inch of Syrian territory defended is a particle of Metropolitan France saved. Every drop of French blood spilled in Syria is a fraction of national honour retrieved,' declared a leading Vichy journalist.[23] Fired up by propaganda that played on Dunkirk and Mers el-Kébir, the French in the Levant fought fiercely.

Including the Free French in the invasion force proved to be a grave mistake, because it made the conflict internecine. To the Vichy French, the Gaullists were 'the Devil incarnate, the scapegoats for all the anger, resentment and weakness which had been lurking in the dark places of their consciences for a year', a Free French officer believed.[24] Wherever they were involved, the fighting was especially vicious. In the village of Khirbe in southern Lebanon a Free French officer was shot by Vichy forces in the back as he was returning to his own front line, having failed to persuade his countrymen to surrender. When, in another incident, a Free French officer on a motorcycle drew up beside a Vichy counterpart and invited him to join him against their common German enemy, the Vichy man drew his pistol and shot him dead. In a memoir, Jumbo Wilson called the invasion a 'most unpleasant campaign'.[25]

The Vichy commander Dentz launched a concerted counter-attack on 15 June, a week after the Allied invasion. West of the mountain spine, Vichy forces subjected Marjayoun and Jezzine to an intensive artillery bombardment that obliged the Australians to withdraw. East of the mountains, they attacked forward British positions south of Damascus, causing significant casualties, and recaptured Qunaytirah in the Golan Heights. Legentilhomme was wounded when Vichy pilots identified his temporary headquarters from the vehicles parked unconcealed outside, and bombed it.

Within twenty-four hours the British had fought their way back into Qunaytirah, where an obliterated French tank that was still red-hot, overturned lorries, smashed armoured cars and dead horses remained as smouldering testimony to the ferocity of the struggle. But they did not have the firepower or the numbers to dislodge the French forces further west. The British found that their anti-tank guns could not penetrate French tanks, but the hard, rocky ground meant that French artillery inflicted heavy casualties on them. Fighting in the summer temperatures was harsh. 'Exceedingly accurate' shooting by Vichy's Foreign Legionnaires frequently kept them pinned down during the long hours of daylight.[26] As a consequence, there were numerous cases of heatstroke, while the summer haze made identifying and targeting the enemy very difficult. It was only when the Australians finally received a rangefinder that they discovered that the distance to the enemy's positions across a valley was just half what they had estimated. At ten past midnight on 18 June, their commander rang headquarters to ask for reinforcements.

Wavell now committed more Indian Army units from Iraq as well as the Transjordanian Arab Legion in a bid to force Dentz to disperse his forces eastwards. The Indians followed the Euphrates towards Aleppo while the Arab Legion, under its British commander

John Glubb, advanced towards Palmyra following a send-off by
Abdullah, who recognised the pregnant symbolism in Wavell's resort
to Arab troops to liberate Syria. Glubb offered money to the tribes
along the Euphrates if they would harass the Vichy French. Several
Arab tribes responded to Glubb's overtures, sniping at Vichy outposts, shooting up supply columns and cutting telegraph poles and
roads – 'perhaps more for loot,' reflected Glubb, 'than love of us'.[27]
One of those who answered his call was a tribesman named Zaal.
Now middle-aged and grey-haired, Zaal had distinguished himself as
a crack shot when he accompanied T. E. Lawrence to Aqaba a quarter of a century earlier.

This eastern expansion of the campaign helped. After further
heavy fighting, the British and Free French forced their way into
Damascus on 23 June. Richard Dimbleby, then a young reporter,
witnessed the moment when the senior Vichy officer surrendered
the keys to the city to his Free French opponent. The ceremony
was 'ironic', he reported on the BBC, 'for the two colonels had
studied together at the French military academy of St Cyr and, of
course, knew each other well'.[28] In an effort to stop the British
taking advantage of the situation, de Gaulle immediately accorded
Catroux the ornate title 'Delegate General and Plenipotentiary and
Commander-in-Chief in the Levant', and ordered him to begin
treaty negotiations with the Syrians and the Lebanese, while in the
meantime 'the work of France must be continued'.[29] He published
his decision on the assumption that the British would not dare criticise him in public.

Lebanon was now the focus, and here the Australians faced determined opposition in the dense banana groves that grew along the
coast. While the British advanced up the road from Damascus to
Beirut, the Australians tried to crack the last obstacle south of the
Lebanese capital, the Damour river, which was heavily fortified like
the Litani further south. After patrols spent four nights looking for
a crossing point, early on 6 July two Australian battalions made
their way down to the river in the darkness, crossed it under heavy
fire, and clawed their way up the formidable northern bank. Two
days later Dentz sued for peace.

A month had passed since the beginning of the campaign and in that time the world had changed, because Hitler had invaded Soviet Russia. A Syrian politician, reflecting the general pro-German feeling in his country, quipped that the Nazi leader would be in Moscow before the British reached Beirut. Fortunately, he turned out to be wrong. British forces reached the city by the 12th. By then the British and Free French had lost 4,500 men; Vichy's losses were even larger, at about six thousand.

De Gaulle tried to put the best possible construction on the situation by claiming that the duration of the fighting was 'another proof of the courage of my countrymen, whatever cause they serve', but in private he blamed Britain's 'somewhat feeble and not very appropriate resources' for the length of time it took to beat the enemy.[30] The British, on the other hand, believed that they could have dealt with Dentz's forces all the faster had the Free French not been involved at all. 'Militarily they proved a handicap,' was one British diplomat's blunt appraisal.[31]

Sometime afterwards a British officer, John Hackett, who had been wounded in the advance towards Damascus, met a Vichy officer he knew who had been hurt in the same encounter. As they dissected the engagement over lunch at the Hôtel St Georges in Beirut, the Frenchman claimed that his side had been the better of the two. 'Well, Jacques, in the end we did win, we did win,' replied Hackett. 'Yes,' his counterpart grimaced, 'and that is the least satisfactory aspect of the whole squalid episode.'[32]

With the Germans in control of Crete and Rhodes, the British needed to agree an armistice with Dentz as fast as possible so that they could redeploy their troops elsewhere to face the growing German threat. But Dentz refused to negotiate with Jumbo Wilson while the Free French were also in the room. Faced with the prospect of renewed fighting if he could not agree the terms of an armistice, Wilson priced human life higher than de Gaulle's self-esteem. Backed by Churchill, who was annoyed by de Gaulle's attempt to insert Catroux as high commissioner and felt strongly that negotiations should not collapse 'merely on the point of form as to who Dentz will surrender to', Wilson decided to exclude the Free French from the armistice talks, while keeping Catroux informed of what was going on.[33]

As a consequence the British general was able to reach agreement with Dentz at Acre on Bastille Day – 14 July. The armistice included an additional secret protocol preventing the Free French from contacting the Vichy personnel, to which Catroux had agreed. 'At the signing the French officers were all in tears,' Wilson wrote the following day, 'but a glass of champagne cheered them up afterwards.'[34] The effect, though, was brief. The peace terms soon caused a hangover.

18

COMPLETELY INTRANSIGENT,
EXTREMELY RUDE

As winning over the Armée du Levant was central to his strategy of revival, de Gaulle was outraged when he found out about the secret annexe to the July 1941 armistice agreement. He arrived in Cairo on 21 July – 'in the worst mood I have ever known him in,' said Spears – and threatened to publish the terms of the deal that Wilson had reached with Dentz.[1] When the same day he met Oliver Lyttelton, whom Churchill had charged with handling relations with the Free French, he handed Lyttelton a letter stating that the Free French would no longer submit to British command from 24 July, because the armistice and its secret protocol were both unacceptable. His threat was to draw significant concessions from the British.

Lyttelton was the polar opposite of de Gaulle. A businessman who had made a fortune trading metals before the war, he was known for his level-headedness and ready sense of humour. He took the letter from the general and, with considerable panache, tore it up in front of him. At a further meeting later the same day when de Gaulle had calmed down, they edged closer. De Gaulle acknowledged the need for a seamless transfer of power in Syria, which was the main British concern, and Lyttelton suggested that the secret protocol forbidding Free French contact with Vichy prisoners of war could be rendered void if Dentz violated any of the terms of the armistice.

Lyttelton let off steam with Spears over dinner that evening. He told a funny story of how he had reacted when he once received a letter from a man that ended with the classic refrain: 'I have no choice but to place the matter in the hands of my solicitor.'[2] He had replied, he said, stating that he had no objection to 'your placing it in any such part of his person as your ingenuity or his complacency will allow'. But, much as both men privately agreed on where de Gaulle might insert his ultimatum, neither felt confident enough to call his bluff in public. For as long as a German invasion of Syria remained a threat, security was the British priority; and security required stability. Spears had already witnessed the depth of Syrian hatred towards the French in Damascus, and the combination of this poisonous atmosphere plus the possibility that the Free French leader might do what he called a 'Samson act' alarmed him. Unnerved by de Gaulle's 'completely intransigent and often extremely rude' behaviour earlier that day, he feared that were the Free French leader 'given a free hand in Syria in the mood in which he now is, the country would be out of hand within a fortnight'.[3]

Lyttelton agreed with Spears that they had no choice but to appease the general. In a bid to avert a crisis he proposed an 'interpretative agreement' that quietly rewrote the terms of Wilson's armistice. This gave the Free French a chance to convert the Vichy French before they were repatriated to France, and defined the future division of responsibilities in Syria and Lebanon. Hereby the British, in view of the preponderance of their forces, took charge of the defence of the region against the external German threat, while the Free French would control the organs of internal security in the Levant: the native *troupes spéciales*, the Sûreté and the police.[4] Letters exchanged on 24–25 July confirming this arrangement became known as the Lyttelton–de Gaulle agreement. To allay French fears, Lyttelton reiterated that Britain had 'no interest in Syria or in the Lebanon except to win the war'.

De Gaulle was undoubtedly delighted by what his outburst had achieved. He could not resist a parting shot days later, thanking Lyttelton for acknowledging 'the dominating and privileged position of France in the Levant when these States shall be independent'.[5] And, thanks to the numerical rationale used for allocating the respective responsibilities, the letters left open the possibility that at some point in the future, if the French troops outnumbered the British, they might take charge of the defence of Syria as well.

When soon afterwards Lyttelton visited Lebanon to see the situation for himself, he realised that the division of responsibilities that he had proposed was deeply flawed. In practice, he admitted, it was not 'possible precisely to define the frontier which separates military requirements from civil administration' because of the complexity of the situation.[6] He told Churchill that what he had seen resembled a scene contrived by the famous thriller writer E. Phillips Oppenheim. His Beirut hotel lobby was 'full of Generals, the Syrian Government, Vichy officials, Free Frenchmen, Arabs, some fifth column, and a Druze Princess and only required the presence of Sir Basil Zaharoff* to complete the picture'.[7]

The Vichy officials owed their continued presence in the Levant to de Gaulle. Already angry at the way he had been treated by the British during the armistice negotiations, the Free French leader was determined not to have to ask his allies for assistance in administering Free France's new possessions. When his appeal to the Armée du Levant to join him then failed miserably, he was left with no choice but to reinstate the majority of the officials who had served in the Vichy administration, despite the fact that most of them refused to swear allegiance to the Free French cause.

The British were aghast at de Gaulle's unexpected move. Not only would they now be forced to work with French officials who had been 'until recently avowedly anti-British' but, by guaranteeing Catroux's declaration, they had made themselves responsible for French actions.[8] They immediately foresaw the consequences. 'We urged the Arabs to help us against the Vichyites. Now suddenly we confirm the Vichyites in their posts, and entrust to their tender mercies the future of those Arabs who have just shot them up at our request. This is a nightmare!!' groaned Glubb, the leader of the Arab Legion.[9]

Back in their jobs, former Vichy officials behaved exactly as

---

* An infamous arms dealer, who had died in 1936.

Glubb feared, pursuing vendettas against Arabs who had collaborated with the British. The French governor of Dara – the man who joined the Free French only when his getaway car broke down – returned to his old job and promptly sacked the Arab mayor, who he now realised was a British agent. In Dayr az Zor, the main town in eastern Syria, the first action of the new Free French political officer, guided by the Vichyite chief of police, was to punish the tribes who, at Glubb's instigation, had attacked Vichy forces in the desert. They had 'proved themselves scandalously disloyal to one French government and would doubtless be equally unfaithful to another', the French political officer said.[10]

After their hopes of being rid of the French for ever crashed to earth, the Syrians quickly began to press the British to intervene, as it was clear to them that the French had only re-established themselves in Syria by means of British help. In Dayr az Zor angry tribal shaykhs summoned a British political officer to a meeting, where they harangued him. If the British were not willing to take control, they told him, then they wanted their 'independence as promised'.[11] He predicted that he would soon be forced to make the unpleasant choice 'whether of standing by and watching the French have their throats cut, or of shooting down Arabs in defence of a detested French administration'.[12]

The prospect of a tribal uprising against the French in eastern Syria unnerved the British. Good relations with the Bedu, they believed, were key to mastery of the desert. In turn, control of the desert was crucial to the defence of Syria, as it was across the flat, stony steppe of eastern Syria that the British expected the German onslaught to come, once the Soviet Union surrendered and the German army had crossed the Caucasus. This was why the British officer in Dayr az Zor argued: 'We must control the desert, not only for the safety of our military communications, but because who holds the desert also, in the end, holds the sown.'[13] He believed that the stakes justified robust tactics. 'The French ... seldom "play the game" and certainly they never believe that we are doing so. I suggest that we might for once incline to live down to their opinion of us, and for the sake of the safety of our Army, be most determinedly *rusé* in keeping them out of the desert.'

Glubb agreed. He hurried to Dayr az Zor and set about trying to restore relations with the angry tribesmen.[14] He handed out more money to calm them down and, interpreting the Lyttelton–de Gaulle agreement, reassured them that the British would take charge of the desert zone because it was strategically important. He well knew that this work among the shaykhs 'probably annoys the French', but he did not greatly care.[15] 'The only thing that deeply concerns me,' he told a colleague, 'is what attitude these people will take when the Germans come.'[16]

It did not take long before reports of Glubb's activities reached de Gaulle's ears. The news that 'Major Grubb', as the French tended to call him, was roaming the desert, showering money on the tribesmen and predicting a British takeover, confirmed French suspicions that he was trying to oust them. De Gaulle believed that Glubb was one of 'a fanatical group of British Arabophiles' who 'saw in the Syrian affair the opportunity of driving France out', and he insisted on the removal of him, his Arab Legion and two other British officers, Kenneth Buss and Gerald de Gaury, whose decidedly murky roles during Operation Exporter had included winning over Druze support.[17] Although Lyttelton correctly guessed that de Gaulle was 'pitching his demands high in order to try to render his price secure', the breakdown in relations between British and French officers at a local level was such that he saw no choice but to cave in and remove all three men, together with the Arab Legion.[18] 'We must remove the ingrained suspicions which three weeks ago were making it impossible to concert on a sensible basis plans regarding security, propaganda and other essential matter,' he wrote on 28 August, to justify his decision.[19]

At the same time the British minister circulated a headmasterly memorandum to British officers serving in Syria, encouraging them to be more sympathetic to the Gaullists' situation. 'Never forget that the Free French are more than allies who are fighting by our side,' he reminded them.[20] 'They are men who have resisted the demoralisation and defeat of their country, men who have risked reprisals on their families and relations, men who have had their property sequestrated, men who are under sentence of imprisonment and sometimes death.' Optimistically, he ended: 'Good manners and good sense will see us through.'

De Gaulle, however, had reached the opposite conclusion. Bad manners and foul temper had wrung significant concessions from the British. As he left the Middle East to start a tour of the other French colonies under Free French rule, he told Catroux to refuse to deal with either Lyttelton or Spears, who was to be the British representative at any treaty talks between the French and Arabs. Any gratitude that de Gaulle felt towards the man who had aided his escape from France had disappeared. He now believed that Spears, like many of his British counterparts, was playing a 'mischievous and disconcerting' role in Middle Eastern politics.[21] En route for London he gave an interview to the *Chicago Daily News* in which he accused the British of being scared of Vichy France and alleged that they used the Vichy government as a channel to communicate with Hitler.

Churchill was apoplectic when he heard about this interview. He ordered that no one was to meet de Gaulle when the general returned to London – 'he should stew in his own juice,' the prime minister decreed – and set about preparing a public statement of Britain's policy in Syria that he would deliver in the House of Commons before he met the Free French leader.[22]

That task was complicated by the competing pressures on Churchill. Four weeks earlier, as part of his campaign to draw the United States into the war, he had sailed to Newfoundland to meet the American president, Franklin D. Roosevelt, and agree the wording of an Atlantic Charter. The charter – which bore close similarities to the pledges made by Woodrow Wilson and the Allies in the previous war – committed both countries to 'seek no aggrandizement, territorial or other' and to 'respect the right of all peoples to choose the form of government under which they will live'. Britain's approach in Syria would be an early test of Churchill's dedication to this pact, which assumed great significance when the United States entered the war on Britain's side after the Japanese attack on Pearl Harbor later in the year.

An unequivocal pledge of Syrian independence would have been in keeping with the Atlantic Charter, but by September 1941 reports of de Gaulle's growing popularity in France were reaching Britain, and Churchill could not afford the rupture with de Gaulle that such a forthright declaration might cause. Accordingly, when he addressed the Commons on 9 September, the policy he announced was contradictory. Although he stated that 'Syria shall be handed back to the Syrians, who will assume at the earliest possible moment their independent sovereign rights', he also acknowledged that when the war was over, 'among all the nations of Europe the position of France in Syria is one of special privilege, and that in so far as any European countries have influence in Syria, that of France will be pre-eminent'.[23]

'Why?' demanded several members of parliament. 'Because,' Churchill answered back, 'that is the policy which we have decided to adopt.'

When Churchill met de Gaulle privately three days later, on 12 September, he could take a much more menacing line. Making reference to rumours that 'some British figures' thought that the Free French leader had 'moved towards certain Fascist views', he accused de Gaulle of leaving 'a trail of Anglophobia behind him' and threatened to cut him loose if his hostility continued.[24] After the general was forced to grovel over his incendiary interview in the *Chicago Daily News*, Churchill turned immediately to Syria. He made it clear that Britain would not accept the possible spreading of Arab discontent in the Levant to neighbouring Palestine.[25] In order 'to give the Arab world a real measure of satisfaction', the British prime minister continued, there had to be 'a transfer of many of the functions previously exercised by France in Syria to the Syrians'. De Gaulle had no choice but to agree.

No sooner had de Gaulle left Number 10, however, than he changed tack. He knew that as soon as he had concluded treaties of alliance with Syria and Lebanon the mandate authorising France to rule both countries would end, and was therefore desperate to procrastinate for as long as possible. Fortunately for him, the nationalists refused to enter talks with him, because they would not recognise his legitimacy. It was a reflection of de Gaulle's guile that, rather than take umbrage at this slight, he saw the opportunity that it gave him. When, on 1 October, he met Churchill again, he told him that it would be impossible to negotiate a treaty because the Free French movement had 'no international status and no power to negotiate the termination of the mandate'.[26]

This sudden volte-face, by a man who normally claimed he was the personification of *La France* and who, in the next breath, complained about the 'humiliation' heaped on his officers in the Levant by British officials, did not amuse Churchill at all – not least because, in legal terms, de Gaulle was right. Nevertheless, the British prime minister insisted that no 'juridical considerations' should be allowed to delay the granting of independence to the Levant states, which he told de Gaulle he expected to follow rapidly.[27]

In a bid to ward off British interference, Catroux did declare both Syria and Lebanon independent that autumn, but in practice neither country enjoyed any more autonomy than it had done previously. As president of each state the French deliberately chose men they could control. In the meantime the situation in eastern Syria had deteriorated sharply following the removal of Glubb. The trouble started when French troops on a tax-collecting mission in the region shot dead a village shaykh. The dead man's tribe retaliated and in the ensuing fire-fight some of them, and as many as thirty French soldiers, were killed. When Catroux immediately alleged that the British political officer had been encouraging the local people to pay a quarter of the tax the French demanded, two officers, one British, one French, were sent to Dayr az Zor to find out what had happened. The British officer reported that the tribes in the area were 'in a state bordering on insurrection'.[28]

Early in October in Amman, Glubb received a deputation of shaykhs from Dayr az Zor who corroborated the worrying report from eastern Syria. If the Bedu supported the British in the event of a German invasion, one shaykh told him, the British army would have 'as safe communications as if it were fighting in the British Isles'.[29] If, on the other hand, the British insisted on 'giving the Free French a free hand to ruin Syria', he continued, then 'the lines of communication of the British army would run through enemy country'.

In Cairo Wavell had been replaced as commander-in-chief in the Middle East by Claude Auchinleck, who was sufficiently alarmed by the reports coming from Syria that he turned his attention from planning a new British offensive against Rommel to go to Beirut to meet Catroux on 6 October. During two hours of talks Catroux

accused the British of encouraging one shaykh to stir up trouble
and deliberately trying to exploit mistakes made by the inexperienced French officer supervising the district. A clearly exasperated
Auchinleck dismissed both these allegations. 'The French have been
given every chance,' he reported back to London. 'They have failed
with the Natives, they have failed to cooperate with us, they are so
short of personnel that they have no choice but to appoint Officers
of very poor quality.'[30]

British impatience with the French, which had been slowly sim-
mering through the summer, now reached boiling point. It was
obvious that French priorities and their own could not be reconciled
and that, at heart, there was little or no difference between men they
had previously distinguished as 'Free' and 'Vichy' French. Both, as
Glubb put it acidly, were 'inclined to forget the War is against
Germany, in their desire to exclude British interference in Syria'.[31]
As Arab anger at French government escalated, British officials
were increasingly uncomfortable at their own role in keeping the
French in power in the Levant. 'One feels as if we were holding
down the Lebanon to be raped by Free France,' wrote one.[32] That
November, Glubb wrote a lengthy assessment of the situation. As
the British and French approaches to imperial rule were so different,
he argued, efforts 'to ensure mutual cooperation between French
and British in governing or administering Arabs' were 'bound to
lead to failure'.[33]

While the British government dithered over how to deal with the
situation, at the end of 1941 British officers serving in the Levant
received a note providing them with platitudinous responses to the
awkward questions they were liable to face from local people. If the
Syrians criticised the puppet Syrian and Lebanese regimes the French
had put in place to govern them, the British were advised to say that
'governments are not immortal and that in due course no doubt
Ministries more to their liking will take the place of the present
ones'. If the Arabs argued that the independence offered to them was
not genuine, they were to reply: 'We have received assurances from
General Catroux that he intends to make the independence a real
one,' and then the caveat, 'so far as circumstances permit.'[34]

By now, however, the British had begun to wonder whether

Catroux really would stand up to de Gaulle. Writing to the foreign secretary at the end of November, Lyttelton quoted Spears's impression that there had been a 'marked change in General Catroux's attitude lately' because the British had let him down by failing to stand up to de Gaulle.[35] Catroux had 'given up the struggle', Spears concluded. 'His attitude is now one of complete subservience.'

As it became clear that, far from diverting and defusing Arab anger, French policy in the Levant was making matters worse, the British realised that simple faith in Georges Catroux was no longer enough; constant pressure on him to honour his promise was now necessary. The man the government chose to take on the role of invigilator was de Gaulle's own liaison officer, Spears himself. Despite a warning from Lyttelton that Catroux would find Spears's appointment 'quite intolerable', Spears was told to prepare to return to Beirut as minister to the Levant States.[36] His job would be 'to foster the independence of the Republics while maintaining the Free French shop front', he told a colleague who had already begun working in Beirut.[37] 'We will have a lot of fun when I get back.'

19

ENVOY EXTRAORDINARY

NEWLY CREATED A BARONET, AND RESPLENDENT IN A BRILLIANT white diplomatic uniform, Britain's new 'Envoy Extraordinary and Minister Plenipotentiary' stepped ashore at Beirut on 21 March 1942. Sir Edward Louis Spears feared that his ornate job title meant that he would not be taken seriously. But in fact the responsibilities conferred by it were relatively clear-cut. As envoy he continued to work for the minister of state in Cairo as liaison officer with the Free French, while as minister he was responsible to the Foreign Office in London, since he was effectively the first British ambassador to the states of Lebanon and Syria, which he was determined to make meaningfully independent of the French. A hint of how he planned to do so was betrayed by the substantial extra power that he had acquired for himself during his time in London. This was to decide where the dividing line between British and French responsibilities lay, and to bring to the attention of the military authorities in Cairo any matters that, in his view, should be dealt with by them.[1] But in Beirut that spring morning the fervour with which he would set about this task had yet to become clear; he looked – misleadingly – as if he had stepped from the set of a comic operetta.

'Louis' to his friends, 'Edward' to his enemies, Spears was 'a thickset powerfully built man ... with thinning blond hair with touches of grey, a strong nose and a rat-trap gash of a mouth'.[2] Aged fifty-five, he preferred not to use the term 'liaison' to describe that aspect of his role. He disliked its connotation of 'illicit relations between the sexes' (perhaps because he was having an affair with his secretary at the time), and the fact that the word denoted 'only ... some sort of postman' in the military world.[3] But, throughout the First World War, the Paris-born, bilingual Spears had been the liaison officer between the British and French armies. He had probably saved the British Expeditionary Force very early in the war, when he alerted its commander to the danger that the French were withdrawing on his flank. Having been wounded four times at the front, in 1917 he was moved to a safer job behind the lines, as head of the British military mission to the French War Office in Paris. As the then recently concluded Sykes–Picot agreement showed, the British government regarded the maintenance of good relations with the French as paramount if the Allies were to win the war.

By then Spears had made the friendship that would shape the rest of his career. In 1915, at the age of thirty-nine, he had met Winston Churchill during the latter's brief spell on the front following the Gallipoli fiasco. Spears, who had just won a Military Cross for bravery, impressed the maverick politician who, when the war was over, suggested that he run for parliament. Spears did so. He was briefly Liberal MP for Loughborough and, having followed Churchill into the Conservative Party, was then elected to represent Carlisle in northern England in 1931.

Spears had represented the border market town ever since but, with his 'brilliant mind and a sharp but unkind wit', he never made great headway at Westminster. He was mocked as the 'member for Paris' for his pro-French views, while his support for Churchill's opposition to appeasement confirmed his membership of the awkward squad.[4] He never gave up that combative mindset, even now that he was a government minister. 'What upsets Government machinery is that once you have made up your mind that a course is right you go all out and damn the consequences,' a colleague once reminded him. 'Such a line creates instinctive hostility in Whitehall.'[5]

The final leg of Spears's journey to the Levant began in 1940 when Churchill, now prime minister, rewarded him for his loyalty by making him his personal liaison officer to the beleaguered French government. The stakes at that moment seemed impossibly high for, as Spears later explained, 'I was persuaded, as nearly all of us were, that a war with Germany was impossible unless we had a friendly and strong France at our side.'[6] The French collapse would test that theory to destruction, but in the meantime Spears took strength from Charles de Gaulle's refusal to give in. It was Spears who had hauled de Gaulle aboard his aircraft that June, enabling the Frenchman's escape to London, and it was Spears who then became his most belligerent champion when both men reached the British capital. 'Whatever propaganda we put forward should aim at strengthening the hand of de Gaulle, since the French will only trust a fellow Frenchman,' he argued at the end of 1940.[7] As Churchill later put it, 'if there had not been a General Spears there might never have been a General de Gaulle'.[8]

The unfamiliar and agreeable sensations of importance and control that Spears gained from his role in de Gaulle's establishment evaporated when the Frenchman started to exert himself. For the first half of 1941 Spears remained a forceful advocate for the Free French leader, but his attitude changed sharply when he visited Damascus after the Vichy French surrender and had an argument with de Gaulle over the future administration of the Levant. 'Do you think I am interested in England's winning the war? I am not – I am interested only in France's victory,' de Gaulle said provocatively.[9] 'They are the same,' retorted Spears. 'Not at all,' replied de Gaulle. 'Even I was taken aback,' Spears admitted as he noted down the disconcerting conversation.

De Gaulle's subsequent behaviour suggested that he was serious. Spears was dismayed to realise that both the Free French leader and his lieutenant, Catroux, saw the 'assertion of French sovereignty in Syria as far more important than taking measures to win the war'.[10] He went on to predict, accurately, that the Free French would 'fight, quarrel and impede us at every point where military security may impinge, however slightly, upon French prestige'. When Churchill began to bristle at de Gaulle's attitude, Spears felt both responsible and exposed. 'I have created a Frankenstein monster,' he confided to a colleague. 'Can I strangle it, or will it strangle me?'[11]

Spears returned to Beirut determined to win that struggle. A member of his staff wrote that he had 'never known what was meant by animals eating their young until he had seen ... Spears devouring the Free French Movement'.[12] When Spears met Catroux on 2 April, he told him that he was about to inform Alfred Naccache, the man Catroux had installed as Lebanese president, that the British government supported full Lebanese independence. Playing on his recent stay in London and his friendship with the prime minister, he tried to unnerve the Frenchman by painting a dark impression of relations between the British and de Gaulle. According to Catroux he claimed that 'everyone' had 'stopped believing in the usefulness and the effectiveness of Free France'.[13]

Catroux, already annoyed that Spears had not immediately come to see him after landing at Beirut, saw what his British counterpart was trying to do. He reported the encounter to de Gaulle, telling his chief that Spears had 'tried this manoeuvre to unsettle me and to leave me thinking that the situation of the Free French leaves me unable to resist the plans that he is making here'.[14] In his memoirs, however, he admitted how much Spears had disconcerted him. 'We feared the effects of his vindictive and combative temperament, his quick temper, his suspicious authoritarianism and his snap judgements, all of them the more dangerous because he had Churchill's ear.'[15]

De Gaulle rapidly reassured Catroux that Spears's claims about the Free French were 'thoroughly false and tendentious', and said he was convinced that Spears's push for full independence was not supported by the British Foreign Office.[16] Although both men were wary of risking Churchill's ire by taking on his friend, they knew that Spears's appointment as Britain's chief diplomat in the Levant was highly controversial back in London. If they were to thwart their determined new opponent, they needed to fortify the Foreign Office's deep concerns about the man the prime minister had foisted on them. De Gaulle asked Catroux to keep him 'constantly au fait' with what Britain's man in Beirut was telling him.[17]

Spears now tried to put pressure on Naccache.[18] He went to see the president soon after he had visited Catroux and, going far beyond his diplomatic remit, recommended that elections should be held before the year was out. Naccache reported this conversation to Catroux, but the French general had a spy inside Naccache's office anyway, and through him he also learned that Spears had told Naccache that Britain might be forced to intervene if Catroux's actions contravened the promise of independence he had made the year before.[19] Catroux asked de Gaulle to try, without giving away his source, to find out whether Spears's policy, which was 'designed to oust us', was also the British government's. His assumption was that it was not: he hoped that, by bringing Spears's conduct to the attention of the Foreign Office, he could undermine him.

Whether or not Spears was disobeying the British government's orders, however, Catroux's immediate problem was that the British minister's call for democratic elections was bound to galvanise the opponents of the puppet governments that he had set up in Lebanon and Syria to bring 'a democratic look to the institutions of these countries ... without recourse to elections'.[20] By then he was well aware that Naccache and the Syrian president, Tajeddin Hassani, were both deeply unpopular and would not win elections if he were forced to call them.

Tajeddin, in particular, was under pressure because the price of bread was rocketing in Syria. Before the war the country had been a net exporter of wheat, but since 1939 Syria's semi-feudal landlords, the *notables*, had been hoarding grain so that they could profit from the price rise that they expected a long war would cause. An attempt by Spears the previous year to ruin the speculators by flooding the market with Australian grain had failed dismally. The hoarders simply sucked the excess up, and the wheat price went on rising.

When Spears returned to Beirut in 1942 the threat of bread riots made tougher action against the speculators pressing. 'Probably nothing less than hanging a few of them will do,' he wrote, although he hoped 'to be able to arrange that the Free French will make themselves responsible for this'.[21]

Catroux proposed the creation of a French monopoly to buy the wheat crop wholesale and sell it at a subsidised price, but Tajeddin refused to endorse a venture that the *notables* – who still backed him – would oppose. Spears saw his chance to interfere. He bullied Tajeddin's prime minister, Husni al-Barazi, into supporting the scheme by threatening him with exile to the desolate Red Sea island of Kamaran if he did not comply. Then he told Catroux that the British would need to have a role in the administration of the scheme as they would be backing it financially, and because in the last resort it would have to be enforced by Jumbo Wilson's Ninth Army. Over several days' talks in May in Cairo, Catroux was obliged to compromise. It was a significant concession. He had been forced to accept British involvement in an area that, under the Lyttelton–de Gaulle agreement, should have been the responsibility of France alone.

By now, however, Lyttelton had been succeeded as minister of state, and therefore as Spears's boss, by Richard Casey, a good-looking, straight-talking Australian politician who chaired the wheat talks days after his arrival in Cairo on 5 May. After de Gaulle's complaint about Spears's activities, the Foreign Office had foolishly tried to present Casey's appointment to the French as an attempt to put a brake on Spears, but Casey failed to live up to this billing. Closing ranks with Spears, the debonair Australian 'did much to demolish what had become a principle of Gaullist policy – that you could always rely on finding a British Minister or Department prepared to oppose another, if need be at short notice', Spears chuckled later.[22] Casey backed him fully.

During the wheat talks, Spears grasped the opportunity to enlist Casey's help over the question of elections. Together the two men bludgeoned Catroux into conceding that it might be possible to hold polls in Lebanon and Syria before the end of 1942, on the grounds that there were plans to hold elections in both Egypt and Iraq to defuse pressure from the Arab nationalists in each country. Nearly ten days passed before Catroux plucked up the courage to tell de Gaulle that he had made another significant compromise, this time to Casey, the man who the Foreign Office had claimed had come to restrain Spears. 'Casey has turned out to be a real rock,' Spears wrote gratefully, sometime later.[23]

In London, de Gaulle took Catroux's news predictably badly. Replying that he wished Catroux had not caved in, he told him to try to ensure the British did not take charge of the timing of any announcement that elections would take place. He wanted to delay the news as long as possible, because he knew it would destroy the authority of the governments of both Naccache and Tajeddin, 'since everyone knows that they will not survive'.[24]

In the event it was Rommel who temporarily saved de Gaulle. On 26 May, the German general launched an offensive in the Libyan desert with the aim of capturing Tobruk, which he did almost a month later, on 21 June, after the British failed to counter-attack effectively. When, at the end of the month, the British retreated to their prepared defences at El Alamein, Rommel's Afrika Korps was just sixty miles from Alexandria and a hundred and twenty-five from Cairo. 'You have over 700,000 men on your ration strength in the Middle East,' Churchill reminded his Middle East commander-in-chief, Auchinleck. 'Every fit male should be made to fight and die for victory.'[25]

While it was a disaster for Churchill – who had repeatedly stressed that, whatever the outcome of the battle, Tobruk would be held at all costs to stop Rommel advancing so confidently towards Egypt – the fall of the Libyan port represented a stroke of luck for de Gaulle. Two days afterwards, Catroux told Casey that de Gaulle was not willing 'to expose the Levant countries to the vicissitudes of political battles while the military situation has not brightened, full-stop'.[26] This was to be the line that de Gaulle maintained throughout the remainder of the year.

There was another reason for the new spring in de Gaulle's step that summer. Not only did the Germans' proximity to Egypt postpone elections in Lebanon and Syria indefinitely, but his own troops, under ('Bloody English') Koenig, had performed impressively in the battle for Tobruk. Without their tenacious defence of the southern extremity of the British line at Bir Hakim, Rommel would have reached Tobruk faster than he had, and British losses consequently would have been even greater than they were. The Free French argued that the Germans might even have broken through into Egypt. Before the battle was even over, Churchill agreed that Britain should recognise the Free French as the 'Fighting French', to acknowledge Koenig's efforts. In his memoirs de Gaulle wrote that having heard the news of Koenig's stand at Bir Hakim, he had gone to his office, closed and locked the door, and wept.

Having exorcised one demon that had haunted him since May 1940, de Gaulle arrived in the Middle East at the beginning of August, planning to spend a month there. In Cairo he met Churchill, who had flown out to assess whether he needed to replace Auchinleck after Tobruk, and asked him to look into the situation in Syria. Churchill, his mind on more important matters, said he would. The next day de Gaulle parried an attempt by Casey to force him to confirm that elections would take place in the Levant. 'The Mandatory Power,' he told the Australian aloofly, 'does not intend to have the people vote while Rommel is at the gates of Alexandria. Are there to be elections in Egypt, Iraq or Transjordan?'[27] Then, after his arrival in Beirut on 14 August, he sent Churchill a formal complaint about the 'constant interventions of the representatives of the British Government' in the Levant, which he said were 'not compatible with the political disinterestedness of Great Britain in the Lebanon and Syria or with respect for the position of France'.[28]

There was certainly truth in de Gaulle's allegation. Since Spears had arrived in Beirut his mission had grown rapidly. It now comprised political, economic and financial, army, navy and air force sections, press and propaganda functions, and ultimately ran a network of as many as a hundred and twenty political officers across the Levant. A team photograph of the mission – filed away by the French, and dating to the end of 1943 – shows a pale-suited Spears surrounded by over seventy men in khaki.[29] The French rightly suspected that the mission also provided cover for a range of clandestine activity, from training saboteurs who would stay behind should the Germans invade, to outright espionage. 'I was associated with the Spears Mission for some time,' was all one man would say as late as 1983, when pressed about his wartime role.[30]

Spears, though feeling isolated, was determined to fend off any attempt to pare his empire down. 'De Gaulle is undoubtedly out to extract from us yet another document which he can quote against us,' he said, after the general's complaint reached Cairo.[31] De Gaulle's letter went unanswered for eight days while Churchill secretly visited Moscow, and the pause gave time for Spears to ensure that the prime minister's response rejected de Gaulle's complaint.

On his return to Cairo, Churchill backed Spears up. 'Louis Spears has a great many enemies,' he remarked over lunch in the Egyptian capital; then, thumping his chest: 'but he has *one* friend.'[32] His response to de Gaulle rejected the general's complaints robustly and gave Spears carte blanche to continue to interfere. 'Our principal concern in the political sphere,' Churchill told de Gaulle, 'is to ensure that no policy is adopted which may jeopardise our military security or interfere with our prosecution of the war. It is for this reason that we expect to be fully consulted beforehand on major political developments.'[33]

Suspecting, rightly, that Churchill and Spears intended to use military security and the wheat shortage as pretexts to intervene in the administration of the Levant, de Gaulle tried a different ruse.[34] If military security gave Britain the excuse to meddle, then France should take control of military security in the Levant. Under his agreement with Lyttelton a year earlier, Britain assumed responsibility for the defence of Syria because its forces outnumbered those of the French.[35] De Gaulle now totted up the different forces in the Levant and, by counting the Syrian gendarmerie and native levies (the twenty-thousand-strong *troupes spéciales*) as French, arrived at a total that suggested the majority of troops in the Levant were French. He then wrote to Churchill demanding the transfer of the military command.

The British initially treated de Gaulle's request seriously, but they changed their mind when the Free French leader then annoyed them with a speech in the Lebanon in which he publicly ruled out the need for an election. Spears, revived by Churchill's open support for him in Cairo, gleefully seized on de Gaulle's announcement.[36] He reported to the Foreign Office that the news that there would be no vote had made the Lebanese 'completely despondent', and warned Casey that such an anti-democratic move threatened to drive the Arab populations of the region into the arms of Hitler.[37] But he was already preaching to a convert: although the minister of state had begun to wonder whether sacrificing Spears might calm the situation, he realised that to do so now would only reward de Gaulle's petulance. Casey had already told London that de Gaulle's presence in the Levant was a 'serious menace', because the French general was openly taking advantage of Britain's reverse in the Libyan desert by 'saying to all and sundry that His Majesty's Government want the elections to be held, but that in view of the military situation in the western desert, no election will be held this year'.[38]

Desperate to shut de Gaulle up before he could infuriate the Arabs further, Churchill called him back to London for talks. When the general refused on the grounds that he was too busy, the British prime minister ordered that the monthly subsidy supporting the French in Syria be cut off. Before de Gaulle reluctantly left Beirut for London, he gave an interview to an American journalist, Wendell Willkie. 'We talked for hours in the general's private room, where every corner, every wall, held busts, statues and pictures of Napoleon,' reported Willkie, who asked de Gaulle whether he realised the depth of local opposition to the French mandate.[39] 'Yes I know,' admitted de Gaulle. 'But I hold it in trust. I cannot close out that mandate or let anyone else do so. That can be done only when there is a government again in France.' Willkie asked about Syria. 'I cannot sacrifice or compromise my principles,' replied the Free French leader. 'Like Joan of Arc,' his aide bizarrely added.

De Gaulle's meeting with Churchill on 28 September in Downing Street was even stormier than their encounter there one year earlier. When de Gaulle again claimed to represent France and flatly refused to accept Churchill's demand for elections in Lebanon and Syria, the British prime minister started ranting. 'You claim to be France! You are not France! I do not recognise you as France! France! Where is France now?'

'If, in your eyes, I am not the representative of France,' de Gaulle came back at him, brilliantly, 'why and with what right are you dealing with me concerning her worldwide interests?'[40]

Churchill had no answer, according to de Gaulle. But the British leader had other means to make his counterpart comply. The British government simply cut off de Gaulle's telegraphic links with his outposts around the world. After a week's being held incommunicado, the French diplomatic representative in London, Maurice Dejean, informed the Foreign Office that the Free French would announce before the end of the year that elections would take place the coming spring.[41] They did so on 27 November.

'If only de Gaulle had controlled himself,' wrote one British official in the Foreign Office, 'we could have got Spears out by now thanks to the complaints we have received from all sides. But de G. has played into his hands and put more than enough rope round his own neck to hang himself with.'[42] Spears had survived de Gaulle's efforts to remove him. He was being shielded from his enemies in the Foreign Office by Churchill. Now he had to make preparations for the next year's poll.

20

DIRTY WORK

ENSURING THAT THE FRENCH DID NOT INTERFERE DECISIVELY in the forthcoming elections was Spears's main concern by the spring of 1943. Early in the year he had had a disconcerting conversation with the newly appointed American consul in Beirut, George Wadsworth. Wadsworth, a former lecturer at the American University in Beirut, told him that he had heard that the French were going to try to rig the votes and then force the newly elected parliaments to ratify treaties binding Lebanon and Syria to France. The rumour worried Spears because he had heard it, too.[1] It fitted the British expectation that the French would not give up their influence without a fight. 'Goodness knows the dirty work that will go on,' was the reaction of another British official when he first heard that polls were to take place later in the year.[2]

There was great pressure on Spears to succeed because his boss, the minister of state Richard Casey, saw the election of nationalist governments in both Levant states as key to a much larger plan to assuage Arab anger: not just in Syria or Lebanon, but in Palestine next door, where the situation was deteriorating sharply. Tensions that had been stilled by the threat of a German invasion had reappeared since the decisive British victory at El Alamein in November 1942 and the simultaneous Anglo-American invasion of French North Africa. 'Every informed observer ... who has been in contact with Palestine during the last twelve months is now convinced of one thing,' Casey wrote on 21 April 1943. 'The country is heading for the most serious outbreak of disorder and violence which it has yet seen, and ... the explosion is timed to go off as soon as the War ends in Europe, or possibly a few months earlier.'[3]

By the spring of 1943 it was evident that a growing number of Jews in Palestine were no longer resigned to accepting the draconian limits on immigration imposed by the British to placate the Arab population in 1939, but preparing to fight for recognition. The first signs had come at a conference at the Biltmore Hotel in New York in May the previous year. There, Zionist representatives had attacked the immigration restrictions as 'cruel and indefensible', and called for the Jewish Agency, the authority set up in 1929 to represent Jewish interests in Palestine to the British, to be given control of immigration into Palestine as a prelude to the establishment of a 'Jewish Commonwealth integrated in the structure of the new democratic world'.[4]

Then, towards the end of 1942, reports that confirmed the rumours of the horrifying scale of German efforts to exterminate the Jewish race started to reach Palestine. They provoked Jewish militancy just as the ebbing German threat weakened the argument that a confrontation with the British would be self-defeating. Casey noted that the Jewish Agency was now spending 15 per cent of its £1 million budget on the training and equipping of its defence organisation, the Haganah. And he quoted a member of the executive of the left-wing Zionist labour organisation, the Histadrut, to demonstrate how what had once been right-wing views were now mainstream. 'We all know that the Zionist problem will have to be solved one day by force of arms,' Eliahu Golomb had stated at a private meeting on which the British eavesdropped. 'It can never be solved by political arguments; only by a fight. We must prepare ourselves, both spiritually and materially, for this decisive struggle.'[5]

Desperate to stop an 'open revival of the Jew v. Arab conflict in Palestine', Casey and his colleagues came up with a new idea.[6] This was to win the Arabs' acceptance of the Jewish presence by compensating them with an Arab federation, for which the British government had promised its support in 1941. Seemingly oblivious to the growing opposition to Britain's presence in the Middle East, they believed that such a federation might form the outer of two zones – the Jews would form the inner – that would protect Britain's position astride the Suez Canal, after the war, like the concentric rings around the bull's-eye on a target.

The Middle East War Council – which drew together Britain's leading officials in the region – reviewed this strategy at a conference in Cairo in May 1943, chaired by Casey's deputy Lord Moyne, who was the project's keenest advocate. It was at this meeting that the group recognised that the plan's success depended on the outcome of the elections in Lebanon and Syria. Since 'any form of closer political association between the Arab States' was 'hardly possible as long as the French maintain any direct influence, political or military, in Syria and the Lebanon', the election in both countries of nationalist and anti-French governments which could be relied upon to throw out the French was central to their hopes of averting a conflagration in Palestine.[7]

In Beirut Catroux was doing his utmost to ensure that the idea of 'Greater Syria' never happened. Having spent 1942 insisting that the German threat made elections most unwise, he now tried to argue that 'elections were now less urgent because the Axis menace had been driven further off'.[8] When, predictably, that line elicited howls of protest from Spears, he was forced to reconcile himself to the fact that the elections were now unstoppable and that the governments elected were likely to be nationalist. Ever the realist, he decided that it would be best to offer support for governments who were willing to negotiate treaties that gave France preferential treatment. He was confident that, once elected, they would bicker over which of them should lead a future Arab federation – which was, as the British knew deep down, that dream's fundamental flaw.

The man with whom Catroux hoped to strike a deal in Syria was the leader of the party bound to win the ballot, the veteran nationalist politician Hashim Bey al-Atassi. Although 'very anti-French' when he had served as prime minister of Feisal's short-lived kingdom in 1920, al-Atassi had since then recognised the need for an accommodation with France.[9] He supported the abortive 1936 treaty, describing the day of its agreement as 'the date on which Syria rediscovered France'.[10] Catroux hoped that al-Atassi could ensure that the National Bloc would support a similar new agreement. 'A noble character and a gallant man whose dignified attitude inspired respect', in Catroux's opinion, al-Atassi personally promised to do just that, so long as Catroux did not interfere in the Syrian election.[11] Before Catroux stepped down as delegate-general at the end of March, he agreed that the French would keep their distance, and the election date was set for July 1943.

This self-denying ordinance did not extend to the Lebanon, where the French were determined to maintain their grip. From the beginning of 1943 they had been making efforts to swing the election there, which Catroux wanted to hold simultaneously with the Syrian vote. They recruited malleable candidates to stand and drew up lists of pro-British and nationalist candidates whom they planned to stop from putting themselves forward. Spears would later allege that the French used 'every form of intimidation, from the suppression of food cards to that of arrest' to bolster their own candidates' chances.[12] The first sign of the lengths the French were going to came that April in Tripoli, when the British military police uncovered a drug-smuggling ring run by a man named Rashid Mukkadam, who was the 'French' candidate for the port in the approaching election. When the French heard about the discovery they tried to persuade the British to postpone Mukkadam's arrest, 'so as not to trouble the town's security', but the British ignored them.[13]

Under the Lyttelton–de Gaulle agreement, the French were responsible for criminal justice, and so the British were obliged to hand over Mukkadam to them. Mukkadam's trial was perfunctory and he escaped on a technicality, although there was ample evidence that he had been bribing British soldiers to transport opium to Egypt for him. Eventually, the British managed to persuade the French to place Mukkadam under house arrest, but he was still allowed to stand in the election. He was 'an excellent example of the way in which the French political system worked in the Levant', said Spears, who now tried to extract the maximum possible advantage from the affair.[14]

Having judged the new French delegate-general to be 'a sensible sort of chap' who looked 'as if he will be easy to deal with', Spears

mistakenly expected Jean Helleu to cave in swiftly when he complained that the French administration was allowing Mukkadam to
stand at the election. But Helleu was unwilling to do anything about
Mukkadam, not least because he suspected that the timing of the
arrest was a deliberate attempt to frame his candidate.[15] Previously
the Vichy ambassador to Turkey, Helleu had approached the Free
French after he was sacked by the Vichy government. The reason
why Vichy had been happy to be shot of their man in Ankara
became apparent only when it emerged, as Spears put it, that Helleu
was 'far too addicted to strong alcohol refreshment from breakfast
time onwards', and had a tendency to disappear into a shed at the
end of his Residency's garden, armed with a bottle of whisky, when
times were tough.[16]

That disabling predilection mattered, because behind Helleu there
was a powerful cabal of advisers. The British were particularly suspicious of an alliterative triumvirate named Boegner, Baelen and
Blanchet, who, according to the head of British counter-espionage in
the Levant, had been 'openly or secretly ... frustrating and double-
crossing us'.[17] Like Helleu, Boegner and Baelen had defected from
the Vichy embassy in Ankara, while Blanchet had fought for Vichy
during the invasion and remained 'openly Anglophobe'.[18] By nefar-
ious means Spears had obtained proof that Blanchet was still in
touch with Vichy, and he believed that Blanchet's two colleagues
and other French officials probably were as well.

As the evidence mounted that this 'small, ambitious, and fundamentally anti-British clique' had seized control of political affairs
from the incapable Helleu, Casey intervened.[19] At the start of May
the Middle East War Council, which he chaired, concluded that,
because the French were 'unco-operative and unreliable', their continued presence in the Levant was 'incompatible with our political
and military interests in the Middle East as well as with the peaceful
development and well being of the Arab countries'.[20] The council
recommended that Britain should actively try to frustrate French
efforts to sign treaties with either Syria or Lebanon.

Since this pronouncement made it clear how far Cairo was diverg-
ing from the Foreign Office line that Britain should support Free
French rule in the Levant, Casey volunteered to return to London

with Spears for further discussions. On their arrival at the end of June both men had an awkward meeting at the Foreign Office (where the head of the Eastern Department privately noted his regret that Casey had 'sold himself to Sir Edward Spears in the manner of Doctor Faustus') before going on to see the prime minister at Chequers.[21] Much as Churchill now disliked de Gaulle, he was unwilling to endorse the Middle East War Council's strategy, because the British government's interest in the Arabs had quickly waned following the Allied victory in North Africa. The day after he met Casey and Spears he issued a directive saying that, although he wanted 'a complete show-down about Syria', he would 'not hear under any circumstances of our taking the place of the French in the Levant ... We must be able to say that we fought this war for honour alone and have gained nothing whatsoever by it.'[22]

Churchill's message was mixed, but Spears was only briefly disconcerted. At a further meeting in the Foreign Office he was invited to write an indictment of the French, a challenge he responded to with gusto. On 5 July he submitted a memorandum that portrayed the French administration in the Levant as 'proving itself more dictatorial every day, exceeding by far Vichy's unpleasant record', and argued that the Mukkadam affair and French interference in the elections were evidence that Helleu was 'falling more and more under the sway of the extremists in his entourage'.[23] The problem, Spears implied, was that the Free French were seen locally as being backed by Britain. Knowing that Churchill would read the memo, he tried to persuade the prime minister to take action by insinuating that his reputation was on the line. Spears claimed that the question of whether the British would force the French to give the Syrians and Lebanese independence was now 'widely regarded as a test of the sincerity of the Atlantic Charter', which of course Churchill had signed.

'I had no idea the French were behaving so tyrannically,' Churchill wrote, after he had read Spears's counterblast.[24] He reprimanded Eden when the foreign secretary tried to dismiss Spears's arguments. 'I am quite clear that we are being knocked about unduly and unfairly by the French and that a stiffer line should be taken with them in Syria. ... our pledges to the Syrians and Lebanese are serious and must be made good.'[25]

This intervention gave Casey and Spears the support they needed for a meeting with René Massigli, the Free French representative on foreign affairs, two days later, on 17 July. There, they complained about both Boegner and Blanchet; Spears added that while both men remained in place there was little hope of meaningful cooperation. Massigli, who had been planning to say much the same about Spears, was unnerved by Churchill's evident support for the British envoy, and kept quiet. The talks ended with neither side's concerns about the other's personnel being solved in any way.

During Spears's absence in London, Helleu had been uncharacteristically busy. In the hope of swaying the outcome of the election at the end of May, he had approved a proposal from the Christian Lebanese president to increase the number of parliamentary seats in such a way that there would be significantly more Christian representatives than Muslim in the new parliament. The predominantly Christian Lebanese diaspora would also be allowed to vote. The Muslims, predictably, complained and, by threatening to boycott the elections, wrecked the French plan to hold the Syrian and Lebanese elections simultaneously.

While Helleu tried to resolve the dispute, Syria went to the polls. The result was, as predicted, a triumph for the National Bloc. But it did not represent the breakthrough that the French had wanted, for at the last moment Hashim Bey al-Atassi mysteriously decided not to stand, and Syria's new president, Shukri al-Quwatli, immediately made it clear that he did not see himself as bound by the promise that his predecessor had made. Embarrassed French officials vainly tried to present the result as positive, arguing that the National Bloc's greatly expanded parliamentary presence was a potential weakness, since its many newly elected members would 'doubtless be particularly sensitive to influences which can be exerted on them from outside'.[26]

In truth, the result was a significant setback for the Free French, and it also buoyed up the nationalist candidates in the Lebanon, where the vote still had to take place. There, in what the French called 'a confrontation less of ideas than of personalities', two men were vying for office.[27] France's preferred candidate – 'a man capable of accomplishing a policy of appeasement and of defending the French position against Anglo-Saxon ambitions' – was the clever Beirut lawyer Emile Eddé, who had already served as president once.[28] His association with the French went back many years, for he had been a member of the delegation that had long-windedly lobbied the Paris Peace Conference in 1919 for a French mandate for Syria, and then an adviser to François Georges-Picot. Eddé's opponent was another lawyer, his former protégé Beshara al-Khoury, who had himself been prime minister. He enjoyed more broadly based support, not only from the Maronite Christian community but among many Sunni Muslims too. As an open supporter of an Arab federation, he was clearly Britain's preference, and that of the new Syrian government too.

Al-Khoury had fallen out with Eddé when the French backed the latter for the presidency in 1936. Goaded on by Spears, he now raised the question of whether his former patron was eligible to stand once more. Under a 1937 law brought in by the French, a retiring president had to wait six years before he could offer himself as a candidate again, and al-Khoury argued that Eddé, who had been president between 1936 and 1941, was clearly contravening this law.

With lawyerly dexterity Eddé countered that, at the time, the Lebanese constitution had been suspended, and so that earlier period in office should not count; but by doing so he probably only reminded many voters how close to France he was. French legal advisers in Helleu's administration predictably agreed with his interpretation, but Spears sealed the matter when he made it clear that the controversy surrounding the legitimacy of Eddé's candidature was such that Britain would not be prepared to recognise him if he were elected.[29] From that point, Eddé's campaign was doomed.

Meanwhile in Tripoli Rashid Mukkadam remained under house arrest. When it became clear that, even in the venal world of Lebanese politics, this confinement was limiting his ability to influence the electorate, the French tried to persuade him to make his son-in-law Mustapha stand instead. Mustapha, however, had already seen which way the wind was blowing. He had found himself a place on the list of his father-in-law's ancient rival, Abdul-Hamid Kerameh, who had been going around for months claiming his own election was assured because he had the backing of the British. This seemed plausible enough, since Kerameh was a long-term opponent of the French and supporter of wider Arab unity, but Spears denied he had any interest in the election of Kerameh over and above the fact that, compared to Mukkadam, he had 'a relatively good reputation'.[30]

Although establishing the exact truth of the allegations that the British and French then traded is impossible, it is clear that the vote itself was marred by widespread bribery and intimidation. In the countryside the mukhtars used to take the identity cards of their villagers to the polling station and vote en bloc. 'Quite a number used to take them to the highest bidder and collect their payments,' one British witness recalled. He heard that 'Some of the candidates would ... pay with British gold guineas to make the Muktars think that they were endorsed by the British.'[31] Spears accused the French authorities of distributing paper – which was rationed – only to those newspapers that toed their line. More seriously, he alleged that agents of the French Sûreté had murdered one voter in a polling booth.[32] The French rejected this interpretation, claiming that 'armed intervention' had been necessary after al-Khoury's supporters had tried to steal some ballot boxes.[33] In turn they accused British officials in the Spears Mission of openly assisting their own preferred candidates. There was certainly truth in their claims, for Casey later admitted that Spears was 'largely responsible' for the nationalists' success.[34]

Helleu realised that, thanks to Spears's 'flagrant intervention', Eddé had no chance of being elected. He now tried instead to organise a compromise that would make him look like the kingmaker when the president was elected by the new parliament.[35] He suggested to both candidates that they might find a third man, whom they could both support, and who would form a government made from members of both their parties.

Al-Khoury would do so only on condition that the notoriously anti-French Camille Chamoun became president. But there was no way that Helleu could accept a man who he was certain was a British agent, and with Eddé's presidency blocked by Spears he had no choice but to persuade al-Khoury, now the lesser of two evils, to re-enter the election. Al-Khoury did so, and on 21 September was elected by parliament as Lebanon's new president. Every member present voted in his favour, though Eddé and seven others stayed away.

This was not quite the disaster for the French that it appeared to be. Helleu tried to convince the Free French leadership that the election of al-Khoury was 'from the French point of view ... far from being the setback that certain people wanted to see', and to some extent Spears agreed.[36] The British minister had his own doubts about just how resolute a defender of Lebanese independence the new president would be, and realised that it was paramount that he secure his preferred candidate as prime minister. Under Lebanon's complex confessional constitution the president is always Christian, while the prime minister is always Sunni Muslim. There were four potential candidates for the prime-ministership. One was Kerameh, who had beaten Mukkadam in Tripoli; but the man who impressed Spears the most was Riad as-Sulh, a rich and brilliant lawyer from the southern Lebanese port of Saida. Spears was determined to make sure that as-Sulh got the job.

Riad as-Sulh had been working closely with Spears's mission since the British threatened to jail him because of his support for German intervention in Rashid Ali al-Gaylani's coup in Iraq in 1941. Imprisoned by the Ottomans in 1915 after he was arrested while acting as a courier between Feisal and Arab leaders in south Lebanon, he probably only escaped the gallows because of his family's good connections. His reputation as 'one of the most influential leaders of the Arab National Movement' was thus impeccable.[37] Promisingly, given British hopes of joining Lebanon and Syria together, he was married to the niece of Saadallah Jabri, the new prime minister of Syria, and he was virulently anti-French. Eager to avoid incarceration again, he offered to do a deal with Britain. 'If you help us end the French Mandate, we will be on your side,' he told Spears's political adviser, Geoffrey Furlonge.[38]

On the day that al-Khoury was elected, as-Sulh went to see Furlonge again to tell him that, if and when he formed his ministry, his first acts would be to call on Helleu 'to tell him exactly where he got off', and to meet Spears 'to ask for British guidance and support'.[39]

When none of the other three potential candidates was initially willing to endorse as-Sulh, Spears waded in. Gathering all four men together, he managed to persuade the other three to support as-Sulh as prime minister. On leaving the meeting, one of those three met a friend. 'It's done,' he told him. 'We have been obliged to support Riad, after General Spears firmly told us to.'[40]

Spears was ecstatic. The appointment of as-Sulh, he crowed to Casey, 'means that everything has ended infinitely more satisfactorily than I ever dared hope for. I have felt all along as if I were building a house of cards and that an additional card was likely to bring down the whole structure. Yet until the last tier was in position nothing had been achieved.'[41]

As-Sulh agreed with al-Khoury that they would work to create 'a homeland with an Arab face seeking the beneficial good from the culture of the West'. On 7 October he set out his plans for closer ties with other Arab countries, the revision of the constitution to reflect Lebanon's new national sovereignty and – in case that subtle reference to the termination of the French mandate was not clear enough – the abolition of French as an official language. Given the cultural element of French imperialism, this was an incendiary move, and one to which the French took violent exception.[42]

By now Helleu knew how far Spears had interfered in the formation of as-Sulh's new government. He was aware that a go-between had 'shuttled between the President of the Republic and General Spears in order to convey Spears's desires concerning the choice of ministers and to obtain his approval of the final composition of the cabinet'.[43] Stiffened by his cabal of political advisers and strong drink, he decided it was time to take a stand. So on 13 October Helleu issued a directive to his chief administrators across Lebanon and Syria, telling them that it would not be possible to 'accord the attributes of independence to the States until we are absolutely certain that the granting of this independence will not enable the installation of a power other than France in the Levant'.[44] Eight days later, he wrote to President al-Khoury to inform him that his government's plans were incompatible with the French mandate.

Riad as-Sulh quickly made it clear to Helleu that he had no intention of backing down. On 28 October he privately told the French that the Lebanese government would take over all the functions of their Délégation-Générale. Two days later he formally told Helleu, again in private, that the French delegate-general's claim did not correspond with the declaration Georges Catroux had made two and a half years earlier. He also threatened to publicise Helleu's refusal to accept his manifesto.

While Helleu hurried to Algiers to seek directions from de Gaulle, the man he left in charge, Yves Chataigneau, made his own appraisal of the situation. 'It's not a question, strictly speaking, of collusion between the British and the Government,' Chataigneau wrote to Massigli, the Free French foreign affairs spokesman, arguing that the Lebanese government were simply 'obedient servants of English policy, from which they get a personal profit'.[45] Drawing strength from this analysis, he was optimistic that it was not too late to stop France's ejection from Lebanon, if the French took forceful action against those whose only loyalty to the British was financial.

'Be in no doubt,' Chataigneau finished, 'that a display of firmness in this country will be met with enthusiasm by the majority of Lebanese opinion.'[46] What happened next would prove him horribly wrong.

21

ANOTHER FASHODA

IT WAS THE BLOOD-SPATTERED SON OF THE LEBANESE PRESI-
dent who woke Louis Spears before dawn on 11 November 1943
with news of what had happened overnight. Kalil al-Khoury told
Spears that French Sûreté agents had barged into his family's home
at four o'clock that morning and abducted his father. His own head
wound, he explained, was inflicted when the Sûreté had bludgeoned
him into the cellar with their rifle butts, yelling 'Son of a dog, son of
an Englishman!' at him.[1]

As relatives of other ministers converged at his front door,
Spears soon established that al-Khoury was not alone. The prime
minister, Riad as-Sulh, had also been dragged from his bed, in
which he had been asleep with his wife, and all but two members
of his cabinet had been seized as well. Soon afterwards, Helleu
came on the radio. In a 'new voice, strident, harsh and high-
pitched', he announced that he had suspended the constitution,
dismissed the government and appointed Emile Eddé president.[2]
The coup was to spark an eleven-day-long crisis as the British government wondered whether to acquiesce in what Helleu had done,
or to threaten to restore Lebanese democracy by force if he would
not back down. 'By the time this incident is over either your prestige or ours will be zero in Syria and the Lebanon,' one Frenchman
correctly predicted.[3]

Rumours that the French were on the point of taking forceful action against the new Lebanese government had been flying around for days. The first sign of trouble had come from Algiers, where Helleu had gone to seek from de Gaulle support for 'a display of firmness'.

At that moment, de Gaulle was locked in a battle for control of the French Committee for National Liberation, a steering committee for the Free French movement which had been set up with British encouragement in a bid to water down the general's influence. De Gaulle was vying with the Americans' preferred candidate, General Giraud, for the chairmanship of the group. The situation encouraged grandstanding behaviour and in these circumstances there was no chance that de Gaulle would meekly accept Lebanese independence without a fight.

Until that point the exchanges between the French and the Lebanese had been private. But then on 5 November the French Committee for National Liberation made the disagreement public by issuing a communiqué stressing that the Lebanese had no right to change the constitution unilaterally, because the mandate remained in place. When the Lebanese replied to this unyielding statement the same day, with the observation that draft legislation to do so had already been tabled for discussion in parliament on the 8th, it was clear that relations between the French and Lebanese had curdled irreversibly. A confrontation was now inevitable.

A French attempt to organise a boycott of the parliamentary session flopped. The Lebanese, ignoring a message from Helleu requesting a delay, passed the bill amending the constitution the same day. Helleu returned to Beirut on the 9th, under the impression that de Gaulle 'wished to see him act vigorously if the need arose'.[4] In Beirut he imposed complete censorship of the local press in a forlorn attempt to stop the parliament's decision becoming widely known. He also announced that he had withdrawn the customary invitations to the Lebanese government to attend the annual Armistice Day parade that was due to take place two days later, on 11 November. When, on the evening of the 10th, Spears collared him about the persistent rumours he was hearing, Helleu had 'looked the very picture of shocked deprecation'.[5] Although he drunkenly let slip that he was going to make a broadcast the following morning, he gave Spears his 'word of honour that nothing would be done to disturb public order'.[6]

Once Spears had absorbed the news of the coup the following dawn, he decided that unflattering publicity was the best stick with which to beat the French. In its previous altercations with the Free French, the British government had kept its criticisms private, but Spears felt that this simply encouraged de Gaulle's bad behaviour. In London that summer he had raised the possibility of bringing some British newspaper reporters out to the Levant 'to get the story of French misdeeds ... published to the world as the best means of stopping them', and this was the idea he now put again to Casey when he telephoned the British minister in Cairo.[7] Casey agreed to Spears's plan, and also told the British envoy to deliver a written protest personally to Helleu. No job could have delighted Spears more. Soon afterwards he dropped an inflammatory note round to the delegate-general that accused him of being 'inadmissibly dictatorial' and, given the two men's conversation the night before, cast aspersions on his honour.[8]

The rousing reception that Spears received from the Lebanese wherever he went in Beirut that day made the British envoy feel extremely confident. But although he was ready to confront the French head on, he knew that his counterparts in the Foreign Office were not. During his visit to London earlier that year he had taken an instant dislike to the two principal officials in the Eastern Department, describing its head as 'big, flabby, with sunken eyes, cloaked with a hostility that will I feel never disappear', and his deputy as 'the wettest thing I have ever come across'.[9] Moreover, as the theatre of the war had shifted from the Middle East to Europe following the Allied conquest of North Africa and the invasion of Italy, Britain's diplomatic corps now fretted more about upsetting the French than about honouring a two-and-a-half-year-old guarantee of independence when the Lebanon was no longer under direct threat. Now that the Arabs no longer seemed so critical, just as in the First World War, the British government was happy to renege on its promise.

When the Foreign Office tried to create the basis for a compromise in Lebanon by blaming 'grave blunders and lack of judgement on both sides' for the crisis, Spears retorted sarcastically that the Lebanese people had only 'made the "grave blunder" (your words) of assuming that, as a "sovereign and independent people" (our own words) they were entirely free to change their own laws as they saw fit'.[10]

Spears's well-known dislike of the French led the Foreign Office to discount his reports that the situation had the potential to deteriorate. The British minister responsible for relations with de Gaulle in Algiers, Harold Macmillan, was more inclined to believe French claims – which relied on Helleu's assurances – that Spears and Casey were exaggerating events in Beirut. 'I feel that Spears is out for trouble and personal glory, and Casey is so weak as to be completely in his pocket,' he wrote.[11] Having been badly wounded in the First World War, Macmillan preferred negotiation to confrontation. 'Spears wants a Fashoda,' he wrote in his diary, 'and I do not.'[12]

While Macmillan's estimate of Spears's aim was spot on, Spears's assessment of the situation in Lebanon was right as well. On 13 November in Tripoli, French Senegalese soldiers in armoured troop carriers ran down a crowd protesting about the French kidnap of their government, crushing seven and shooting dead another. In Saida – home town of the prime minister Riad as-Sulh – four were killed and between fifty and sixty wounded when the French governor of the port ordered his troops to open fire to disperse rioters. A boy was shot dead when he was spotted tearing down a poster of de Gaulle in Beirut. When Casey visited to make his own appraisal he confirmed that tensions were increasing and the situation would 'soon be potentially very dangerous'.[13]

Two years earlier Spears had claimed that the 'peoples of the Levant and the immense Arab populations behind only have me to express their fears and apprehensions', and it was into this role that he now threw himself.[14] He spoke at a demonstration of Lebanese women who, according to one onlooker, 'went wild when he addressed them'.[15] He visited the aftermath of demonstrations that took place across Beirut, reporting that he had found bullet marks in the tarmac proving the French were not shooting in the air as they had claimed. And in case the Foreign Office were not inclined to take his word for it, he helped the journalists whom Casey had sent to

Beirut wire their reports home, while exercising what he called 'an unofficial censorship to ensure objectivity'.[16] Separately, he persuaded two members of parliament who had previously worked for him on the mission to ask awkward questions in London about the crisis.

In a situation where diplomacy had failed, Spears's raw courage suddenly became an asset. When his car was held up by a French soldier at gunpoint, he leapt from the vehicle and broke his swagger stick over the soldier's head. One of his officials, who had previously described him as 'completely vain, selfish and full of a politician's trickery', was won over.[17] 'The Gen behaved like a roaring lion,' he wrote, impressed by the way that Spears 'took part himself in the fight and smashed his walking stick'.[18]

Once again, Casey also came to Spears's aid. He gave Georges Catroux a chilly reception when, on 15 November, the French general passed through Cairo on his way to Beirut to try to solve the crisis. The Australian listened unsympathetically as Catroux 'ploughed over a lot of old ground' and rehearsed the argument de Gaulle had told him to make, which was that British interference would force the French to pull out of the Levant altogether – de Gaulle assumed that Britain would not want to devote more resources to defending and administering the region on its own.[19] Casey insisted that the French must quickly release and reinstate the Lebanese ministers *and* remove Helleu before the Lebanese revolted. In a second, private, meeting Catroux was reduced to pleading. If Helleu was recalled and the Lebanese government restored, he said, it would represent 'a complete loss of face' for the French.[20] In his diary, Casey recalled that he had told Catroux that he did not really care. 'The composite picture wasn't a very rosy one for him, but, as I said, the complex wasn't of my making.'[21]

Spears dismissed the threat that the French might leave the Levant as 'sheer blackmail', and reacted angrily to what he suspected was an effort to buy time.[22] Having already reminded London that the two cabinet ministers who had escaped the dawn arrests were organising armed resistance in the mountains outside Beirut, he argued that the British 'simply cannot afford to plunge these countries in bloodshed and chaos out of regard for French "face". To do so would be quite incompatible with our good name throughout the world.'

Crucially, Churchill agreed with his old retainer. The prime minister would not allow the French to have their way because he believed that his own reputation was at stake. A clause in the Atlantic Charter that he had signed committed him 'to see sovereign rights and self government restored to those who have been forcibly deprived of them'. Awkwardly, he was also trying to persuade a sceptical Roosevelt to recognise the French Committee for National Liberation as a French government-in-waiting, which effectively meant accepting de Gaulle as president-to-be since the latter had by now outmanoeuvred Giraud for the chairmanship of this body.

Given that de Gaulle's apparent support for the coup in Lebanon reinforced Roosevelt's concerns that the Frenchman had dictatorial tendencies, there was no way that Churchill could accept what de Gaulle had done. When the news reached him that the Free French leader had again publicly dismissed the Lebanese government's move and privately threatened to resign, the British prime minister decided it was time to call the general's bluff. At Churchill's insistence, the war cabinet informed Casey that if there was still no progress by the end of 18 November he was to fly to Beirut the following day and present Catroux with an ultimatum. The French would have until 10 o'clock in the morning of the 22nd to release the ministers, or the British would declare martial law.

Casey was astonished when he received his order, though, since it made no mention of the *reinstatement* of the ministers. Rightly suspecting that Macmillan was trying to save de Gaulle's face, he immediately protested to Churchill and Eden. Eden initially tried to justify the omission, saying that to demand the ministers' reinstatement would simply ensure deadlock, but Churchill sided with Casey. 'Have the ministers been released and reinstated?' he pungently repeated later the same day.[23] The war cabinet agreed to fudge the issue for the moment, agreeing that release alone was not enough, but asked Casey to avoid explicitly demanding reinstatement for the time being.

Casey met Catroux in Beirut in the afternoon of the 19th. 'This is another Fashoda,' Catroux replied when Casey presented him with the ultimatum.[24] As at Fashoda, the French had no choice but to concede, because a British armoured brigade had taken up position on the Beirut golf course. Late the following morning Catroux went to see Spears to tell him that the French Committee for National Liberation had agreed to release and reinstate the president, but would only release the prime minister and his cabinet. Late the same day the Committee voted to recall Helleu. There were only three dissenters who held out against the return of Riad as-Sulh to office. The British believed that one of them was de Gaulle.

In the meantime, Eden came round to the prime minister's view. He resented his lack of control over Macmillan, who was responsible for liaison with the Free French in Algiers, and relished the opportunity to put his junior minister back in his place. The same day he bluntly told Macmillan that the idea of releasing but not reinstating the government was 'no solution', and reassured Casey that there was 'no question whatever' of negotiating with the French to set up a new and unconstitutional government, as de Gaulle evidently hoped might be arranged.[25]

The closure of the split within the British government left the French Committee with no choice. Late on 21 November it bowed to the inevitable. They announced that they were recalling Helleu and releasing and reinstating the president, Beshara al-Khoury. In Beirut a crowd of forty thousand people celebrated when the president and his ministers were released the next day.

The French Committee's statement contained what Macmillan described as 'an intentional ambiguity' about the position of the cabinet, whom it hoped the president would not reinstate.[26] But when al-Khoury refused to appoint a new government, Catroux had no option but to acquiesce. Catroux ignored de Gaulle's order and reinstated the cabinet. Helleu's cabal of advisers left soon afterwards.

Catroux still hoped that it might be possible for France to agree a treaty with the Lebanese, and Eden, reverting to his normal pro-French posture, concurred. The British foreign secretary told Spears that he should work for a situation in which the French would have

Churchill and de Gaulle in Paris, Armistice Day 1944. Days after the assassination of Lord Moyne, de Gaulle insisted that France was not conspiring against Britain in Palestine, but during the next three years Paris was to provide a safe haven for Zionist terrorists operating against Britain.

Avraham Stern. The help Stern and his gang received from the Vichy French was maintained by the Free French.

Lord Moyne. Moyne, the most fervent backer of Britain's Greater Syria plan to oust France from the Levant, was murdered by the Stern Gang in November 1944, just as the plan appeared to be coming to fruition. © Getty Images

Bevin and Attlee, January 1946. 'Clem,' Bevin said to Attlee one day, 'about Palestine. According to the lads in the Office, we've got it wrong. We've got to think again.' © Getty Images

Betty Knout. The Jewish former member of the French Resistance tried unsuccessfully to bomb the Colonial Office in London in 1947.
© *Daily Express*, 25 August 1948

Jewish refugees, survivors of Buchenwald, leave France by ship for Palestine in June 1945. Despite promising the British otherwise, the French government made no attempt to stop Jews emigrating to Palestine in large numbers after the war. On the right, wearing the armband, is a representative of the Oeuvre de Secours aux Enfants, a French Jewish charity. © Memorial de la Shoah/CDJC

Marlon Brando, Paul Muni and Celia Adler in *A Flag Is Born*. Premièred in September 1946 ahead of the mid-term elections, the Broadway play raised funds for the Irgun, and Palestine as a political issue in the United States. © Time & Life Pictures/ Getty Images

Jewish refugees are forced to disembark from the *Exodus* in Haifa, 20 July 1947. The ship carried a large number of pregnant women and young mothers to emphasise the brutality of Britain's unyielding policy on immigration in Palestine. © Getty Images

Georges Bidault (centre) at the United Nations, September 1947. To retaliate for Britain's wartime intrigues in the Levant, the French foreign minister authorised arms shipments to the Irgun.

Fawzi Qawukji, March 1948. Arab infighting in 1948 ruined the veteran
rebel's hopes of defeating Jewish forces. © Time & Life Pictures/Getty Images

King Abdullah (in white) visits Jerusalem, June 1948. Britain vested its hopes of maintaining Middle Eastern influence in 'Mr Bevin's little king' after its position in Palestine became untenable.
© Time & Life Pictures/Getty Images

W. F. Stirling in conversation with an Arab shaykh in Syria. After the Lebanese gained their independence from France in 1943, the British tried hard to engineer a similar outcome in Syria.
© Time & Life Pictures/Getty Images

a position in the Levant corresponding to Britain's in Iraq. But Spears instantly rejected this. It would be a 'mockery', he said, to force the Lebanese to sign a treaty that conferred 'strategic advantages in their own territory upon a Power which from long experience they dislike and fear'.[27] In fact, when the legally trained al-Khoury met Catroux, he used a neater argument that was both less emotional and more humiliating. Turning de Gaulle's familiar argument about his powerlessness to end the mandate back against him, al-Khoury said that the Lebanese government would not negotiate a treaty with the French Committee, 'since that body could not bind a future French government'. Catroux returned to Algiers looking 'rather tired and depressed'.[28]

Spears reported al-Khoury's put-down to London with unconcealed relish. Triumphantly, he reminded the Foreign Office of the three threats that de Gaulle had made but never carried out, and reported the petty humiliations to which the Lebanese cabinet had been subjected by the French during their captivity. On Christmas Eve his lover and secretary summed up the situation as she saw it in a letter home. 'British prestige is now sky high in the whole of the Middle East, and the people say that General Spears has achieved what Lawrence failed to do – he has made Arab unity a reality.'[29] This was hyperbole, but it reflected what Spears thought of himself.

Although the security apparatus remained under French control, the civil functions of the French Délégation-Générale were finally transferred to the Lebanese and Syrian governments on 1 January 1944. Later in the month, *The Times* reporter Gerald Norman wrote a long appreciation of events in the Levant and their significant implications. Without naming Spears specifically, he acknowledged the role that the British envoy had played in reporting news that neither the British nor the United States governments could then ignore. Both governments 'certainly were in part prompted by the fear of jeopardizing allied credit elsewhere. They were also encouraged by the indignation which the first Press messages about the crises had provoked. By their decision in this case they set a precedent to which appeal will certainly be made.'[30]

Spears was triumphant, but the victory came at considerable

personal cost. Once the crisis had passed, other British officials in the Levant began to think that he had overstepped the mark. One wrote that he believed Spears was 'at least 75% responsible for all the trouble here', while another was disturbed by the powerful emotions that Britain's envoy had managed to arouse: 'Our popularity here is so great that it is almost alarming.'[31] *The Times*'s correspondent Norman, too, was perturbed by the behaviour of Britain's senior representative in the Levant. While censorship prevented him from making his concerns public, he told the new British ambassador to the French Committee for National Liberation, Duff Cooper, that he believed Spears had exaggerated the incidents he reported, and confirmed that the French regarded the British minister with 'the most intense and violent hatred'.[32] What he did not know was that some within the French administration had already made an astonishing alliance as a means of getting their revenge.

FRIENDS IN NEED

ON 29 FEBRUARY 1944 THE FRENCH CONSUL IN JERUSALEM, Guy du Chaylard, informed his boss René Massigli that he had been contacted by two Jewish terrorist groups, the Irgun Zvai Leumi and the Stern Gang. The Irgun had originally been formed in the 1930s to fight the Arabs; the Stern Gang had splintered from it in a dis-agreement over policy. Both had just launched violent campaigns against the British in Palestine. The Irgun, which sent du Chaylard a copy of its 'declaration of war' against the British, had bombed the customs and excise offices in Jerusalem, Haifa and Tel Aviv. Not to be outdone, the Stern Gang shot dead two policemen in Haifa. Under cover of a letter in which he described these latest attacks, du Chaylard sent copies of the items he had received to Free French headquarters in Algiers.

From the Stern Gang du Chaylard had received an article on the previous November's Lebanese crisis which had been published in the Gang's newsletter, *Hechazit*. While it is easy to see why terrorists fighting for independence would be interested in the precedent the Lebanon had set, the article was surprising, for quite deliberately it took a line that was very sympathetic towards the French. Blaming the British for precipitating the crisis, it praised France's 'swift and energetic' effort to arrest the Lebanese cabinet, who were 'the agents of England'.[1] It ended: 'The Zionist Resistance Movement and Free France have very clear common interests. Sooner or later the French will recognise it.' If that seemed a bold prediction, its note of confidence arose from the fact that the Gang knew it was already halfway there. For by then, some members of the French administration in the Levant were already secretly supporting Zionist terrorists who shared their determination to root the British out of Palestine.

That confluence of interest dated back to September 1940, when David Hacohen, whose company had built Tegart's fence, agreed to put up three Free French activists in his Haifa home. At that point Vichy still controlled neighbouring Syria and Lebanon, and the Free French and the Haganah, the secret Jewish defence organisation, both agreed that Britain was not treating its threat seriously enough. When the British refused to allow the Free French to broadcast propaganda into Syria, Hacohen, who was a Haganah member, allowed the three to set up a secret radio transmitter in his house so that Radio 'Levant France Libre' could go on air regardless. There was a simple reason why the Zionists were willing to help. As the head of the political department at the Jewish Agency put it, 'despite the difficulties of today, the Free French will play an important role in the France of tomorrow and we are right to hope that they will not forget the sympathy shown them by Jewish Jerusalem when France found itself in distress'.[2]

As Hacohen's house overlooked the harbour in Haifa, the three Frenchmen were eyewitnesses to a tragedy that took place there on 25 November 1940. In the dock that day a large cruise ship named the *Patria* was preparing to set sail for Mauritius. Her passengers were unwilling, however, for they were Jewish refugees from Germany who had attempted to claim asylum in Palestine. On arrival they had been detained by the British authorities, who were determined to enforce the immigration restrictions of the 1939 White Paper and argued that among the refugees there might be German agents provocateurs set on stirring up an ethnic conflagration in Palestine.

The *Patria* never left the port. On the morning of the 25th, as the last deportees were being pressed up the gangway, there was a resounding explosion aboard and the ship rolled on to its side. Despite frantic efforts by the British to extract those trapped within, in all two hundred and sixty-three died.

It was immediately obvious that sabotage was likely, and the Frenchmen cornered Hacohen, since they knew that the Haganah opposed British efforts to deport incoming Jewish refugees. 'We stood there mouths open,' recalled one of them, Raymond Schmittlein, as Hacohen admitted that the cause of the blast had been a mine that Haganah had smuggled aboard to cripple the vessel so that it could not depart.[3] Hacohen then asked them whether they thought that modern Jews lacked Samson's courage. 'That won us over,' Schmittlein said. 'A national determination of that order could not but triumph.'

Cooperation between these two minorities, which were both frustratingly dependent on the British and both struggling to win their freedom, grew from there. The Haganah put its intelligence network in Syria at the disposal of the Free French, and provided valuable intelligence until its leading agent gave himself away to the head of the Sûreté Générale in the Levant, Colombani. Hacohen himself took a message from the Free French to Damascus, inviting the chief French official in the city to defect. And when the invasion of the Levant was finally agreed in 1941, the Haganah provided members of its elite commando unit, the Palmach, to act as guides when the advance began on 8 June. Although, as one of them, Moshe Dayan, recalled, 'not one of us knew Syria' and the Palmach in turn hired an Arab to show them the way, it was the thought that counted.[4] At a time of crisis the Zionists had shown their willingness to help the French.

The relationship between the Free French and the Zionists was to develop significantly over the next year, as Jewish anger at Britain's immigration policy grew following a further maritime catastrophe that involved another ship crammed with Jewish refugees, the *Struma*. After the *Patria* disaster, the British would not allow the overladen *Struma*, which set sail from Romania in December 1941, near Palestinian shores. The ship spent eight weeks in port in Istanbul, while the British government, by now well aware of the awful fate that its passengers were desperate to flee, argued over what it should do. When the British finally announced that they would not allow the ship to proceed to Palestine, it was towed back into the Black Sea. Barely had it left Istanbul when there was an

explosion, probably caused by either a mine or a torpedo of uncertain origin. All but one of the *Struma*'s 769 passengers drowned. Not
surprisingly, there was an outcry in Palestine.

Speak
the
Truth

While the British prevaricated about the *Struma*, one man decided
to take action. Thirty-four-year-old Avraham Stern was a dandyish
classical scholar and poet whose hero was Eliezer ben Yair, one of the
zealots who in the first century AD had held out against the Romans
at Masada before committing suicide to avoid capture. Previously
responsible for the Irgun's foreign relations, Stern had left after dis-
agreeing with the group's early policy of collaborating with the
British. He believed that the Jews should aid the British war effort
only after the British had given the Zionists their independence. When
it became clear that they had no such plans, in 1940 Stern had passed
a message into Vichy Syria, offering to fight for Germany if Hitler
would support 'the re-establishment of the Jewish state in its historic
borders, on a national and totalitarian basis, allied to the German
Reich'.[5] Stern's strange offer seems to have come to the attention of
Colombani, who relayed it to the German embassy in Ankara.

After waiting in vain for a reply from Hitler, at the start of 1942
Stern launched a short-lived campaign of violence by which he hoped
to force the British government to give the Jews in Palestine their
independence. Desperately short of money, his gang robbed a bank
run by their ideological opposites, the Histadrut, but killed two
Jewish bystanders. Two of the three Palestine policemen they murdered in a bombing days later were also Jewish. The Gang had
quickly made a lot of enemies, and when the police offered a reward
for information they soon received a tip-off about its members'
whereabouts. A week after the bank robbery the police raided a house
in Tel Aviv, killing two men and wounding two more, one of whom,
from his hospital bed, then inadvertently gave away Stern's location.

On 12 February Stern was found hiding in a wardrobe at a flat in the
same city, after his damp shaving brush betrayed his presence. As he
made a lunge for a window while putting on his clothes, he was shot
dead on the spot by two British policemen, Stanley Hancock and
Geoffrey Morton. In a report the following day Morton claimed that he
and Hancock had fired "practically simultaneously" and justified their
action by quoting a note written by Stern declaring, 'I shall not keep

quiet until I fall in battle', that he had found *afterwards* on the prem-
ises.[6] The circumstances of the killing remain murky. Hancock soon
after left the police and Morton never mentioned his colleague's involvement again. But as he later put it, 'I was no armchair policeman.'[7]

The Palestine Police closed in quickly on the remnants of the
Gang, which was in a state of turmoil after its charismatic leader's
death. Following another tip-off, at the end of April the police
arrested twelve more members. By 19 May the chief of the force
believed that only two 'known important members' of the Gang
were still at large, but he urged against complacency.[8] Alive, Stern
had been almost friendless, but the controversial circumstances of his
death and the uproar over the *Struma*, which sank days afterwards,
seemed belatedly to justify his anger, the police chief suggested, and
had led some Zionists 'to wonder if Stern's "idealism" was not, after
all, worthy of serious thought'.

It was at this point that the British police discovered that it was not
just other Zionists who were giving the Stern Gang serious thought.
One day in the spring of 1942, as relations between the British and
the French deteriorated following the return of Spears to Beirut, the
head of the Palestine Police's Criminal Investigation Department,
Arthur Giles, strode into the office of Patrick Coghill, Britain's chief
counter-espionage officer in the Levant. 'My God,' exclaimed Giles.
'These French are the bloody limit. Do you know what they are up to
now?'[9] Coghill did not, so Giles went on to explain.

Three days earlier, said the veteran detective, his department had
received a tip-off that a taxi had just left Jerusalem carrying three
members of the Stern Gang northwards. His detectives had caught
up with the car in Tiberias and had followed it from there to the
Lebanese border. There, they had seen three Jews being welcomed
into Lebanon by a French officer. Coghill immediately appreciated
Giles's implication. It looked 'as if the French were helping and using
the Stern Gang – a matter of such seriousness that it could not be
laughed off. Giles was indeed spitting with rage.'[10]

Giles could not nip this shocking association in the bud, however,
because Coghill needed to cover up an embarrassing incident himself. Far from sharing Giles's anger, Coghill was secretly delighted,
for the timing of the discovery was a godsend. Relations between

him and his opposite number in the Sûreté Générale, already awkward, were about to become a great deal worse. The Sûreté had just
caught an agent of Britain's Special Operations Executive acting far
beyond his remit by trying to entice a French soldier into selling arms
to him illegally. Not only did the incident encapsulate French allegations of British intrigue, but worse still, the same individual had
days earlier taken potshots at Catroux's car when it had passed him
while he was on a drinking spree in Damascus. Coghill was praying
that the French would not connect the two. If they did, they were
bound to accuse the British of trying to assassinate Catroux.

Seeing an opportunity to draw a line under this affair, Coghill
raised Giles's similarly grave allegations with the head of the French
intelligence service in the Levant, Colonel Emblanc. Clearly horri-
fied, Emblanc said he knew nothing about the matter but would
investigate. 'The next day,' recalled Coghill, Emblanc 'arrived all
smiles and announced that our SOE Englishman would be handed
over at once and nothing more said'.[11] The French intelligence chief
explained that the French had been recruiting stay-behind agents
from the Jewish population, just as SOE had been, and that it was
three of these men who had crossed the border.

Relieved that 'a major row had been avoided', Coghill was left to
persuade the CID that the three Stern Gang members had got out of
the taxi in Tiberias and, conveniently, the three Jews recruited by the
French had then hailed the same cab and taken it to the frontier. This
implausible explanation was left looking flimsier still by the fact
that, at about this time, one of the Gang members who was still at
large was arrested inside Syria.[12]

Years later a former member of the Stern Gang confirmed that the
Vichy administration in Beirut had 'gladly supplied us with arms of
all kinds, knowing that they were intended to attack their British
enemy'.[13] What the episode proves is that this traffic did not stop following the 1941 invasion: it was maintained by the former Vichy
officials whom de Gaulle had retained in post. Indeed, it was when
Colonel Emblanc, who had joined the Free French, resigned soon
afterwards in protest at the activities of Blanchet, the Anglophobe
military adviser within the Délégation-Générale, that the British first
realised the baleful influence of the cabal of former Vichy officials

running the French government of the Levant. By the end of 1942 the local representative of Britain's security service, MI5, believed that it was the 'small minority of determined and cunning Vichyists' in the French administration, and not the Germans, who were now the 'chief danger' to Britain in the Levant.[14]

Boegner and Baelen resigned when Helleu was replaced at the end of 1943, and this was why the Stern Gang was having to look for French support again by the beginning of 1944.[15] Having nearly been snuffed out by the British police in 1942, the Gang's prospects had dramatically improved when in November 1943, just as France was embroiled in the Lebanese crisis, twenty of its members tunnelled their way out of a prison camp in Latrun, fifteen miles west of Jerusalem. But when it restarted its terror campaign the following January, it still had the same basic problem. As one of its leading members, Yitzhak Shamir, later recalled, 'we badly needed financial resources, to build up bases, to buy arms, to pay for our broadcasts and pamphlets, to keep ourselves alive'.[16] Robbery seemed again to be the only option, but, as Shamir acknowledged, 'however essential the break-ins and hold-ups were for us, they added markedly to public indignation and lack of sympathy'.[17]

The answer, the Stern Gang decided, was to appeal to the French for help. It hoped that the French, having been so recently humiliated by the British in the Lebanon, might make common cause against the enemy they shared. This was why they sent du Chaylard first the article dissecting the Lebanese crisis, and then, in April 1944, the first issue of their new French-language publication, *Front de Combat Hébreu*. This described itself as being aimed at 'the French, and people of French culture, in the countries bordering on Israel', and it portrayed 'England, all the while flying the flag of democracy', as 'our main enemy'.[18] That was a sentiment with which many Frenchmen in the Levant could heartily agree. They would also have noticed that the appeal was written by a native French speaker.

The Gang was quick to highlight similarities between itself and the French Resistance. The next issue of *Front de Combat Hébreu* described one Zionist emerging from the *maquis* – the scrub from which the Resistance in the south of France took their name. It also made a reference to the communist French Resistance group, the

Francs-Tireurs Partisans, in a comment on the difficulty the British would have in dealing with the Stern Gang's campaign in Palestine 'with a sledgehammer, because the *francs-tireurs* fire their shot and disappear'.[19] A later Stern Gang publication circulated in France made the comparison more explicitly still. 'Our approach is simple. It is to work clandestinely in an occupied country: an underground war, where invisible, elusive soldiers undermine the immense imperialist machine.'[20]

These efforts to win French favour became public in June that year, at the trial of two of the Stern Gang's young members who had been arrested in Tel Aviv. The trial attracted significant publicity because, for the first time, one of the defendants was female, but it was a document found on her male accomplice that was of just as much significance. Written in French, it explained the goals of the Stern Gang, and asked for help from 'foreign powers whose interests were identical to theirs'.[21] The president of the court tried unsuccessfully to persuade the defendants to admit whom this appeal was destined for, although the language of the missive made it starkly obvious.

The defendant in another trial days later also hinted that the French were supporting the Stern Gang. Twenty-four-year-old Raphael Birnbaum was the first person to be arrested after the restoration of the 1938 law that made possession of a firearm a capital offence. Birnbaum refused a lawyer and in an eloquent defence commented that he had no doubt that, had he been Lebanese rather than Jewish, the British would have armed him to fight the French regime in the Levant. 'If Palestine itself was under the mandate of France, or another Nation,' he suggested, 'I am convinced that you, the British, would have given me arms.'[22] Birnbaum's death sentence was commuted to life imprisonment.

In July a worried du Chaylard wrote again to Massigli, to warn him that in a Hebrew-language publication the Stern Gang had all but admitted they were receiving foreign support.[23] He had also heard 'echoes of rumours' that Jewish terrorists in Palestine were being supplied by the French, and blamed the Stern Gang's French-language propaganda for sparking these reports. The Gang itself was blasé about its association with the French. At about this time they agreed on a tune that they could whistle to identify themselves to one another on an operation. It was the Marseillaise.[24]

Having grown increasingly confident, the Stern Gang now attempted its most audacious coup so far. On 8 August it tried to murder the outgoing high commissioner of Palestine, Sir Harold MacMichael, on his way to a farewell party given by some Arabs on the coast.[25] The invitation was public knowledge, as MacMichael's willingness to accept it had been criticised in a right-wing Jewish newspaper the day before, and the Gang had time to plan an ambush.

They set their trap at the point where the road from Jerusalem began its serpentine descent from the hills on to the coastal plain. On a wide bend they shot up the high commissioner's motorcycle out-riders, who were out in front, and the police car bringing up the rear. By simultaneously setting fire to a slick of oil across the road, they brought the MacMichaels' old Rolls-Royce to a standstill at a point where there was seemingly nowhere to hide: to the right was precipice, to the left, a cliff. It was MacMichael's driver who saved their lives. He rammed the car into the left-hand side of the road where it was better protected from the bullets coming from above by a slight overhang in the cliff, and hard to push over the precipice to the right. A friend of the MacMichaels recalled, 'They had a very narrow escape'.[26]

Perhaps because MacMichael survived, or because he was shortly due to leave, the British reacted lethargically to the attack on their chief representative in Palestine. The police imposed a collective fine of £500 on the nearest settlement, but three months later had still not enforced its payment. Although the attack was clearly political in motivation, no sanctions were imposed on the wider Jewish community, even though the Jewish Agency's condemnation of the ambush was mealy-mouthed.

From Cairo, Casey's successor as minister of state, Lord Moyne, argued that both these failings were unwise. 'Opinion in these countries can hardly fail to draw a comparison with the prompt and stern action taken against the Arabs after the assassination of Mr Andrews in 1937,' he said.[27] A few days later, after he had failed to stir up London, he sent a further telegram. To demonstrate his fears, this time he quoted from a speech just given by David Ben-Gurion, in which the Jewish Agency executive's chairman stated: 'We shall migrate to Palestine in order to constitute a majority here. If there be need – we shall take by force; if the country be too small – we shall expand the boundaries.'

Ben-Gurion's statement was, Moyne worried, 'in effect an incitement to violence'.[28] Little did he know that he was soon to be its highest-profile victim.

23

TROP DE ZÈLE

'A QUIET LITTLE MAN, WEARING A BOW TIE AND AN AERTEX shirt', who was 'interested in most things, wild flowers and animals, Colonial administration, New Guinea, yachting', Lord Moyne did not look like the most formidable threat to Zionist and French aspirations in the Middle East.[1] But, as Britain's leading advocate of a 'Greater Syria', that was what he was by August 1944. Like Spears, the new minister of state in Cairo owed his job to the fact that he was an old friend of Churchill, but unlike Spears, whose credibility was by now waning fast, Moyne was a member of the cabinet and wielded real influence. In particular, his colleagues respected his zealous backing of an Arab state that was designed to protect British interests in the Middle East and defuse tensions over Zionism in Palestine.

Although an unassuming man, Moyne personified the confidence of the British Empire at its height.[2] He had been born into the Guinness brewing family in 1880, and his career had followed a familiar trajectory. After Eton he joined the British army, and after active service in South Africa he entered parliament. His passions were big-game hunting and adventure. 'Frequently,' the author of his obituary later marvelled, 'he travelled accompanied only by natives.'[3] When he stepped down from parliament after the Conservatives lost the 1929 election, he returned to exploration, bringing back live Komodo dragons to London Zoo.

Moyne's friendship with Churchill dated to the period in the 1920s when he had served as a Treasury minister while Churchill was chancellor of the exchequer. With their shared appetite for adventure the two men got on well, and Churchill cajoled his 'most agreeable, intelligent and unusual friend' back into the government in 1941, as secretary of state for the colonies – a job that made him responsible for Palestine.[4]

It was as colonial secretary in September 1941 that Moyne circulated a memorandum on 'Jewish Policy' in which he wondered whether British support for a Greater Syria might ease the tension that renewed Jewish immigration into Palestine was bound to cause. 'I have every sympathy with the plight of the Jews and I am sure we must give our minds seriously to a solution of their problems,' he wrote. 'But the more I think about it the more convinced I become that Palestine alone cannot provide the solution.'[5] One option to reduce the pressure that such an influx was bound to cause was to create the Arab federation to which Eden had referred in his speech in May that year. Although Moyne did not think it was the complete answer, he thought the idea was 'attractive'.

Three months later, he failed to show any sympathy for the plight of the Jewish refugees aboard the *Struma*, however, insisting that to allow them to proceed from Istanbul to Palestine would be 'in flat contradiction to government policy'.[6] When he was moved out of the Colonial Office soon afterwards, he made a speech in parliament that has since been criticised as anti-Semitic because of comments he made about the Jews' ethnic purity.[7] Yet this is to miss the far more striking point that he made – that the Zionists were 'far too narrow in their outlook' and that the British government should investigate whether the neighbouring governments of Lebanon, Syria and Transjordan would be willing to offer asylum to Jewish immigrants.[8] 'It would be physically possible for those States, if they were willing, to absorb large numbers of Jews to mutual advantage, and without any threat to their own political independence,' he argued. In this respect, he proposed that 'a Federation of the Northern Arab States might well assist such a solution'.

Thus Moyne made his support for 'Greater Syria' public, in a speech that was as thoroughly radical as it seemed impracticable. Yet it was not entirely far-fetched. Although his idea that the Arab states surrounding Palestine might accept Jewish immigration was surely wishful thinking, the president of the Hebrew University in Jerusalem and other Jewish academics told the British government the same year that they supported the idea of an autonomous Jewish entity within a broader Arab federation.[9]

Soon afterwards, when Moyne was appointed deputy to Richard Casey in Cairo, he was able to give the Arab federation much more thought, not least because he had little else to do. 'The only alternative to the White Paper,' he mused at the start of 1943, 'seems to be a bargain with the Arab States and we have no inducements to offer unless we could link up a Palestine settlement with the evacuation of Syria by the French.'[10] That May, the Middle East War Council, which he chaired, decided that France's presence in the region was no longer in British interests.

At this point, British support for 'Greater Syria' was not official policy. But that July Moyne was invited to join a secret cabinet committee set up by Churchill to rethink the government's approach on Palestine when the 1939 White Paper lapsed in April 1944. When the committee reported five months later it recommended that, once Germany had been defeated, Palestine should be divided between the Arabs and the Jews, along similar lines to those proposed by Peel seven years before. To defuse the 'heartburning and disappointment' that such a split would inevitably provoke, the committee also proposed that the British government should back the creation of a Greater Syria comprising 'Syria, Trans-Jordan, the Arab residue of Palestine and the portion of Lebanon south and east of Sidon' – evidence of Moyne's influence on the report.[11] This would put Britain on a crash course with France, but then, as another member of the committee wrote to Moyne, 'only the elimination of the French influence can mean anything like a satisfactory settlement of the Middle East'.[12]

When the cabinet finally discussed the plan in January 1944, Moyne said it was crucial that work to create a Greater Syria should start immediately. The minutes of the meeting record him arguing: 'It would be very unfortunate if, owing to a delay in dealing with [the] matter, we missed an opportunity of transferring the Arab areas in Palestine to Greater Syria as a concession, and waited till we were faced with a demand on the matter.'[13] Although the cabinet formally endorsed the plan, and sanctioned 'other necessary preliminary action' required to implement it, the fear of uproar in the Middle East if its details leaked out made it impossible to do more for the time being. The Colonial Office introduced an ad hoc arrangement permitting some Jewish immigration and, amid hopes that the war might end within the year, British policy was left to drift.

When Moyne succeeded Casey as minister of state at the start of 1944 his task was therefore complex. He interpreted 'other necessary preliminary action' to include work on his pet project, but the need to maintain the strictest secrecy tied his hands. He also quickly realised that many of his colleagues in the Middle East had doubts about the plan. The ambassadors in Cairo and Baghdad registered their reservations after encouragement from Eden, who was himself now sceptical about Greater Syria, and in Palestine Harold MacMichael raised his worry that the Syrians would not accept Abdullah as their king.

Moyne accepted this concern and, that April, he agreed with MacMichael that while they should continue to support the Greater Syria project, they would not actively encourage it until France's future position in the Levant was clearer. To guard against the possibility that the French might take advantage of Greater Syria to extend their influence 'half-way to the Suez Canal', they also decided to break the plan in two.[14] The first step would be the union of the Arab areas of Palestine with Transjordan, under Abdullah's leadership. The second stage would be a broader union of this area with Syria and Lebanon. Given both men's fears that French influence might spread, the ousting of their ancient rival was the unspoken prerequisite of that second step. That prospect does not seem to have perturbed Lord Moyne. Reportedly, he was willing to 'throw the French to the wolves – or to the Arabs – in order to put our Palestine settlement across'.[15]

Soon afterwards the British in the Levant began working to assess and encourage Arab support for the two stages of the Greater Syria plan, despite the fact that there was no deep support in London for the policy. One of those involved in this work was W. F. Stirling, the man who had driven into Damascus with T. E. Lawrence just over a quarter of a century earlier. Called back to serve in Syria as a political officer in 1941, Stirling was posted to Damascus at the beginning of June 1944 to act as Commander of the Desert and Frontier Areas and liaison officer between the British army and the Syrian president, Shukri al-Quwatli.[16] His close friendship with leading shaykhs and his connection with Lawrence disturbed the French, who were alarmed when he immediately met the Syrian prime minister for dinner and was dubbed 'Chief of the tribes of Syria and Transjordan' by one local newspaper.[17]

Recently declassified French archives show that French agents trailed Stirling wherever he went. Their surveillance generated a fat file on the British colonel, and confirmed that their suspicions were well founded, for Stirling was clearly interested in matters that went far beyond his vague remit. In a series of meetings with Syrian dignitaries he asked leading questions like What do you think about Arab Unity? What is your opinion of the current government? How do you see the future of Syria?[18] Usually, the French observed, the respondents asked for British help.

Stirling asked another shaykh – a significant religious leader – a question hinting that the British were also interested in negotiating a treaty directly with the Syrians that would preserve their influence in the country. 'If there was an appeal to your excellency for an effective or consultative collaboration,' Stirling asked, 'could Great Britain count on your personal influence to serve your country while also safeguarding general British interests?'[19]

'If Great Britain sincerely recognises this country's legal rights and its independence ... I think that all honest people will extend it a loyal hand,' the shaykh replied.[20]

Secret British government files, which have similarly only recently been declassified, now explain why Stirling had asked this question.[21] Days before Stirling's arrival in Damascus, Spears had received a letter from the Syrian foreign minister, Jamil Mardam, proposing 'an official agreement' between Syria and Britain to prevent the French regaining control over the Levant.[22]

The clue to why Jamil Mardam wrote the letter lies in his

description in it of President Shukri al-Quwatli as a 'creature of colonisation'.[23] Just as the French had hoped, the new nationalist government in Syria was bitterly divided over the question of how to make Arab unity a reality. The pro-Saudi al-Quwatli, who fiercely disliked the Hashemites, was a potential stumbling block to Britain's plans to join Arab Palestine with Transjordan, and ultimately Syria and Lebanon. Mardam, on the other hand, favoured the Hashemite Abdullah as the monarch of a united Iraq, Syria and Transjordan, and had already signed a declaration with the Iraqi prime minister in April committing both men to 'strive for the formation of an Arab Hashemite state including Syria'.[24] That was why Mardam wanted British help, and why the increasingly ebullient Spears was willing to assist him. 'My goal is simple,' the British minister was reported to have told a journalist at about this time. 'I want to chase the French out of the Levant. France is completely decadent. It would be stupid to believe that it would be good policy after the war to associate with her.'[25]

On 5 June 1944 (the day before D-Day) Spears met secretly with Mardam and the Syrian prime minister, Saadallah Jabri. He told both men that, in the event that they agreed to sign a treaty with Britain alone, the British government would support whichever form of Arab federation they wanted. In exchange for commercial advantages for British companies he also promised Syria membership of the 'sterling bloc' to counter inflation, which was a growing problem. And finally he said that in further discussions they could explore other matters, including what rights other foreign companies should have and the question of the rearmament of the Syrian army.[26] Mardam wrote again the same day repeating his keenness to reach a deal. Expectantly, he now awaited a response.

By 9 July the French had found out about this secret meeting. Soon afterwards through an agent they acquired copies of the two letters Mardam had sent the British minister, and a summary of what Spears had promised Mardam. As Spears was simultaneously pressing the French to provide weapons for the Syrian gendarmerie, the information provided by the documents suggested that the purpose of these two tracks of activity was to give the Syrians both the incentive and the means to throw out the French themselves. The new delegate-general in the Levant, Paul Beynet, who replaced the alcoholic Jean Helleu and had served in the Levant as an intelligence officer during the Druze revolt, warned the French Committee for National Liberation that, if the Syrians tried to do so, he did not have sufficient troops to fight back.[27] And when he tried to parry Spears's demand, Spears prevailed upon the British army to offer the Syrians an arsenal of seven thousand rifles – seven times more than they had asked for – and several hundred automatic weapons, instead.

Other intelligence gleaned by the French, reinforced by the general sense that the war in Europe had entered its final phase, suggested that a climactic moment was approaching. The Syrian foreign minister, Jamil Mardam, stated in public that the plan for Arab unity was 'on the point of being realised', and through a spy in the British diplomatic legation in Beirut the French found out that the British were putting heavy pressure on the Syrians and the Lebanese to unite.[28] On 5 August, Gilbert MacKereth, who had by now joined Spears's mission, sent the Lebanese prime minister, Riad as-Sulh, to Damascus with a proposal responding to Mardam's June letter. It pledged that Britain would protect Syria from outside aggression, promised 'to put a complete stop to Jewish ambitions' and stated British support for the unification of Syria, Transjordan and Palestine under Abdullah.[29] Four days later the pro-Zionist newspaper the *Palestine Post* ran a story claiming that representatives of several Arab states would shortly meet in Alexandria to discuss a proposal that was uncannily similar. Although the Syrian government denied this newspaper report, the article fitted with France's secret intelligence and with the news days later that the Iraqi prime minister Nuri Said had met his Syrian and Lebanese counterparts and other nationalists at the end of July. One of them had pressed for action as fast as possible, while the British army remained in Syria and 'with England supporting this project'.[30] Reporting these various snippets to Massigli, the new delegate-general, Beynet, commented that together they all suggested that Arab unity was an idea of 'British origin'.[31]

In London the foreign secretary had no idea what was going on, although he could see that events in Syria were 'really troubling' Massigli.[32] 'I have no doubt,' he told the new British ambassador to the French Committee, Duff Cooper, 'that he is sincerely convinced, however mistakenly, that our local authorities are out to destroy what remains of the French position in Syria and never miss an opportunity in doing so.'

Although Eden did not yet know exactly why Massigli was so certain, he was aware that the French already had some embarrassing evidence of Spears's activities. In February that year Spears had sent Duff Cooper a colourful letter in which he claimed that the new counsellor in the Beirut Délégation-Générale, Stanislas Ostrorog, was an opium addict, and that Boegner and several others had been Cagoulards* before the war. Instead of being opened by the ambassador, however, the letter found its way to the *ambassadeur*, René Massigli, who read it. 'No more unfortunate document could possibly have come into French hands,' wailed Cooper when he discovered what it said.[33]

Spears could not care less, for he had long stopped bothering to disguise his contempt for the French. During the First World War, the assumption behind his liaison work had been that an effective alliance with the French was the only way to defeat the Germans, but his recent experience had made him question his earlier *raison d'être*. A month after D-Day, once the Allies had successfully established a bridgehead in Normandy, he told a friend that the experience of the past four years had proved 'that we can fight and win a war with a hostile France, or at least a France in hostile occupation'.[34] Since there was consequently no need 'to buy French friendship at all costs', he now argued that there was no need to propitiate de Gaulle, not least because he did not think the Frenchman would be 'reliable enough, if left in charge of the Levant to give us the absolute security we need for the Canal'.

Eden was by now desperate to be rid of this diplomatic liability, but so far Churchill had continued to protect his friend. When Eden

---

* The Cagoulards, who were named after the hooded coats they wore, were an extreme right-wing gang who murdered communists in pre-war France.

warned him that 'one of Spears' more pungent reports' had been intercepted by the French, the prime minister countered ten days later that Spears's input was 'very valuable'.[35] 'I look forward indeed to the day when we shall have the representatives of a clean France, decent, honest Frenchmen with whom we can work, instead of the émigré de Gaullists.'

Eden's opportunity arose over Spears's announcement that Britain would arm the Syrian gendarmerie, which he did without consulting London. Blocking the transfer of the weapons, Eden openly admitted to Massigli that he had twice asked Churchill in recent days for Spears's recall, and offered the Frenchman a compromise that involved the transfer of only two thousand rifles of the seven thousand the British envoy had originally promised to the Syrians. Days later he persuaded Churchill that it was time to call Spears back to London for a reprimand.

Massigli was aware of the pressure building up in London for Spears's removal, and the strenuous efforts being made in the Levant to achieve Arab unity, and decided that the moment had come to reveal to Eden his knowledge of the British minister's secretive activities. When he arrived in London for talks on the Levant on 21 August, days before the liberation of Paris, he submitted a note in which he accused the British of taking advantage of French weakness to extend their influence in the region. He refused to discuss the agenda further until Eden both addressed these concerns about British officials' interference and acknowledged (yet again) that France should have a privileged position in the Levant when the war was over.

Unaware of the trap that Massigli had dug for him, Eden denied the accusations his French counterpart had made. It was 'no part of the policy of His Majesty's Government', Eden told him, 'to supplant French influence in the Levant States', although he qualified that by saying that the government did not 'intend' that British personnel should be used against French interests.[36] Now, declaring himself unhappy with Eden's response, Massigli flourished the letters from Mardam and the transcript of what Spears had told the Syrian foreign minister, and put these to Eden as proof that 'Spears, while opposing the conclusion of a treaty between France and the States, was running negotiations for the conclusion of a treaty between the States and England'.[37] Eden, clearly mystified, denied that Spears's actions had official support. To ward off the implication of bad faith, he again told Massigli that he supported France's efforts to secure a treaty with both Levantine states. He immediately sent a telegram to the Spears Mission in Beirut ordering it not to satisfy Jamil Mardam's demands.

'Spears is compromised in writing,' Eden warned Churchill the following day. 'We cannot expect him to carry weight with the French any longer.'[38] Churchill, finally, agreed. The prime minister had warned Spears earlier in the year that, while he admired the 'efficiency and vigilance' of his old friend's work, 'surtout pas trop de zèle'. He now reproached Spears for failing to take his advice 'to try to keep your Francophobia within reasonable bounds'.[39] Observing that there was 'no doubt that great irritation is being felt by the French', he finally served Spears his notice. 'Two or three months will be the limit of your tenure out there.'

And so it proved. Spears returned to Beirut in September, but he no longer had the powers he had previously enjoyed. With Paris free, France and de Gaulle were both resurgent, and Spears now had very specific instructions from Eden to assist the French in achieving treaties with Lebanon and Syria. Moreover, while he had been in London, his mission had been dramatically pared down by his second-in-command, MacKereth. Spears railed against MacKereth, but MacKereth refused to budge. By now Spears was regarded as a handicap by many of his colleagues – even those who broadly shared his views. Towards the end of November, he finally received a request from Churchill for his resignation, which he offered on the 24th.

In the meantime the Foreign Office tried to clear up the mystery of Spears's meeting with Mardam that summer. 'I cannot help thinking that there must be some fire behind all this smoke,' one British diplomat wrote as the Eastern Department wondered how best to pursue the matter.[40] Briefly, they contemplated disguising the source of the documents and confronting Spears with the allegations they raised. But then they worried that Spears might claim that he had been recalled on the basis of false French accusations. The Foreign

Office decided it was best to let the matter rest. Although there was a danger of looking furtive by not responding directly to Massigli's allegations, as another member of the department put it, 'I think that the French would accept mentally that if these June talks were ever sponsored by HMG, they no longer represent our policy.'[41]

By the end of 1944, Spears was back in Britain. As it turned out, it was a good time to leave.

24

THE MURDER OF LORD MOYNE

As LORD MOYNE'S CAR SWUNG THROUGH THE GATES OF HIS Cairo home at lunchtime on 6 November 1944, the two young men who had been expecting the British minister's return slipped off the wall outside and hurried up the drive behind it. Ahead of them, the car had stopped, and Moyne's aide-de-camp and driver had already got out: the aide was heading towards the front door of the house, the driver passing around the back of his vehicle to open the car door for the minister of state.

'Don't move. Stay where you are. Don't move,' one of the two youths, Eliahu Hakim, told Moyne's aide, waving a long-barrelled revolver at him.[1] Hakim's accomplice, Eliahu Beth Tsouri, shot the driver dead at point-blank range. Hakim then thrust his pistol through the car door's open window, pointed it at Moyne, and fired three times. According to Moyne's secretary, who was sitting beside him in the car, 'Lord Moyne put his hand to his throat and said "Oh, they've shot us."'[2] The minister's last words were 'When will the doctor arrive?' Despite a blood transfusion, he died at eight o'clock that evening.[3]

By then both Hakim and Beth Tsouri were in police custody. As they fled the scene, Moyne's aide had run out on to the road after them and flagged down an Egyptian policeman on a motorcycle. The policeman gave chase, and rammed both assailants off the road as they tried to make their getaway. Hakim made no attempt to deny that he had killed the cabinet minister. 'I was sent by the organisation expressly to kill Lord Moyne,' he told police.[4] That organisation was the Stern Gang.

Almost three weeks later Duff Cooper, the British ambassador to de Gaulle's government, which had returned to Paris following the Allied liberation of the city, received a high-priority telegram from London instructing him to ask the French not to send a warship to the Levant. The message mystified him. 'They are worried,' he wrote, 'because the cruiser *Emile Bertin* is visiting Beirut, which they think may cause complications at a time when the situation in the east is strained as a result of the murder of Lord Moyne.' When he responded huffily that he 'could not see the connection between the murder of an English minister in Cairo by Jewish terrorists and the visit of a French ship to Syria', he rapidly received a reply from Eden telling him, obliquely, to do as he was told.[5] For there *was* a link, and recently declassified government files make it clear that it had been established by Britain's secret intelligence service, MI6.

Eight weeks earlier, and days after the liberation of Paris, MI6's station in the Levant had produced the first of three reports about a French intelligence officer named Colonel Alessandri. As a young officer Alessandri had served in Syria during the Druze revolt. Early in the war, he had been the military attaché at the Vichy French embassy in Tehran. Now, having swapped sides, he was in charge of a section of the Free French intelligence service known as the Bureau Noir. The Bureau's job was to counter British influence in the Middle East, and MI6 initially believed that Alessandri and his subordinates were only trying to stir up Arab anger in Palestine in retaliation for Britain's involvement in the Lebanese crisis the previous November.

Alessandri was no stranger to the British. Having allegedly defected to the Free French only because he wanted 'to enjoy the favours of some Frenchwoman in Syria', in 1943 he had clashed with a British political officer in Dayr az Zor over which of the two of them should be in control of the town, the most important in eastern Syria.[6] Like de Gaulle, Alessandri had argued that the fact that French troops outnumbered British in the area meant that he should be in charge, but his British counterpart disagreed. According to the British, Alessandri was a 'man of narrow outlook' who not only paid 'no attention to the implications of a world-wide war' but had openly vowed to protect French interests 'foot by foot and with his life'.[7] Alessandri seemed to be so deliberately trying to undermine British authority in the sensitive desert zone that in April 1943 the British had asked the then delegate-general, Helleu, to remove him.

Helleu acknowledged that Alessandri had 'always been violently anti-British'.[8] But although he was willing to withdraw the Anglophobic colonel from the town, he could not banish him from the Levant because of pressure from the all-powerful cabal of advisers behind him, who turned their colleague's treatment into a *cause célèbre*. As a consequence Alessandri remained in the Levant, and spent some time in command of a mountain brigade in the Lebanon. There, unlike his protectors in the Délégation-Générale, he managed to avoid being banished when Helleu was sacked in 1943. French army records for 1944 show that he was one of two heads of the intelligence service in the Levant.[9] He 'certainly comes under the heading "undesirable Frenchmen"', the British had noted, back in August 1943.[10]

What MI6 could not immediately say was whether Alessandri enjoyed official backing for his work within the Bureau Noir. Here, Spears's deputy, Gilbert MacKereth, was able to assist. No stranger to covert work himself from his time in Damascus before the war, he wrote to the Foreign Office, saying that he could clear up this uncertainty. 'From an indiscretion on the part of a French acquaintance of one of us we should say that the Delegation know of and approve them [Alessandri's activities],' he told London. He suggested that 'a pointed hint should be given ... that we do not care for the smell of this business'.[11]

MacKereth's colleagues in the Foreign Office agreed with him, but they dared not immediately register a complaint with the French. Barely a week had passed since Massigli had confronted Eden with Spears's secret correspondence with the Syrian government. The British knew that the French would ignore any protest they made about Alessandri until they could say that they were replacing their maverick representative in Beirut. Once the French knew that Spears was leaving, the atmosphere would be better. In the meantime, the Foreign Office asked MI6 if it could 'collect any more dope by then'.[12]

When MI6 dug further, it discovered that Alessandri's activities were not confined to encouraging the Arabs to make trouble. From a French officer they found out that the Bureau Noir was backing Jewish terrorists as well. Not only was Alessandri selling weapons to the Jewish defence organisation the Haganah, but from November 1944 – the month that Moyne was murdered – he started providing funds to the Stern Gang, which is significant because one of Moyne's attackers, Beth Tsouri, admitted at that time that 'the chief trouble of the organisation at the moment was money'.[13] MI6 officers shared the Palestine Police's two-year-old suspicion that members of both the Stern Gang and the Irgun used Lebanon and Syria as a safe base for operations, 'if not with French connivance at least with their tacit approval'.

MI6 believed that Alessandri's motive was 'to back any movement in opposition to the Greater Syria scheme, which, if brought about, would undermine French influence'.[14] Alessandri was almost certainly spurred on by the intelligence his colleagues were receiving from their spy inside the British diplomatic legation. Together with other information this convinced them that Spears was, despite orders to the contrary, still doing his utmost to stop President al-Quwatli from signing a treaty with the French, and that the Greater Syria plan was on the verge of becoming a reality.[15] At the Arab conference in Alexandria, which opened on 15 September, the British were so obviously trying to orchestrate a deal between the parties that a Syrian delegate reported: 'our Congress is British and not Arab'.[16] Lord Moyne met Jamil Mardam and the Iraqi premier, Nuri Said, several times, and the two Arabs secretly renewed their vows to unite their countries under a Hashemite monarch and 'deliver Syria from the yoke of the colonisers'.[17] Simultaneously, a vigorous campaign promoting Abdullah as head of such a state started in Damascus.[18]

Reviewing these events in late September 1944 Alessandri's colleague, the head of French military intelligence, described an alarming change of tempo in British policy. He believed that the

British were presenting themselves 'as the only power capable of guaranteeing Syrian independence ... against a return of the French, and against the Turkish and Russian threats' and putting pressure on the Arabs to unite.[19] It was against this backdrop that Moyne, the foremost advocate of 'Greater Syria', was murdered on 6 November by the Stern Gang. Intriguingly, Alessandri appears to have been in Cairo at the time.[20]

There is no doubt that Moyne was already unpopular with the Jews because of his involvement in the *Struma* disaster. But evidence from the time suggests that it was his support for Greater Syria that sealed his fate. Just over a week before his death, leaflets began to circulate accusing him of authorising the 'distribution of arms among the Arabs' so that the latter could attack the Jews.[21] This was a reference to the decision by the British to arm the Syrian gendarmerie weeks earlier. Knowledge of it, and Moyne's support for the Greater Syria plan, is most likely to have come from the French, who were by then sharing with the Zionists intelligence they received through their spy within the British legation. There is an intriguing possibility that the information may even have come from a source inside Moyne's office, for in May that year the British security service MI5 had found out that an intelligence network operating in Cairo whose members included several French nationals had an agent on the switchboard at Moyne's office. In theory, the network was friendly, but MI5 wondered whether 'the present strain on Anglo-French relations and the likelihood of further political disputes generally in our relations with de Gaulle' might have encouraged the French members of the network to pass information to their fellow countrymen instead.[22] It certainly believed that a number of top-secret British papers acquired by the Jewish Agency had come from the minister of state's office.

Undoubtedly, it occurred to the British that the French might be connected to Moyne's murder. This explains the Foreign Office's strange decision to ask the British ambassador in Paris to object to the arrival of the French cruiser *Emile Bertin*, off Beirut, days after MI6 revealed the link between Alessandri and the Stern Gang. And when de Gaulle met Churchill in Paris five days after the murder he was uncharacteristically defensive about French activities in the

Levant. 'We are doing nothing nor will we do anything against you in Iraq, Palestine or Egypt,' he told the British prime minister.[23]

Moyne's murder shocked Churchill, whose support for Zionism had been a constant since his inspiring encounter with the Jewish 'beauties of the groves' in Palestine in 1921. When, after his meeting with de Gaulle, he returned to London he made a statement suggesting that the murder of his friend was testing that support. 'If our dreams for Zionism are to end in the smoke of assassins' pistols and our labours for its future are to produce a new set of gangsters worthy of Nazi Germany, many like myself will have to reconsider the position we have maintained so consistently and so long in the past,' he told the House of Commons.[24] 'If there is to be any hope of a peaceful and successful future for Zionism these wicked activities must cease and those responsible for them must be destroyed, root and branch.'

Though angry in its tone, Churchill's speech contained no sanction because his options were very limited. While many British officials in the Middle East were out for blood, demanding widespread searches for arms and a block on further Jewish immigration, the scale of military needs elsewhere and the fear of a backlash made both ideas impracticable. The chiefs of staff in London said that searches would 'entail a military commitment which could be met only at the direct expense of operations against Germany', while Churchill felt that suspending immigration would 'simply play into the hands of the extremists'.[25] Worried too about Zionist criticism in America, he preferred to warn Chaim Weizmann privately that immigration would have to be suspended if terrorism continued.

A worried Weizmann now put pressure on the Jewish Agency, which speedily renewed its offer of support to track down terrorists in Palestine. The Agency had begun cooperating with the Palestine Police in the summer after its executive began to realise its authority was ebbing because younger Jews increasingly supported the terrorists' campaigns. The police rapidly came to depend on the liaison officer the Agency supplied it with, the future mayor of Jerusalem, Teddy Kollek, since it had had no success whatsoever in penetrating either the Stern Gang or the Irgun, which used a three-man cellular structure and recruited recent refugees from Eastern Europe to reduce the risk of being infiltrated.

In numerical terms, the consequences of this collaboration looked impressive. At a time when MI5 believed that the Stern Gang had five hundred members, within a month of Moyne's death the Jewish Agency had supplied five hundred names of suspects for the police to arrest. When, however, MI5 sent out a senior officer, Alec Kellar, to assess the progress of the police investigation, he was unimpressed. Some of those named turned out to be innocent, he observed, which suggested that the Agency had simply 'taken the opportunity of paying off old scores by giving the Authorities names of persons more of a nuisance to themselves than to us'.[26] Police records were inadequate, the political intelligence section of the Criminal Investigation Department undermanned, and barely any British detectives had a grasp of Hebrew; the CID's leading Hebrew speaker had been murdered by the Irgun in 1939. In these circumstances, the police had no choice but to chase the suspects whose names the Agency supplied.

The police and MI5 wanted more details of the organisation of both the Stern Gang and the Irgun, but the Jewish Agency would not supply them. Kollek provided no hard information beyond names, although he did describe how Haganah conducted many arrests on its own initiative and characterised its interrogation methods as '"unorthodox" but fruitful of result'.[27] Kollek's reticence was deliberate. He wanted to capitalise on the power he now wielded over the police, and he wanted the British to think that neither the Jewish Agency nor the Haganah had anything to do with either the Stern Gang or the Irgun. But he failed to hoodwink Alec Kellar of MI5, who concluded when he got back to London that the Jewish Agency was 'quite certainly following their own interests rather than ours' and that its cooperation would only last as long as it believed that Britain would ultimately enable the creation of a Jewish state.

Belatedly, Kollek did corroborate the core of MI6's conclusions. 'The French,' he said, 'are in collusion with right-wing Jews, and known terrorists have lunched with Colonel Alessandri.'[28] He claimed that the Agency had been reluctant to give up this useful piece of information earlier because it feared that the British would immediately raise the matter with the French and thereby compromise its sources in Beirut.

Once Spears's departure date had been confirmed, at the end of December 1944 the Foreign Office finally had the opportunity to ask for Alessandri's removal. By then, however, the mysterious French officer had already gone to ground after the French realised that the British were interested in the work of the Bureau Noir. MI6 had one last snippet of information about the colonel. In March 1945 they reported that he was returning to Paris to continue the same work from there.[29]

With Lord Moyne died the policy he had so keenly advocated. In April 1945 his successor as minister of state, Sir Edward Grigg, argued that Britain should abandon partition as a policy and instead seek a revised mandate to govern Palestine as a 'peaceful bi-racial state'.[30] Grigg portrayed this approach as more appropriate for a 'victorious Empire with a prestige far higher than it had before this war', but in truth Britain's position was weakening all the time. The real reason why Britain could no longer support partition, or its counterpart Greater Syria, was due to the new Arab League's clear opposition to the Zionists. Formed in Cairo on 22 March 1945, the League had not emerged in the way the British government had hoped. Far from feeling confident enough to accept the creation of a Jewish state, its members were utterly divided. About the only policies they could agree upon, observed the British ambassador in Cairo, were 'getting rid of the French from Syria and ... preventing the Zionist domination of Palestine'.[31] On this the League issued an explicit threat: 'Palestine constitutes an important part of the Arab world and the rights of Arabs [there] cannot be touched upon without prejudice to peace and stability in the Arab world.'[32]

Given that the British had thrown their weight behind creating a Greater Syria as a way to persuade the Arabs to accept the Jews' permanent settlement in Palestine, the strategy had backfired. When Eden reviewed the government's approach on Palestine in April 1945, he suggested that Moyne himself had begun to wonder about the wisdom of the strategy he had championed. 'The late Lord

Moyne warned me ... that we must face the new fact that the main idea of the leaders of the Arab States was to arrange to present an united front on anything that they regarded as an attack on any Arab State.'[33] As Arab unity had failed to develop in a way that served British interests, Eden argued that promoting Greater Syria was 'no longer current politics'.

Moyne's killers were hanged on the same day that the Arab League was formed, but Britain's weakness had been devastatingly revealed. Confronted by the murder in broad daylight of a member of his cabinet, the prime minister had merely threatened to reconsider his support for Zionism. The consequent attempt by the British authorities in Palestine to round up those who lay behind the murder had revealed them to be almost totally dependent on the Jewish Agency for information. One long-serving British official predicted the conclusion that the Zionists would reach when they saw the hesitancy of British policy: 'The longer HMG does nothing, the harder it is to resist the conclusion that terrorism pays, and that if only the pressure is kept on, the Jewish State – which is the official aim of the whole Zionist movement – will very soon be gained.'[34]

PART FOUR

EXIT: 1945–1949

The aftermath of the King David Hotel bombing, July 1946.

25

TIME TO CALL THE SHOTS

ON 5 APRIL 1945 CHARLES DE GAULLE SUMMONED HIS foreign minister Georges Bidault and the delegate-general to the Levant, Paul Beynet, to discuss the Syrian government's latest request – a demand for the transfer of the *troupes spéciales*, the twenty-thousand-strong Syrian militia which remained under French command. Disparaged as 'a useless mass of wogs dressed up as soldiers' by a British officer, the militia mattered to the French because their forces in the region otherwise totalled only 3,200 poor-quality colonial infantry – all their best troops had returned to participate in the liberation of France.[1] The *troupes* were the 'last element of authority that we have at our disposal at the moment'.[2] The Syrians knew it too. 'When we have the army France will be nothing in our country,' Jamil Mardam wrote, in a message intercepted by the French.[3] And that was why de Gaulle was so determined not to hand it over.

Since receiving a hero's welcome on his return to a newly liberated Paris in August 1944, de Gaulle had done his utmost to re-establish France as a great power, treated as an equal by the United States, the Soviet Union and Great Britain. He had ignored Bidault, the chairman of the fractious Conseil National de la Résistance, when the latter, a former history teacher, had advised him to proclaim the Republic from the balcony of the Hôtel de Ville, as had happened after other turbulent eras in the country's past. 'Why should we proclaim the Republic?' he asked Bidault. 'It never ceased to exist.'[4]

'De Gaulle has his head in the clouds and his feet in the shit', to quote one Parisian graffiti artist on the general's unwillingness to acknowledge his country's dire situation.[5] That attitude also coloured de Gaulle's analysis of his options in the Levant. 'We are far from having lost our cards in the Syrian game,' he had already insisted to a sceptical Bidault, and in the 5 April meeting he argued that he had been vindicated by what had happened in recent months.[6] Spears had gone, and the British government, beset by French-sponsored Jewish terrorism in Palestine, was now 'preaching calm' in the Levant.[7] The Syrians had fallen out with the Lebanese, and their Greater Syria project seemed to have been abandoned for the time being.[8]

In de Gaulle's opinion, the circumstances were therefore favourable for France to dismiss the Syrians' demand outright. In that April meeting he claimed the latter had missed 'le moment psychologique', and that, because the British needed good relations with the French in Europe and as quiet a life as possible in Palestine, they would help restrain the Syrians. 'You can count on them to urge caution,' he said.[9] It was a misjudgement that directly led to France's departure from the Levant.

Although Georges Bidault openly confessed that 'he knew nothing and had no experience' of foreign policy, he could have predicted that outcome.[10] Despite being driven to drink by his infuriating boss, even he could clearly see that an outright refusal to hand over the *troupes spéciales* was bound to lead to trouble. To maintain France's 'thousand-year tradition' in the Levant, he favoured more subtle tactics.[11] He proposed that France should offer the Syrians the transfer after a delay, instead. Six months after the end of the war and one month after the British had departed was his suggestion. This would give the Syrians an incentive to force out the British, and once the British were out of the way, France could then go back on the deal.

Delegate-General Beynet was similarly nervous about de Gaulle's plan. He said that it would spark a crisis and asked the general to authorise the dispatch of reinforcements to contain it. He had spent the past year doing what he could to claw back French influence in the Levant, but he had been utterly unable to persuade the Syrians

that they should negotiate a treaty with him.[12] He was far less san-
guine about the situation than de Gaulle, and predicted that the
troupes would mutiny if the French did not provide a timescale for
their transfer to Syrian control. Nor was he so certain about the
position the British would take if the Syrians refused to accept the
French government's proposal and the *troupes* revolted.

For months the British had sent conflicting signals about their
willingness to tolerate an ongoing French presence in the Levant. At
the end of January that year, the foreign secretary had told Duff
Cooper to leave the French in no doubt that 'there were limits to the
extent to which we were prepared to incur mistrust and hostility or,
still more, endanger our position in the Middle East on their
behalf'.[13] But one month later René Massigli, now the French ambassador to London, drew attention to a speech by Churchill in which
the British prime minister seemed to be retreating from the idea that
Britain was the guarantor of Syrian and Lebanese independence. It
was not for Britain 'alone to defend by force either Syrian or
Lebanese independence or French privilege. We seek both, and we do
not believe that they are incompatible. Too much must not be
placed, therefore, upon the shoulders of Great Britain,' Churchill
had said.[14]

A top-secret British telegram that the French had mysteriously
acquired reinforced their hope that the British were too preoccupied
and overstretched to interfere in the Levant. In it Britain's
commander-in-chief in the Middle East, Sir Bernard Paget, made it
clear that while the Foreign Office had said it planned to 'deal firmly'
with the French in the event of a crisis, he had 'little confidence in the
realisation of that intention'.[15] The deteriorating situation in
Palestine, he went on to explain, meant that he did not have the
troops available to back up a diplomatic threat with force. The
French military attaché at the embassy in London was asked if he
could discreetly verify this information. Although his best source at
the War Office was off sick, he told Paris that Paget's worries
sounded plausible. In his opinion, Britain's position was: 'We will
not stir Syrian affairs while their repercussions across the Arab world
could endanger our security in the Middle East and the route to
India.'[16]

From this inaccurate assessment the French mistakenly inferred that even if their refusal to hand over the *troupes spéciales* led to trouble, the British would probably not intervene. Even Catroux, who was about to become French ambassador to Moscow, weighed in. As he passed through Beirut on the way to his new posting, he argued that France should send troops to the Levant to impose its will. 'No doubt there would follow serious international complications, but, locally, the salutary effect would be considerable.'[17] In the past, the British had joked that Catroux was 'a past master at evolving face-saving devices', but since his carpeting in Lebanon in November 1943 even he now seemed to be spoiling for a fight.[18]

Set on saying *Non* to the Syrian government's request for the handover of the *troupes*, de Gaulle accordingly approved Beynet's request for three further battalions to deal with the trouble that the announcement would provoke, and made arrangements for the reinforcements to sail to Beirut. Before these troops set out he told Bidault, who had gone to San Francisco to represent France at the conference that would give birth to the United Nations, that their departure marked 'the end of the period of France's obliteration and Britain's supremacy'.[19] To reinforce that message, de Gaulle advised his minister that the troops would sail aboard the *Montcalm*, one of the French navy's largest ships. He also told Bidault to ignore the inevitable British anguish that their appearance off Beirut was bound to cause. It was 'now time to call the shots', he said.

When news that eight hundred Senegalese troops were on their way to Beirut reached London, the British government asked de Gaulle to divert the *Montcalm* to Alexandria immediately. But Duff Cooper, who bore the message to de Gaulle on 30 April, privately felt that it was 'very hard for us to argue that the French mustn't send troops while we ourselves retain such large forces there'.[20] De Gaulle spotted the British ambassador's diffidence, and launched into a tirade against their mutual adversary, Spears, saying that it was clear that the British government still shared the former minister's determination to see France ousted from the Levant. He needed to send troops precisely because he was handing over the *troupes spéciales* to Syria, he said.

After Cooper reported de Gaulle's unyielding attitude back to Whitehall, Churchill tried to calm the situation. On 4 May he sent a telegram to de Gaulle, telling him that the British government was willing to withdraw its troops as soon as the war was over and France had agreed treaties with both states.

However, the friendly tone of this message was fatally undermined by intelligence the French had received, which suggested that the British had not given up on their Greater Syria ambition, and a coincidence: at the same time, the British commander, Paget, sent a brigade of his Arab Palestinian troops to Lebanon for rest and training.[21] Churchill was furious when he heard what Paget had done. 'Why should such steps, of great political consequence, be taken at this time without my being advised?' he complained to his officials, for the appearance of more British troops in the Levant gave de Gaulle the excuse to ignore him.[22] The French leader fired a message back at Churchill on the 6th, telling him that he was sending Beynet back to negotiate treaties – which, he added, might already have been signed, had the governments of Damascus and Beirut not felt that 'they could avoid any commitment by leaning on you against us. The presence of your troops and the attitude of your agents helps them in this unfortunately negative politicking.'[23]

As a consequence, when the *Montcalm* docked in Beirut the same day and disgorged its Senegalese soldiers, the British did not immediately comment. The French were delighted, believing that the British silence would make the Syrians and Lebanese feel isolated and more willing to give in to their own demands. Capitalising on the lack of British protest and the announcement of Germany's surrender on the 7th, overnight the French plastered Beirut with posters of de Gaulle. On VE-Day itself they organised lorry-loads of their troops to tour the city shouting slogans including 'Vive de Gaulle! We are your children!' and 'This country is yours, de Gaulle!'[24]

The following day the Arab nationalists organised a counter-demonstration in which some of Paget's Arab troops took part, parading a large picture of the Mufti, who had fled to Germany during the war and offered his services to Hitler. When a stone was thrown at the Mufti's portrait, the demonstration turned violent.

The protesters damaged a nearby convent, and tore down the *tri-colores* the French had hoisted across the city. The French seized on the affair, saying that it was the Arab troops, who they claimed had been waving a swastika flag, who were responsible for the growing tension in Syria and Lebanon.

De Gaulle had argued that he needed to send troops to the Levant to make up for the transfer of the *troupes spéciales*, but he sent Beynet back to Beirut with explicit instructions not to hand over any of the Syrian militia until he had a commitment from the Syrians that France would have the military bases he wanted. Beynet arrived in Beirut on 12 May to find that neither the Lebanese nor the Syrian government would negotiate with him until he turned away the reinforcements. The French delegate-general would not do so, and on 17 May another cruiser, the *Jeanne d'Arc*, arrived to offload five hundred more French soldiers. Beynet justified its arrival by pointing at the brigade the British had just sent to the Levant.

The killing of three French soldiers in a riot in Aleppo on 20 May gave Paget the excuse he needed to intervene. As the French blamed the deaths on the failure of the Syrian gendarmerie to keep order, when the British commander-in-chief met Beynet two days later he called the French delegate-general's bluff by offering to provide the gendarmes with the extra arms and transport they needed. Beynet, of course, refused to take up the offer, but by doing so he confirmed Paget's suspicion that France's true priority was to improve its position in the Levant rather than to restore security.

On 27 May fighting erupted in Homs and Hama, the two main cities between Damascus and Aleppo. In Hama a dispute between the French and the Syrian gendarmes about who controlled the railway station escalated. After the Syrians ambushed a French relief column outside the town, capturing artillery and armoured cars, the French retaliated by mortaring, machine-gunning and bombing the town. Eighty people died.

'It will be a miracle if Damascus does not go up too,' observed the British minister to the Levant, Terence Shone, who had replaced Spears at the end of 1944.[25] A career diplomat, Shone appeared rather anodyne in comparison to Spears, but he was just as keen as his predecessor to see the action. Putting on his old school tie and taking his wife's pistol because he could not find his own – he 'seemed a little dubious as to how it worked', she wrote – Shone drove to Damascus in an armoured car emblazoned with the Union Jack to see President al-Quwatli and try to persuade him not to rise to the French provocation.[26] Meanwhile his assistant, Gerry Young, went to see Beynet once again. He found the French delegate-general 'calm and cheerful', but in a clearly combative mood. 'The Damascus abscess must be lanced,' the Frenchman declared. As if one metaphor were inadequate, he added that 'now the barrel had been broached the wine must be drunk'.[27]

'It might prove somewhat bitter,' Young suggested.

The French bombardment of Damascus began at seven o'clock on the evening of the 29th, on the orders of General Fernand Oliva-Roget, Beynet's representative in the city. W. F. Stirling, the British liaison officer to President al-Quwatli, was in Damascus at the time. According to him, artillery and machine-gun fire broke out simultaneously across the city, followed soon afterwards by heavy artillery and mortar fire. Within minutes, 'Pandemonium reigned.'[28] As darkness fell he watched a French bomber circling the old city, dropping bombs on its citadel, the headquarters of the gendarmerie.

While Stirling took refuge in his house, a few blocks away in the Government Palace the Syrian finance minister, Khalid al-Azm, tried to find out what was going on. But the telephone line from his office was dead, and after he received news that French Senegalese soldiers had fired artillery point blank at the Parliament, then used their machetes to butcher the surviving gendarmes who were guarding it, it seemed wise to leave. Having barricaded the palace with office furniture, he and his colleagues slipped away to his home near the Great Mosque in the old city.

The Syrian government's location seems to have remained unknown to the French until Jamil Mardam tried to use al-Azm's home telephone. The French, who had tapped the line, relayed the news of the cabinet's position to their artillery on the heights above Damascus. The Druzes had attacked al-Azm's home during their revolt in 1925; now it was the turn of the French to bombard this pretty eighteenth-century enclave in the heart of the old city. Shells began to fall in the palace courtyard shortly afterwards, forcing al-Azm and his colleagues to take cover.

Not all the telephone lines were cut, as yet. From the British consulate, which was also hit by machine-gun fire, Shone managed to get through to his assistant, Young, in Beirut to tell him what had happened. Young passed the message on to Cairo, and that evening Paget's headquarters informed London that the French had 'run riot in Damascus and there is indiscriminate shooting and shelling in the town', adding that Oliva-Roget appeared to be 'wholly irresponsible and the French Military Authorities either cannot or will not control him'.[29]

As Stirling later put it, 'I suppose we shall never know what instructions General Oliva-Roget had been given by de Gaulle.'[30] Oliva-Roget had served most of his career in the Levant, originally in the Jabal Druze; an odd and humourless character, he told people he barely knew that he had an Oedipus complex.[31] The British intelligence chief, Coghill, described him as 'one of the worst types of French Colonial Officers'.[32] But by May 1945, despite being Beynet's chief representative in Damascus, Oliva-Roget had little of significance to do. He had been sidelined completely by the Syrians and he was ill and constantly in pain – the British speculated from his yellowish hue that he had liver trouble. At the end of that month, it seems, he finally snapped.

Oliva-Roget had always been suspicious of the British. After the invasion of Syria in 1941, he had lunch with the British official Alec Kirkbride, who had been secretly involved in buying Druze support beforehand. He asked Kirkbride directly whether he had been sending over any rifles to the Druzes of late. No, Kirkbride replied, 'but we have had some attractive lines to offer lately in the way of light machine-guns'.[33] He learned afterwards that Oliva-Roget had reported his aside to Beirut as concrete evidence that he was gun-running.

Judging by recently declassified French files, Oliva-Roget reserved his deepest distrust for one man in particular. When W. F. Stirling arrived in Damascus to liaise with President al-Quwatli, Oliva-Roget had immediately complained that the veteran British officer's role was a slight on the French government. After sending intelligence officers to trail the *homme au chien*, as he called him (since Stirling was rarely seen without his large black dog), he rapidly concluded that the British officer was effectively the successor to Louis Spears.[34] Warning his colleagues not to be misled by Stirling's 'good natured appearance', he argued that the ageing colonel was 'one of the most dangerous British agents in Syria', and that his job title was simply cover for his true responsibility which was to coordinate British efforts to bring about a Greater Syria.[35] French briefing notes on Stirling invariably mentioned another fact: Stirling's friendship with T. E. Lawrence.

Convinced that the tensions in Damascus were of Stirling's making, Oliva-Roget announced that he was going to teach the Syrians 'a good lesson' – and allowed the shooting to continue throughout 30 May.[36] Those who bore the brunt of that attack describe fighting of unparalleled ferocity. One Russian holed up inside the Orient Palace Hotel, who had been at Stalingrad, said afterwards that he had 'never been through such an experience as this'.[37] When Stirling visited the hotel, which was once the finest in the city, he remarked: 'Every window was shattered; there was at least an inch of broken glass all over the ground floor; the dining-room tables were scored with bullet marks; almost every water pipe was leaking, pierced by bullets; and the walls of the bedrooms on the outer side of the building were pockmarked by bullets.'[38] The hotel's guests spent two days cowering in a basement; a British officer was killed when a French soldier lobbed a hand-grenade into the building.

An ill and desperate al-Quwatli called Shone to see him the same day, and asked him how long Britain was willing to let de Gaulle 'wreak his will uncurbed'.[39] In a last-ditch bid to encourage the British to act, he wrote a series of notes promising that he would pursue Arab unity and offering Britain a privileged position in an independent Syria.[40] Shone dictated a message down the telephone to Beirut for transmission to the foreign secretary in London. 'The French have instituted nothing short of a reign of terror in Damascus. Apart from indiscriminate shelling their troops, black and white, are behaving like madmen, spraying the streets with machine-gun fire from vehicles and buildings.'[41] Amid reports that the French had run out of food and were issuing their troops with wine alone, Shone implored his government to let Paget intervene.[42]

Churchill was reluctant to do so because he feared how British intervention might look abroad, and in a cabinet meeting the same day he said that he wanted American support first. His old ally Franklin D. Roosevelt had died eight weeks earlier, and the new president, Roosevelt's deputy Harry S. Truman, did not instantly respond with his backing. Churchill was obliged to send his message to de Gaulle regardless. In what amounted to a direct order, he told the French leader that, as Paget was going to intervene, 'to avoid collision between British and French forces we request you immediately to order the French troops to cease fire and to withdraw to their barracks'.[43] Before the telegram had even reached Paris, Eden announced its message to parliament, making the ultimatum evident to the world.

Having received news of Churchill's demand at six o'clock the same evening, the British in Damascus found Oliva-Roget and handed him an order from Paget to cease fire. The French general, however, refused to accept Paget's authority and it was not until early the next morning, after he had heard directly from Beirut, that he finally reined in his forces. To cheers from the people of Damascus, British tanks and armoured cars rolled into the city centre the same afternoon.

In less than three days, as many as eight hundred Syrians had been killed and the damage to the capital was extensive. The Parliament itself was a smoking shell. A large area of the centre of town had been destroyed by fire, and the streets were pitted with shell holes and gravelled with broken glass and chunks of masonry. Twenty missing Syrian gendarmes were found in a mass grave at the French aerodrome: they had been mutilated before being murdered. 'This generation of Syrians,' President al-Quwatli predicted afterwards, 'will not tolerate seeing one Frenchman walk through the streets of Damascus.'[44] He wanted Beynet and Oliva-Roget tried as war criminals.

Although, as in November 1943, France had brought the problem on itself, the British did not render France's situation any easier. Paget imposed a curfew on all French citizens, and prevented French ships and aircraft from moving. French soldiers were not allowed to shoot, except in self-defence. Although the curfew was probably in the best interests of the French – 'If we had not been here and inter- vened when we did, practically every Frenchman would have had his throat cut,' Coghill believed – these draconian steps added insult to self-inflicted injury.[45] Beynet described the measures as 'a stab in the back'.[46]

Bidault called Duff Cooper in to see him, saying that 'whatever mistakes France had committed, she had not deserved such humili- ation as this'.[47] Cooper sympathised. Paget's orders, he admitted, did 'sound more like terms imposed on a defeated enemy whom it is desired to humiliate, rather than on an Ally whom we are trying to help'. When Oliva-Roget, who was sent home to Paris shortly after- wards, was asked how he was treated by the British following their takeover, he replied sarcastically: 'They were very nice to me. They escorted me with a machine-gun at my back.'[48]

At a hastily convened press conference in Paris on 2 June de Gaulle blamed the 'activities of numerous British agents in the Levant' for what had happened.[49] He insinuated that the British had deliberately armed the Syrian gendarmerie earlier that year to enable them to confront the French. He also claimed a ceasefire was already in place by the time the British intervened. Even Duff Cooper, a man who usually gave the French the benefit of the doubt, described de Gaulle's performance as a 'mixture of false- hoods, half-truths, suppressions of inconvenient facts and insinuations against Britain'.[50] He was bemused when he met the French leader the following day to find him 'genuinely convinced' that the whole incident had been 'arranged by the British in order to carry out their long-planned policy of driving the French out of the Levant in order to take their place'.[51] Oliva-Roget backed up de Gaulle's claims. He said that he had been provoked into reacting by the gendarmerie, who were encouraged by British agents whose identities were 'perfectly well known'.[52] One of them, he added, was Colonel Stirling.

Stirling was swiftly given a month's home leave by the British army. 'In the eyes of every Frenchman,' he wrote afterwards, 'I was tarred with the Lawrence brush and assumed to be working against the interests of France.'[53] To rebut Oliva-Roget's version of events, he pointed to the fact that there was no physical evidence to support the French contention that they had been attacked first. After touring the city for himself, he observed that 'neither the French Delegation, nor the offices of the Etat-Major,* nor the French general's residence had a single broken window or a sign of a bullet mark, whereas the Banque de Syrie and the British Officers' Club were pockmarked all over with bullets'.[54]

Al-Quwatli himself dismissed as a 'comical lie' the idea that Stirling lurked behind the violence.[55] He described French accusations about British agents stirring up trouble as 'an old song we heard during the last twenty-five years whenever they want to oppress us and whenever Great Britain stands in their way'. But there is no doubt that, around this time, the Syrian government did ask Stirling and his colleagues what their attitude would be if they tried to mount a coup to remove the French. Confronted by this question, one British officer 'told them to lay off that sort of thing since we were the guarantors of internal security in Syria as long as we were there'.[56] Of course, such an answer only encouraged Syrian brinkmanship. For regardless of Churchill's effort earlier that year to claim that Britain was not responsible for policing relations between the Syrians and the French, every British officer in Damascus believed that if trouble erupted there, they would have to intervene before the unrest spread. Had the British stood back, Coghill believed, 'Thousands of Syrians would have been killed, Iraq and possibly TJ would have joined in and the whole ME would have gone up as the Jews in Palestine would surely have thought this was their chance too.'[57]

The Syrians' undisguised delight at how matters had turned out reinforced the French conviction that they were right to suspect British motives, and in a meeting with Cooper on 4 June de Gaulle hinted that he was considering revenge. 'We are not, I admit, in a position to open hostilities against you at the present time. But you have insulted France and betrayed the West. This cannot be forgotten.'[58]

De Gaulle's fulmination was immediate and predictable; Bidault's

* The French general staff.

slower-burning malice took longer to become clear. Midway through June, the French foreign minister was obliged to make an embarrassing statement to France's provisional assembly on what had happened in the Levant a fortnight earlier. 'To sum up,' he concluded, 'the world, particularly the East, has roared with laughter, laughter at our expense, and from which, I am driven to believe, some think they will benefit.'[59] Rejecting the British government's claim that its officials had in no way contributed to the problems France had faced, he ended with an ominous threat. 'Hodie mihi, cras tibi,' he proclaimed, quoting a Latin proverb often carved on gravestones: Today my fate, tomorrow yours.

The collapse of French influence in Syria was immediate and total. By the end of the month a French official in Beirut wrote that neither he nor his colleagues dared travel to any of the major Syrian towns without an escort, for fear of being murdered. The *troupes spéciales* were transferred to Syrian and Lebanese control the following month, but, predictably, neither the Syrians nor the Lebanese were willing to guarantee their former ruler the military bridgehead in the Middle East that de Gaulle desired. The British and French hammered out a deal to leave simultaneously – 'This should end French intrigues in Palestine,' the foreign secretary noted optimistically – and both sides' troops withdrew from Syria in April 1946, and from the Lebanon that August.[60] After twenty-six years, the French mandate in the Middle East was over.

The loss of Lebanon and Syria paved the way for a new, pro-Zionist French policy. At the end of June 1945, the French delegate-general in the Levant, Paul Beynet, had written to de Gaulle to point out that throughout the Damascus crisis 'only the Jews of Palestine' had been supportive of the French.[61] Many Jews in Palestine felt reassured by the presence of a Christian Lebanon next door, since they knew that the Christians would share their fear about being surrounded and outnumbered by Muslims. Now deeply alarmed at the prospect that France was going to be thrown out of the Levant, both the Jewish Agency and the terrorist organisations had made contact to 'offer their services', Beynet explained. 'I have given orders for contacts to be maintained.'[62]

Initially, the Jews wanted very little in exchange. 'A verbal reassurance, not necessarily to support the Zionist movement and its demands, but to refrain from adopting a hostile attitude, especially when it comes to the question of immigration to Palestine, would be enough,' Beynet told de Gaulle.[63] Personally, he felt that 'the injustices and suffering of the French Jews under German occupation make it difficult for us to take any other stand'. Nor was Beynet the only Frenchman whom the Zionists had met. Henri Bonnet, the ambassador in Washington DC, had also been approached. He too argued that 'the Zionist groups can represent an element of support for our country which we should not neglect'.[64] The Zionist representative who had visited his embassy summarised the argument very simply: 'Jews and Christians must defend themselves against the Arab menace backed by England.'

Two months later, a man named Tuvia Arazi met the director of the Europe Department at the Quai d'Orsay in Paris, François Coulet. The minutes of the meeting record that the purpose of the encounter was for both men to renew their friendship, which dated back to 1940.[65] Then, Arazi was the Haganah's main spy in Vichy-occupied Syria, while Coulet was one of the three men put up by David Hacohen in Haifa, who had watched the sabotaged *Patria* keel over.

After reminiscing about those earlier times, which had seen him jump from a fourth-floor window to escape detention by the Vichy French Sûreté, Arazi moved the conversation on to the future relationship between France and a Jewish state. Recalling a speech that Spears had made a few months earlier, in which the British politician had said that France and the Zionists were the main hindrances to Britain's Middle Eastern policy, Arazi suggested that there was a more positive basis than a shared dislike of Britain for an alliance between the two. All that was required was for France to rethink its foreign policy. For compared to the widespread hatred that France now evoked across the Arab Middle East, he said, there were coherent Zionist organisations that recognised France's rightful place in the world, and hoped that the French would assume it once again.

Although De Gaulle had no great sympathy for the Jews, he had not forgotten the June 'insult' and could immediately see how the

Zionists might be useful in avenging it. When he met the French representative of the Zionist movement, Marc Jarblum, in Paris later in the year, he mused that 'the Jews in Palestine are the only ones who can chase the British out of the Middle East'.[66]

Bidault had been arguing for months that the French needed to abandon the delaying tactics that had failed in the Levant for what he called a 'grand policy' that would enable France to regain the initiative, particularly in its dealings with its remaining Arab colonies in North Africa.[67] In what the Zionists were proposing he saw the germ of such a scheme. France could use the Zionists not just to give the British a bloody nose in Palestine, but to defeat the Arab League, which had made Palestine its *cause célèbre*, since Arab nationalism was a growing force in French North Africa as well.

On 10 November, Bidault quietly told David Ben-Gurion that France would support the Zionists' cause. Eighteen months earlier Ben-Gurion had offered up the hope in public that, after the war, the Jews would find that a rejuvenated France would 'have an understanding attitude towards us'.[68] That prayer had now been answered. It was not long before France's grand policy of covert support for the Zionists would emerge, and the British would realise that Bidault's epitaph was meant for them.

26

GOT TO THINK AGAIN

THE WAR LEFT EUROPE WITH AN UNPRECEDENTED HUMANITAR-
ian crisis. About a quarter of a million 'displaced people' were living
in camps across the continent. Some – those forced to work in Nazi
Germany, and children separated from their parents – wanted to go
home. Others, like the Eastern Europeans fleeing Soviet rule and
the Jews who had been liberated from the concentration camps,
wanted anything but. The Zionists were quick to advocate that they
should be allowed to live in Palestine.

Briefly, it looked as if the new British government might agree. In
the general election of July 1945 Churchill's Conservatives were
resoundingly defeated by Clement Attlee's Labour Party which, two
months earlier, had decided that Palestine should provide a home for
Jewish survivors of the Holocaust. That May the man who was now
the chancellor of the exchequer, Hugh Dalton, had argued that 'the
unspeakable horrors that have been perpetrated upon the Jews of
Germany and other occupied countries in Europe' meant that it was
'morally wrong and politically indefensible to impose obstacles to
the entry into Palestine now of any Jews who desire to go there'.[1]
The party's membership agreed. A resolution it adopted at that time
called for the Arabs to 'be encouraged to move out as the Jews move
in'.[2] The assumption was that the Arabs were essentially a nomadic
people who would be prepared to leave.

Putting this resolution into practice was the task that lay ahead of

Ernest Bevin, the new British foreign secretary. In stark contrast to his debonair predecessor Eden, he was a bruiser who had left school at eleven and worked his way up from farmhand to the Foreign Office, via the chairmanship of the trades union movement. His break had come in 1940 when Churchill, impressed by Bevin's hostility to trade union pacifism and his seemingly limitless appetite for work, invited him to join the cabinet as minister of labour. Churchill thought Bevin was by 'far the most distinguished man that the Labour Party have thrown up in my time'.[3] Foreign Office officials, who had initially regarded their new chief with horror, quickly realised that the former prime minister was right. 'He knows a great deal, is prepared to read any amount, seems to take in what he does read, and is capable of making up his own mind and sticking up for his (or our) point of view against anyone,' wrote Bevin's permanent secretary.[4]

So far as the Foreign Office was concerned, this was a real asset, because the British government was facing heavy pressure from the United States government to relax its tight restrictions on Jewish immigration into Palestine. Whereas the former president, Roosevelt, had maintained an even-handed line that had greatly helped the British, his successor Harry Truman decided that continuing equivocation was politically unwise. The horrors of the Holocaust were by now evident, and Zionist leaders of America's five-million-strong Jewish population were pressing him for action.[5]

A former farmer and unsuccessful businessman who had never been to college, Truman instinctively distrusted the advice given him by the Ivy League-educated 'striped-pants boys' of the State Department, who argued that a pro-Arab, not pro-Zionist, policy was in America's best interests in the long term, given the United States' dependency on Middle Eastern oil. Truman afterwards claimed his motive was humanitarian. 'It was my feeling that it would be possible for us to watch out for the long-range interests of our country while, at the same time, helping these unfortunate victims of persecution to find a home,' he wrote.[6] But the evidence from the time suggests that electoral mathematics were considerably more important in determining his position. 'I'm sorry gentlemen,' he told a group of Arab ambassadors who came to complain about his bias, 'but I have to answer to hundreds of thousands who are anxious for the success of Zionism; I do not have hundreds of thousands of Arabs among my constituents.'[7]

In mid-August 1945, Truman deliberately made his position public at a press conference. In response to a question that had been planted with a reporter, he announced that his goal was 'to let as many Jews into Palestine as possible and still maintain civil peace'.[8] After receiving a report on the plight of displaced persons and news that the British government's immigration permits for Palestine were about to run dry, he then put a number on that aspiration. When two weeks later he privately wrote to Attlee to say that Americans felt that immigration to Palestine should not be closed, he proposed that the British government should issue a hundred thousand more immigration visas. That large round number, first advocated by the Jewish Agency, was to acquire a totem-like significance in the debate that followed. Out of an estimated quarter of a million displaced persons, about 138,000 were Jewish.

It probably never dawned on Truman that his overture would be rejected, because in the run-up to the general election the Labour Party had been ardently pro-Zionist. Once in the Foreign Office, however, Bevin – unlike Truman – was swayed by his advisers. 'Clem,' he said to Attlee one day, 'about Palestine. According to the lads in the Office, we've got it wrong. We've got to think again.'[9]

Bevin's lads had told him not to yield to the calls to accept a large number of Jewish immigrants – who were bound to call for independence and antagonise the Arab population – because in their view Britain's failing relationship with the nationalist Egyptian government made Palestine all the more important. Egypt had been Britain's powerbase in the Middle East for more than fifty years, but the country's new prime minister, Ismail Sidqi, now seemed determined to bring that era to a close. The more likely Sidqi's success in this endeavour seemed, the more the British convinced themselves that it was strategically crucial that they keep hold of Palestine. From there they would still be able to dominate the Suez Canal, and the mandate would be a useful base for projecting British power around the world.

The fundamental flaw in this grand plan was that Palestine, in its

present state, was utterly unsuitable as a base. At the end of August
the chief secretary of the Palestine administration warned that tensions in the mandate were close to breaking point. Truman's press
statement had 'further stimulated Arab apprehensions', he
explained, while Jewish leaders appeared to be 'deliberately pushing
extremism to a point when an explosion can no longer be avoided
and [they] do not scruple to use the plight of the Jews in Europe as
a main political cause'.[10] Nor did war-weary Britain have the
resources to deal with trouble: the Palestine Police was more than a
third under strength. Bevin understood the problem perfectly, and
came up with a plan. 'Let us wait until our strength is restored and
let us meanwhile, with US help as necessary, hold on to [our] essential positions'.[11]

After Attlee told Truman flatly that to let a hundred thousand
Jews into Palestine would 'set aflame the whole Middle East' and
cause 'grievous harm to relations between our two countries', Bevin
set out to find a way to bring the United States administration
round to the British point of view.[12] British diplomats in Washington DC argued that Britain's ongoing control of Palestine was in the
interests of both governments as they tried to contain the Soviet
threat. A few weeks later Bevin proposed that a joint Anglo-
American Committee of Inquiry should investigate where the
displaced persons might settle, and recommend an interim solution
to both governments until the United Nations could address the
matter. Truman, who agreed to this idea so long as it specifically
examined whether Palestine would provide the answer, subsequently accused the British of 'dilatory tactics', but the outcome
suited him as well.[13] He did not want to admit that his attempt to
force an instant change to British immigration policy had failed
before mayoral elections in New York took place, in case the city's
large Jewish population reacted badly.

In fact, the Jews already knew that the British were not planning
any fundamental change of policy, thanks to intelligence provided
to them by the French. In October 1945 the chairman of the
Jewish Agency's executive, David Ben-Gurion, therefore quietly
told the Haganah leader, Moshe Sneh, to start cooperating directly
with the Irgun and the Stern Gang as a combined Jewish

Resistance Movement. So far as he was concerned, now that the war was over, there was no need for further restraint. From the French capital he declared that the 1939 White Paper limiting immigration had no moral or legal basis. 'There are two things that the Jews will not accept: minority status in their own country and immigration into Palestine under tolerance. They do not want to live under foreign rule in their homeland.'[14] In Palestine, the new British high commissioner, Lord Gort, wrote to his predecessor: 'I am afraid Dr Weizmann and his counsels of moderation are out of fashion and that Ben-Gurion and the wilder men have taken over control.'[15]

Sneh began meeting the leaders of the Irgun Zvai Leumi and the Stern Gang, Menachem Begin and Nathan Friedman-Yellin, to coordinate their efforts. Deciding not to wait for Bevin to make a formal statement on the new government's policy on Palestine, which was expected imminently, on the night of 31 October they carried out their first combined attack, sabotaging Palestine's railway network in more than a hundred and fifty places, as well as the Haifa oil refinery. The attacks killed four, but that was not their point. Their unprecedented scope was designed to be a warning to the British government of what, united, all three groups could do.

Bevin chose to ignore the threat. Loud cheers greeted him when he finally told the House of Commons on 13 November that the United States government had accepted his invitation to join an Anglo-American Committee of Inquiry investigating the prospects for Jewish immigration into Palestine. For what he really meant by this announcement was that he was not going to be bullied into changing Britain's stringent immigration policy by outside pressure: not by the Zionists, nor by America. With little apparent grasp of how the survivors of the Holocaust might feel, Bevin took the view that they should return home. To give in to the demands that the Jews should receive special treatment, he argued in a press conference immediately after his statement in the Commons, raised the 'danger of another anti-Semitic reaction' from other displaced persons who were also waiting to go home.[16] The argument would have looked logical, even virtuous, in its refusal to discriminate, had Bevin's motive not been utterly transparent: he was determined that large-scale Jewish immigration to Palestine, which would only further weaken Britain's mandate, must not go ahead.

Bevin's announcement and these insensitive comments caused uproar in the United States and were followed by a further spate of violence. 'The basic principle,' wrote one member of the Stern Gang, 'was that the more British officials, soldiers and policemen were eliminated, the sooner the foreign occupier would have to leave our land.'[17] In the next eight months Jewish terrorists killed twenty-seven, wounded a further one hundred and sixty-four, and caused an estimated £4 million worth of damage.[18] At the end of November the Jewish Resistance Movement blew up two coastguard stations. At the end of December, they turned their attentions to the police, bombing their headquarters in Jerusalem and a police station in Jaffa, then hosing the survivors with machine-gun fire as they emerged from the shattered buildings. Ben-Gurion effectively justified this assault when he said, soon afterwards, that it was 'difficult to appeal to the Yishuv to observe the law at a time when the Mandatory Government itself was consistently violating the fundamental law of the country embodied in the Palestine Mandate'.[19]

The violence continued into 1946. The Irgun, some of whose members had been trained by the Polish army before the war, ambushed a train on 12 January, capturing £35,000 earmarked for the payment of railway staff. Seven days later they destroyed an electricity substation in Jerusalem and, the following day, attacked the coastguard once again. In February Jewish terrorists raided a military depot for more arms, and attacked police and military encampments and an airstrip, destroying on the ground twelve British aircraft worth three-quarters of a million pounds. Two Jews involved in the police encampment attack were killed. Fifty thousand people attended their funeral.[20]

At about this time, a French journalist visiting Palestine recounted a conversation he had had in a café in Tel Aviv after a young man at a nearby table finished his lunch, paid and left.

'You know who that was?' his guide from the Jewish Agency asked.

'No,' said the reporter.

'It's Untel, one of the members of the Irgun. The CID has a price on his head.'

'Everyone knows who he is?'

'Yes, me, the other customers, the waitress, everyone – you too now. He has lunch every day here.'

'And no one hands him over to the police?'

'No. No one.'[21]

A British officer, trying to explain the army's failure to gain the upper hand, protested: 'None of these chaps wore any uniform so could not be distinguished from law-abiding citizens, so the initiative was almost entirely in their hands.'[22]

From London, the government insisted on restraint while the Anglo-American Committee was deliberating, and British troops demonstrated a laughable appreciation of what counter-insurgency involved. On one occasion, when 6th Airborne Division officers were told to dress casually for an attempt to locate an illegal radio transmitter in Tel Aviv, they appeared, each 'disguised, as he thought suitably, in a regimental blazer and grey flannels, but this was soon put right'.[23] That search was fruitful. The building from where transmissions were being aired was found, surrounded, and the radio and its armed presenters seized. 'Appropriately enough, the script was open at a paragraph which swore that their announcers were prepared to defend their radio to the last man. However, they thought better of this.'[24]

Minor successes of this sort were few and far between. In the meantime, the British death toll kept rising. Early in March the Irgun attacked the arms depot on the British army's Sarafand base, killing one policeman. In an attempt to seize more weapons, it attacked the police station in Ramat Gan late in April, killing three police and losing four of its own men, wounded. Then on the night of 24 April the Stern Gang took on the Parachute Regiment at its vehicle park in Tel Aviv. With a force including at least six women, the Gang killed six soldiers, two of whom were still in bed.

'The Jews, especially the IZL, proved the bravest and most cunning guerrilla fighters I have ever met,' one 6th Airborne Division officer recalled.[25] But the Division's ability to fight them was deteriorating. Made up entirely of regular army officers and men who had volunteered for the new parachute force, it began to suffer when, once the war was over, demobilisation started. As demobilisation operated on the principle of 'first in, first out', the Division's longest-serving non-commissioned officers went home first. They were replaced, but by men who were less experienced. These did not command the same respect among the men, whose discipline began to suffer as they waited for their own discharge. Following the vehicle park attack, there was a minor mutiny. The outgoing chief of the imperial general staff, Lord Alanbrooke, feared that the troops 'might get out of hand' if the relentless attacks continued but the troops were not allowed to fight back.[26]

Meanwhile, the Anglo-American Committee failed to deliver the report that Bevin had desired. Far from sympathising with the British predicament, most of the six Americans on the twelve-man panel believed that the problem would be solved if Britain accepted the hundred thousand, as Truman had requested. The Committee's British members reluctantly accepted this recommendation; but they managed to persuade their American colleagues to agree to the insertion of a sharp criticism of Ben-Gurion's half-hearted condemnation of the police station attacks the previous December, and a call on the Jewish Agency to resume cooperation with the British government in stopping terrorism and illegal immigration. The report also recommended that terrorism should be 'resolutely suppressed'.[27]

Without conferring with Attlee, Truman immediately endorsed the Committee's immigration proposals, but pointedly refused to offer any further American assistance to enforce a policy that was bound to lead to Arab uproar. Attlee did not conceal his anger. The truth was, he told the cabinet, that the United States wanted 'her interests at our expense' and, to achieve them, had put substantial pressure on the American members of the Committee.[28] As the government's anger with their ally mounted, Bevin later bluntly told a gathering of the Labour Party that the Americans were pressing the British to accept Jewish displaced persons 'because they do not want too many of them in New York'.[29] That comment predictably caused fury in America but, in fact, Bevin was only paraphrasing what he said the American secretary of state, James Byrnes, had told him.[30]

The report's only useful aspect, so far as the British were concerned, was its criticism of the Jewish Agency, because the Agency's malign influence in Palestine had been bothering them for months. Created in 1929, it had long outgrown the advisory and subordinate role envisaged for it in the mandate. From its fortress-like stone headquarters in west Jerusalem it was now operating as a parallel government to the British administration, which made do with the south wing of the King David Hotel half a mile away. The Agency already had an elected legislature, a council, executive departments and a semi-secret army of its own. Latterly the British authorities' reliance on it for information about the terrorists had endowed it with something more precious still: authority. It had, said MI5's Alec Kellar, 'something of the status of an imperium in imperio' – a state within a state.[31]

The discomfort the British felt at the Agency's burgeoning power grew as its chairman Ben-Gurion dropped unsubtle hints that the Yishuv needed to be ready for a fight. As the chief secretary in Palestine commented, the Jewish Agency might 'deplore terrorism; but every immoderate speech ... the flagrant disregard on the one hand for the authority of Government in maintaining law and order and on the other for the Arab case, the chauvinism and intolerance of their educational system, all contribute to an atmosphere in which the fanatic and the terrorist flourish'.[32]

By the end of 1945 the British had established that the Jewish Agency was not simply condoning terrorism, but actively colluding with the terrorists. Through interception and their sources inside the Agency, the British acquired a number of telegrams in the autumn of that year which showed that the Agency's executive had approved the large-scale railway attacks of 31 October and that it had come to a 'working arrangement with the dissident organisations according to which we shall assign tasks to them under our command'.[33]

An idea began to crystallise in British minds. If they could not penetrate the terrorist networks directly, then perhaps, by raiding the Jewish Agency, they could not only deal the terrorists a fatal blow but, by demonstrating the Agency's direct links with terrorism, make it harder for the Truman administration to support its views. They even hoped they might find documents incriminating the French.

The idea appealed to the armed forces' combative new chief,

Bernard Montgomery. On a tour to familiarise himself with Britain's overseas commitments before he took up his post at the end of June 1946, Montgomery visited Palestine, where he was dismayed to find 'a state of affairs in which British rule existed only in name, the true rulers being the Jews whose unspoken slogan was "You dare not touch us."'[34] The true state of affairs was vividly demonstrated days later, when the Irgun kidnapped five British officers while they were having lunch at their club in Tel Aviv. The organisation rapidly released two and made it clear that the freeing of the others depended on whether the British carried out the execution of two of its own members, who had recently been sentenced to death. When the British swiftly commuted both sentences, the Irgun dumped the remaining three in a crate outside the club from where they had been taken. 'Most undignified!' wrote one officer.[35] Kidnap was used by the Irgun to devastating effect thereafter.

Montgomery, by now a field marshal and a viscount, was determined to turn the tables. Before the war in Palestine he had used overwhelming military force to crush the Arab revolt, and he now proposed similar methods to deal with the Jews. By now Attlee's cabinet agreed. 'We can't go on protesting and making Parliamentary statements,' the deputy prime minister, Herbert Morrison, accepted.[36] As preparations for a massive operation, codenamed 'Agatha', against the Jewish Agency and the Haganah were finalised amid great secrecy, at the end of June Montgomery ordered Sir Evelyn Barker, the British general in command in Palestine, to 'strike hard and with great speed and determination, with the object of completely and utterly defeating the Jews as soon as possible ... Now that the Jews have flung the gauntlet in our face, they must be utterly and completely defeated and their illegal organisations smashed for ever.'[37]

The British chose a Saturday, the Jewish Sabbath, for their strike. At a quarter past four in the morning of 29 June, a combined force of seventeen thousand British soldiers of the 6th Airborne Division and the Palestine Police swooped on the Jewish Agency and, simultaneously, on the members of its executive at their homes, as well as those they believed were members of the Haganah's elite Palmach commando unit. The British collected three truck-loads of documents from the Agency and, in all, 2,718 people were detained, including most of the Jewish Agency's executive and many members of the Palmach, whose leadership was shocked by how 'amazingly accurate' British intelligence was.[38] British officers could not understand the hostility they encountered. 'These bloody Jews,' said one. 'We saved their skins in Alamein and other places and they do this to us.'[39]

The operation was unprecedented in its scale, but it failed to deliver the coup the British wanted. For, through a tip-off from a sympathetic British army officer, the Jews' own intelligence service had known for weeks that a crackdown was coming, and had broadcast a warning the week before the operation finally took place. As a result, although British soldiers uncovered a large and ingeniously concealed arms cache in one settlement, their search of the Jewish Agency itself yielded nothing that was truly damning.

The British were initially mystified. 'We failed to get the evidence to connect the Agency with Jewish terrorism. We failed to get the evidence, I'm sure it was there, before we arrived, to connect them with the illegal immigrant traffic,' complained the CID's head of political intelligence, Dick Catling. 'We failed. We got nothing.'[40] Meanwhile the French savoured the moment when MI5's officer in Palestine told them, 'with some astonishment', that Britain had found nothing compromising them among the paperwork seized from the Agency.[41] The only evidence of the increasingly close links between the French government and the Zionists is a photograph taken on the day of the operation. It shows two of the men most wanted by the British, the chairman of the Jewish Agency and the head of the Haganah, relaxing at a table at a pavement café. David Ben-Gurion and Moshe Sneh were more than two thousand miles away, in Paris.

Nevertheless, the scale of Operation Agatha unnerved the Zionists, who could not immediately be certain that the search of the Jewish Agency had *not* yielded any incriminating evidence. On 1 July Sneh sent a message to the Irgun leader Menachem Begin ordering him to bomb the headquarters of the British administration in Palestine where, he assumed, the seized documents were being analysed.[42] Just after midday on 22 July seven Irgun members, disguised as Arab milkmen, passed through the hotel's oppressive security and wheeled milk churns containing 250 kilograms of explosive through the hotel's kitchens and into La Régence, a nightclub directly beneath the British quarters. They shot their way out of the hotel, jumping into a getaway car parked outside the French consulate just around the corner. At 12.37 p.m. the bomb exploded, and the south wing of the hotel collapsed. In all ninety-one people were killed, and forty-five more injured.

One of the survivors, Robert Newton, worked on the fifth floor of the hotel. 'Instead of the wall behind my chair, I found that I was on the brink of a drop of five storeys,' he recalled. 'The lift well and the staircase on the other side of the destroyed wall had gone, and with them the typists' room I had just visited and the adjacent room of one of my colleagues, who was sharing my house in the absence of our respective wives. He, of course, was somewhere under the rubble, dead, and with him the loyal and cheerful girls who had worked for him.'[43]

'I lost nearly 100 of my best officers and old friends,' the chief secretary, Sir John Shaw, wrote bitterly. 'I have been in Palestine off and on for 11 years: these people meant a lot to me, not only the British officers by any means, but also the loyal and faithful Palestinians including several Jews. My own police escort who had been my inseparable companion and friend for 20 months, my own Armenian chauffeur, and many other humble persons of this type were among the dead. I helped to dig out their stinking putrefying bodies and I attended about 14 funerals in 3 days.'[44] Shaw, who narrowly escaped being killed by a falling chandelier in his office, had then just managed to stop himself stepping from his office into the abyss left by the bomb. He had been specifically warned eight months before that La Régence was a threat to his staff's security, but he had opposed moves to close down the nightclub because, since the onset of the terror campaign, there were so few places for off-duty staff to go.[45]

'Just like the Gunpowder Plot of 1605, the British neglected to think about the basement,' the French consul in Jerusalem reported, a little too cheerily, two days later.[46] He blamed the British for believing that they had 'checkmated' the Jews in Operation Agatha. But he soon found himself having to deny the Irgun's claim that the French consulate, like the hotel, had received a telephone warning before the bomb exploded, and that his staff had been given vital seconds to open all the building's windows, minimising the threat of flying glass. Well aware that the British were trying to link the French with Jewish terrorism, the consul insisted that it was the pressure wave of the explosion that had opened the windows; the warning had come eight minutes after the blast, at 12.45 p.m, he said.

General Barker now issued a crass order to his officers to cut all ties with the Jewish population – 'punishing the Jews in a way the race dislikes as much as any – by striking at their pockets and showing our contempt for them' – and ordered another, massive search.[47] British soldiers discovered five arms caches, including a Stern Gang hoard in the basement of the main synagogue in Tel Aviv. A sharp-eyed police sergeant also identified the leading Stern Gang member, Yitzhak Shamir, by his distinctive eyebrows, although he was disguised as a rabbi. But they did not find the man responsible for the bombing, Menachem Begin. Begin, who was hiding in a secret compartment in his ground-floor flat in Tel Aviv, went for nearly four days without food or water because there was a platoon of British soldiers camped in the garden outside. They thoroughly searched the flat, at one point banging on the wall behind which he was hiding. 'They knocked so hard,' he remembered, that 'I could hardly restrain myself from knocking back.'[48]

Although the bombing of the King David Hotel was an enormous blow to the British administration in Palestine, it backfired on the Irgun and the Jewish Agency politically. Amid international condemnation of the attack, the Agency hurriedly broke off contact with both the Irgun and the Stern Gang, and felt obliged to 'express its horror at the dastardly crime perpetrated by the gang of desperadoes' who had blown up the hotel, although it still did not explicitly condemn the outrage.[49] Ben-Gurion's denial that the Agency was colluding with the terrorists was undermined when the British government rushed out a White Paper publishing what evidence it did have, which suggested that the Agency was colluding with both terrorist organisations.

The Agency dismissed the White Paper as a 'jumble' and, in a bid to undermine it, challenged the British government to prove its allegations by revealing its intelligence sources, a step it knew the British would not take.[50] But, reeling from the arrest of most of its executive, it had no choice but to agree to further talks.[51] Bevin noted in cabinet on 25 July with some satisfaction that 'the Jews' had 'come round to Partition'.[52]

The Jewish Agency's abrupt volte-face left the leaders of the Irgun and the Stern Gang, Begin and Friedman-Yellin, feeling isolated. Convinced that Ben-Gurion was now going to betray them, they looked abroad to carry on their fight.

27

THE AMERICAN LEAGUE FOR
A FREE PALESTINE

EXACTLY ONE WEEK AFTER THE BOMBING OF THE KING DAVID Hotel, a group calling itself the American League for a Free Palestine published an open letter to Harry S. Truman in the *New York Post*, goading the president to prove himself. Since the president had called on the British to let a hundred thousand Jews into Palestine, it noted, almost a year had passed without result. 'The million and a half Hebrews in Europe are waiting in blood-soaked ghettoes, in DP camps, on the highways, and in the seaports. They are waiting for a sign from the United States, from you, Mr President, that they are not being abandoned but given the fundamental right to live in dignity and freedom.'[1]

The League, which had been set up two years earlier by a man called Peter Bergson and had an office on West 49th Street in New York, made the challenge partly because it scented blood. The midterm November elections were approaching and it was obvious that Truman's presidency was in trouble. America had expected prosperity to follow peace, but the end of round-the-clock industrial production had led instead to unemployment and wage cuts. Pay cuts brought on strikes, which caused power cuts. Early in 1946, Truman's administration was forced to admit that the demobilisation of many servicemen would be delayed. Those who did come home found everything in short supply, especially housing. Divorce rates soared, Truman's popularity plummeted and, as the poll drew near, his Republican opponents boiled their message down to just two words. 'Had Enough?' their posters asked.

The slight, myopic and short-fused Harry Truman could never hope to match his predecessor Roosevelt. He had been vice-president for less than twelve weeks when he was told that Roosevelt was dead. The former farmer later described the moment when he realised that he was now president of the most powerful nation on earth as like having 'a load of hay fall on you'.[2] His discomfiture was obvious. 'He looked to me like a very little man as he sat ... in the huge leather chair,' wrote one contemporary, remembering Truman as he waited to be sworn in.[3] Roosevelt's wife Eleanor was openly sceptical to Truman's face. When, after the news of her husband's death came through, Truman asked her if there was anything he could do to help her, she replied, 'Is there anything *we* can do for *you*? For you are the one in trouble now.'[4] Policies that Roosevelt had made coherent and convincing now sounded reedy and muddled when they came from Truman. What would Roosevelt have done were he still alive? people wondered. In the summer of 1946 they began joking: What would Truman do if he were alive?[5]

With elections in the offing, the American League was deliberately trying to play on Truman's image as a man who had no drive. There had been no headway since the Anglo-American Committee reported that April. Attlee had made his willingness to implement the Committee's recommendations conditional on the Jewish terrorist groups disarming, and had then insisted that the recommendations be discussed by a panel of experts from both countries. When Truman went along with this idea, the British delegation came up with a list of forty-three more points they felt worthy of consideration. When, at last, the experts were on the verge of issuing their report, their proposal to make the United Nations trustee of a federal state comprising autonomous Arab and Jewish provinces was leaked, and under heavy criticism from both sides it fell apart. Frustrated by the lack of headway and by continuous pressure from the Zionists, Truman told his cabinet that he had 'no use' for the Jews 'and didn't care what happened to them'.[6]

But there was a second, crucial reason why the American League decided to intervene to keep the spotlight fixed on Britain's restrictive immigration policy and the pressure on the president. The day after the King David Hotel bombing, Truman issued a forceful statement in which he called on 'every responsible Jewish leader' to join with him 'in condemning the wanton slaying of human beings'.[7] He went on to say that the bombing 'might well retard' Jewish immigration into Palestine. The American League had more reason than most to be alarmed that the outrage might generate American sympathy for the British. For in reality it was a front for Menachem Begin's Irgun, the bombers of the hotel. 'Peter Bergson' was a pseudonym. The real name of the American League's organising genius was Hillel Kook, a senior member of the Irgun.

Kook, the son of a well-known rabbi in Palestine, had arrived in the United States in 1940, expecting that the country held the key to the fulfilment of Zionist ambitions, given its five-million-strong Jewish population. But he found the main Zionist body there, the American Zionist Emergency Committee, divided. Its co-chairmen, the rabbis Stephen Wise and Hillel Silver, disagreed on tactics: Silver, a Republican, wanted to put more pressure on Roosevelt to come off the fence; Wise, a Democrat like Roosevelt, did not.

Kook was disenchanted by the bickering between the two men. Convinced that it was the reason why the Zionists were not having more success, he set up the American League for a Free Palestine in 1944. The League's aim, which reflected the increasingly militant attitude of Zionists in Palestine, was to raise money for the Irgun and sympathy for its violent methods by drawing parallels between the Zionists' struggle against the British and the Americans' own war of independence, a century and a half before. 'As a nation born in revolution against the same brand of Britannic despotism, we know that no matter how hard and bitter the struggle, it is the Hebrew David that will beat the British Goliath,' another advert from the American League thundered in July 1946.[8] A week later Kook held a press conference. 'The civilised nations of the world must take sides in this conflict,' he said. 'They must side with the British Aggressor or the Hebrew victims.'[9]

Kook's greatest gift was securing celebrities willing to endorse this view. Frank Sinatra, Bob Hope, the Marx brothers and Leonard Bernstein were among many who signed up to his campaign. So too, significantly, did Eleanor Roosevelt. They, and the money Kook splashed on full-page advertising, guaranteed the League coverage in the press. But to ensure that he had clout in Washington DC as well, he hired Guy Gillette, a former Democratic senator who had lost his Iowa seat in 1944. Described by a member of his staff as 'probably one of the best looking men who ever served in this body', the white-haired Gillette had the charm and presence necessary to give the League plausibility on Capitol Hill.[10]

As yet unaware of the American League's connection with the Irgun, the British allowed Gillette to visit Palestine just after the King David Hotel bombing. From Jerusalem that August the former senator joined calls for the abandonment of the proposal that the United Nations could act as trustee of a federal state of Palestine. In a telegram to Truman Gillette claimed that this idea, which had emerged out of the Anglo-American Committee's report, would 'have the effect of turning this nation from an independent state under temporary mandate into a province of the British Empire'.[11] On his return from Palestine Gillette rubbished the idea that Britain was a stabilising presence in the Middle East. 'If the British would clear out, there would be no hostility between the Jews and the Arabs,' he insisted.[12]

As the mid-term elections approached, Kook came up with a brilliant way to ensure that Palestine stuck in both voters' and politicians' minds. In September 1946, with nine weeks to go before the poll, the American League premièred a new play on Broadway. *A Flag Is Born* capitalised on Kook's show-business connections to the full. Written by Ben Hecht, scored by the composer Kurt Weill and narrated by the war reporter Quentin Reynolds, *A Flag Is Born* told the story of three Jewish concentration camp survivors trying to reach Palestine. Thwarted by all the great powers – but most especially Britain – only one, 'David', played by Marlon Brando, survives the final act to do so. 'Where were you?' Brando repeatedly asks the audience in the last climactic moments of the play. 'Where were you ... when the killing was going on? When the six million were burned and buried alive in lime, where were you? ... Nowhere!

Because you were ashamed to cry as Jews! A curse on your silence. And now you speak a little. Your hearts squeak – and you have a dollar for the Jews of Europe. Thank you. Thank you.'[13]

This closing speech set the scene for an appeal. At the end of each performance, the manager would stand up with the spotlight on him and declare that any money raised that evening would be immediately telegraphed abroad to purchase ships to take Jewish refugees to Palestine. The play raised at least $400,000 – a little over half the League's $740,000 expenditure in 1946.[14] The souvenir programme, with a cover illustration likening Jewish pioneers in Palestine to American revolutionaries in 1776, hinted at what this money also bought, for it included the emblem of the Irgun – a rifle in a clenched fist over a map of Palestine and Transjordan.[15]

The play stoked the febrile political atmosphere in New York, where Kook and other Zionists played on the Democratic and Republican Parties' uncertainty about whether their respective policies on Palestine were enough to win the city's 'Jewish vote'. As a British official put it afterwards, the Zionists were 'apt to claim that their voting strength is decisive in certain areas and the Administration seems all too willing to believe them'.[16] But there was no question that the Jews mattered in New York. When the Democrats discovered that the Republican governor of the city, Thomas Dewey, was going to declare his support for Jewish immigration to Palestine on 6 October, they panicked. Truman's adviser, David Niles, urged the president to go one step further than the governor. On 4 October – the eve of Yom Kippur – Truman did so, by calling for the creation of 'a viable Jewish state'.[17] Two days later Dewey went still further, calling for 'hundreds of thousands' to be allowed into Palestine.

Truman's declaration failed to swing the outcome of the November elections. Dewey was easily re-elected as governor of New York, and the Republicans won a majority in Congress for the first time since 1928. Truman himself was fed up with being badgered by 'selfish' Jewish delegations. 'Jesus Christ couldn't please them when he was here on earth,' he moaned, 'so how would anyone expect that I would have any luck?'[18] Laughably, he tried afterwards to claim that the timing of his Yom Kippur declaration had nothing to do with the election, but the following February Bevin disclosed that the State Department had told him the president's statement had been an attempt to outbid Dewey. To cheers, he told the House of Commons that 'in international relations he could not settle things if his problem were made the subject of local elections'.[19] Bevin's snide revelation outraged Truman. The same day, the president's spokesman put out a barely disguised rebuke, claiming that Truman's statement was nothing new, and simply reflected 'the desire of the President to advance a just solution of the Palestine problem'.[20]

Yet it never escaped Truman that support for a Jewish state was good politics. His stance resonated not only with Jewish Americans, but with the much larger population of Bible-reading Protestants, who saw it as their duty to help the Israelites regain the Promised Land. This was why Kook's propaganda always referred to 'Hebrews' rather than to 'Jews'. Many Americans recognised the Zionists as fellow settlers, and black Americans were also drawn to Truman's willingness to support the underdog. By 1947 the polls showed that, by two to one, Americans were in favour of the creation of a Jewish state.[21] And, as the British quietly insinuated, Truman's policy was one that even anti-Semitic Americans might rally around, since otherwise the United States might have to find a home for the dispossessed Jews of Europe.

Strategic calculations mattered too. In early March President Truman addressed the House of Representatives in Washington and set out his foreign policy. A year earlier he had been advised by a brilliant young official in the State Department, George Kennan, that the United States should embark upon the 'long-term, patient but firm and vigilant containment of Russian expansive tendencies'.[22] Now the president announced that his government would provide financial support to Greece and Turkey – a job that Britain had done in the past – and outlined what was to become known as the Truman Doctrine. It 'must be the policy of the United States to support free peoples who are resisting attempted subjugation by armed minorities or by outside pressures', he stated. America 'must assist free peoples to work out their own destinies in their own way'.[23] The comments were aimed at Soviet Russia, but of course they also had a barbed relevance for Britain in Palestine, where Truman worried that the 'crackpots' might 'turn the country over to Stalin if they had half a chance'.[24]

The American League had achieved its goal. Not only had it forced both main parties in the United States into a bidding war over Jewish immigration, but it had sparked tensions between the United States administration and the British that were to prove important in due course. Kook was shaping American opinion: his arguments had started to be repeated back to him. 'The brave men and women of the Resistance Movement in Palestine are no more extremists than the American colonists who staged the Boston Tea Party or the Irish rebels of the 1920s,' wrote one Christian activist in a message to the Zionist Conference. He went on to propose that 'the resistance against British tyranny in Palestine be continued with the same spirit – and in greater strength – in the difficult days that lie ahead'.[25]

In December 1946 Kook launched an offshoot of the American League in Paris, in a similar bid to win French sympathy by drawing parallels between the Irgun's struggle and wartime French resistance. Whereas in America the League had sought the autographs of Hollywood's stars, the Ligue Française pour la Palestine Libre predictably offered cigarettes to the nicotine-stained intellectuals of the Rive Gauche: it even based itself nearby, at the Hôtel Lutétia in St Germain.

The Ligue's greatest coup was to gain the backing of Simone de Beauvoir and Jean-Paul Sartre, who had written during the war for *Combat*, the Resistance newspaper which the foreign minister Georges Bidault had once edited. Through them it won support from many other writers and philosophers, whose thoughts it paraded in a weekly publication, *La Riposte*. Former members of the Resistance, notably Edgar Faure and Daniel Mayer, who had served with Bidault on the Conseil National de la Résistance, also signed up, as did many French politicians who were anxious to atone for France's complicity in the deportation of Jews to Germany during the war. From these various directions Kook made his most important connection – with Georges Bidault himself, whom he did his best to reassure that the Irgun would look after the Christian holy places in a new Jewish state.

Britain's treatment of one man probably did more than anything else to win Kook's battle for him. Dov Gruner, a member of the Irgun, had been captured by the British after being seriously wounded during the attack on the police station at Ramat Gan in April 1946. His jaw was badly shattered and he spent months in hospital before he came to trial. But when he finally did so, the outcome was predictable. On 2 January 1947, he was condemned to death. As he did not recognise the legitimacy of the British court, he refused to appeal against his sentence. What made Gruner so unusual was that, before joining the Irgun, he had fought for the British army in the war. Born in Hungary, he had emigrated to Palestine in his youth and volunteered to fight for Britain after war broke out in 1939. When he was posted to an auxiliary unit he deserted and rejoined so that he could fight in the front line, which he did – across North Africa and then through Europe.

The idea that the British would execute a man who had fought to preserve their freedom drew international astonishment and condemnation. To stay Gruner's execution, the Irgun kidnapped two British officials on 26 January. One of them, a judge named Sir Ralph Windham, they seized from the court where he was hearing a 'rather boring' case. Discovering a shared interest in classical music, Windham and his captors 'were quite friendly with each other', the judge recalled after his release, which came when the British decided to put off Gruner's hanging.[26] Gruner remained in the condemned cell throughout February and March while the British government made one last, unsuccessful, effort to broker a deal between the Arabs and the Jews, and then briefly brought in martial law following a further bombing. After the civil legal process resumed, Gruner was hanged without warning early on 16 April, before his sister, who lived in Philadelphia, was able to see him one last time. 'I do not want to be a martyr for my religion,' he wrote, in a letter he left to be opened after his death, 'but I am ready to offer myself in sacrifice for my people, just as Jesus Christ did.'[27]

'It was a sneak murder,' declared the American League for a Free Palestine in another advertisement the same week that invited readers to 'Build Dov Gruner's Memorial' by donating to its 'Palestine Freedom Drive'.[28] '$7,500,000 applied now in the right places will win the battle for Palestine ... This victory will not depend on charity or upon editorial praise in the world's press. It will be won by Hebrews fighting with their blood and courage ... and your dollars.'

And the dollars flowed in. The League looked anywhere for money. It even held a fund-raising event for members of the West Coast mafia.[29] One of them, the gangster Mickey Cohen, later boasted that he had helped raise $1 million for the Irgun; the true sum was probably about a tenth of that, but significant nonetheless.[30]

The British government, which had been following the League's work with growing fury, had already tried to persuade Truman's administration to find a way to prevent it advertising in the press. It finally snapped when that May Kook published another open letter in the *New York Post*, this time 'to the terrorists of Palestine', written by Ben Hecht.[31] 'Every time you blow up a British arsenal or wreck a British gaol, or send a British railroad train sky-high, or rob a British bank, or let go with your guns and bombs at British betrayers and invaders of your homeland, the Jews of America make a little holiday in their hearts. Not all Jews of course. The only time Jews present a united front is when they lie piled in massacre pits.'

'What if British communists did the same in the British press?' fumed the permanent secretary at the Foreign Office when he met Lewis Douglas, the American ambassador to London.[32] He apparently 'begged' Douglas to do what he could to stop the League from advertising, but without success. Initially, the British felt that the administration was running scared of the American Jewish lobby, but it transpired that more prosaic factors were at work. 'The real trouble, over and above the internal political aspect, is the apparent lack of legal sanctions which can be invoked by the United States Government,' a British official admitted.[33] As a result, not only did the League continue to place advertisements in the press, but it was also exempt from paying tax because it was a non-profit-making body.

Truman did issue an appeal the following month, asking US citizens 'to refrain ... from engaging in or facilitating any activities which tend further to inflame the passions of the inhabitants of Palestine, to undermine law and order in Palestine or to promote violence in that country', but the League was unperturbed. Asked whether it intended to take any notice of Truman's request, its spokesman's answer was short and blunt.

'Definitely not,' he said.[34]

28

FRENCH AND ZIONIST INTRIGUES

HOURS BEFORE DOV GRUNER WAS EXECUTED, ON 15 APRIL 1947 a well dressed, coquettish young woman carrying a smart blue handbag and a parcel wrapped in newspaper stepped up to a guard at the Colonial Office's headquarters on Whitehall and asked whether she might urgently use the lavatory. When he seemed reluctant she admitted that she had a ladder in her stocking that she needed to repair. His chivalry – or possibly his imagination – roused by this added detail, the guard relented and directed her towards the cloakrooms in the basement. It was only later in the day, long after the girl had been and gone, that a cleaner found the parcel abandoned on a loo seat. Picking it up and tearing away the newspaper, she pulled out a wire and realised that she was holding a bomb. It had not exploded only because its timer had jammed.

Once defused, the device provided Scotland Yard with two important leads. It comprised twenty-four sticks of French-made gelignite which were covered in the fingerprints of a man who had escaped from prison in Palestine in 1943. The guard recalled another significant detail. The anxious young woman who had left it behind spoke English with a French accent. A Chief Inspector Jones of the Special Branch rapidly flew to Paris. The newspapers cryptically reported that 'after making certain inquiries' he had gone into conference with senior officers of the French police.[1] It is likely that he also spoke to John Bruce-Lockhart, the highly regarded head of MI6's Paris station.

Although the British government had known for some time that the Irgun and the Stern Gang were planning to use Paris as a base for assassinations of key British politicians including Churchill and Bevin, Bruce-Lockhart was unable to provide more useful information.[2] British intelligence officers in Palestine had worried, after Colonel Alessandri of the Bureau Noir got wind of their interest in him and returned to France, that it would be not be easy to keep 'as close a watch on French and Zionist intrigues ... in Paris as it is in the Middle East', and the subsequent lack of meaningful intelligence had proved them right.[3] At the start of 1947 the Paris MI6 station reported that the French Sûreté had seen Menachem Begin in Paris. A month later it added that the Irgun's leader was believed to have undergone plastic surgery to alter his appearance, admitting, 'we have no description of the new face'.[4] Begin, who was in Tel Aviv throughout, had indeed gone to some effort to change how he looked, but he had only grown a beard.

All this made Chief Inspector Jones's appearance the more welcome, for he finally brought concrete information. He was able to tell Bruce-Lockhart and the French that the man whose fingerprints were on the bomb was Yaacov Levstein, a member of the Stern Gang.

Born in Russia, thirty-year-old Levstein was a brilliant bomb-maker who had been wounded and arrested in the first police raid after the betrayal of the Gang in February 1942. It was his mother who then inadvertently led the police from his hospital bedside to Stern's hiding place in Tel Aviv, where the British detective Geoffrey Morton shot the Gang's charismatic leader dead. Levstein recovered from his injury and was sentenced to life imprisonment, but he did not serve much of his term. After eight months he escaped and remained at large until the war was over, whereupon he made his way from Palestine, via Egypt, to France. Chaotic and shattered, dotted with sympathisers and awash with arms, the country was the perfect place for him to open a new front against the British.

On his arrival in Paris Levstein went to the Quai d'Orsay and tried to contact Alessandri, but was told that the French intelligence officer had been temporarily posted to Tunisia. About a month afterwards, he later recalled, the concierge of his hotel informed him that he had an important-looking guest to see him. 'I quickly put on my coat and tie,' Levstein later recalled, 'and went downstairs. A tall, aristocratic-looking Frenchman stood there, with a stick, a monocle and a top hat. After he had verified my identity he embraced me like an old friend. We chatted for a few minutes, and he told me he would put me in touch with certain French institutions to begin negotiations.'[5] Levstein reported back to Palestine that Colonel Alessandri had found him.

Levstein and Alessandri met again a few days later. By then the Stern Gang's emissary to the French in Beirut, Gabriel Messeri, had joined Levstein, and Alessandri brought with him André Blumel, a lawyer and adviser to the former French prime minister Léon Blum, France's first Jewish leader. Levstein and Messeri now asked Alessandri and Blumel for 'arms and for a secret base for war against London'.[6] According to Levstein, 'Blumel told us he was authorized to tell us in the name of the French government that the government was willing in principle to sign an agreement with the LEHI [Stern Gang], and only needed a few days to fully study the matter.' Although Blumel was ultimately unable to deliver the deal because the French government 'might get into political trouble with the British', he reported that the French were still investigating whether clandestine support could be provided. 'He ... hoped that LEHI got all the assistance it needed in its struggle against the British.'[7] In return, the Stern Gang agreed not to launch attacks on Britain from France itself.

Levstein also contacted a man named David Knout, another Russian Jew and a poet, who had helped establish a Jewish resistance organisation called the Armée Juive in January 1942. After the Vichy government banned the Jews from public life and began to deport them, from July 1942, Jews in France had every incentive to join the Resistance, in which they played a disproportionately vital role. The Armée smuggled Jews out of France and money in, and tried to murder informants who betrayed Jews. In autumn 1943 it established a 'maquis' of its own in the Montagne Noire, a rugged part of south-west France where Resistance activity was most intense. For

Knout, however, the Armée had an important further purpose. After the war he expected it to help create a Jewish state in Palestine. The Jews, he wrote, could 'either come back to life collectively or perish individually'.[8]

To help Levstein, Knout volunteered his daughter Betty, a pretty nineteen-year-old who had already risked death working as a courier for the Armée. Together Levstein and Betty Knout reinvigorated the Armée's wartime networks, locating arms caches, recruiting new members and producing a bulletin, *L'Indépendance*.

Levstein also claimed the support of Jean-Paul Sartre, who had just signed up to Hillel Kook's Ligue Française pour la Palestine Libre, and he managed to recruit one of Sartre's students at the Sorbonne, Robert Misrahi, to carry out his first bombing on the British mainland. On 7 March Misrahi left the bomb – a coat in which the shoulder pads had been replaced with gelignite – at the Colonies Club, a social club for servicemen, off Trafalgar Square in London. Police blamed the explosion on a gas leak, but in a statement a day later the Stern Gang proclaimed its responsibility and promised that the attacks would continue until Britain had been driven from Palestine.

'No security measures can stop sophisticated, imaginative planning,' Levstein later wrote, delighted by the ease with which Misrahi had carried out his mission.[9] What he did not plan for was what would happen if one of his bombs failed to explode. As a consequence, when his next bomb did not go off, he provided Jones of the Special Branch in London with enough evidence to come to Paris to press the French to hunt him down. On 18 April *Le Monde* reported that the British were hunting for a French woman in connection with the bomb discovered at the Colonial Office. They did not know at this point that she was Betty Knout.

Persuading the French police to crack down on Jewish terrorism was not easy because the minister of the interior at the time, Edouard Depreux, sympathised with the Zionists. A lifelong socialist, Depreux was also a great admirer of the former prime minister, Blum. Blum, who had spent two years of the war in Buchenwald and then Dachau, daily expecting to be executed, had declared after the King David Hotel bombing that Jewish terrorism was 'nothing but a desperate form of revolt'. The former French prime minister blamed the British government for provoking terrorism 'by closing, one after the other, all the avenues of hope to the Jews of Palestine and the Zionists across the world'.[10]

Depreux took the same line. When a Zionist consignment of arms was impounded by the police in south-west France in 1946, he intervened and ordered the release of the weapons so that they could be shipped to Palestine. He was also instrumental in ensuring that the French government decided, in the spring of 1947, that its officials should not waste much effort checking the visas of those who were leaving France, and when five members of the Irgun and the Stern Gang escaped from the British prison camp in Eritrea and managed to reach the neighbouring French colony of Djibouti, it was Depreux who offered them asylum in France. One of the five, Yitzhak Shamir, remembered how, on arrival in Toulon, he and his Stern Gang comrade Arieh Ben-Eliezer had received 'the warmest possible reception ... There were old friends from Lehi and the Irgun, and Arieh and I were given permission to stay in France for as long as we liked.'[11]

After it was revealed that the British were hunting Betty Knout, and her wartime role within the Resistance was disclosed, it rapidly became clear that the Sûreté were not going to expend too much energy in finding her. As one Parisian newspaper characterised the tensions between Scotland Yard and the Sûreté, 'The former want to hang Betty, the latter seek to save her.'[12] Five weeks after Chief Inspector Jones's appearance in Paris French police finally raided a flat in the Latin Quarter, arresting five students, some of whom were enrolled at the Sorbonne nearby. Plastic-explosive wrappings and bomb-making equipment found there matched the Colonial Office bomb, but there was no sign of either Levstein or Knout.

In keeping with his deal with Blumel not to wage war from French soil, Levstein had a courier heft a rucksack full of letter bombs addressed to prominent British politicians across France's alpine frontier with Italy so that they could be posted from Turin. The letters arrived in Britain in the first week of June, and by luck none of them detonated, for forensic tests afterwards found that, despite the packages' deceptive slimness, Levstein had created a bomb powerful enough to blast a hole through a piece of steel plate. The chancellor of the exchequer's secretary felt her letter growing hot as she began to open it, and the messenger who had just delivered it grabbed it back from her and threw it in a fire bucket. Anthony Eden carried his around with him all day on a visit to the annual 4th of June celebrations at his old school, Eton. The least deserving recipient was the manager of the Norwood and Dulwich Laundry in Gipsy Hill, south London, whose misfortune was to share his name with the paymaster general, Arthur Greenwood. Louis Spears, interestingly, was another of the recipients.

By then both Levstein and Knout had been arrested. On a mission to Belgium to post further letter bombs and to try to blow up a visiting British destroyer, they were stopped at the border by Belgian customs officials who discovered that Knout was wearing a corset made of dynamite and that their trunks had hidden compartments containing letter bombs identical to those that had been turning up in Britain. Knout was carrying the same blue handbag she had been seen with at the Colonial Office.

The British government now began to put pressure on the Belgians to extradite both Knout and Levstein to Britain, but the Belgians refused to do so, describing their crime as 'political'. The pro-Zionist lawyer André Blumel visited them both, and organised their defence. That September a court in Mons fined Knout 1,000 francs and sentenced her to twelve months in prison. Levstein, who had given Knout most of the explosive to take across the border, received eight months and a fine half the size of Knout's. His sentence, at least, meant that his most diabolical idea – to poison London's water supply with cholera bacteria supplied by sympathisers working at the Pasteur Institute in Paris – was never carried out. [13]

Taking account of the time he had already spent in prison on remand, the Belgians freed Levstein four months later. But when the bomb-maker crossed back into France he was promptly rearrested. 'I know all about you. You cannot hide anything from me,' the local French police chief told him when he was brought to the police station. 'Tell me, *entre nous*, did you really try to kill Englishmen?' When Levstein tried to deny his involvement in the Stern Gang, the conversation took an unexpected turn. 'One should kill the British wherever one can find them,' the policeman told him. 'They are pathological liars, and this is how they have ruled the whole world. I saw it myself. I served in Lebanon and Syria in de Gaulle's Free France army. We spilled our blood helping the British in the Levant, and after they took over Lebanon and Syria they threw us to the dogs.'[14] And with that he produced a bottle of wine and poured Levstein and himself a drink.

Levstein's Paris operation folded but, a short distance away, the Irgun's was still active. Its leader Eli Tavin, a graduate in philosophy from the Hebrew University in Jerusalem, had been the organisation's head of intelligence in Palestine until he was kidnapped and tortured by the Haganah during its crackdown on the terrorist organisations following the murder of Lord Moyne. Released at the end of war when Ben-Gurion decreed that the Haganah should start collaborating with the Irgun and the Stern Gang, Tavin went to Italy to find displaced Jews, train them as terrorists and organise their illicit entry into Palestine. There he stayed until one day in October 1946 he was contacted by a courier, a young South African Jew named Samuel Katz. The heel of one of Katz's shoes contained a hidden message for Tavin telling him to go to Paris and take over leadership of the Irgun's operations there. Before he did so, he was to bomb the British embassy in Rome, which was at that point the centre of Britain's attempt to disrupt Jewish immigration to Palestine.

In the early hours of 31 October the Irgun left two suitcases packed with high explosive outside the British embassy. The resulting explosion gouged the façade from the building and, once reinforced by a series of menacing anonymous telephone calls to British politicians and military officers, it sparked alarmist headlines in the British newspapers. Katz, who after his rendezvous with Tavin proceeded to the British capital to assess the consequences of the Rome attack, was pleased to see billboards proclaiming, 'Irgun threatens London.'[15] As he reflected later, this was a wild, and therefore helpful, exaggeration of the Irgun's offensive capability at that moment. 'Until the spring of 1947 there was not even any specific plan for operations there, nor anyone in England who could carry it out.'

Tavin arrived in Paris to find that his predecessor, Shmuel Ariel, had reached an understanding with the French government, of a similar type to that negotiated by the Stern Gang through Alessandri. The Irgun and the Stern Gang could use Paris as their base providing they did not carry out any action against the British on French soil: before Princess Elizabeth – the present queen – visited in 1948, the French police met the Irgun face to face to double-check that they would not try to kill her. Ariel had also based himself at the Hôtel Lutétia, the grand hotel in St Germain where that other Irgun front, the Ligue Française pour la Palestine Libre, was already based. This choice of accommodation contributed to the Irgun leadership's decision to replace Ariel with Tavin – on the grounds that Ariel was living too extravagant a lifestyle for a representative of an organisation pleading poverty – but in fact the location was inspired. The hotel, which had been requisitioned by German military intelligence in the war, had now become a clearing house to receive former inmates of the concentration camps as they returned to France. Survivors posted photographs and descriptions of missing family and friends on large boards outside the hotel lobby. It was here that the scale of the Holocaust became apparent: the Lutétia was the ideal place to recruit supporters for the Irgun's cause in Palestine.

One of the first men to approach Tavin was not a returning survivor of the death camps but a thirty-three-year-old rabbi from New York. Baruch Korff had emigrated to the United States when he was twelve. There, when the war began he became associated with Kook's American League for a Free Palestine, and took charge of trying to ensure that the League, and other like-minded organisations, received the lion's share of the street-collections licences that were issued by the city's Public Solicitations Division. He was evidently a persuasive man. A woman who worked for the city later told the British that '"higher ups" in the Department and in the Municipal government frequently stretched the regulations to enable Jewish groups to have more collection days, and also reserved dates long in advance for favoured groups'.[16]

In the late summer of 1947, Korff moved to Paris to see if he could make progress on a hare-brained scheme to parachute Jews into Palestine, thus circumventing the British efforts to stop Jewish immigration by sea. When, however, he put the idea of raining Jews into the Promised Land to France's acting foreign minister, he received a polite rebuff. So Korff revised his plan. He decided to hire a private aircraft to drop first propaganda and later bombs on London, instead. Having produced ten thousand copies of a leaflet declaring that the British government had 'dipped His Majesty's crown in Jewish blood and polished it with Arab oil', and inviting recipients to press the British government to 'quit ... Israel now', Korff hired a pilot and arranged to rendezvous with him at an aerodrome ten miles outside Paris early on 4 September.[17] The pilot, however, tipped off the French Sûreté, and, in an appropriately absurd dénouement, when he and Korff met at the airstrip they were arrested by a squad of twenty policemen disguised as mechanics.

The French, though, made no effort whatsoever to try to hinder Zionist efforts to organise mass illegal immigration into Palestine from the south of France. In March that year the French cabinet had decided not to impose stringent checks on people wishing to leave the country, with consequences that became immediately obvious. Before the month was out the British ambassador, Duff Cooper, visited the Quai d'Orsay to register a protest at 'French slackness in preventing illegal departures of Jews for Palestine'.[18] Bidault, on the surface sympathetic, continued to do nothing to help Cooper. One newspaper quoted an exchange between a group of Jewish would-be émigrés and a policeman in the summer of 1947. Where were they going? the policeman asked. 'We are going to Bolivia,' the group's leader replied, presenting their collective visa to him to demonstrate it. 'A lovely country,' the *flic* remarked, as he glanced at the document and handed it back. 'I know it well. I served three years in Syria.'[19]

Soon there were Jews coming from across Europe to board ships docked in France's southern ports. By mid-1947 convoys of trucks bearing between a hundred and five hundred Jews were arriving at the ports every other night. Initially they timed their crossing of the French frontier at the weekends, when border posts were short-staffed and the officials present keen for as quiet a life as possible.

Gradually, they realised that many of the officials were sympathetic. So too was a network of fishermen, dockers and shipping agents in the ports. At one point the communists even interrupted a hauliers' strike to enable a convoy of Jews to reach Marseille.

At the port the refugees were helped to board a strange variety of ships that the Haganah, through its emigration service Mossad, had managed to acquire. 'What the hell,' said the Haganah's man in Paris when the seaworthiness of some of the vessels he had bought came in for scrutiny, 'Columbus discovered America in a 49-ton barge.'[20] French newspaper readers came to appreciate the conditions that the émigrés underwent en route to Palestine through French reporters whom the Haganah embedded aboard the ships. 'If I live to a hundred, I will never forget these sinister hours, in which death hovered over the *Theodore Herzl*, a floating ghetto covered by filth and blood, of groans and swearing,' wrote one, Pierre Joffroy, for *Le Parisien Libéré*.[21]

The British resorted to extreme measures to try to stop the traffic. At the end of 1946 the government sought the assistance of MI6, which came up with a range of plans, including tampering with ships' water and food supplies and arson, to be blamed on an invented new Arab terrorist organisation. On 14 February 1947, the government gave it permission to go ahead with attacks on empty ships in Italian, but not French, waters. Five ships were attacked.[22]

The most famous ship of all to leave Marseille was the *Exodus* which, in an earlier incarnation as the *President Warfield*, had plied the Chesapeake Bay from Baltimore. Its captain was the Danzig-born Yitzhak Aharonovitch, who had qualified as a sailor in London, then returned to Palestine to join the Palmach's sister naval unit, the Palyam. Aharonovitch had risen quickly through its ranks, though only perhaps because the Palyam had no other professional sailor. At the end of 1946 he was sent to Baltimore to supervise the refit of the former pleasure steamer, including a substantial upgrade of its engines. Under Aharonovitch's command and flying the Honduran flag, the *President Warfield* chugged across the Atlantic and reached Marseille on 12 June 1947, where it spent the next three weeks. Following the execution of Dov Gruner, the Haganah now wanted to provoke the British into heavy-handed action while the international press was still interested. Renamed the *Exodus*, the *President Warfield* was to be the means by which they did so.

Having taken on supplies at Marseille, Aharonovitch now sailed the *Exodus* west to the port of Sète to take aboard its passengers. The port was well known for its willingness to help the Jews. The local *député* was the Jewish minister of transport, Jules Moch, whose son had been murdered by the Gestapo during the war, while Moch's cousin was the prefect of the town. Over the next three days more than 4,500 passengers embarked. These the Haganah had chosen, thinking of the spotlight that would soon be cast upon them. It was a well-known secret, one of those selected later said, that the ship contained a high proportion of heavily pregnant women, mothers with young children, the elderly and the sick. Packed into the ship in bunks three storeys high, they set off for Palestine on 12 July. Aharonovitch's plan was to sail as close as possible to Palestine, and then try to outrun the Royal Navy by opening the battered-looking ship's engines up to their reconditioned maximum – an astonishing twenty knots.

The British government knew that a confrontation was coming. Their agents in the south of France had warned them that Mossad had as many as thirty thousand displaced persons ready to set sail, and MI6 had a yacht carrying saboteurs shadowing the *Exodus*. By then, however, the Foreign Office had vetoed further sabotage operations, and MI6 was never given permission to try to destroy the vessel. As soon as the *Exodus* sailed for Palestine on the 12th, Bevin formally complained to Bidault. When Bidault indicated that, if the Royal Navy were able to intercept the ship, her passengers might be returned to France, the British government decided to rise to the Haganah's challenge. The colonial secretary, Arthur Creech Jones, told the British high commissioner in Palestine to turn the *Exodus*'s passengers away so as to 'clearly establish the principle of *refoulement*', French for 'repulsion'.[23]

Britain's handling of the episode did indeed achieve repulsion, although not quite in the way Creech Jones had envisaged. The *Exodus* was followed by the Royal Navy down the length of the Mediterranean, but Aharonovitch was never able to order full steam ahead. In the small hours of 18 July she was rammed by two British destroyers twenty miles off Gaza while still in international waters. British sailors armed with coshes boarded the hemmed-in ship, but when the Jews aboard turned steam jets on them and threw smoke bombs, fireworks and tear-gas canisters, the British started shooting.

Below deck, Aharonovitch still hoped to beach the ship, but he was overruled by the Haganah commander aboard, for by now the *Exodus* was slowly sinking. After three hours' resistance – details of which the ship broadcast by radio to the shore – Aharonovitch surrendered. The *Exodus* was towed to Haifa, where three vessels were ready to deport her passengers to France. By nightfall the same day, the first of them were on their way back to Marseille, but not before two members of the United Nations Special Committee on Palestine, Emil Sandström and Vladimir Simic, had witnessed what had happened. Their minder felt that the scenes of the wounded being stretchered from the *Exodus* marked a turning point in the two men's attitude towards the British mandate.

The three ships' return to Port-de-Bouc, at the mouth of the river Rhône, triggered friction between the British and French governments. Duff Cooper was incandescent at the French, who he said had 'behaved abominably. They had undertaken to inspect visas with care and to enforce the provisions of the safety of life at sea convention – and they allowed five thousand Jews with obviously forged visas to sail in a ship that was unfit, by their own admission, to carry any passengers.'[24] Bidault, who was quietly angry that the British and American governments had just agreed a deal to boost German industrial output behind his back, claimed that he felt as strongly about the matter as Cooper did. But again he resisted the latter's pressure to do anything to help the British. Camouflaging his own true feelings, he blamed the problem on his socialist counterparts in the cabinet, Depreux and Moch, and the influence of Léon Blum.

From Whitehall Bevin instructed Cooper to ask the French to help land the returning Jews by force, but Cooper thought this was a mad idea. On 30 July, the day after the three ships reached French shores, the French press stood universally against the British. 'We are all with you,' the manager of a Paris hotel told Samuel Katz of the Irgun. Katz was not so sure. 'Don't you think your government may

give in and force the people to land from the boats?' he asked.
'Impossible!' the manager retorted, 'The Government would fall' –
he snapped his fingers – 'like that.'²⁵ 'The French were furious,'
wrote another member of the Irgun. 'Their old animosity towards
the English was rekindled. No expression seemed too strong to
express the feelings of horror and of disgust towards those who
were inflicting such suffering on the passengers of the *Exodus*. No
one could have thought that France and Britain were allied countries. The views taken in restaurants, on the métro, even on the
pavements of the boulevards could have left the impression that the
two peoples were at war with one another.'²⁶

Just thirty-one of the émigrés accepted a French invitation to disembark, and the remainder ignored a British threat that, if they did
not do so, they would be shipped to Germany where they would be
forcibly removed instead. After a three-week stand-off, on 23 August
the ships sailed again, this time, as the British had threatened, to
Hamburg. There, one thousand British troops, backed by a further
fifteen hundred German police, used water hoses, truncheons and
tear gas to remove the passengers from the ships. This episode
demonstrated that Britain could no longer effectively rule Palestine,
and reinforced the UNSCOP's judgement, a few days earlier, that the
mandate should end and the country be split between the Arabs and
the Jews, with Jerusalem an international zone. As the Jews were
taken away to be housed in two former concentration camps, in
the background a military band was playing. Designed to drown
out the screams of protest, its brassy tunes were effectively the finale
of the British mandate in Palestine.

29

LAST POST

When a subdued Ernest Bevin announced on 18 February 1947 that, after the breakdown of last-ditch talks with Arab and Jewish representatives, the only course remaining for the British government was to submit the problem to the United Nations, few believed that this was the beginning of the end of Britain's rule in Palestine.[1] Not since 1776 had the British given up any part of their empire, and never voluntarily.

The British government itself could not quite believe it. In private, Bevin told the cabinet: 'We still have to find a means of holding the Middle East', and he hoped that if the United Nations backed a federal solution for Palestine it might task Britain with running it.[2] A week later his colleague the colonial secretary, Creech Jones, made it clear that Britain's decision to refer the problem did not mean that it would be giving in quite yet. 'We are not going to the United Nations to surrender the Mandate,' he confirmed. 'We are going to the United Nations setting out the problem and asking for their advice as to how the Mandate can be administered. If the Mandate cannot be administered in its present form we are asking how it can be amended.'[3] Creech Jones's implication was inflammatory, leading both the Irgun and the Stern Gang to redouble their efforts to dislodge the British.

Four days after Creech Jones's statement the Irgun bombed the British Officers' Club in Jerusalem, an attack which killed thirteen and injured sixteen more. At the end of March the Shell oil refinery was attacked, causing a quarter of a million pounds' worth of damage, and on 22 April a train on the Cairo–Haifa line was derailed by a landmine, killing eight and wounding a further forty-one. Two days later the head of the Special Branch in Haifa, A. E. Conquest, was shot dead by two young Jews as he parked his car at home after another long day at the office.

The Jewish Agency again promised to campaign against terrorism, and although the Haganah did save lives by alerting the British that the Irgun was about to blow a mine beneath the police headquarters in Tel Aviv, the Agency's broad offer came far too late to help the British to reverse the growing opposition to their presence. The sustained anti-British rhetoric of its leadership had long since shaped the minds of a generation of young Jewish people. As *The Times* observed, 'The youths who shot Superintendent Conquest were possibly not born' when the detective joined the Palestine Police eighteen years earlier, in 1929.[4] Furthermore, the British had long since lost the battle with the terrorists, for it was clear that they could not protect even sympathetic Jews from the terrorists' threats. They came up with the notion of publishing photographs of wanted terrorists in the local newspapers, but the idea foundered when the papers' editors then received anonymous telephone calls detailing exactly what would happen to them personally if they did. When the British news wire Reuters tried to set up a Palestine office, the Irgun frightened it away, but it was happy simultaneously to allow Agence France Presse, at that time an arm of the French government, to establish a bureau in Tel Aviv.

On 4 May, the Irgun launched a spectacular attack on Acre prison. Disguised as British soldiers, they blew a hole in the curtain wall of the jail – the supposedly impregnable crusader castle – allowing hundreds of Arab prisoners, and nearly thirty Jewish terrorists, to escape. British soldiers who had been swimming at the beach south of the town hurriedly carried out an ambush of the escaping Irgun force, killing nine and capturing eight. But most of the convicts got away.

By now the Palestine Police was being heavily criticised and, in London, the War Office resorted to extraordinary measures to try to take the war to the terrorists themselves. With the backing of Montgomery, whose demand for permission to use 'robust' measures had just been approved by the cabinet, it picked a Guards officer named Bernard Fergusson to recruit special squads to operate against Jewish terrorists.[5] Fergusson, who had served in Palestine, then with the Chindits in Burma, and knew Orde Wingate well, hoped that Wingate's tactics from ten years earlier might be made to work in the streets and alleyways of Jerusalem and Tel Aviv. He started drafting good men for dirty work. One of those he chose was a twenty-six-year-old officer he had taught at Sandhurst. Roy Farran was a highly decorated former squadron commander in the Special Air Service, with extensive experience of combat behind enemy lines. Like many former war heroes, Farran contemplated peace with deep unease and leapt at his old tutor's promise that he would soon see violent action once more.

Farran arrived in Palestine in a policeman's uniform in March 1947, and selected a squad; after a few weeks' target practice in the Arab city of Jenin, he set out to try to trap the terrorists. On 6 May he came unstuck. Circling the suburb of Rehavia in west Jerusalem in plain clothes and an unmarked car, his squad came upon a six-teen-year-old boy named Alexander Rubowitz, who was pasting up posters for the Stern Gang. Farran himself chased Rubowitz down the street, losing his trilby as he ran, and having caught him, bundled the teenager into the car and raced away. Rubowitz was never seen again.

The following day Farran confessed to Fergusson that he had murdered Rubowitz while trying to interrogate him, and Fergusson warned the new chief of the Palestine Police, Nicol Gray, of what had happened. Gray, an army officer like both Fergusson and Farran, initially tried to avoid an investigation, but after the press reported Rubowitz's disappearance, and Farran's hat, in which he had inked his name, was found at the scene, a cover-up was impos-sible – even though by now the Palestine Police had denied knowing anything about Rubowitz's disappearance. Reluctantly, Gray passed the matter to his deputy Arthur Giles for further action.

Giles – the man who had first established the connection between the Stern Gang and the French – had no time at all for Gray, who had been parachuted in above him and knew nothing about police work. He immediately told the chief secretary to the Palestine administration about the murder. An investigation started but made little progress because Farran, fearing that he was about to be made a scapegoat, fled to Syria where he was offered political asylum. Eventually his former commanding officer persuaded him to give himself up.

Farran returned to Palestine just as the twenty-three members of the United Nations Special Committee on Palestine arrived to assess what should happen to the British mandate, but he did not stay long. Two days later he escaped again and, as the press made the connection between him and Rubowitz's disappearance, members of the Palestine Police who disliked the military's interference in their work began to leak to reporters what he had really been doing. As the UNSCOP delegates toured Palestine, it was becoming increasingly apparent that the British had resorted to terrorism themselves, despite strenuous denials from the government in London. The Stern Gang exacted its revenge, killing five soldiers and wounding two more in two separate shootings on 28 June. One of those killed was a friend of Farran, who gave himself up once more soon afterwards. When eventually Farran came to trial that autumn, Fergusson refused to repeat what the young SAS officer had told him on 7 May; and a notebook, in which Farran had plainly stated his responsibility for Rubowitz's death, was ruled inadmissible as evidence. Despite overwhelming evidence to the contrary, he was acquitted of the murder.[6]

The verdict in the Farran case caused jubilation in the British press, for by then the mood in Britain had turned venomously against the Zionists – indeed, in certain places, against the Jews in general. On 29 July, the British had disregarded calls from members of the UNSCOP to show clemency, and hanged three of the Irgun they had captured in the ambush following the Acre prison break. This time the Irgun retaliated in kind. In a secret meeting with the chairman of the UN Committee, Emil Sandström, Menachem Begin had warned that 'if the British execute Irgun men, Irgun will execute British men – also by hanging'.[7]

Begin carried out that threat on 30 July. That day the Irgun announced that it had executed two British sergeants, Cliff Martin and Mervyn Paice, whom it had kidnapped a fortnight earlier as they walked home from a bar. A communiqué it issued parodied British legal jargon, stating that the two dead men had been found guilty of 'illegal entry into the Hebrew Homeland', of membership of a 'criminal terrorist organisation' – namely, 'the British Occupation Army in Palestine' – and of 'illegal possession of arms'.[8] Propaganda the group devised soon afterwards aimed at ordinary British soldiers noted that when, on previous occasions, they had kidnapped officers, the British had swiftly commuted or postponed death sentences, but when it was only sergeants' lives at stake, they had not bothered.[9] The tactic worked. The British carried out no more executions in Palestine.

The two sergeants' bodies were found hanging in a eucalyptus grove near Netanya the following day, and before they were retrieved the press was allowed to photograph them. The *Daily Express* ran its photograph above the caption, 'Hanged Britons: Picture That Will Shock the World'.[10] The ground beneath the hanging corpses had been mined so that there was an explosion when they were cut down. One body was mangled and blown twenty yards; small pieces of the other were found as far as two hundred yards away. Press reports of the gruesome discovery and the aftermath of the booby traps triggered rioting in more than a dozen towns and cities across Britain during the first week of August. In Liverpool over three hundred Jewish properties were attacked and police made eighty-eight arrests. Caught in the act of using a half-brick to smash two shop windows in Salford, two women were unrepentant. 'We did it,' they said, 'because the owner is a Jew.'[11]

A week later, the chancellor of the exchequer Hugh Dalton wrote to Attlee arguing that it was time for Britain to leave Palestine, whatever UNSCOP's decision was. 'The present state of affairs is not only costly to us in manpower and money, but is, as you and I agree, of no real value from the strategic point of view – you cannot in any case have a secure base on top of a wasps' nest – and it is exposing our young men, for no good purpose, to abominable experiences and is breeding anti-Semites at a most shocking speed.'[12]

UNSCOP, some of whose members had also been eyewitnesses to the *Exodus* fiasco that was playing out simultaneously, agreed that the British mandate had to end. When it reported on 1 September, it announced that representatives of eight of the eleven-nation body supported the partition of the country into Arab and Jewish states and the creation of an international zone in Jerusalem. The three dissenters, India, Iran and Yugoslavia – all of which had substantial Muslim populations – preferred a unified federal state instead.

Convinced that the proposal was both unfair to the Arabs and unworkable because of the hatred between the two sides, Attlee did not wait for it to be debated in the United Nations' new General Assembly. On 26 September the government announced that Britain would withdraw unilaterally from Palestine the following year, on 14 May 1948, regardless of the United Nations' decision. It was effectively a snub to the new international body, for it signalled that, whatever the General Assembly decided, partition of some sort would take place immediately after the British withdrew. As Bevin put it, 'Nature may partition Palestine.'[13]

The partition proposal, which needed a two-thirds majority to be carried as a resolution, was debated that November at the UN General Assembly at Flushing Meadow in New York. It was a home game for the Zionist delegation, which organised crowds of local supporters to demonstrate outside the building, and lobbied brilliantly within. Their organisation and arguments contrasted strikingly with the disunited representatives of the Palestinian Arabs and the surrounding Arab states who, in the words of one disappointed British official, were 'rather second-rate'.[14] Even so, it was clear that the Zionist delegation could not yet command the majority necessary to pass the resolution they so desperately needed. By filibustering they managed to delay the vote three days, until 29 November. This bought time for their New York supporters to put extra pressure on wavering states, by emphasising their power over the president – the man who had been forced to make such a blatant play for the Jewish vote just one year earlier. There was one undecided country to which they devoted particular attention: France.

About 26 November – the date on which the vote had been supposed to take place – France's short and undistinguished-looking delegate to the United Nations, Alexandre Parodi, received a visit from a Jewish businessman named Bernard Baruch, a tall and handsome man who had made a fortune years earlier short-selling in the foreign exchange markets. Now in his late seventies, Baruch had long been connected with the Democratic Party. He had helped to bankroll Woodrow Wilson's 1912 presidential campaign – when Parodi would have been eleven years old – and during the war had been an informal, though clearly influential, economic adviser to Franklin D. Roosevelt. Now appointed by Truman as the United States' ambassador to the fledgling UN Atomic Agency Commission, Baruch milked his reputation as a powerful *éminence grise*. But his most important association at that moment was one about which he was uncharacteristically discreet. He was a backer of the Irgun and its front, the American League for a Free Palestine. At the point when others had begun to dissociate themselves from the League's more lurid advertising copy, Baruch had sought out its author, Ben Hecht. 'I am on your side,' he told Hecht. 'Think of me as one of your Jewish fighters in the tall grass with a long gun.'[15]

Baruch told Parodi bluntly that if France failed to support partition – a policy that he knew President Truman personally supported – French stock was bound to fall in the United States. A French *Non* would antagonise Truman, he implied, and he suspected that, as a consequence, the administration might divert aid it had been planning to pump into France to other, worthier causes.[16] Parodi immediately warned the French ambassador, Henri Bonnet, about the threat, and he in turn informed Bidault that same day.

Until this point, Bidault had made certain that France's public position on Palestine was a deliberately cautious one. Aware of the likely reaction in France's remaining Arab colonies in North Africa if the country backed partition, he had deep misgivings about finally making French support for the Zionists public, not least when the British government had said it would abstain. In a bid to appear to be catering for Arab interests, when UNSCOP was constituted eight months earlier Parodi had appealed in the United Nations for a 'conciliation formula'. In mid-October, when it became clear that there was pressure to vote on UNSCOP's report, Bidault had instructed Parodi to do his utmost to postpone the vote if possible.

The Quai d'Orsay was also deeply divided on the matter. Although Bidault himself could see the wisdom of pursuing a policy that would cut Britain down to size, and oblige France's oldest rival to start treating its neighbour as an equal, many on his staff did not. In particular, Jean Chauvel, the most senior official in the Quai, argued against voting for partition. In September he had explicitly told the envoy of the Arab Higher Committee – representing the Palestinians – that France would avoid taking a position that was contrary to Arab interests.

The danger that a vote for partition might produce anger in French North Africa had now to be weighed against a second risk: of the United States withholding money that France desperately needed for reconstruction. France had no remaining currency reserves, and a balance of payments deficit of ten billion francs. True, the United States had given France almost $2 billion more in credit since the liberation. But, since the new secretary of state, George Marshall, had announced the reconstruction fund that bore his name that summer, there had been worrying signs that his top priority was Germany. In the middle of the *Exodus* affair, the Americans and the British had stitched up a deal that benefited Germany, not France, and the communist-inspired trouble in France that autumn would certainly not encourage the State Department to be more generous.

The outcome of Bidault's assessment of these relative dangers became apparent on 29 November. After calling a day earlier for a further twenty-four-hour delay so that a compromise might be reached – a gesture to assuage the colonies – on the 29th Parodi cast France's vote in favour of partition. So too, as the Zionists had hoped, did France's neighbours, Belgium, Luxembourg and the Netherlands.

The resolution required a two-thirds majority to be passed, so these four votes mattered as they helped ensure it was then narrowly carried, by 33 votes to 13. Ten more states abstained, including Britain. The reaction in Palestine was immediate. The Jews were 'hysterically jubilant', the Arabs 'stunned with disbelief', Britain's general in command in Palestine recorded.[17] In Tel Aviv the cry went up: 'Vive la France!'[18]

Truman afterwards admitted that he had been subjected to a

'constant barrage' from 'a few of the extreme Zionist leaders' who 'were even suggesting that we pressure sovereign nations into favorable votes in the General Assembly'.[19] But he denied that he had succumbed to this unprecedented pressure and refuted allegations that his country had put pressure on other states before the vote. 'I have never approved of the practice of the strong imposing their will on the weak, whether among men or among nations. We had aided Greece. We had in fact fathered the independence of the Philippines. But that did not make satellites of these nations or compel them to vote with us on the partitioning of Palestine or any other matter.' The pressure that his ambassador, Baruch, put on Parodi, however, contradicts that pious claim. Either Truman was lying, or he was not fully in control of his administration. Interestingly, he did not mention France in his denial.

The euphoria of the General Assembly's vote rapidly wore off as the Zionists quickly realised that they would now have to fight for their survival. Arab attacks on Jewish settlements began the day after the vote, and it was clear to the Zionists that they could soon expect a coordinated onslaught from all sides. To blunt the greatest threat, which was the British-armed and -trained Arab Legion of Abdullah across the Jordan, they had already secretly begun talks with the Arab king with a view to a mutually advantageous partition of Palestine on very different lines from those envisaged by the United Nations Special Committee. And to resist the other Arab states, they needed better weapons. 'I carry only a kind of toy pistol of the kind used by ladies to shoot their lovers,' wrote one unhappy member of the Haganah.[20]

An Austrian Jew who had emigrated to Palestine named Ehud Avriel was sent to Paris in November 1947 to buy arms for the Haganah, which the Jewish Agency was hurriedly reorganising as a regular army. It did not take long before he was approached. 'We hit a gold mine practically the day after my arrival in the form of ... a gentleman who came to see me ... with a catalogue of arms from the Czechoslovak arms industries, which before World War Two he had represented in his native Rumania.' But there was a catch: the Czechoslovak government would only deal in government-to-government transactions. This stipulation did not inconvenience Avriel for long, though. 'Very fortunately we were in the possession from the old days of illegal immigration of both the stationery and the rubber stamp of a very dignified government that put these things at our disposal,' he explained, 'and we used some of these.' Once purchased, the arms were flown from Czechoslovakia to Palestine via French territory, with the French government's approval.[21] The French also used borrowed American dollars to finance arms sales directly to the Zionists. In January 1948 Georges Bidault approved a $26 million deal to arm eight thousand Haganah soldiers.

France's willingness to assist the Zionists directly resulted partly from the prevailing belief in the Quai d'Orsay that the British had no intention of pulling out of Palestine. The British government again insisted on 11 December that the mandate would end on 14 May the following year, but a hoard of secret British documents captured by the Haganah four days later suggested very differently. On 15 December the Haganah intercepted a British truck travelling from Beirut, which was transferring archives from the defunct Spears Mission to Haifa for shipment home. When the Haganah became aware of the importance of what it had discovered, it notified the French. Within hours, a French intelligence officer pretending to be a newspaper reporter was on his way to Tel Aviv to go through the material.

The documents revealed the extent of British espionage in Lebanon and Syria during the war and confirmed long-standing French suspicions. They indicated, apparently, that Muhsin al-Barazi, who was the private secretary to the Syrian president al-Quwatli, was a British agent being run by W. F. Stirling, who had stayed on in Damascus at the end of the war. The British were also receiving information from Ibn Saud's doctor. His handler was a man the French had suspected of clandestine work since the outbreak of the Druze revolt. In the intervening period Walter Smart, the praying mantis-like former consul in Damascus, had not gone far. He was now the oriental secretary at the British embassy in Cairo.[22]

The intelligence the French thus gleaned reinforced the suspicion that, in the words of one observer, the British were 'leaving through the door and returning through the window'.[23] That impression was absolutely accurate for, as Bevin had admitted within the confines of a cabinet meeting, Britain was looking for a way to maintain influence in the Middle East, not least to spite the United States. By the end of 1947, the man in whom they had invested all their hopes of doing so was King Abdullah.

Thirty-one years had passed since T. E. Lawrence had deliberately disparaged the 'more businesslike' Abdullah in order to persuade his chiefs to back his more malleable younger brother Feisal. But Lawrence and Feisal were now both dead, and the British government had long since transferred its faith to Feisal's elder sibling. Dependent on British gold and military expertise, by 1939 Abdullah had become Britain's most reliable Arab ally. As French rule in neighbouring Syria and Lebanon ended, in March 1946 Britain finally signed a treaty with Abdullah that brought the mandate to a close. Transjordan – renamed Jordan – became an independent country, but the British negotiated a twenty-five-year deal to retain military bases on Jordanian territory and Abdullah remained reliant on British money. In a secret annexe to the treaty that the two countries signed, Britain agreed to pay for the military force that made Abdullah a formidable threat: the Arab Legion, commanded by the British officer John Glubb. Foreign Office diplomats dubbed Abdullah 'Mr Bevin's little king'.[24]

The servile nature of Jordan's relationship with Britain was not a well-kept secret. Neither the United States nor the Soviet Union, which was trying to gain influence in the Middle East, would initially recognise Jordan as an independent state. But Abdullah's closeness to the British did have one advantage. He had known since early 1946 that the British were considering withdrawing from Palestine, and in this he saw an opportunity to realise his long-held ambition to create and rule a Greater Syria. In the chaos that would follow Britain's departure he would seek to merge Jordan with the Arab areas of Palestine. Then, when he had control of Jerusalem, and some political momentum, he would seek to bring in Syria and Iraq as well.

In August 1946, Abdullah tried to win the support of the Jewish Agency for his move. 'I am sixty-six years old,' the king told Elias

Sasson, the Agency's leading expert on the Arab world. 'My remaining years are numbered. You do not have any realist Arab leader like me in the entire Arab world. You have two paths: to join with me and work together, or to give me up.'[25] In April 1947 Abdullah concluded a treaty of 'Brotherhood and Alliance' with Iraq, and by the end of the same year he was busy trying to persuade the Druzes to secede from Syria.

The Zionists were not the only people to whom Abdullah confided his ambition. He talked freely about his hope of ruling Greater Syria with Britain's chief representative in Amman, Sir Alec Kirkbride. Kirkbride fully appreciated the king's dream for, as a young man, he had fought alongside Lawrence and the Arabs in the 1916–18 revolt; but he doubted that Abdullah could achieve it, given his unpopularity in neighbouring Arab states. Nevertheless, he could see the advantages if Jordan did annex the Arab parts of Palestine. As he put it diplomatically to London, such a move 'would not be contrary to British interests' since, if Abdullah succeeded, he might gain an outlet to the Mediterranean Sea at Gaza, which would satisfy Britain's own strategic interests nicely.[26]

Twelve days before the United Nations General Assembly voted for partition, a representative from the Jewish Agency, the future Israeli prime minister Golda Meir, made a dangerous journey into Jordan to visit Abdullah. Although she flatly dismissed his suggestion that the Jews might want to take part in his big idea, the two agreed to the division of Palestine between them. They shared an overwhelming determination to stop a takeover of the Arab areas of the country by the Mufti, who had now bobbed up again in Syria, having mysteriously escaped from house arrest in Paris following his support for Hitler through the war.

This was a deal the British could support, discreetly. When Bevin secretly met Abdullah's prime minister, Tawfiq Pasha, in London on 7 February 1948, he made it clear that the British government were relaxed about Abdullah's plan. When Tawfiq said that the Arab Legion was planning to occupy the Arab areas when Britain left, Bevin answered: 'It seems the obvious thing to do. But do not go and invade the areas allotted to the Jews.'[27]

In the meantime, the violence in Palestine was growing worse. At the end of December 1947 Irgun terrorists had thrown grenades into a crowd of Arabs at the oil refinery in Haifa. The Arabs ran amok, killing forty-one Jews and injuring a further eleven. Three days later the Jews exacted their revenge, killing fourteen Arabs in an attack in Haifa. Amid reports that hundreds of well-armed Arabs, including the flamboyant guerrilla leader Fawzi al-Qawukji, were entering Palestine unchallenged, the Zionists accused the British of standing by. The British hotly denied the accusation. Were it not 'for the efforts of the security forces over the past month, the two communities would by now have been fully engaged in internecine slaughter', the high commissioner claimed.[28]

But that already appeared to be the case. The Palestine Commission, which the United Nations had created to implement the partition resolution, reported on 16 February 1948 that, in the three months following the General Assembly's vote, 2,778 people had been killed or wounded in Palestine, the overwhelming majority of them Jews or Arabs. It warned that a collapse in security was possible unless 'adequate means' were made available 'for the exercise of its authority', since the Arab Higher Committee had said that it would resist any attempt to create a Jewish state by force, and Arab morale was rising.[29] The Commission's implication was clear: Palestine would be the first major test of the authority of the United Nations. If the UN could not impose its will, it might also be the last.

No one, however, was willing to send troops. The US representative to the United Nations, Warren Austin, argued that armed force could not be used because the United Nations Charter only permitted the use of force to restore peace in international conflicts; but the administration's true concern was that sending American forces would not be popular at home, and would invite intervention by Soviet troops as well. The French were similarly reluctant. Although the North African reaction to their vote for partition was surprisingly subdued, they did not want to be involved in imposing that policy on the Palestinian Arabs by force. Bevin was simply determined not to give any other member of the UN Security Council the impression that Britain would be willing to take responsibility for security in Palestine beyond 14 May.

On 24 February, Austin proposed one last attempt at reaching a compromise, but this idea was rapidly rejected by the other members of the Security Council. The French delegate, Parodi, told his government that he believed the partition plan was 'dead', and that a temporary trusteeship would have to be set up in Palestine to bridge the period from the end of the mandate to the point where a settlement was achieved. In a speech on 5 March he declared that France was withdrawing its support for partition. Then, in the absence of agreement between the Arabs and the Jews, or within the Security Council, the US secretary of state George Marshall called a press conference on the 20th. Faced with the prospect that the United Kingdom would abandon the mandate midway through May, leaving no successor to guarantee law and order, Marshall proposed a trusteeship, just as Parodi predicted.[30] The State Department then approached the British government to see whether it would be willing to assume it.

The short answer was no. In a cabinet meeting on 22 March Bevin savoured the Americans' alarm. The situation, he smugly told his colleagues, was what happened when Truman 'allowed U. S. electoral needs to influence U. S. foreign policy', and he did not want British troops to be caught up in the consequences.[31] At that moment the legislation to end the mandate was passing through parliament. Bevin initially wanted to delay it, so that he could at least go through the motions of giving Marshall's idea some thought. But when it was suggested that this might imply that Britain was willing to stay on in Palestine, he changed his mind. 'Very well then,' he finished. 'Ram it through.'

Three days later, Shmuel Ariel, the Irgun's representative in Paris, handed in a memorandum at the Quai d'Orsay. The document proposed an agreement between the Irgun and the French government, asking France to arm and equip two Irgun brigades, and provide one of them with a base somewhere on French territory until they were required after 14 May.[32] In a covering letter to his contact in the ministry Ariel expressed his hope that Georges Bidault might rapidly approve the measure. 'In light of the urgency of the matter,' he ended, 'I would appreciate it if you could inform me soon of a favourable outcome.'[33]

The approach marked the revival of good relations between the Irgun and the French government which, a fortnight earlier, had seemed close to breaking point. The previous December, the United States had declared that it was imposing an embargo on arms shipments to the Middle East, and had pressed its allies to do likewise. On 5 March 1948, French officials had seized a supply of arms near Marseille and arrested its couriers, who were members of the Irgun. Until that point the Irgun manufactured its weapons using the machinery in a zip factory: it desperately needed a source of new and better arms. 'We were far from being jubilant,' recalled Samuel Katz, 'knowing as we did that the gulf between our needs and our resources was large and forbidding. It was not enough to decide to convert the five-thousand-strong Irgun into an effective army; we also had to arm our men.'[34]

In the hope of persuading the French government to release the consignment and its couriers, a representative of the Irgun went to see the French government's special envoy in Palestine, René de Lacharrière. Having reminded him that the British were helping to arm Abdullah, he warned de Lacharrière that 'the fact that the French police, which for a long time was not unaware of our activities, chose, at this time of ordeal, to arrest our friends, can only be seen by the Irgun as a sign of hostility ... We would be deeply sorry to have to conclude that France is abandoning its traditional policy of supporting oppressed peoples.' The release of the impounded arms consignment, he said, was 'a matter of life or death'.[35] De Lacharrière was evidently troubled by the encounter. 'The Irgun,' he reminded Paris, 'is a force of crucial importance now in Palestine. It is a fact that it would be better not to have them as opponents and, in fact, its activity until now has sometimes been indirectly favourable to French interests.'

In Paris, Bidault and his advisers agreed. They had been similarly lobbied by Hillel Kook, the founder of the Ligue Française pour la Palestine Libre, and well knew that Britain was trying to find ways around the embargo that was in place. Earlier that year French intelligence officers had managed to thwart an attempt by Britain to broker an arms deal between a Swiss company and Ethiopia, after they established that the true recipients of the weapons were to be

Egypt and Jordan. They were determined that Britain should not emerge from the chaotic final months of the mandate in a stronger position than they did. The Irgun had ambitions to extend the Jewish state beyond the Jordan, and using it as a way to counter Glubb's Arab Legion now seemed a good idea.

Bidault's adviser Jacques Boissier was especially keen on the Irgun. At the start of May he wrote a memorandum arguing that France should back the group, which he described as 'not just a handful of terrorists or guerrillas' but 'very disciplined troops, well trained and well commanded to fight and win'.[36] The French authorities should be encouraged to 'turn a blind eye to the arms purchases that the Jews were secretly making in France, or to the transit of war equipment across French territory', in defiance of the American-led embargo. Bidault took Boissier's advice. At the end of May he reached a secret deal with Ariel. France would supply 153 million francs' worth of weaponry, in exchange for influence in the newly independent Jewish state. The arms were delivered to Ariel at Port-de-Bouc in early June and shipped to Tel Aviv aboard a landing craft the Irgun had purchased, the *Altalena*. Although the *Altalena* was sunk on Ben-Gurion's orders off Tel Aviv to prevent the Irgun becoming too powerful, the transaction marked the beginning of a sustained relationship: France would be Israel's leading arms supplier until 1956.

In a bid to break through to Jerusalem, which was surrounded by hostile Arab forces, on 1 April 1948 the Zionists had launched Operation Nachshon to try to end the Arab siege of the Holy City. The Arab armies seemed formidable – an impression that the Zionists encouraged so as to spur donations of arms and money – but in fact they were completely disunited. After the Arab League convened to decide its tactics, a British officer of the Arab Legion asked an Iraqi how the meeting had been. 'Splendid,' came the answer. 'We all agreed to fight separately.'[37] In northern Palestine, Fawzi al-Qawukji was operating in familiar territory, the triangle of hill country between Nablus, Jenin and Tulkarm, which had been the epicentre of the Arab insurgency ten years before. To the south Abdul Qadir al-Husayni, the man the Mufti had appointed as his main commander in Palestine, held the important town of Qastal overlooking the Jerusalem–Jaffa road, but he was short of weapons. In the background, both the Syrians and the Jordanians refused to arm him adequately. The Syrian president Shukri al-Quwatli was backing Fawzi al-Qawukji, while Abdullah placed his faith in Glubb, whom the British had abruptly disowned in a feeble effort to pretend they had nothing to do with what was going on.

It was not simply that al-Quwatli and Abdullah did not want the Mufti, Hajj Mohammed Amin al-Husayni, to take control of the West Bank: each wanted to deny the region to the other. Abdullah, of course, regarded the annexation of the Arab areas of Palestine as the first stage of his grand plan. Al-Quwatli, who still felt deeply threatened by Abdullah's open advocacy of a Greater Syria, was determined to use al-Qawukji to stop the ambitious Jordanian king in his tracks. And the consequence of all this infighting was that, after the Haganah's elite Palmach captured Qastal on 3 April, Abdul Qadir tried to retake the hill town without adequate supplies. 'We began to run short of ammunition,' wrote one of his officers, but 'our appeals for help to the ALA* and the Transjordanian Arab Legion forces nearby went unanswered'.[38] A direct appeal by Abdul Qadir himself was met by silence. 'You're all traitors,' he railed at them, 'and history will record that you lost Palestine!' He was killed in the Arabs' attempt to retake the town. The Arabs killed their fifty Jewish prisoners.

Then, early on 9 April, the day of Abdul Qadir al-Husayni's funeral in Jerusalem, a force of Irgun and Stern Gang fighters attacked the Arab village of Dayr Yasin, just west of the city. After capturing it, they murdered 250 – about a third – of its inhabitants, and paraded the survivors through Jerusalem. Eyewitnesses who reached the village soon afterwards recorded terrible sights. One man saw a pregnant woman who had been disembowelled: her foetus was lying on the ground beside her. The atrocity was immediately condemned by the Jewish Agency, but it had clearly been

* The Arab Liberation Army – the name given to the irregular force commanded by Fawzi al-Qawukji.

premeditated. One of Glubb's officers had already asked a Jewish official whether there would be irreconcilable tensions between the Jews and Arabs after the British left on 14 May. 'Oh no,' the official had replied. 'That will be fixed. A few calculated massacres will soon get rid of them.'[39] Four days later the Arabs replied in kind, ambushing a medical convoy and murdering over seventy doctors, nurses and students at the Hebrew University.

Wealthier Arabs were already fleeing Palestine, but the spreading news of what had happened at Dayr Yasin sparked a much more general exodus. On 18 April in Haifa, the British commanding officer, Hugh Stockwell, called in the Jewish Agency official and told him he was about to evacuate British positions in the city, prior to the final withdrawal the following month. 'We so clearly were handing over the city to the Jews,' recalled Edward Henderson, one of Stockwell's junior officers, 'and almost all the Arab citizens were driven out by the Jewish irregular armies under our noses in not much over twenty-four hours on 21 and 22 April 1948.' For days the Haganah broadcast messages telling the Arabs to leave the town before it was too late. But, according to Henderson, they then 'complained to us on the 23rd that they were having difficulty in providing municipal services as the Arab municipal workers appeared "strangely" to have left'.[40] The Arabs who left were wise to do so, for the Haganah entered the port with orders to 'Kill any Arab you encounter; torch all inflammable objects and force doors open with explosives', in an operation codenamed 'Scissors'.[41] By the end of April the Zionists controlled Tiberias and Jaffa too.

'It is quite beyond me to describe the present situation. Our nights are almost sleepless on account of the incessant machine gun and rifle fire, coupled with the heavy detonations of mortars,' a British officer, James Pollock, wrote of the last apocalyptic days of British rule.[42] At the end of April the British paid off their local staff and prepared to leave themselves. The chief secretary, with no further work to do, found time for tennis amid the noise of constant shooting. On 14 May, as promised, the British high commissioner left Jerusalem by plane, the mandate ended, and on Allenby Bridge King Abdullah raised his revolver, fired, and shouted 'Forward!'

Overnight Truman recognised the state of Israel, and on the 15th the first Arab-Israeli war formally began.

Years later Sir John Shaw, the former chief secretary of Palestine who survived the King David Hotel bombing, was asked to assess Britain's record in the mandate.

'In many cases we thought that we were doing good to the people concerned, and indeed we were,' he said.[43] 'I mean we stamped out all sorts of abuses and malpractices and things but,' he hesitated, 'if you look at it from a purely philosophical, high-minded point of view, I think it is immoral, and I think it's ... it's not only immoral but it's ill-advised.'

'Why?' Shaw was asked.

'Why? Well ... because it's not your business or my business, or British business, or [for] anybody else to interfere in other people's countries and tell them how to run it, even to run it well. They must be left to their own salvation.'

Epilogue

A Settling of Scores

When, late on 6 November 1949, three Arabs hammered on his door and insisted that they see him, W. F. Stirling was initially not inclined to meet them. It was a Sunday evening, the three were unexpected, and he and his wife Marygold already had two guests for dinner.

Sixty-nine-year-old Colonel Stirling, the former liaison officer with the Syrian government and now *The Times*'s correspondent in Damascus, should have trusted that initial instinct. But he tended to live beyond his means and was always short of money. He knew that he could not afford to miss a scoop because *The Times* had fired his predecessor for missing stories. And from personal experience going back over thirty years to that euphoric October day when he had reached Damascus with Lawrence of Arabia, he knew how unpredictable Syria could be.

Since finally winning its independence in 1946 after a quarter of a century of French rule, Syria had proved notoriously unstable, even by the standards of the region. By November 1949 there had already been two *coups d'état* that year. Shukri al-Quwatli, who had steered the country to independence, was overthrown in March by an army officer, Husni Zaim, who in turn was murdered when the then current president Sami al-Hinnawi seized power in August. Seeking to draw a line under his brutal removal of his predecessor, al-Hinnawi – 'a fat, slug-like creature with no brain', according to one diplomat – had called a general election that was now only days away.[1]

The poll was controversial because al-Hinnawi, who came from the ancient city of Aleppo in the north, had banned the semi-nomadic Bedu tribesmen of eastern Syria from voting on the grounds that they were vulnerable to foreign manipulation from beyond the country's porous desert borders. This tension between the settled peoples of the urbanised, fertile west and the wild nomads of the eastern desert was one of several that now made Syrian politics so volatile. The tribesmen were deeply angry that they had been disen-franchised – Stirling was well aware of it, because he had gone deep into the desert to report on their resentment eight weeks earlier.[2] So when the three men standing at the door claimed they had been sent by the shaykh of a large and influential tribe who was an old friend of his, Stirling took their persistence to mean they brought vital news that might have a bearing on the imminent vote. He relented, and told his servant Ali to let them in. It was to prove a fatal error.

The three men entered Stirling's study in single file, but declined their host's invitation to sit down, and instead advanced towards him. When Stirling got up from behind his desk to proffer a silver cigarette box their leader interrupted, ominously asking him whether he was Colonel Stirling. When Stirling nodded, the man produced a Colt automatic pistol.

It was established afterwards that his first shot must have blown the cigarette case from Stirling's hand. The next two hit him in the stom-ach, one puncturing his liver. The fourth hit him in the chest. The fifth grazed his jugular. It took the sixth, which smashed through his right forearm, spinning him around, to send him crashing to the floor.

Stirling's assailant then turned and shot Ali, who had heard the gunfire and rushed into the study. Then he and his accomplices fled downstairs, out of the door and down the street.

Stirling's wife Marygold found Ali first, lying on the Persian carpet in the study, blood soaking his white jacket. He was dying, but trying to speak.

'Ali, Ali, what is it?' Marygold Stirling pleaded, kneeling down beside him.

'Madame, the Colonel, the Colonel,' gasped her servant.

From across the room there was a groan. Marygold Stirling leapt up. Behind the desk she found her husband sprawled and quickly losing consciousness.[3]

Several days after the shooting of *The Times*'s correspondent in Damascus, two Arabs were overheard discussing the attack in a café in the city. 'Did they really think they could kill Colonel Stirling with only six shots?' one asked the other.[4] For Stirling, miraculously, had survived the attempt to kill him.

'Well, I suppose I am dead, or at least dying, but I'm damned if I feel like it,' Stirling recalled thinking as he lay bleeding and losing consciousness on the floor of his study.[5] It was not willpower, though, but one of his two guests who saved his life. Ernest Altounyan, who had arrived just twenty minutes earlier asking if he might stay the night, was a well-known doctor who ran a small private hospital in Aleppo that had been set up by his father. The Altounyans admired Britain. Altounyan's father had sent him to Rugby School in England, where Ernest trained as a doctor and married an Englishwoman, Dora. They were friends with the author Arthur Ransome, and their children went on to become the models for Ransome's Swallows. Ransome, it has recently been revealed, had worked for the British intelligence service, MI6. After the British invaded Syria in 1941, Altounyan volunteered his services. He worked for military intelligence throughout the war in northern Syria, which was how he had come to know Stirling.

Altounyan operated on Stirling within half an hour of the attack. Having successfully extracted two of the six bullets from his old friend's body, he decided that the other four would have to stay in place. Stirling demonstrated that he was well on the way to recovery when, days later, after he had asked a nurse in hospital for some water, he was presented with a full glass on a tray. He took the tumbler, gulped from it, and shuddered. 'That is not soda water,' he remarked.[6] It turned out that the nurse had inadvertently filled the glass with methylated spirits. The alcohol seemed to do no harm, and within days he was discharged from hospital. Shortly afterwards he flew to Cairo, never to return.

*

The vital clue to who wanted Stirling dead and why lay in the rumours that had been swirling before the shooting. These alleged that Stirling was a British agent who was trying to skew the outcome of the general election due to take place nine days after he was shot. Such was the rumours' potency that, when four Arabs were finally put on trial for the attack early in 1951, the Syrian chief prosecutor suggested that the motive of the four accused was that 'they believed that [Stirling] had played an important role in the assassination of … Zaim and he carried out espionage activities among the tribes'.[7]

When Husni Zaim seized power from Shukri al-Quwatli on 30 March 1949, Syria's economy was in a parlous state and its army had been beaten the previous November by the Israelis. Zaim knew that he needed to take action on both fronts fast. After overthrowing al-Quwatli bloodlessly, he set out to open peace talks with the Israelis and mend relations with the French via a currency agreement and an arms deal that would pave the way for renewed French influence in the former mandate. But Zaim's reign did not last long. One hundred and thirty-seven days after he had taken power, on 14 August he too was overthrown and executed.

It was Stirling's counterpart in neighbouring Israel, a well-known *Times* reporter named Louis Heren, who drew attention to the source of the rumours that his colleague had played a part in Zaim's removal. The man who later coined that axiom of dogged journalism, 'Always ask yourself why these lying bastards are lying to you', Heren pointed out that it was not the Syrians but the French news agency Agence France Presse that had first alleged that Stirling was a spy, reviving the claims made by the French general Fernand Oliva-Roget after the failed French coup in Damascus in June 1945.[8] In Heren's view the shooting of Stirling related to this old feud. It was, he said, part of a 'rather stupid and unnecessary and certainly dangerous unofficial struggle being waged between certain Frenchmen and Englishmen in these parts'.[9] And he suggested that 'the Colonel knows more about the reason for the attempt than he cares to admit', a diplomatic way of suggesting that Stirling was rather more than a newspaper reporter.

Earlier that year Heren had thought it would be 'a very good idea' if Britain was covertly trying 'to finally oust the French from the Levant', but his realisation that Stirling was involved in such clandestine activity seems to have changed his attitude.[10] Perhaps he was worried what might happen to him if rumours persisted that his newspaper was providing a front for British espionage. 'There are too many would-be successors to Lawrence; too much unnecessary bitterness between the two groups of nationals,' he now decided, arguing that 'something ought to be done about it'.[11] 'I do not mean to infer that a Frenchman was responsible,' Heren added, but he did suggest that Agence France Presse had created a climate of suspicion that would encourage others to target Stirling. His colleague in Cairo, Cyril Quilliam, went further. Quilliam, a former intelligence officer who now ran *The Times*'s Middle Eastern operation, argued that Agence France Presse's involvement implied that the attack on Stirling did have official backing because the news wire depended on a subsidy from the French government worth about 800 million francs. Blaming AFP for perpetuating the 'bogey' of the 'mysterious anti-French British agent', he noted that in turn it funded the Syrian newspaper that had repeatedly criticised Stirling.[12]

As to the motive, Quilliam thought it was revenge. The French, he said, had 'banked a lot upon Zaim', believing that through him they could re-establish the influence they had lost after they were forced out of Syria when the country gained its independence.[13] When Zaim's overthrow and murder dashed these hopes, they were furious. A fortnight after the coup, Quilliam reported, they were 'still telling anyone who will listen that it was the British who were responsible for the assassination of Zaim'.[14]

Quilliam may have felt responsible for what then happened to Stirling, because it was he who had encouraged him to dig deeper into the circumstances of Zaim's demise. Stirling spoke to the murdered president's foreign minister, and filed an article reporting that earlier in the year the French ambassador to Damascus, Jean-Charles Serres, had deliberately poisoned the possibility of a pact with neighbouring Iraq by telling Zaim that the Iraqis were preparing to invade.[15] Stirling also drew attention to the fact that France had flouted the United Nations arms embargo by selling weapons and ammunition to Zaim in its bid to win him over. Accepting this materiel, he suggested, was Zaim's 'grave error', because it reminded

his opponents of France's heavy-handed intervention in Damascus in
1945.

The article – bylined only 'From Our Damascus Correspondent'
and published on 26 August – touched a nerve. Quilliam was
amazed that the Syrian authorities had not censored it. Not only did
it earn Stirling a great deal of praise from people who believed it was
an accurate representation of events, but it infuriated the French
foreign ministry, the Quai d'Orsay. The French angrily called in *The
Times*'s Paris correspondents to complain that they saw 'the hand of
Colonel Stirling' in the piece, which they dismissed as 'entirely
untrue'.[16]

It was Serres – rather incongruously, he was the author of a book
on diplomatic protocol – who orchestrated the attempt to smear
Stirling. He had already described the *Times* correspondent as
'ready to order the charge of the cavalry of St. George'* to establish
British influence at French expense in Syria, and did not try to camouflage his efforts.[17] An American diplomat reported back to
Washington that Serres 'loses no opportunity to try [to] arouse in
Middle East distrust [of] Britain'.[18] Agence France Presse reported
that Stirling was a British agent, a charge that was repeated in the
Syrian press and echoed in *Le Monde*, which alleged that British
money and influence lay behind Zaim's killing. 'The French, ever
since I came into Syria in 1941, have been convinced that I am an
extreme Francophobe and have been working against them – possibly due to my connection with T. E. Lawrence,' Stirling wrote to
his boss at *The Times*, shortly before he was shot.[19] Stirling believed
that his assailants were not local men, for otherwise they would
have known that he took his dog out for a nightly walk, and would
have waited until then to try to kill him. When he reached the relative safety of Cairo he told Quilliam that he thought his would-be
killers had been 'agents of the Mufti of Jerusalem in the pay of the
French', who were trying to dispense with him because of his support for the political union of Iraq and Syria.[20] Quilliam apparently
agreed.

---

* The nickname given to British gold sovereigns, because of the St George and dragon
design on their reverse.

By then both *The Times* and the British government had tried to distance themselves from Stirling and the clandestine struggle that had nearly killed him. Ahead of a state visit to Britain by the French president, at the end of November the newspaper's Paris correspondent – who had been carpeted at the Quai d'Orsay over Stirling's article that August – remarked that, in the 'so-called conflict of Anglo-French interests in the Middle East ... great progress towards a common understanding' had been made, but he admitted that 'agreement in London and Paris is one thing and the activities of both French and English on the spot is another'.[21] The British foreign secretary, Bevin, apparently asked his French counterpart Robert Schuman not to confuse the British government's policy with that of 'irresponsible individuals such as General Spears or Colonel Stirling', effectively cutting Stirling adrift.[22]

The French remained tight-lipped about the shooting. When, on 10 November 1949, the French chargé d'affaires in Damascus informed Paris that Stirling had been shot, he could not resist describing him as 'officially working as a correspondent of *The Times*'.[23] The 'most fanciful explanations have been concocted to explain this attack', he continued. 'However,' he added as an afterthought, it was 'most generally accepted' that 'it was the result of a settling of scores'.

The departure of W. F. Stirling to Cairo marked the end of a thirty-year-long last gasp of empire that aggravated the conflict that remains unsolved today. It was the struggle between Britain and France for the mastery of the Middle East that led the two countries to carve up the Ottoman Empire with the Sykes–Picot agreement, and it was British dissatisfaction over the outcome of this deal that led them, fatefully, to proclaim their support for Zionist ambitions in the Balfour Declaration. And so the Jews' right to a country of their own became dangerously associated with a cynical imperial manoeuvre that was originally designed to outwit the French.

The Balfour Declaration was an acknowledgement of the fact that the zenith of empire had now passed. Frontiers like Sykes's – 'drawn with a stroke of a pencil across a map of the world', according to one of his contemporaries – which had seemed so assured when they were used to divide up Africa in the nineteenth century, looked arrogant when applied to the Ottoman Empire in the twentieth.[24] It was the flimsiness of their entitlement to redraw the political map of the Middle East that explained why the British now had to use a commitment to a stateless people to camouflage their determination to take over Palestine. When the French realised the depth of Arab opposition to their rule they quickly followed suit, hiving off the Lebanon in supposed deference to the wishes of the Christian community there.

Britain's sponsorship of the Jews in Palestine and France's favouritism of the Christians in the Lebanon were policies designed to strengthen their respective positions in the region by eliciting gratitude from both minorities. The appreciation they generated by doing so was short-lived, but they deeply antagonised the predominantly Muslim Arab population of both countries, and the wider region, with irreversible effects. As Britain and France became increasingly unpopular, they were forced into oscillating alliances that only polarised Arab and Jew, Christian and Muslim further. The mandatories' abrupt changes of policy under pressure, and their refusal to institute meaningful, representative government, made it clear to those they ruled that violence worked.

Until the Second World War the British reluctantly accepted the presence of the French as what their ambassador to Cairo, Lord Killearn, termed 'an unnecessary evil which we must just make the best of'.[25] While a further war with Germany looked possible, then likely, and finally inevitable, Britain's relations with metropolitan France were more important. 'The plain fact was that the presence of the French in the Levant States was a perpetual irritant which upset British policy in the Middle East,' Killearn acknowledged, 'but I had always realised that we here ought to conform and adapt our local policy to the needs of our higher interests in regard to metropolitan France which was our neighbour just across the channel.'

The collapse of France in 1940 destroyed the assumption on which that policy was based – that France would be a vital ally in any fight with Germany. The vacuum gave British officials the opportunity to press for the independence of Syria and Lebanon, to provide the Arabs with the representative government they were still unwilling to supply in Palestine. This effort at distraction briefly worked, but ultimately its consequence made it self-defeating. As onlookers immediately recognised, Lebanese and Syrian independence set a precedent in the countries immediately to the south, and it was not long before the British were ousted too.

The wrangling between Britain and the Free French throughout the war years had a further, far-reaching consequence when de Gaulle returned to power in 1958. As president of France it was he who infamously vetoed Harold Macmillan's application to join the Common Market. In tracing exactly why de Gaulle said *Non*, it is, surprisingly, to the hot and noisy cities of Beirut and Damascus that we should look. The general's experience of British machinations in both places profoundly shaped his reluctance to allow his wartime rivals to join his European club. It is a tale from which neither country emerges with much credit.

PERMISSIONS

For permission to quote from copyrighted published and unpublished records I would like to thank: Patrick Aylmer for Sir Edward Louis Spears; Professor Caroline Barron for Professor David Hogarth; Mrs Shirley Gould-Smith for Captain Paul Vanson; Lord Moyne for Lord Moyne; Jane Jefford for Lt Col J. K. Windeatt, Lord Killearn for Sir Miles Lampson; Professor David Morgan for Lord Cecil of Chelwood; Lord Raglan for F. R. Somerset; Lord Robertson of Oakridge for Sir William Robertson; Sir Tatton Sykes for Sir Mark Sykes; the Howard Gotlieb Archival Research Centre at Boston University for William Yale; News International for papers relating to W. F. Stirling; and the Seven Pillars of Wisdom Trust for T. E. Lawrence.

For permission to quote from holdings in their respective collections I would like to thank: the Trustees of the Liddell Hart Centre for Military Archives and the Imperial War Museum; the Parliamentary Archives for David Lloyd George's papers; the Master and Fellows of Churchill College, Cambridge, for Leo Amery's and Maurice Hankey's papers; the Master and Fellows of Pembroke College, Cambridge, for Ronald Storrs's papers; and the Librarian, Robinson Library, Newcastle University, for Gertrude Bell's diaries and letters. Quotations from Crown Copyright records held in all of the archives that I consulted appear by permission of Her Majesty's Stationery Office.

Extracts from *La révolte Druze et l'insurrection de Damas* by Charles Andréa are reprinted by permission of Editions Payot; from *The Story of the Malakand Field Force, The River War, Great Contemporaries* and *The Second World War* by Sir Winston Churchill by permission of Curtis Brown Group Ltd; from *Going Solo* by Roald Dahl by permission of David Higham Associates; from *The Duff Cooper Diaries* by permission of Weidenfeld and Nicolson; from *Mémoires de Guerre* and *Le Fil de l'Epée* by Charles de Gaulle by permission of Amiral Philippe de Gaulle and Editions Plon; from *Summing Up* by Yitzhak Shamir by permission of Samuel Hayek.

ACKNOWLEDGEMENTS

I am deeply grateful to the many people who have helped me during the four years it has taken me to write this book, starting with the archivists and staffs of the National Archive, Bodleian Library, British Library, Churchill Archives, Imperial War Museum, India Office Records, Liddell Hart Centre for Military Archives, London Library, Parliamentary Archive and American Jewish Historical Society. Simon Offord and Richard Hughes at the Imperial War Museum, Patricia Aske at Pembroke College, Cambridge, and Jane Hogan at the Sudan Archive at the University of Durham all helped me obtain permissions to use material I had found. I would particularly like to thank Debbie Usher at the Middle East Centre Archive in Oxford, and Nick Mays at the Times Archive for their help. During my research trips to France I was heavily dependent on the goodwill at both the archives I visited. The staff at the Centre des Archives Diplomatiques de Nantes and the Service Historique de l'Armée de Terre in Paris bent the rules to enable me to achieve a lot in a relatively short time.

I was extremely fortunate to be elected to a visiting fellowship at St Antony's College, Oxford, during my research, and to be made so welcome by everybody there. I would especially like to thank the Warden, Margaret MacMillan, as well as Avi Shlaim, Eugene Rogan, Ahmed al-Shahi, Peter Mangold and Mastan Ebtehaj for their encouragement and advice, Jeevan Deol for his expertise on Freedom of Information requests, and Jeff Short, a fellow visitor at the same time as me, for his friendship.

The Rory Peck Trust helped me gain a place on a hostile environments and first-aid course. Jonathan Lehrle accompanied me on my visit to Lebanon. Caroline and Hassan Farran were hugely hospitable in Damascus, where Fatie Darwish joined in the hunt for information about Colonel Stirling. Patrick and Françoise Pierard welcomed me to their home in snowy Paris. I am grateful to Henri Laurens for sharing the reports of Antonin Jaussen with me, and to Roberto Mazza for his paper on the French archaeologist. I would also like to thank Maurice Larès and Christophe Leclerc for their perspectives on T. E. Lawrence, and Blandine Guegan for confirming my suspicions about the French authorship of some Stern Gang propaganda. Lesley Barnes, Marilyn Checkley, Sir James Craig, Terry Dean, Samantha Ellis, Alison Hudson, Alex

Roberts, Steven Wagner, Philip Walker and George Williamson also supplied a range of other help.

Jean-Michel de Tarragon and Ben Smith helped me with picture research. Tracking down a photograph of François Georges-Picot involved a human chain that linked Tom Tugendhat, Roland Giscard d'Estaing, Eric Georges-Picot, Bruno Georges-Picot and finally Anne Parent, who provided me with the photograph of her grandfather which is included in the illustrations. I am very grateful to Mme Parent for allowing me to do so.

I wrote, and rewrote, much of the book in Cape Town. When Lord Moyne's significance as the force behind the Greater Syria idea dawned on me while I was there, 6,000 miles away in Britain Tim Jinks generously agreed to investigate further, saving me a long and costly trip. I am also grateful to Veronica Belling, Jewish Studies Librarian at the University of Cape Town, for allowing me access to the library during my time in the city. Long-distance history is being made much easier by digitisation projects now in progress. The Cabinet Papers online archive at the National Archive, the Gertrude Bell archive and the London Library's electronic library, which includes access to the Times Digital Archive, were all extremely useful. So too was Jeremy Wilson's online database of T. E. Lawrence's writings. I gratefully acknowledge all of them.

I inflicted early versions of the book on Matthew Keen, Paul Kenward and Derek Parsons: thank you to all three for their responses; Ivor Lucas generously read and commented on the final draft, and drew my attention to new research that otherwise I would have missed. The judgements in the book, and any errors you may find, are my responsibility alone.

I should like to thank my agents, Catherine Clarke and George Lucas, and the team at Simon and Schuster: the commissioning editor, Mike Jones, my editors, Katherine Stanton and Talya Baker, as well as Hannah Corbett, Joanne Edgecombe, Emily Husain, Viki Ottewill and Rory Scarfe. Thanks too to my copy editor, Sue Phillpott, and proofreader, Margaret Histed. Reg Piggott drew the superb maps. Talya Baker deserves special recognition, as she patiently and expertly steered the book from manuscript to finished book.

On my computer I kept the files relating to this book in a folder I entitled 'Phoenix', for this project grew out of an earlier idea that foundered when I discovered that a rival book, with the same title and a similar subject was on the point of publication. Dismay gave way to excitement when, on my return to the archives, I found the Security Service files I mention in the Prologue to this book – which is much more ambitious, and ground-breaking, than its abortive predecessor would ever have been. On the trek it has taken me to reach this point, my greatest debt is to my wife, Anna, for her love, patience, encouragement and support.

NOTES

ABBREVIATIONS USED IN THE NOTES

AJHS   American Jewish Historical Society, New York
BL   British Library, London
CAC   Churchill Archives Centre, Cambridge
CADN   Centre des Archives diplomatiques de Nantes
DDF   *Documents Diplomatiques Français*
FRUS   *Foreign Relations of the United States*
GBA   Gertrude Bell Archive, Newcastle
HC Deb   House of Commons, Debates
HL Deb   House of Lords, Debates
IOR   India Office Records, London
ISA   Israel State Archives
IWM   Imperial War Museum, London
LHCMA   Liddell Hart Centre for Military Archives, London
MAE   Ministère des Affaires Etrangères, Paris
MEC   Middle East Centre Archive, Oxford
PAL   Parliamentary Archives, London
PCC   Pembroke College Archive, Cambridge
SAD   Sudan Archive, Durham
SHAT   Service Historique de l'Armée de Terre, Paris
TNA   The National Archives, London
TTA   The Times Archive, London

1 VERY PRACTICAL POLITICS

1 TNA, FO 882/2, Sykes to Clayton, 28 Dec. 1915.
2 N. N. E. Bray, *Shifting Sands* (London, 1934), pp. 66–7.
3 HC Deb, 27 Nov. 1911, vol. 32, c. 102.
4 BL, Add 63040, Crewe to Bertie, 17 Dec. 1915.
5 BL, Add 63040, Crewe to Bertie, 17 Dec. 1915. Lord Crewe described Sykes as 'knowing I think both Turkish and Arabic'.
6 GBA, Bell to Mary Bell, 1 Feb. 1905.
7 *The Times*, 'Death of Sir Mark Sykes', 18 Feb. 1919.
8 Roger Adelson, *Mark Sykes, Portrait of an Amateur* (London, 1975), pp. 108–9.
9 SHAT, 6N 76, 'Note sur les intérêts moraux et matériels de la France en Syrie',

1 Feb. 1919. Total French government revenue in the period 1904–14 was 2,577 million francs, according to Hew Strachan, *The First World War*, vol. I (Oxford, 2001), p. 856.

10 Sykes, *The Caliphs' Last Heritage* (London, 1915), p. 298.

11 Sykes, *The Caliphs' Last Heritage*, p. 482.

12 Sykes, *The Caliphs' Last Heritage*, pp. 338–9

13 Sykes, *The Caliphs' Last Heritage*, p. 299.

14 Sykes, *The Caliphs' Last Heritage*, pp. 471–2, 522.

15 Edwin Pears, review of *The Caliphs' Last Heritage*, *English Historical Review*, vol. 31, no. 122 (Apr. 1916), p. 300.

16 W. Crooke, review of *The Caliphs' Last Heritage*, *Man*, vol. 17 (Jan. 1917), p. 24.

17 TNA, CAB 24/1, 'Meeting held at 10, Downing Street, on Thursday December 16 at 11.30am: Evidence of Lieutenant-Colonel Sir Mark Sykes, Bart, MP, on the Arab Question'.

18 Charles Townshend, *When God Made Hell: The British Invasion of Mesopotamia and the Creation of Iraq, 1914–21* (London, 2010), p. 82.

19 TNA, FO 882/2, Sykes to Clayton, 28 Dec. 1915.

20 HC Deb, 28 Mar. 1895, vol. 32, c. 406.

21 Winston S. Churchill, *The River War* (London, 1899), p. 318.

22 BL, Add 63040, Bertie to Crewe, 21 Dec. 1915. On French suspicions about British activities in Syria see W. I. Shorrock, *French Imperialism in the Middle East: The Failure of Policy in Syria and Lebanon 1900–1914* (Wisconsin, 1976), p. 124.

23 Amanda L. Capern, 'Winston Churchill, Mark Sykes and the Dardanelles Campaign of 1915', *Historical Research*, vol. 71, no. 174 (Feb. 1998), p. 117, quoting Sykes to Churchill, 27 Jan. 1915.

24 David Garnett, ed., *The Letters of T. E. Lawrence* (London, 1938), pp. 193–4, Lawrence to Hogarth, 18 Mar. 1915.

25 MAE, Guerre 1914–1918, 868, Defrance to Delcassé, 13 Feb. 1915.

26 Martin Gilbert, *Winston S. Churchill*, companion volume part 1 to vol. III, p. 458. Grey's annotation on Churchill to Grey and Kitchener, 26 Jan. 1915.

27 TNA, FO 800/48, Grey to McMahon, 8 Mar. 1915.

28 A. J. Barker, *The Neglected War: Mesopotamia 1914–1918*, London, 1967, p. 472.

29 C. M. Andrew and A. S. Kanya-Forstner, *France Overseas: The Great War and the Climax of French Imperial Expansion* (London, 1981), p. 74.

30 Robert de Caix in *L'Asie Française*, Jan.–Mar. 1915, quoted in C. M. Andrew and A. S. Kanya-Forstner, 'The French Colonial Party and French Colonial War Aims, 1914–1918', *Historical Journal*, vol. 17, no. 1 (1974), pp. 79–106.

31 Andrew and Kanya-Forstner, *France Overseas*, p. 40.

32 Cloarec, *La France et la question de Syrie, 1914–1918* (Paris, 2002), p. 115; Edward Peter Fitzgerald, 'France's Middle Eastern Ambitions, the Sykes–Picot Negotiations, and the Oil Fields of Mosul, 1915–1918', *Journal of Modern History*, vol. 66, no. 4 (Dec. 1994), p. 704.

33 MEC, Barbour Papers, Groupe Sénatorial pour la défense des intérêts français à l'étranger, *Rapport sur la Syrie et la Palestine, présenté par M Etienne Flandin*, 1915.

34 Sykes, *The Caliphs' Last Heritage*, p. 468.

35 Cloarec, *La France et la question de Syrie*, p. 126, de St Quentin to Millerand, 'Visées anglaises sur la Syrie', 28 July 1915.

36 Andrew and Kanya-Forstner, *France Overseas*, p. 76.

37 J. K. Tanenbaum, 'France and the Arab Middle East 1914–1920', *Transactions of the American Philosophical Society*, vol. 68 (1978), Part 7, p. 8; Delcassé to Cambon, 24 Aug. 1915.

38 Andrew and Kanya-Forstner, *France Overseas*, p. 77.

2 MONSIEUR PICOT

1   C. M. Andrew, 'The French Colonialist Movement during the Third Republic: The Unofficial Mind of Imperialism', *Transactions of the Royal Historical Society*, vol. 26 (1976), p. 149. The speaker was the Comité's president, Auguste Louis Albéric, Prince d'Arenberg.

2   T. E. Lawrence, *Seven Pillars of Wisdom* (London, 1935), p. 464.

3   Andrew and Kanya-Forstner, *France Overseas*, p. 99. For an outline of Georges-Picot's career see F. W. Brecher, 'French Policy toward the Levant 1914–18', *Middle Eastern Studies*, vol. 29, no. 4 (Oct. 1993), pp. 654–6.

4   SAD, Wingate Papers, 148/4, Lloyd to Wingate, 2 Feb. 1918.

5   Gérard Khoury, *La France et l'Orient Arabe: Naissance du Liban Moderne* (Paris, 1993), p. 66.

6   Khoury, *La France et l'Orient Arabe*, p. 66.

7   Cloarec, *La France et la question de Syrie*, p. 116, Georges-Picot to Defrance, 5 Oct. 1915.

8   PCC, Storrs Papers, letter to Φιλτατε ['Dearest'], 22 Feb. 1915.

9   McMahon to Husein, 30 Aug. 1915; Husein to McMahon, 9 Sept. 1915, in G. Antonius, *The Arab Awakening* (London, 1938), p. 417.

10 TNA, FO 371/2486, piece 153045, McMahon to Grey, 18 Oct. 1915.

11 SAD, Wingate Papers, 135/6, Sykes to Callwell, 21 Nov. 1915.

12 TNA, FO 371/2486, piece 152729, Clerk, minute, 19 Oct. 1915.

13 James Barr, *Setting the Desert on Fire: T. E. Lawrence and Britain's Secret War in Arabia, 1916–1918* (New York, 2008), p. 28.

14 TNA, FO 371/2486, piece 155203, Grey to McMahon, 20 Oct. 1915.

15 Elie Kedourie, *In the Anglo-Arab Labyrinth* (Cambridge, 1976), p. 119.

16 TNA, FO 371/2486, piece 163832, McMahon to Grey, 26 Oct. 1915. Piece 153045 contains the early draft.

17 MEC, Cox Papers, Hirtzel to Cox, 29 Dec. 1920.

18 Ronald Storrs, *Orientations* (London, 1937), p. 179.

19 TNA, FO 371/2486, piece 158561, Nicolson to Crewe, 30 Oct. 1915.

20 Fitzgerald, 'France's Middle Eastern Ambitions', p. 708.

21 Andrew and Kanya-Forstner, 'The French Colonial Party and French Colonial War Aims', p. 84, Cambon to Viviani, 21 Oct. 1915.

22 Andrew and Kanya-Forstner, *France Overseas*, p. 89.

23 TNA, FO 371/2486, piece 161325, McMahon to Foreign Office, 28 Oct. 1915.

24 Tanenbaum, 'France and the Arab Middle East', p. 11, Hardinge to Nicolson, 28 Dec. 1915.

25 TNA, FO 882/2, 'Minutes of the second meeting of the Committee to discuss the Arab Question and Syria, 23 Nov. 1915'.

26 BL, Add 63039, Bertie to Grey, 17 Dec. 1915.

27 TNA, FO 882/12, Clayton to Wingate, 28 Jan. 1916, and FO 882/2, Clayton's annotations on the 'Minutes of the second meeting of the Committee to discuss the Arab Question and Syria, 23 Nov. 1915'.

28 BL, Add 63039, Bertie, note, 24 Oct. 1915.

29 BL, Add 63039, Bertie to Grey, 30 Nov. 1915.

30　SAD, Wingate Papers, 135/6, Parker to Clayton, 19 Nov. 1915.

31　TNA, FO 800/380, Nicolson to Hardinge, 16 Dec. 1915; Polly A. Mohs, *Military Intelligence and the Arab Revolt:The First Modern Intelligence War* (London, 2008), p. 31.

32　BL, Add 63040, Crewe to Bertie, 17 Dec. 1915.

33　Tanenbaum, 'France and the Arab Middle East', p. 11.

34　Cloarec, *La France et la question de Syrie*, p. 146, Briand to Cambon, 14 Dec. 1915.

35　Andrew and Kanya-Forstner, 'The French Colonial Party and French Colonial War Aims', p. 85, Georges-Picot to de Margerie, 2 Dec. 1915.

36　Cloarec, *La France et la question de Syrie*, p. 147.

37　Sykes, *The Caliphs' Last Heritage*, p. 596.

38　SAD, Wingate Papers, 135/6, Sykes to Callwell, 21 Nov. 1915.

39　Isaiah Friedman, *The Question of Palestine* (London, 1973), p. 113.

40　Cloarec, *La France et la question de Syrie*, p. 115, Georges-Picot to Defrance, 30 May 1915.

41　Cloarec, *La France et la question de Syrie*, p. 151, Briand to Cambon, 5 Jan. 1916.

42　TNA, FO 371/2767, Macdonogh to Nicolson, 6 Jan. 1916.

43　MEC, Samuel Papers, 'Palestine', Mar. 1915.

44　BL, Add 63041, Grey to Bertie, 11 Mar. 1916.

45　Andrew and Kanya-Forstner, *France Overseas*, p. 128. The minute was by Jean Goût, n.d.

46　*The Times*, 'Allies Reply to Mr Wilson', 12 Jan. 1917.

47　Woodrow Wilson, speech to the Senate, 22 Jan. 1917.

48　Woodrow Wilson, speech to Congress, 2 Apr. 1917.

49　Martin Gilbert, *Exile and Return: The Emergence of Jewish Statehood* (London, 1978), pp. 83–4.

50　MEC, Sykes Papers, note of a conference at 10 Downing Street on 3 Apr. 1917.

51　MEC, Sykes Papers, Sykes to Graham, 6 Apr. 1917.

52　Andrew and Kanya-Forstner, 'The French Colonial Party and French Colonial War Aims', pp. 94–5.

53　Charles Seymour, ed., *The Intimate Papers of Colonel House*, vol. III (London, 1928), p. 48.

3 ENTER T. E. LAWRENCE

1　SAD, Clayton Papers, 693/11, Lawrence to Sykes (unsent), 7 Sept. 1917.

2　MEC, Sykes Papers, Sykes to Drummond, 20 July 1917.

3　Lawrence, *Seven Pillars of Wisdom* (1935), p. 57.

4　Jeremy Wilson, *Lawrence of Arabia: The Authorised Biography of T. E. Lawrence* (London, 1989), p. 138, Kenyon to Watson, 21 Nov. 1913.

5　GBA, Bell, letter, 21 May 1911.

6　Malcolm Brown, ed., *Lawrence of Arabia: The Selected Letters* (London, 2005), p. 81, Lawrence to E. T. Leeds, 16 Nov. 1915.

7　Garnett, ed., *The Letters of T. E. Lawrence*, pp. 90–1, Lawrence to Vyvyan Richards, 15 Dec. 1910.

8　Brown, ed., *Lawrence of Arabia: The Selected Letters*, p. 40, Lawrence to Sarah Lawrence, 24 June 1911.

9　Garnett, ed., *The Letters of T. E. Lawrence*, pp. 193–4, Lawrence to Hogarth, 18 Mar. 1915.

10 M. R. Lawrence, *The Home Letters of T. E. Lawrence and his Brothers* (Oxford, 1954), p. 303, Lawrence to his family, 20 Feb. 1915.

11 Jeremy Wilson, *Lawrence of Arabia*, p. 178, Lawrence to E. T. Leeds, 9 Mar. 1915.

12 Garnett, ed., *The Letters of T. E. Lawrence*, pp. 195-6, Lawrence to Hogarth, 22 Mar. 1915.

13 Christophe Leclerc, *Avec T. E. Lawrence en Arabie, La Mission militaire française au Hedjaz 1916-1920* (Paris, 1998), p. 34, 'Note to the President of the Council', 19 July 1916.

14 Edouard Brémond, *Le Hedjaz dans la première guerre mondiale* (Paris, 1931), p. 46. The official was Philippe Berthelot.

15 Lawrence, *Seven Pillars of Wisdom* (1935), p. 57.

16 Lawrence, *Seven Pillars of Wisdom* (1935), p. 63.

17 Leclerc, *Avec T. E. Lawrence en Arabie*, p. 68. The source is a dispatch Brémond sent to the Quai d'Orsay on 28 Oct. 1916. SAD, Clayton Papers, 470/6, Wilson to Clayton, 16 Jan. 1917, reports Brémond's partiality to whisky.

18 TNA, FO 882/25, *Arab Bulletin* 32, 26 Nov. 1916.

19 TNA, FO 141/510/4, Foreign Office to high commissioner, Egypt, 6 Apr. 1920.

20 BL, Add 45914, f. 29.

21 TNA, FO 882/25, *Arab Bulletin* 32, 26 Nov. 1916.

22 Lawrence, *Seven Pillars of Wisdom* (1935), pp. 91 and 67.

23 LHCMA, Joyce Papers, 1/258, Joyce to Clayton, 25 Sept. 1917.

24 Wilson, *Lawrence of Arabia*, p. 610, quoting Feisal's diary from the peace conference, 1919.

25 SAD, Clayton Papers, 693/11, Lawrence to Sykes, 9 Sept. 1917 (unsent).

26 SAD, Clayton Papers, 693/11, Lawrence to Sykes, 9 Sept. 1917 (unsent).

27 SAD, Clayton Papers, 693/11, Lawrence to Sykes, 9 Sept. 1917 (unsent).

28 BL, Add 45915, f. 54.

29 BL, Add 45915, reverse f. 55.

30 BL, Add 45915, reverse f. 57.

31 IWM, Stirling Papers, Stirling, letter, 12 Sept. 1917.

4 ALLENBY'S MAN

1 MEC, Sykes Papers, Sykes to Clayton, 22 July 1917.

2 IOR, L/PS/11/124, Wingate to Robertson, 13 July 1917.

3 T. E. Lawrence, 'The Changing East', *The Round Table* (Sept. 1920), pp. 756-72.

4 Brown, ed., *Lawrence of Arabia: The Selected Letters*, p. 71, Lawrence to Sarah Lawrence, 12 Feb. 1915.

5 Henri Laurens, 'Jaussen en Arabie', in *Photographies d'Arabie: Hedjaz 1907-1917* (Paris, 1999), p. 30; MAE, Guerre 1914-1918, 1703.

6 MAE, Guerre 1914-1918, 878, 173-181, Defrance to Ribot, 30 Aug. 1917, enclosing 'Note sur le mouvement arabe à la frontière du désert syrien Akaba-Amman', 13 Aug. 1917.

7 Leclerc, *Avec T. E. Lawrence en Arabie*, p. 147; Doynel de St Quentin, report, 20 Aug. 1917.

8 Doynel de St Quentin, report, 20 Aug. 1917.

9 SAD, Clayton Papers, 470/5, Wilson to Clayton, 22 Nov. 1916.

10 Matthew Hughes, 'Allenby, Edmund Henry Hynman, first Viscount Allenby of Megiddo (1861-1936)', *Dictionary of National Biography* (Oxford, 2004), quoting Raymond Savage, *Allenby of Armageddon* (London, 1925), p. 24.

11 TNA, WO 158/634, Allenby to Robertson, 19 July 1917.

12 LHCMA, Robertson Papers, 8/1/73, Allenby to Robertson, 17 Oct. 1917.

13 SAD, Clayton Papers, 693/11, Lawrence to Sykes, 9 Sept. 1917 (unsent).

14 SAD, Clayton Papers, 693/12, Clayton to Lawrence, 20 Sept. 1917.

15 MEC, Sykes Papers, memorandum, 18 July 1917.

16 MEC, Sykes Papers, Sykes to Clayton, 22 July 1917.

17 Lawrence, *Seven Pillars of Wisdom* (1935), p. 359; TNA, FO 882/4, Clayton to general staff, enclosing Lawrence's report, 29 Sept. 1917.

18 Lawrence, *Seven Pillars of Wisdom* (1935), p. 367.

19 Garnett, ed., *The Letters of T. E. Lawrence*, pp. 237–8, Lawrence to Leeds, 24 Sept. 1917.

20 LHCMA, Liddell Hart Papers, 9/13/42, Lawrence to Stirling, 25 Sept. 1917.

21 LHCMA, Joyce Papers, 1/300, Dawnay to Joyce, 12 June 1918.

22 Leonard Stein, *The Balfour Declaration* (London, 1961), frontispiece.

23 Lawrence, *Seven Pillars of Wisdom* (1935), p. 423.

24 Lawrence, *Seven Pillars of Wisdom* (1935), p. 431.

25 Brown, ed., *Lawrence of Arabia: The Selected Letters*, p. 140, Lawrence to his parents, 14 Dec. 1917.

26 TNA, WO 33/946, Robertson to Allenby, 26 Nov. 1917.

27 LHCMA, Allenby Papers, 1/8/32, Allenby to Lady Allenby, 11 Dec. 1917.

28 Lawrence, *Seven Pillars of Wisdom* (1935), p. 455.

29 Lawrence, *Seven Pillars of Wisdom* (1935), p. 527.

30 *The Times*, 'British War Aims: Mr Lloyd George's Statement', 7 Jan. 1918.

31 Andrew and Kanya-Forstner, 'The French Colonial Party and French Colonial War Aims', p. 101, Sykes to Clayton, 3 Mar. 1918, Sykes to Wingate, 3 Mar. 1918.

32 BL, Add 51094, Cecil to Sykes, 7 Sept. 1918.

33 Otto Liman von Sanders, *Five Years in Turkey* (Nashville, 2000), p. 290.

34 Service Marine Q86, Jaussen, report, 1900hrs, 20 Sept. 1918.

35 Wilson, *Lawrence of Arabia*, p. 553.

36 Maurice Larès, *T. E. Lawrence, La France, et Les Français* (Paris, 1980), p. 403, *Echo de Paris*, 24 Sept. 1918.

37 W. F. Stirling, *Safety Last*, London, 1953, p. 94.

38 IWM, Stirling Papers, Stirling to his sister, 5 Nov. 1918.

39 Stirling, *Safety Last*, p. 97.

40 IWM, Wilson Papers, HHW2/33A/29, Allenby to Wilson, 9 Nov. 1918.

41 SAD, Clayton Papers, 693/11, Lawrence to Sykes, 9 Sept. 1917 (unsent).

5 I WANT MOSUL

1 CAC, Hankey Papers, HNKY 1/6, diary entry, 6 Oct. 1918.

2 Lord Meston, 'Mr Lloyd George's Memoirs', *International Affairs*, vol. 14, no. 2 (Mar.–Apr. 1935), p. 243.

3 Andrew and Kanya-Forstner, *France Overseas*, p. 162.

4 Andrew and Kanya-Forstner, *France Overseas*, p. 163.

5 CAC, Hankey Papers, HNKY 1/6, diary entry, 6 Oct. 1918.

6 TNA, CAB 21/119, Admiral Sir Edmond Slade, 'Petroleum Situation in the British Empire', 29 July 1918. Slade was a director of the British government-controlled Anglo-Persian Oil Company, which had extensive interests in neighbouring Persia.

7 TNA, CAB 21/119, Hankey to Lloyd George, 1 Aug. 1918.

8   TNA, CAB 21/119, Hankey to Balfour, 1 Aug. 1918 and 12 Aug. 1918.
9   Kenneth O. Morgan, 'David Lloyd George, first Earl Lloyd-George of Dwyfor (1863–1945)', Oxford *Dictionary of National Biography* (Oxford, 2004).
10 Robert Vansittart, *The Mist Procession* (London, 1958), p. 247.
11 John Julius Norwich, ed., *The Duff Cooper Diaries* (London, 2005), p. 45, 1 Jan. 1917.
12 Kenneth O. Morgan, 'Lloyd George's Premiership: A Study in "Prime Ministerial Government"', *Historical Journal*, vol. 13, no. 1 (Mar. 1970), p. 133.
13 Norwich, ed., *The Duff Cooper Diaries*, pp. 88–9, 8 Dec. 1918.
14 Morgan, 'Lloyd George's Premiership', p. 132.
15 CAC, Hankey Papers, HNKY 1/6, diary entry, 6 Oct. 1918.
16 PAL, Lloyd George Papers, LG/F/41/8/22, copy of telegram from Henderson to Northcliffe, 14 Oct. 1918.
17 Erik Goldstein, 'British Peace Aims and the Eastern Question: The Political Intelligence Department and the Eastern Committee, 1918', *Middle Eastern Studies*, vol. 23, no. 4 (Oct. 1987), p. 427. The official was Arnold Toynbee, writing on 19 Dec. 1918.
18 TNA, FO 371/3384, Cecil, note, 28 Oct. 1918.
19 MEC, Hogarth Papers, Hogarth to Clayton, 1 Nov. 1918.
20 Wilson, *Lawrence of Arabia*, p. 585.
21 Margaret MacMillan, *Peacemakers* (London, 2002), p. 384.
22 Andrew and Kanya-Forstner, 'The French Colonial Party and French Colonial War Aims', p. 104.
23 TNA, CAB 27/24, Eastern Committee, minutes, 21 Nov. 1918.
24 TNA, CAB 23/42, Eastern Committee, minutes, 20 Dec. 1918.
25 SAD, Clayton Papers, 694/6, the Weizmann–Feisal agreement, 3 Jan. 1919.
26 Wilson, *Lawrence of Arabia*, p. 596.
27 Andrew and Kanya-Forstner, *France Overseas*, p. 152.
28 SHAT, 6N 76, Cambon to ministère des affaires étrangères, 28 Nov. 1918.
29 SHAT, 6N 76, Cambon, note, 30 Nov. 1918.
30 CAC, Hankey Papers, HNKY 1/6, diary, note dated 11 Dec. 1920 in entry for 4 Dec. 1918. In the most contemporary account of this meeting (TNA, CAB 23/42, Imperial War Cabinet, minutes, 20 Dec. 1918) Lloyd George reported that, when he told Clemenceau that British troops were staying in Palestine and Mesopotamia, Clemenceau replied: 'All right. I don't care.'
31 Harold Nicolson, *Peacemaking 1919* (London, 1933), p. 256, 4 Feb. 1919.
32 Harold Nicolson, *Peacemaking 1919*, pp. 274–5, 1 Mar. 1919.
33 Wickham Steed, review of Clemenceau's *Grandeur and Misery of Victory*, *International Affairs*, vol. 10, no. 1 (Jan. 1931), p. 115.
34 Andrew and Kanya-Forstner, *France Overseas*, p. 137.
35 MacMillan, *Peacemakers*, p. 37.
36 Andrew and Kanya-Forstner, *France Overseas*, p. 137, Bertie to Lloyd George, 9 Dec. 1917.
37 Andrew and Kanya-Forstner, *France Overseas*, p. 207.
38 SHAT, 6N 76, 'La France et l'Angleterre en Syrie', n.d.
39 MacMillan, *Peacemakers*, p. 39.
40 SHAT, 6N 197, 'Note pour Monsieur le Président du Conseil, "A.s. de L'Emir Fayssal"', 9 Jan. 1919.
41 TNA, FO 608/97, Lawrence's note on Feisal's meeting with Goût, 16 Jan. 1919.
42 Henry Cumming, *Franco-British Rivalry in the Post-war Near East* (Oxford, 1938), p. 72.

43 Michael B. Oren, *Power, Faith and Fantasy: America in the Middle East, 1776 to the Present* (New York, 2007), p. 373; Wilson, *Lawrence of Arabia*, p. 605.

44 Lord Hardinge of Penshurst, *Old Diplomacy* (London, 1947), p. 232.

45 SHAT, 6N 76, 'Note sur les intérêts moraux et matériels de la France en Syrie', 1 Feb. 1919; MacMillan, *Peacemakers*, p. 401.

46 MacMillan, *Peacemakers*, p. 401.

47 PAL, Lloyd George Papers, LG/F/205/3/1, report on French press, 7 Feb. 1919.

48 Larès, *T. E. Lawrence, La France, et Les Français*, p. 403, *Echo de Paris*, 7 Feb. 1919.

49 SHAT, 6N 76, 'Comparison of the French and British Military Effort during the Years 1917 and 1918', n.d.

50 TNA, CAB 24/75, Foreign Office Political Intelligence Department, 'Currents of Opinion in France', 16 Feb. 1919.

51 TNA, FO 608/107/1, Curzon to Balfour, 21 Feb. 1919.

52 PAL, Lloyd George Papers, LG/F/89/2/8, Lloyd George to Kerr, 12 Feb. 1919.

53 MacMillan, *Peacemakers*, p. 402.

54 TNA, FO 608/107/2, note by the Comité de l'Asie Française, n.d. but stamped 13 Feb. 1919.

55 TNA, CAB 24/75, Foreign Office Political Intelligence Department, 'Currents of Opinion in France', 16 Feb. 1919.

56 Tanenbaum, 'France and the Arab Middle East 1914–1920', p. 32.

57 MEC, Yale Papers, Yale, 'Interview with Mr Jean Goût', 13 Sept. 1919.

58 *Time*, 'France: Grandeur and Anecdotes', 21 Apr. 1930.

59 Andrew and Kanya-Forstner, *France Overseas*, p. 189.

6 DEADLOCK

1 *FRUS*, The Paris Peace Conference, vol. 5, p. 4, *The Council of Four: Minutes of Meetings Mar. 20 to May 24, 1919*, Notes of a Meeting Held in the Prime Minister's Flat at 23 Rue Nitot, Paris, on Thursday, 20 Mar. 1919.

2 *FRUS*, The Paris Peace Conference, vol. 5, p. 7, *The Council of Four: Minutes of Meetings Mar. 20 to May 24, 1919*, Notes of a Meeting Held in the Prime Minister's Flat at 23 Rue Nitot, Paris, on Thursday, 20 Mar. 1919.

3 *FRUS*, The Paris Peace Conference, vol. 5, p. 7, *The Council of Four: Minutes of Meetings Mar. 20 to May 24, 1919*, Notes of a Meeting Held in the Prime Minister's Flat at 23 Rue Nitot, Paris, on Thursday, 20 Mar. 1919.

4 *FRUS*, The Paris Peace Conference, vol. 5, p. 9, *The Council of Four: Minutes of Meetings Mar. 20 to May 24, 1919*, Notes of a Meeting Held in the Prime Minister's Flat at 23 Rue Nitot, Paris, on Thursday, 20 Mar. 1919.

5 PAL, Lloyd George Papers, LG/F/3/4/12, Balfour to Lloyd George, 19 Feb. 1919.

6 Garnett, ed., *The Letters of T. E. Lawrence*, pp. 265–9; Lawrence, 'Reconstruction of Arabia', 4 Nov. 1918.

7 MEC, Cox Papers 5/2, Bell to Cox, 7 Feb. 1919.

8 TNA, FO 608/97/15, Intelligence Department naval staff, 'The Oilfields of Persia and Mesopotamia', 26 Feb. 1919.

9 T. E. Lawrence, *T. E. Lawrence to his Biographers Robert Graves and Liddell Hart* (London, 1963), p. 52, Lawrence to Graves, 28 June 1927.

10 BL, Add 52455 A, Wilson to Cox, 9 May 1919.

11 Nicolson, *Peacemaking 1919*, p. 288, 23 Mar. 1919.

12 PAL, Lloyd George Papers, LG/F/6/6/47, Cecil to Lloyd George, 27 May 1919.

13 Col. R. Meinertzhagen, *Middle East Diary, 1917–1956* (London, 1959), p. 26.

14   MacMillan, *Peacemakers*, p. 447.
15   MEC, Meinertzhagen Papers, diary, 22 May 1919.
16   Matthew Hughes, *Allenby and British Strategy in the Middle East, 1917–1919* (London, 1999), p. 131.
17   *FRUS*, The Paris Peace Conference, vol. 5, p. 812, *The Council of Four: Minutes of Meetings Mar. 20 to May 24, 1919*, Notes of a Meeting Held at Mr Lloyd George's Residence, 23 Rue Nitot, Paris, on Thursday, 22 May 1919.
18   *FRUS*, The Paris Peace Conference, vol. 12, p. 747, The American Section of the International Commission on Mandates in Turkey (The King–Crane Commission), Instructions for Commissioners from the Peace Conference, 25 Mar. 1919; IOR, L/PS/11/157, piece 5878, French (GOC EEF) to Curzon, 30 Aug. 1919.
19   TNA, FO 608/96/11, 'Self-Determination in Iraq', comments by Haji Hasan Shabbut and Shaykh Saud al-Sabbah.
20   *FRUS*, The Paris Peace Conference, vol. 12, p. 849, Crane and King, 'Report of the American Section of the International Commission on Mandates in Turkey', 28 Aug. 1919.
21   MEC, Yale Papers, memoir: 'It Takes So Long'.
22   IOR, L/PS/10/801, Cornwallis, report, 18 May 1919; Eugene Rogan, *The Arabs: A History* (London, 2009), p. 161.
23   MEC, Yale Papers, memoir: 'It Takes So Long'.
24   *FRUS*, The Paris Peace Conference, vol. 12, pp. 798 and 848, 'Confidential Appendix to the Report upon Syria: For the Use of Americans Only', p. 798, Crane and King, 'Report of the American Section of the International Commission on Mandates in Turkey'.
25   *FRUS*, The Paris Peace Conference, vol. 12, p. 794, Crane and King, 'Report of the American Section of the International Commission on Mandates in Turkey'.
26   *FRUS*, The Paris Peace Conference, vol. 12, p. 792, Crane and King, 'Report of the American Section of the International Commission on Mandates in Turkey'.
27   IOR, L/PS/11/155, piece 4393, Grahame to Foreign Office, 26 July 1919.
28   *The Times*, 'The Situation in Syria', 6 Sept. 1919.
29   Peter A. Shambrook, *French Imperialism in Syria, 1927–1936* (Reading, 1998), pp. 41–2.
30   PAL, Lloyd George Papers, LG/F/205/3/15, Grahame to Curzon, 13 Sept. 1919.
31   IOR, L/PS/10/801, Grahame to Curzon, 12 Aug. 1919.
32   *The Times*, 'France and the Persian Treaty', 19 Aug. 1919.
33   TNA, CAB 21/154a, Lloyd George to Clemenceau, 18 Oct. 1919.
34   Brown, ed., *Lawrence of Arabia: The Selected Letters*, p. 175, Lawrence to Stirling, 28 June 1919.
35   MEC, Yale Papers, 'A report on Syria, Palestine and Mount Lebanon for the American Commissioners, prepared by Captain William Yale, Technical Advisor to the American Section of the International Commission on Mandates in Turkey', 26 July 1919.
36   *The Times*, 'Sidelights on the Arab War: Two Turkish Plotters – Emir Said Arrested', 4 Sept. 1919.
37   SHAT, 6N 197, Pichon to Cambon, 20 Aug. 1919.
38   *The Times*, 11 Sept. 1919.
39   Keith Jeffery, 'Great Power Rivalry in the Middle East', *Historical Journal*, vol. 25, no. 4 (Dec. 1982), p. 1031.
40   Jeffery, 'Great Power Rivalry in the Middle East', p. 1031.
41   TNA, CAB 21/154a, minutes of a meeting held on 9 Sept. 1919.

42 This description of the geographical bounds of Palestine can be found in the Bible: 1 Samuel 3: 20; Judges 20:1.

43 PAL, Lloyd George Papers, LG/F/47/8/24, Wilson to Lloyd George, 23 June 1919, enclosing a paper by Gribbon on the significance of Palmyra.

44 Paul C. Helmreich, *From Paris to Sèvres* (Ohio, 1974), p. 70.

45 Garnett, ed., *The Letters of T. E. Lawrence*, p. 288, Lawrence, memorandum, 15 Sept. 1919.

46 Garnett, ed., *The Letters of T. E. Lawrence*, p. 294.

47 Stirling, *Safety Last*, p. 102.

48 TNA, CAB 23/44 B, 'Notes of a Meeting held at 10 Downing Street, on Friday Sept. 19, 1919, at 4 pm'.

49 IOR, L/PS/11/159, piece 6977, Clemenceau to Derby, 14 Oct. 1919.

50 TNA, CAB 21/154a, Lloyd George to Clemenceau, 18 Oct. 1919.

51 Pierre Lyautey, *Gouraud* (Paris, 1949), p. 192.

7 THE CRUSADER

1 MEC, Monckton Papers, Monckton to Evelyn Mary Monckton, 25 Nov. 1919.

2 Vansittart, *The Mist Procession*, p. 246.

3 Lyautey, *Gouraud*, p. 140.

4 Lyautey, *Gouraud*, p. 180.

5 Georges Catroux, *Deux Missions en Moyen Orient, 1919–1922* (Paris, 1958), p. 102.

6 TNA, HW 12/9, Bristol to secretary of state, Washington, 22 May 1920. This comment was made by Robert de Caix, reported by the American consul, and intercepted by British intelligence.

7 PAL, Lloyd George Papers, LG/F/89/4/20, Kerr to Lloyd George, 8 Nov. 1919.

8 Charles Andréa, *La Révolte Druze et l'insurrection de Damas* (Paris, 1937), p. 21. Lyautey, *Gouraud* (p . 192) states that the British withdrew thirty-four battalions, which the French replaced with thirteen battalions, four of them under strength.

9 Lyautey, *Gouraud*, p. 193.

10 This was due to differences in the boundaries of the zones set out in the Sykes–Picot agreement and in the Occupied Enemy Territory Administration (OETA) arrangements established by Allenby at the end of the war, which divided occupied Ottoman territory into north and west, south and east districts, under French, British and Arab administration respectively. In the withdrawal, Britain only agreed to hand over OETA West to the French because it feared that, if it followed the Sykes–Picot arrangement, the implication that a political deal had been reached would anger the Arabs. This left the Arabs in charge of an area which the French claimed under the Sykes–Picot agreement.

11 Tanenbaum, 'France and the Arab Middle East', p. 35.

12 Tanenbaum, 'France and the Arab Middle East', p. 35.

13 IOR, L/PS/11/161, Derby to Curzon, 20 Dec. 1919.

14 Tanenbaum, 'France and the Arab Middle East 1914–1920', p. 36.

15 IWM, Sir Clifford Norton Papers, Brayne, memorandum, 12 June 1919.

16 Andréa, *La Révolte Druze*, p. 18.

17 Tanenbaum, 'France and the Arab Middle East', p. 37.

18 IOR, L/PS/11/170, piece 2202, Curzon to Derby, 13 Mar. 1920.

19 PAL, Lloyd George Papers, LG/F/92/16/1, Bourne to Talbot, 25 Jan. 1919.

20 PAL, Lloyd George Papers, LG/F/3/4/4, Curzon to Balfour, 16 Jan. 1919.

21 PAL, Lloyd George Papers, LG/F/3/4/4, Curzon to Balfour, 16 Jan. 1919.

22 MEC, Samuel Papers, Weizmann to Curzon, 2 Feb. 1920.

23 TNA, CAB 24/154, Foreign Countries Report No. 12, 10 Mar. 1920.

24 Stirling, *Safety Last*, p. 113.

25 Tom Segev, *One Palestine, Complete* (London, 2000), p. 140.

26 Philip Mattar, *The Mufti of Jerusalem* (New York, 1988), p. 17.

27 Segev, *One Palestine, Complete*, p. 128.

28 MEC, Somerset Papers, Somerset to Ethel Raglan, 20 May 1920.

29 Segev, *One Palestine, Complete*, p. 147. The writer was the chief of the imperial general staff, Sir Henry Wilson.

30 TNA, CAB 24/108, 'Notes by the Director of Military Intelligence on his recent visit to Turkey, 21 June 1920'.

31 IOR, L/PS/11/174, Curzon to Cambon, 18 May 1920.

32 Tanenbaum, 'France and the Arab Middle East', p. 40.

33 TNA, CAB 24/131, Colonial Office, Middle East Department, 'Foreign Incitement of the Turks to Attack Iraq', 13 Dec. 1921.

34 TNA, CAB 21/204, Churchill, memorandum, 'French intentions in Syria', 8 June 1920.

35 IOR, L/PS/10/801, piece 5579, Allenby to Feisal, n.d. -

36 Ross Burns, *The Monuments of Syria* (London, 1992), p. 91.

37 MEC, Somerset Papers, Somerset to Raglan, 1 Aug. 1920.

38 Ronald Storrs, *Orientations* (London, 1937), p. 506.

39 SHAT, 7N 2829, 'Propagande Britannique en Orient: Propagande Anglo-Arabe en Syrie', annexe 10, n.d., but *c.* 1927.

8 REVOLT IN IRAQ

1 L/PS/11/175, piece 5655, 'The Proclamation by the Arabs to the Free Mesopotamians', n.d.

2 William Facey and Najdat Fathi Safwat, eds, *A Soldier's Story: From Ottoman Rule to Independent Iraq, The Memoirs of Jafar Pasha Al-Askari* (London, 2003), p. 174.

3 Peter Sluglett, *Britain in Iraq* (London, 2007), pp. 20–1; GBA, Bell to Hugh Bell, 30 Jan. 1921.

4 MEC, Cox Papers, 5/11, Bell to Hirtzel, 11 Oct. 1919.

5 TNA, CAB 24/96, Wilson to Montagu, 15 Nov. 1919, enclosing Bell's 'Syria in Oct. 1919'.

6 MEC, Cox Papers, 5/20, Bell to Hirtzel, 19 Mar. 1920.

7 TNA, FO 608/97/4, Vansittart, minute, 6 Sept. 1919.

8 GBA, Bell to Hugh Bell, 10 Jan. 1921.

9 BL, Add 52455 A, Wilson to Cox, 2 Jan. 1920.

10 IOR, L/PS/11/168, piece 1153, Wilson, New Year speech, Baghdad, 1 Jan. 1920.

11 GBA, Bell to Mary Bell, 14 Mar. 1920.

12 GBA, Bell to Hugh Bell, 19 Sept. 1920.

13 GBA, Bell to Hugh Bell, 1 June 1920.

14 *The Times*, 'Persia and Mesopotamia', 10 June 1920.

15 Sir Aylmer L. Haldane, *The Insurrection in Mesopotamia, 1920* (Edinburgh, 1922), p. 41.

16 BL, Add 52455, Wilson to Cox, 29 July 1920.

17 BL, Add 52455, Wilson to Cox, 29 July 1920.

18 HC Deb, 23 June 1920, vol. 130, c. 2226.

19   HC Deb, 23 June 1920, vol. 130, c. 2235.
20   *The Times*, 'Mr Lloyd George in the Garden of Eden', 24 June 1920.
21   *The Times*, 'Grave Trouble in Mesopotamia', 16 July 1920.
22   TNA, CAB 24/109, Churchill, 'Situation in Mesopotamia', 17 July 1920.
23   Garnett, ed., *The Letters of T. E. Lawrence*, p. 288, Lawrence, memorandum, 15 Sept. 1919.
24   *Sunday Times*, 'A Report on Mesopotamia', 22 Aug. 1920.
25   *The Times*, 'Arab Rights', 23 July 1920.
26   The British government's ordinary expenditure in 1921 was estimated at £947 million, according to Andrew McDonald, 'The Geddes Committee and the Formulation of Public Expenditure Policy, 1921–22', *Historical Journal*, vol. 32, no. 3 (Sept. 1989), pp. 643–74.
27   GBA, Bell to Mary Bell, 5 Sept. 1920; Bell to Hugh Bell, 19 Sept. 1920.
28   IWM, Clarke Papers.
29   TNA, FO 141/444/7, Wilson to Montagu, 31 July 1920.
30   TNA, FO 141/444/7, Wilson to Montagu, 31 July 1920.
31   *The Times*, 'Emir Feisal's Future: Possible Ruler of Mesopotamia', 5 Aug. 1920.
32   IOR, L/PS/10/919, draft instructions for Sir Percy Cox on his appointment as high commissioner.
33   *Observer*, 'France, Britain and the Arabs', 8 Aug. 1920.
34   *The Times*, 'Emir Feisal', 7 and 11 Aug. 1920. Saladin was in fact a Kurd.
35   *The Times*, 'Emir Feisal', 7 Aug. 1920.
36   IOR, L/PS/10/919, Fleuriau to Curzon, 17 Aug. 1920.
37   MEC, Monckton Papers, Monckton to Evelyn Mary Monckton, 21 Aug. 1920.
38   CAC, CHAR 16/34, Churchill to Haldane, 26 Aug. 1920.
39   CAC, CHAR 16/52, Churchill to Trenchard, 29 Aug. 1920.
40   Haldane, *The Insurrection in Mesopotamia, 1920*, p. 331.
41   CAC, CHAR 16/48 Churchill to Lloyd George, 31 Aug. 1920.
42   MEC, Cox Papers, 5/27, Hirtzel to Cox, 29 Dec. 1920.
43   Paul Addison, 'Churchill, Sir Winston Leonard Spencer (1874–1965)', *Oxford Dictionary of National Biography* (Oxford, 2004).
44   Richard Toye, *Rivals for Greatness: Lloyd George and Churchill* (London, 2007), p. 5.
45   Winston Churchill, *The Story of the Malakand Field Force* (London, 1898), p. 172.
46   Ernst Gombrich, 'Winston Churchill as Painter and Critic', *The Atlantic*, vol. 215 (1965), pp. 90–3.
47   John Charmley, *Churchill: The End of Glory* (London, 1993), p. 141.
48   *Morning Post*, 11 Jan. 1919.
49   Gilbert, *Winston S. Churchill*, vol. IV, p. 582. Richard Meinertzhagen attributed the comment to Sir Henry Wilson, chief of the imperial general staff.
50   CAC, CHAR 16/11, Lloyd George to Churchill, 22 Sept. 1919.
51   CAC, CHAR 16/48, Churchill to Lloyd George, 31 Aug. 1920.

9 THE BEST AND CHEAPEST SOLUTION

1   Winston Churchill, *Great Contemporaries* (London, 1939), p. 127.
2   Churchill, *Great Contemporaries*, p. 129.
3   Gilbert, *Winston S. Churchill*, vol. IV, p. 509, Churchill to Lloyd George, 4 Jan. 1921; Catherwood, *Winston's Folly*, p. 162.
4   Lawrence, *Seven Pillars of Wisdom* (1935), p. 21.

5   Wilson, *Lawrence of Arabia*, p. 645.
6   Brown, ed., *Lawrence of Arabia: The Selected Letters*, p. 196, Lawrence to Blunt, 2 Mar. 1921.
7   MEC, Cox Papers, 5/27, Hirtzel to Cox, 29 Dec. 1920.
8   CAC, CHAR 17/16/1, Churchill to Cox, 9 Jan. 1921.
9   CAC, CHAR 17/2/6, Lawrence to Marsh, n.d.
10 LHCMA, Coote Papers. Coote cites Lawrence as the source of the anecdote.
11 Catherwood, *Winston's Folly*, p. 130.
12 CAC, CHAR 17/2/7, Churchill to Curzon, 12 Jan. 1921.
13 Catherwood, *Winston's Folly*, p. 97, Churchill to Cox, 12 Jan. 1921.
14 TNA, FO 141/444/7, Curzon to Hardinge, 24 Jan. 1921, reporting a meeting between the Comte de Saint Aulaire and Sir Eyre Crowe on 21 Jan.
15 CAC, CHAR, 17/2/64, Churchill to Curzon, 16 Feb. 1921.
16 CAC, CHAR, 17/15/57, 'Notes of a conversation at Mr Churchill's house on February 24th'.
17 CAC, CHAR, 17/15/57, 'Notes of a conversation at Mr Churchill's house on February 24th'.
18 LHCMA, Allenby Papers, 1/11, Allenby to Catherine Allenby, 13 Mar. 1921.
19 *T. E. Lawrence to his Biographer Liddell Hart* (London, 1938), p. 143.
20 Catherwood, *Winston's Folly*, p. 131.
21 LHCMA, Coote Papers, diary, 13 Mar. 1921.
22 Brown, ed., *Lawrence of Arabia: The Selected Letters*, p. 196, Lawrence to Sarah Lawrence, 20 Mar. 1921.
23 Gilbert, *Winston S. Churchill*, vol. IV, p. 638.
24 Catherwood, *Winston's Folly*, p. 141.
25 MEC, Somerset Papers, 'Minutes of the First Meeting of the Palestine Political and Military Conference, 17 Mar. 1921'.
26 MEC, Cox Papers, 5/27, Hirtzel to Cox, 29 Dec. 1921.
27 PAL, Lloyd George Papers, LG/F/9/3/21, Churchill to Lloyd George, 23 Mar. 1921.
28 LHCMA, Coote Papers, diary, 24 Mar. 1921.
29 Martin Gilbert, *Churchill and the Jews* (London, 2007), p. 66.
30 PAL, Lloyd George Papers, LG/F/9/3/20, Lloyd George to Churchill, n.d.
31 CAC, CHAR 17/15/68, Churchill to Gouraud, 31 Mar. 1921.
32 Catherwood, *Winston's Folly*, p. 151, Churchill to Lloyd George, 18 Mar. 1921.
33 IOR, L/PS/10/919, Cox to Churchill, 9 June 1921.
34 TNA, FO 141/444/7, Hardinge to Curzon, 25 June 1921.
35 IOR, L/PS/10/919, Cox to Churchill, 1 July 1921.
36 GBA, Bell to Hugh Bell, 31 July 1921.
37 Gilbert, *Winston S. Churchill*, vol. IV, p. 581.
38 Catherwood, *Winston's Folly*, p. 164, Churchill to Cox, 9 July 1921.
39 IOR, L/PS/10/919, Cox to Churchill, 20 Aug. 1921.
40 GBA, Bell to Hugh Bell, 28 Aug. 1921.
41 Andrew and Kanya-Forstner, *France Overseas*, p. 222.

10 THE DRUZE REVOLT

1   Catroux, *Deux Missions en Moyen Orient*, p. 110.
2   MEC, Somerset Papers, 'Minutes of the First Meeting of the Palestine Political and Military Conference, 17 Mar. 1921'.

3　Catroux, *Deux Missions en Moyen Orient*, p. 115.

4　CADN, Mandat Syrie–Liban, Cabinet Politique, I/1531, 'Extract from a summary of intelligence issued by GS "I", GHQ, for the period 11th to 20th Aug. 1921'; Abramson, Amman, to civil secretary, Jerusalem, 1 Oct. 1921, enclosing reports by Alec Kirkbride and Frederick Peake.

5　CADN, Mandat Syrie–Liban, Cabinet Politique, I/1531, Kirkbride, report on the attempt to arrest men wanted by the French government, 24 Sept. 1921.

6　Garnett, ed., *The Letters of T. E. Lawrence*, p. 336, Lawrence to Newcombe, 8 Nov. 1921.

7　MEC, Barbour Papers, Groupe Sénatorial pour la défense des intérêts français à l'étranger, *Rapport sur la Syrie et la Palestine, présenté par M Etienne Flandin*, 1915.

8　Shambrook, *French Imperialism in Syria*, pp. 41–2.

9　Rousseau de Beauplan, 'Où va la Syrie?' (Paris, 1929), in Philip Khoury, *Syria and the French Mandate* (Princeton, 1987), p. 76.

10　TNA, FO 406/75, 'Syrian Personalities', c. 1937.

11　MEC, Glubb Papers, 'A Note on Certain Aspects of the Situation in Syria, 17 July 1941'.

12　MEC, Coghill Papers, 15 July 1945.

13　Catroux, *Deux Missions en Moyen Orient*, pp. 57–8; MEC, Somerset Papers, Somerset to Raglan, 15 July 1920.

14　MEC, Glubb Papers, 'A Note on Certain Aspects of the Situation in Syria, 17 July 1941'.

15　Stirling, *Safety Last*, p. 220.

16　IOR, L/PS/11/193, Fontana to Curzon, 31 Jan. 1921.

17　Catroux, *Deux Missions en Moyen Orient*, p. 39.

18　MEC, Samuel Papers, Samuel, draft letter to Thomas, 25 Jan. 1924.

19　Wilfred Thesiger, *The Life of My Choice* (London, 1987), p. 359.

20　Thesiger, *The Life of My Choice*, p. 360.

21　Charles Andréa, *La Révolte Druze et l'insurrection de Damas* (Paris, 1937), p. 39.

22　Bennett J. Doty, *The Legion of the Damned* (London, 1928), p. 95.

23　Alice Poulleau, *A Damas sous les bombes: journal d'une française pendant la révolte syrienne* (Yvetot, 1930), p. 44.

24　Jan Karl Tanenbaum, *General Maurice Sarrail 1856–1929: The French Army and Left-Wing Politics* (Chapel Hill, North Carolina, 1974), p. 186.

25　LHCMA, Codrington Papers, memoir: 'Gathering Moss', n.d.

26　TNA, FO 371/10835, Salisbury-Jones to GHQ Palestine, 6 May 1925.

27　TNA, FO 371/10835, Salisbury-Jones to GHQ Palestine, 10 Dec. 1925.

28　Poulleau, *A Damas sous les bombes*, p. 24.

29　Joyce Laverty Miller, 'The Syrian Revolt of 1925', *International Journal of Middle East Studies*, vol. 8, no. 4 (Oct. 1977), p. 551.

30　TNA, FO 371/10835, Salisbury-Jones to GHQ Palestine, 30 July 1925.

31　TNA, FO 371/10835, Salisbury-Jones to GHQ Palestine, 30 July 1925.

32　CADN, Mandat Syrie–Liban, Cabinet Politique, I/2389, Gamelin to high commissioner, May 1926.

33　Andréa, *La Révolte Druze*, p. 68.

34　Poulleau, *A Damas sous les bombes*, p. 78.

35　Poulleau, *A Damas sous les bombes*, p. 70.

36　CADN, Mandat–Syrie Liban, Cabinet Politique, I/2389, Gamelin to high commissioner, May 1926.

37 CADN, Mandat Syrie–Liban, Cabinet Politique, I/2389, Gamelin to high commissioner, May 1926.
38 CADN, Mandat Syrie–Liban, Cabinet Politique, I/2389, Gamelin to Sarrail, 31 Oct. 1925.
39 *The Times*, 'Damascus Riots: The Full Story', 27 Oct. 1925.
40 TNA, CO 732/22/1, Vaughan-Russell to foreign secretary, 1 Apr. 1926.
41 Tanenbaum, *Sarrail*, p. 207.
42 Treaty of Mutual Guarantee between Germany, Belgium, France, Great Britain and Italy, 16 Oct. 1925, article 7.

11 THE CRUSHING OF THE DRUZES

1 Poulleau, *A Damas sous les bombes*, 22 Aug. 1925.
2 Michael Provence, *The Great Syrian Revolt and the Rise of Arab Nationalism* (Austin, 2005), p. 79.
3 Paul Coblentz, *The Silence of Sarrail* (London, 1930), p. 229, quoting letter from Sarrail dated 15 Aug. 1924 (sic).
4 Andréa, *La Révolte Druze*, p. 72.
5 Aviel Roshwald, *Estranged Bedfellows: Britain and France in the Middle East during the Second World War* (Oxford, 1990), p. 11.
6 MEC, Smart Papers, Allanah Harper in 'Walter Smart by some of his friends', n.d.
7 MEC, Smart Papers, Julian Amery in 'Walter Smart by some of his friends', n.d.
8 TNA, FO 371/10835, Salisbury-Jones to GHQ Palestine, 10 Sept. 1925.
9 TNA, FO 684/3, Vaughan-Russell to foreign secretary, 2 June 1926.
10 LHCMA, Codrington Papers, 'Gathering Moss' (draft, unedited memoir).
11 TNA, CO 732/22/1, Vaughan-Russell to foreign secretary, 21 Apr. 1926.
12 *The Times*, 'Position at Damascus', 30 Oct. 1925, 'More Unrest in Syria', 2 Nov. 1925.
13 SHAT, 7N 2829, draft report: 'Propagande Britannique en Orient: Propagande Anglo-Arabe en Syrie', dated 1927 in pencil.
14 SHAT, 7N 2829, draft report: 'Propagande Britannique en Orient: Propagande Anglo-Arabe en Syrie'.
15 LHCMA, Codrington Papers, 'Gathering Moss'; TNA, CAB 24/131, Colonial Office, Middle East Department, memorandum, 'Foreign Incitement of the Turks to Attack Iraq', 13 Dec. 1921.
16 TNA, FO 371/10835, Salisbury-Jones to GHQ, 13 Oct. 1925.
17 CADN, Mandat Syrie–Liban, Cabinet Politique, I/2363, 'Proclamation faite aux peuples de la Syrie et du Djebel Druze', 10 Dec. 1925.
18 TNA, FO 371/10835, Salisbury-Jones, 'Report on the relief of Soueida', 6 Oct. 1925.
19 *FRUS*, 1926, vol. II, Keeley to secretary of state, 3 Mar. 1926.
20 TNA, FO 684/3, McFarland to Vaughan-Russell, 29 Apr. 1926; CADN, Mandat Syrie–Liban, Cabinet Politique, I/2389, Gamelin to secretary-general of the high commission, 7 Jan. 1926.
21 TNA, CO 732/22/1, Vaughan-Russell to foreign secretary, 14 June 1926.
22 SHAT, 4H 134, 'Extraits de la traduction des documents trouvés sur le corps du bandit Ahmed Merawed', n.d.
23 SHAT, 4H 134, Gamelin to ministre de la guerre, 1 July 1926.
24 SHAT, 4H 134, Gamelin to ministre de la guerre, 19 Sept. 1926.
25 Andréa, *La Révolte Druze*, p. 187.
26 LHCMA, Codrington Papers, 'Gathering Moss'.

27 LHCMA, Codrington Papers, 'Gathering Moss'.
28 SHAT, 4H 134, 'Interrogatoire de Hamze Derviche', 11 July 1926.
29 SHAT, 4H 134, 'Rapport de mission de Lieutenant-Colonel Catroux', 28 Sept. 1926.
30 SHAT, 4H 134, 'Rapport de mission de Lieutenant-Colonel Catroux', 28 Sept. 1926.
31 SHAT, 4H 134, 'Rapport de mission de Lieutenant-Colonel Catroux', 28 Sept. 1926.
32 TNA, CO 733/22/3, Hole to foreign secretary, 25 Nov. 1926.
33 SHAT 4H 134, Louis Jalabert, 'La France abandonnera-t-elle la Syrie?', Les Etudes, 20 Apr. 1927.
34 TNA, FO 684/3, Smart to foreign secretary, 11 Jan. 1926.
35 SHAT, 4H 134, Maurepas, Jerusalem, to high commissioner, 13 Apr. 1927.
36 SHAT 4H 134, Beynet to high commissioner, 29 June 1927.
37 Shambrook, French Imperialism in Syria, p. 7.
38 SHAT, 4H 134, Gamelin to ministre de la guerre, 23 Aug. 1927.
39 LHCMA, Codrington Papers, 'Gathering Moss'.

12 THE PIPELINE

1 TNA, CAB 24/202, Committee of Imperial Defence, 'Report by the Sub-Committee on the Construction of the Proposed Haifa–Baghdad Railway and/or Pipeline, 13 June 1928: Appendix 1: Cadman, "Evidence of Existence of Oil in Iraq", 28 Mar. 1928'.
2 R. W. Ferrier, The History of the British Petroleum Company Vol. I (Cambridge, 1982), p. 165.
3 IOR, L/PS/11/151, Petroleum Executive, memorandum, 'Petroleum Position of the British Empire', Dec. 1918.
4 PAL, Davidson Papers, Davis to Curzon, 12 May 1920. This was hypocritical, as Curzon pointed out. The United States had cancelled the British concession in Haiti when it occupied the island in 1913.
5 TNA, CAB 24/131, Colonial Office, Middle East Department, 'Foreign Incitement of the Turks to Attack Iraq', 13 Dec. 1921; FO 371/7782, Churchill to Curzon, 1 Feb. 1922.
6 TNA, CAB 27/436, 'Notes for Conference with Sir John Cadman', 2 June 1930.
7 TNA, CAB 24/202, Committee of Imperial Defence, 'Report by the Sub-Committee' 13 June 1928: Appendix 1: Cadman, 'Evidence ...', 28 Mar. 1928.
8 SHAT, 2N 245, 'Note à propos du tracé du 'Pipe-line' des Pétroles de Mésopotamie', 15 Feb. 1928.
9 SHAT 2N 245, 'Note pour le Président du Conseil', 29 Mar. 1928.
10 TNA, CAB 24/202, Committee of Imperial Defence, 'Report by the Sub-Committee' 13 June 1928, Appendix 2: Report by the chiefs of staff sub-committee, 'The Baghdad–Haifa Pipeline and Railway: Strategic Importance and Defence', 24 May 1928.
11 TNA, CAB 24/202, Amery, 'The Oil Position in Iraq', 11 Mar. 1929, Appendix II, Monteagle to Williams, 6 Feb. 1929.
12 TNA, CAB 24/202, Eastern Department, Foreign Office, 'The Attitude of the French Government regarding the proposed Baghdad–Haifa Railway and Pipeline', 9 Mar. 1929.
13 TNA, CAB 24/202, Amery, 'The Oil Position in Iraq', 11 Mar. 1929, Berthelot, aide-memoire, 23 Jan. 1929.

14   TNA, CAB 24/202, Amery, 'The Oil Position in Iraq', 11 Mar. 1929, Appendix II, Williams to Monteagle, 18 Feb. 1929.
15   TNA, CAB 24/206, Trenchard, 'Baghdad and Haifa Railway and Pipeline', Williams to deputy chief of air staff, 11 Apr. 1929.
16   TNA, CAB 23/61, conclusions of a meeting of the cabinet, 25 Sept. 1929.
17   TNA, CAB 24/211, 'Report by the Committee on the Baghdad–Haifa Railway and Pipeline, 1 May 1930'.
18   Fitzgerald, 'Business Diplomacy', p. 222.
19   Fitzgerald, 'Business Diplomacy', p. 223.
20   TNA, CAB 24/211, 'Report by the Committee on the Baghdad–Haifa Railway and Pipeline, 1 May 1930, Appendix: Madden (Chief of the Naval Staff), "Baghdad–Haifa Railway and Pipeline", 5 Apr. 1930'.
21   G. M. Lees, 'The Search for Oil', Geographical Journal, vol. 95, no. 1 (Jan. 1940), pp. 11–12.
22   TNA, CAB 27/436, Passfield, note, n.d.
23   Time, 'Trouble in Paradise', 21 Apr. 1941.

13 REVENGE! REVENGE!

1   The Times, 'Renewed Violence in Palestine', 3 Aug. 1936.
2   IWM, Clarke Papers, memoir, p. 550.
3   This percentage is based on the Peel Commission's belief (report, p. 210) that an industrial workforce of 32,000 represented a total population of at least 80,000. Applying this ratio to the estimated 151,000 Jews in Palestine, the potential workforce at that time was 60,000.
4   LHCMA, Dill Papers, 2/9, Dill to Deverell, 18 Sept. 1936.
5   Segev, One Palestine, Complete, p. 334.
6   MEC, Chancellor Papers, Chancellor to Stamfordham, 27 May 1930.
7   MEC, Chancellor Papers, Chancellor to Stamfordham, 27 May 1930.
8   IWM, Kitson, interview, 26 Apr. 1989.
9   Alfred Bonné, 'The Concessions for the Mosul–Haifa Pipe Line', Annals of the American Academy of Political and Social Science, vol. 164, Palestine. A Decade of Development (Nov. 1932), p. 125.
10   MEC, Monckton Papers, Monckton to Evelyn Mary Monckton, 21 Aug. 1920.
11   Rogan, The Arabs, p. 203.
12   IWM, Morton Papers.
13   IWM, Catling, interview, Sept. 1988.
14   LHCMA, Wheeler Papers, 'Notes on Tactical Lessons of the Palestine Rebellion, 1936', 1937.
15   IWM, Norman, interview, 1 May 1980
16   Segev, One Palestine, Complete, p. 364.
17   TNA, CO 733/383/1, Sir Charles Tegart and Sir David Petrie, 'Memorandum on the future structure and establishment of the Palestine Police', Jan. 1938.
18   IWM, Clarke Papers, memoir, p. 558.
19   TNA, CO 732/81/9, Military Intelligence, summary, 23 Sept. 1938.
20   TNA, CO 733/383/1, Downie, note, 10 Feb. 1938.
21   IWM, Clarke Papers, memoir, p. 572.
22   LHCMA, Dill Papers, 2/9, Dill to Deverell, 14 Oct. 1936.
23   TNA, CAB 24/270, Palestine Royal Commission, report, p. 370.
24   TNA, CAB 24/270, Palestine Royal Commission, report, pp. 394 and 395.
25   Rendel, The Sword and the Olive, p. 123.

26 LHCMA, Dill Papers, 2/9, Dill to Deverell, 14 Oct. 1936.
27 LHCMA, Dill Papers, 2/9, Deverell to Dill, 3 Mar. 1937.
28 *Daily Telegraph*, 29 July 1937.
29 MEC, Tegart Papers, 2/3, Kirkbride to chief secretary, 28 Feb. 1938.
30 TNA, FO 406/75, MacKereth to Eden, 5 Jan. 1937, enclosing 'Damascus Quarterly Report', 1 Oct. to 31 Dec. 1936.
31 TNA, FO 684/10, MacKereth to Eden, 19 Oct. 1937.
32 MEC, Tegart Papers, 2/3, H. M. Foot, assistant district commissioner, Samaria, 'Note on recent terrorist activity in the Samaria Division', 24 Dec. 1937.

14 FIGHTING TERROR WITH TERROR

1   Max Egremont, *Under Two Flags:The Life of Major-General Sir Edward Spears* (London, 1997), p. 259. John Stokes is quoted.
2   *London Gazette*, 18 June 1917.
3   Michael G. Fry and Itamar Rabinovich, eds, *Despatches from Damascus: Gilbert MacKereth and British Policy in the Levant, 1933–1939* (Jerusalem, 1985), p. 99, MacKereth to Rendel, 2 Dec. 1934.
4   Fry and Rabinovich, eds, *Despatches from Damascus*, p. 73, MacKereth to Foreign Office, 3 Jan. 1934.
5   Fry and Rabinovich, eds, *Despatches from Damascus*, p. 210, MacKereth to Baxter, 22 Mar. 1939.
6   Fry and Rabinovich, eds, *Despatches from Damascus*, p. 99, MacKereth to Rendel, 2 Dec. 1934.
7   CADN, Beyrouth Ambassade, B/11/175, 'Chucri Kouatly', description of al-Quwatli, Jabri and Mardam, n.d.
8   TNA, FO 406/75, MacKereth to Eden, 5 May 1937.
9   TNA, FO 371/23251, MacKereth to MacMichael, 5 Sept. 1939.
10 TNA, FO 684/10, MacKereth, 'Memorandum Bludan Congress', 14 Sept. 1937.
11 TNA, FO 684/10, MacKereth, 'Memorandum Bludan Congress', Annexe 6: 'Report of a secret meeting of Syrian and Palestine extremist politicians, held in the house of Hani al Jalad in Suq Sarouja, Damascus, in the early hours of September 12, 1937'.
12 TNA, FO 684/10, MacKereth to Eden, 19 Oct. 1937.
13 MEC, Tegart Papers, 4/7, diary, 4 Feb. 1938.
14 MEC, Tegart Papers, 4/7, diary, 5 and 7 Feb. 1938.
15 In his diary Khalil Eissa wrote that he had decided to murder an Arab auxiliary policeman named Halim Basta. The gun used to kill Basta was the same as that used to kill Andrews (MEC, Tegart Papers, 2/3, British detective sergeant to DIG CID, 29 Sept. 1937).
16 Fry and Rabinovich, eds, *Despatches from Damascus*, MacKereth to Eden, 25 Oct. 1937.
17 Fry and Rabinovich, eds, *Despatches from Damascus*, MacKereth to Eden, 23 Oct. 1937.
18 Fry and Rabinovich, eds, *Despatches from Damascus*, Rendel, minute, 12 Nov. 1937.
19 Fry and Rabinovich, eds, *Despatches from Damascus*, Rendel, minute, 12 Nov. 1937.
20 MEC, Tegart Papers, 4/7, diary, 5 Feb. 1938.
21 MEC, Tegart Papers, 4/7, diary, 3 Feb. 1938.
22 Michael Silvestri, '"An Irishman Is Specially Suited to Be a Policeman": Sir

Charles Tegart & Revolutionary Terrorism in Bengal', *History Ireland*, vol. 8, no. 4 (Winter, 2000), p. 42.

23 Sir Percival Griffiths, *To Guard My People: The History of the Indian Police* (London, 1971), p. 410.

24 Sir Charles Tegart, 'Terrorism in India', lecture delivered to the Royal Empire Society, 1 Nov. 1932.

25 MEC, Tegart Papers, 3/5, Tegart, note, n.d., on his visit to Beirut and Damascus.

26 MEC, Tegart Papers, 3/5, Tegart, note, n.d., on his visit to Beirut and Damascus.

27 MEC, Tegart Papers, 3/5, Tegart, note, n.d., on his visit to Beirut and Damascus.

28 SHAT, 4H 316, Louisgrand to general, Deuxième Bureau, 5 Oct. 1945.

29 TNA, CO 733/383/1, Tegart and Petrie, 'Memorandum on the future structure and establishment of the Palestine Police', Jan. 1938.

30 MEC, Tegart Papers, 2/3, 'Record of a Meeting on Public Security on 7 Jan. 1938'.

31 MEC, Tegart Papers, 4/7, diary, 8 Feb. 1938.

32 MEC, Tegart Papers, 3/2, Tegart to chief secretary, 19 Feb. 1938.

33 MEC, Tegart Papers, 2/3, Tegart to Battershill, 2 Jan. 1938.

34 TNA, CO 733/383/1, Tegart and Petrie, 'Memorandum on the future structure and establishment of the Palestine Police', Jan. 1938.

35 LHCMA, O'Connor Papers, O'Connor to Jean O'Connor, 2 Nov. 1938.

36 IWM, Morton Papers, 'An incomplete and inadequate account of the service of Geoffrey Jackson Morton in the Palestine Police, February 1930 to June 1943'.

37 IWM, Kitson, interview, 26 Apr. 1989.

38 LHCMA, Dill Papers, 2/9, Dill to Deverell, 18 Sept. 1936. In the letter Dill wrote that his 'ultimate solution' to the Arabs' strategy of laying landmines would be 'to carry a couple of Arab mascots on the leading car'.

39 IWM, Lane, interview, 2 Aug. 1988.

40 LHCMA, Mullens Papers, diary, 15 Oct. 1938.

41 IWM, Lane, interview.

42 IWM, Kitson, interview.

43 TNA, CAB 24/278, Macdonald, 'Talks in Jerusalem', 24 Aug. 1938.

44 TNA, CAB 24/278, Macdonald, 'Talks in Jerusalem', 24 Aug. 1938.

45 HC Deb, 5 Nov. 1936, vol. 317, c. 252.

46 J. Bierman and C. Smith, *Fire in the Night: Wingate of Burma, Ethiopia and Zion* (London, 1999), p. 66.

47 Bierman and Smith, *Fire in the Night*, p. 84.

48 David Hacohen, *Time to Tell: An Israeli Life 1898–1984* (New York, 1985), pp. 53–4.

49 Bierman and Smith, *Fire in the Night*, p. 71.

50 LHCMA, Liddell Hart Papers, 15/5/300, Wingate, memorandum, 10 June 1938.

51 LHCMA, Liddell Hart Papers, 15/5/300, Orde Wingate, memorandum on special night squads, 5 June 1938.

52 LHCMA, Liddell Hart Papers, 15/5/300, Orde Wingate, memorandum on special night squads, 5 June 1938.

53 Moshe Dayan, *Story of My Life* (London, 1976), p. 29.

54 Leonard Mosley, *Gideon Goes to War* (London, 1955), p. 58.

55 Bierman and Smith, *Fire in the Night*, p. 100.

56 Bierman and Smith, *Fire in the Night*, p. 103.

57 IWM, Catling, interview, Sept. 1988.

58 Bierman and Smith, *Fire in the Night*, p. 125.

59 TNA, CAB 107/4, MacMichael to Ormsby-Gore, 29 Aug. 1938.

15 PLACATING THE ARABS

1 Yitzhak Shamir, *Summing Up* (London, 1994), p. 18.
2 TNA, CO 732/81/9, Military Intelligence, summary, 15 July 1938.
3 TNA, CO 732/81/9, Military Intelligence, summary, 29 July 1938.
4 *The Times*, 'Jerusalem', 11 Dec. 1917; *The Times*, 'Insecurity in Palestine: Government's Loss of Prestige', 26 July 1938.
5 TNA, CAB 104/7, MacMichael to MacDonald, 2 Sept. 1938.
6 HC Deb, 24 Nov. 1938, vol. 341, c. 1988.
7 TNA, CAB 104/7, MacMichael to MacDonald, 2 Sept. 1938.
8 TNA, CAB 104/7, Wilkinson to Ismay, 21 Oct. 1938.
9 LHCMA, O'Connor Papers, 3/4, Montgomery to O'Connor, 26 Nov. 1938.
10 Rogan, *The Arabs*, p. 206.
11 TNA, CAB 24/280, Halifax, memorandum, 'Visit of British Ministers to Paris', 26 Nov. 1938.
12 TNA, CAB 24/280, Halifax, memorandum, 'Visit of British Ministers to Paris', 26 Nov. 1938.
13 TNA, 371/23251, MacKereth to MacMichael, 5 Sept. 1939.
14 TNA, 371/23251, Eyres, minute, and Baggallay to Shuckburgh, 10 Nov. 1939.
15 Gilbert, *Churchill and the Jews*, p. 154. The speaker was Sir Kingsley Wood.
16 TNA, CAB 104/10, cabinet committee on Palestine, 20 Apr. 1939.
17 TNA, CAB 104/10, cabinet committee on Palestine, 20 Apr. 1939.
18 Segev, *One Palestine, Complete*, p. 436.

16 A KING IN EXILE

1 Robert and Isabelle Tombs, *That Sweet Enemy: The French and the British from the Sun King to the Present* (London, 2006), p. 539.
2 De Gaulle, *Mémoires de Guerre*, vol. I (Paris, 1954), p. 2.
3 Peter Mangold, *The Almost Impossible Ally: Harold Macmillan and Charles de Gaulle* (London, 2006), p. 21.
4 Mangold, *The Almost Impossible Ally*, p. 10.
5 Jean-Raymond Tournoux, *Pétain et de Gaulle* (Paris, 1964), p. 88.
6 Charles de Gaulle, *Le Fil de l'Epée* (Paris, 1944), pp. 81 and 47.
7 De Gaulle, *Mémoires de Guerre*, vol. I, p. 67.
8 Jonathan Fenby, *The General: Charles de Gaulle and the France He Saved* (London, 2010), p. 20.
9 Churchill, *The Second World War*, vol. II, p. 142; MEC, Spears Papers, memorandum: 'De Gaulle and the Free French', 14 Apr. 1954.
10 LHCMA, Dill Papers, 3/1/15, Spears, 'Policy towards the Free French Movement', n.d. but *c.* 7 Dec. 1940.
11 Alec Kirkbride, *A Crackle of Thorns* (London, 1956), p. 145.
12 De Gaulle, *Mémoires de Guerre*, vol. I, de Gaulle to Puaux and Mittelhauser, 27 June 1940.
13 LHCMA, Furlonge Papers, 'The Liberation of the Levant', 1971.
14 Roshwald, *Estranged Bedfellows*, p. 16.
15 Jean Lacouture, *De Gaulle*, vol. I (London, 1990), p. 243.
16 TNA, CAB 66/50/38, 'Relations with General de Gaulle', 1 June 1944.
17 CADN, Mandat Syrie–Liban, Cabinet Politique, I/ 2986, Catroux to de Gaulle, 6 Apr. 1942.
18 Fenby, *The General*, p. 27.

19 François Mauriac, *De Gaulle* (Paris, 1964), p. 68.
20 De Gaulle, *Mémoires de Guerre*, vol. I, p. 70.
21 Tombs and Tombs, *That Sweet Enemy*, p. 569.
22 Edward Spears, *Two Men Who Saved France: Pétain and de Gaulle* (London, 1966), p. 146.
23 Charles de Gaulle, *Mémoires de Guerre*, vol. II (Paris, 1956), p. 102.
24 A. B. Gaunson, 'Churchill, de Gaulle, Spears and the Levant Affair, 1941', *Historical Journal*, vol. 27, no. 3 (1984), p. 697.
25 *Daily Telegraph*, 13 July 1940.
26 De Gaulle, *Mémoires de Guerre*, vol. I, Catroux to de Gaulle, 3 Nov. 1940.
27 LHCMA, Furlonge Papers, 'The Liberation of the Levant', 1971.
28 SHAT, 4H 316, 'Beirut Weekly Appreciation No. 6/40'.
29 Tombs and Tombs, *That Sweet Enemy*, p. 571.
30 De Gaulle, *Mémoires de Guerre*, vol. I, Catroux to de Gaulle, 8 Dec. 1940.
31 Hermione Ranfurly, *To War with Whitaker* (London, 1994), 11–31 May 1941.
32 De Gaulle, *Mémoires de Guerre*, vol. I, Wavell to de Gaulle, 14 Dec. 1940.
33 TNA, PREM 3/422/1, Spears, memorandum, 10 Apr. 1941.
34 MEC, Spears Papers, 1/C, major-general commanding troops Sudan to War Office, 16 Apr. 1941.
35 Winston S. Churchill, *The Second World War*, vol. III (London, 1950), p. 227.
36 Churchill, *The Second World War*, vol. III, p. 227.
37 Churchill to Wavell, 21 May 1941, in Churchill, *The Second World War*, vol. III, p. 290.
38 Churchill to Wavell, 9 May 1941 and 21 May 1941, in Churchill, *The Second World War*, vol. III, p. 289.
39 A. B. Gaunson, *The Anglo-French Clash in Lebanon and Syria, 1940–1945* (London, 1987), p. 37.
40 MEC, Spears Papers, 1/A, commander-in-chief Middle East to War Office, 20 May 1941, forwarding Spears to Spears Mission.
41 MEC, Spears Papers, 1/A, War Office to commander-in-chief Middle East, 20 May 1941.

17 A SQUALID EPISODE

1 De Gaulle, *Mémoires de Guerre*, vol. I, Catroux to de Gaulle, 7 Jan. 1941.
2 MEC, Spears Papers, 1/A, Lampson to Foreign Office, 18 May 1941, forwarding Spears for Spears Mission.
3 De Gaulle, *Mémoires de Guerre*, vol. I, Catroux to de Gaulle, 19 May 1941.
4 MEC, Spears Papers, 1/A, Lampson, Cairo, to Foreign Office, 20 May 1941, enclosing Catroux's statement.
5 Charles Mott-Radclyffe, *Foreign Body in the Eye* (London, 1975), p. 106.
6 De Gaulle, *Mémoires de Guerre*, vol. I, Catroux to de Gaulle, 21 May 1941.
7 MEC, Spears Papers, 1/A, Lampson to Foreign Office, 31 May 1941, forwarding Spears for Spears Mission.
8 TNA, CAB 66/13/39, Eden, 'Our Arab Policy', 27 May 1941.
9 Anthony Eden, *Freedom and Order: Selected Speeches 1939–1946* (London, 1947), pp. 104–5.
10 De Gaulle, *Mémoires de Guerre*, vol. I, de Gaulle to Free French delegation, 31 May 1941.
11 Fenby, *The General*, p. 127.
12 De Gaulle, *Mémoires de Guerre*, vol. I, Churchill to de Gaulle, 6 June 1941.

13 SHAT 4H 314, 'Proclamation du Général Catroux, faite au nom du Général de Gaulle, chef des Français Libres', 8 June 1941; *The Times*, 'Catroux's Call to Arms', 9 June 1941.

14 John Bagot Glubb, *The Story of the Arab Legion* (London, 1948), p. 257.

15 Mott-Radclyffe, *Foreign Body in the Eye*, p. 90.

16 MEC, Spears Papers, I/A, Lampson, Cairo, to Foreign Office, 31 May 1941, forwarding Spears for Spears Mission.

17 MEC, Spears Papers, II/A, Spears to Somerville Smith, 21 June 1941.

18 Kirkbride, *A Crackle of Thorns*, p. 151.

19 Roald Dahl, *Going Solo* (London, 1986), p. 193.

20 TNA, CAB 106/898, Syrian Narratives No. 2 Berryforce (and operations of 2/3 MG Bn Group at Quoneitra).

21 TNA, CAB 106/896, 'Commentary Notes on Syria campaign, by Brigadier L. B. Jones, i/c Col. A'.

22 Grignoire, 11 June 1941, in Jafna L. Cox, 'The Background to the Syrian Campaign, May–June 1941: A study in Franco-German Wartime Relations', *History*, vol. 72, no. 236 (Oct. 1987), p. 448.

23 IWM, Brogan Papers, D. W. Brogan, 'Darlan's Peace means War', 11 June 1941, quoting Jean Luchaire in *Les Nouveaux Temps*.

24 Trevor Royle, *Glubb Pasha* (London, 1992), p. 277.

25 Field Marshal Lord Wilson, *Eight Years Overseas* (London, 1949), pp. 114–18.

26 TNA, CAB 106/898, Syrian Narratives No. 2 Berryforce (and operations of 2/3 MG Bn Group at Quoneitra).

27 MEC, Glubb Papers, Glubb, 'A Report on Operations by the Arab Legion in Syria', n.d.

28 IWM, Dimbleby, report, 23 June 1941.

29 De Gaulle, *Mémoires de Guerre*, vol. I, de Gaulle to Catroux, 24 June 1941.

30 De Gaulle, *Mémoires de Guerre*, vol. I, de Gaulle to Free French delegation, 1 July 1941.

31 LHCMA, Furlonge Papers.

32 IWM, Hackett, interview.

33 Roshwald, *Estranged Bedfellows*, p. 80.

34 MEC, MacMichael Papers, Wilson to MacMichael, 15 July 1941.

18 COMPLETELY INTRANSIGENT, EXTREMELY RUDE

1 MEC, Spears Papers, I, diary, 21 July 1941.

2 MEC, Spears Papers, I, diary, 21 July 1941.

3 MEC, Spears Papers, I, diary, 21 July 1941; Lampson to Foreign Office, 17 July 1941, from Spears to Spears Mission; I/B, commander-in-chief Middle East to War Office, 5 Aug. 1941, forwarding message from Spears.

4 De Gaulle, *Mémoires de Guerre*, vol. I, Lyttelton to de Gaulle, 23 July 1941.

5 De Gaulle, *Mémoires de Guerre*, vol. I, Lyttelton to de Gaulle, 25 July 1941; de Gaulle to Lyttelton, 27 July 1941.

6 CADN, Londres Ambassade, C/144, Lyttelton, memorandum, 20 Aug. 1941.

7 TNA, CAB 120/525, minister of state to prime minister, 12 Aug. 1941.

8 MEC, Spears Papers, I/B, Lampson to Foreign Office, 31 July 1941, forwarding message from minister of state.

9 MEC, Glubb Papers, Glubb, 'A Note on Certain Aspects of the Situation in Syria', 17 July 1941.

10 MEC, Glubb Papers, Lash to Glubb, 27 Aug. 1941.

11   MEC, Glubb Papers, political officer, Deir ez Zor, to Buss, 5 Aug. 1941.
12   MEC, Glubb Papers, Lash to Glubb, 27 Aug. 1941.
13   MEC, Glubb Papers, political officer, Deir ez Zor, to Buss, 5 Aug. 1941.
14   MEC, Glubb Papers, Glubb, 'A Note on a Visit to Damascus, 27–28 Nov. 1941'.
15   MEC, Glubb Papers, report by Glubb on a visit from various shaykhs, 7 Oct. 1941.
16   MEC, Glubb Papers, Glubb to Kirkbride, 29 Sept. 1941.
17   De Gaulle, *Mémoires de Guerre*, vol. I, de Gaulle to Free French delegation, 12 Aug. 1941.
18   MEC, Spears Papers, I/B, Lampson to Foreign Office, 31 July 1941, forwarding message from minister of state.
19   MEC, Spears Papers, I/B, Lampson to Foreign Office, 28 Aug. 1941, forwarding message from minister of state.
20   CADN, Londres Ambassade, C/144, Lyttelton, memorandum, 20 Aug. 1941.
21   De Gaulle, *Mémoires de Guerre*, vol. I, de Gaulle to Free French delegation, 12 Aug. 1941.
22   MEC, Spears Papers, II, Churchill, memorandum, 30 Aug. 1941.
23   HC Deb, 9 Sept. 1941, vol. 374, c. 76.
24   TNA, CAB 66/18/44, 'Record of a meeting between the Prime Minister and General de Gaulle at No. 10 Downing Street on Friday, 12 September, 1941, at 12 noon'.
25   TNA, CAB 66/18/44, 'Record of a meeting between the Prime Minister and General de Gaulle at No. 10 Downing Street on Friday, 12 September, 1941, at 12 noon'.
26   MEC, Spears Papers, II, 'Note of a meeting between the Prime Minister, the Minister of State and General de Gaulle held at No. 10 Downing Street on Wednesday 1 Oct. 1941 at 5.30pm'.
27   MEC, Spears Papers, II, 'Note of a meeting between the Prime Minister, the Minister of State and General de Gaulle held at No. 10 Downing Street on Wednesday 1 Oct. 1941 at 5.30pm'.
28   MEC, Spears Papers, I/C, commander-in-chief Middle East to War Office, 2 Oct. 1941.
29   MEC, Glubb Papers, report by Glubb on a visit from various shaykhs, 7 Oct. 1941.
30   MEC, Spears Papers, I/B, commander-in-chief Middle East to War Office, 8 Oct. 1941.
31   MEC, Glubb Papers, Glubb, 'A Note on the Situation in Eastern Syria', 15 Aug. 1941.
32   MEC, Spears Papers, II, Spears to minister of state, quoting John Hamilton, 25 Nov. 1941.
33   MEC, Glubb Papers, Glubb, 'A Note on a Visit to Damascus, 27–28 Nov. 1941'.
34   MEC, Glubb Papers, 'Guidance Note for Members of the Mission on the Present Political Situation in the Lebanon', 8 Dec. 1941.
35   TNA, FO 954/15, f. 99, minister of state to foreign secretary, 24 Nov. 1941.
36   TNA, FO 954/15, f. 113, minister of state to foreign secretary, 3 Jan. 1942
37   MEC, Spears Papers, Spears to Hamilton, 29 Jan. 1942.

19 ENVOY EXTRAORDINARY

1   CADN, Mandat Syrie–Liban, Sûreté Générale I/7, Spears to Catroux, 7 Apr. 1942.
2   MEC, Coghill Papers.

3   Roshwald, *Estranged Bedfellows*, p. 98.
4   Henry Colyton, *Occasion, Chance and Change* (Norwich, 1993), p. 195.
5   MEC, Spears Papers, II, Somerville Smith to Spears, 4 June 1941.
6   LHCMA, Ismay Papers, 4/31/3, Spears to Ismay, 3 July 1944.
7   LHCMA, Dill Papers, 3/1/15, Spears, 'Policy towards the Free French movement', n.d.
8   TNA, PREM 3/423/14, Churchill's draft response to a question from Attlee, 5 June 1945.
9   MEC, Spears Papers, I, diary, 20 June 1941.
10 MEC, Spears Papers, I/B, commander-in-chief to War Office, 5 Aug. 1941, forwarding message from Spears.
11 Mott-Radclyffe, *Foreign Body in the Eye*, p. 109.
12 Roshwald, *Estranged Bedfellows*, p. 107.
13 CADN, Mandat Syrie–Liban, Cabinet Politique, I/2986, Catroux to de Gaulle, 6 Apr. 1942.
14 CADN, Mandat Syrie–Liban, Cabinet Politique, I/2986, Catroux to de Gaulle, 6 Apr. 1942.
15 Georges Catroux, *Dans la Bataille de Méditerranée* (Paris, 1949), p. 192.
16 CADN, Mandat Syrie–Liban, Cabinet Politique, I/2986, de Gaulle to Catroux, 8 Apr. 1942.
17 CADN, Mandat Syrie–Liban, Cabinet Politique, I/2986, de Gaulle to Catroux, 8 Apr. 1942.
18 CADN, Mandat Syrie–Liban, Cabinet Politique, I/2986, Catroux to de Gaulle, 6 Apr. 1942.
19 CADN, Mandat Syrie–Liban, Cabinet Politique, I/2986, Catroux to de Gaulle, 24 Apr. 1942.
20 CADN, Mandat Syrie–Liban, Cabinet Politique, I/2986, Catroux to de Gaulle, 6 Apr. 1942.
21 Roshwald, *Estranged Bedfellows*, p. 101.
22 Spears, *Fulfilment of a Mission*, p. 181.
23 LHCMA, Ismay Papers, 4/31/3, Spears to Ismay, 2 Sept. 1942.
24 De Gaulle, *Mémoires de Guerre*, vol. I, de Gaulle to Catroux, 26 May 1942.
25 Winston S. Churchill, *The Second World War*, vol. IV (London, 1951), p. 349.
26 TNA, FO 226/246, Catroux to Casey, 23 June 1942.
27 De Gaulle, *Mémoires de Guerre*, vol. II (Paris, 1956), p. 15.
28 De Gaulle, *Mémoires de Guerre*, vol. II, pp. 353–4, de Gaulle to Churchill, 14 Aug. 1942.
29 SHAT, 4H 382.
30 IWM, Harvard Gunn, interview, 1983. Gunn ultimately worked for the sabotage organisation Special Operations Executive in France.
31 TNA, PREM 3/422/10, Spears to minister of state, 19 Aug. 1942.
32 MEC, Spears Papers, I, diary, 23 Aug. 1942, quoting Jacqueline Lampson.
33 TNA, PREM 3/422/10, minister of state to Spears, 22 Aug. 1942, quoting Churchill to de Gaulle.
34 TNA, PREM 3/422/10, British representatives to Fighting French National Committee to Foreign Office, 3 Sept. 1942.
35 De Gaulle, *Mémoires de Guerre*, vol. I, Lyttelton to de Gaulle, 25 July 1941.
36 LHCMA, Ismay Papers, 4/31/3, Spears to Ismay, 2 Sept. 1942.
37 TNA, PREM 3/422/10, Spears to Foreign Office, 29 Aug. 1942; Spears to minister of state, 1 Sept. 1942.
38 TNA, PREM 3/422/10, minister of state to Foreign Office, 26 Aug. 1942.

39 *Life*, 26 Apr. 1943.
40 Charles de Gaulle, *Mémoires de Guerre*, vol. II, p. 33 .
41 CADN, Londres Ambassade, C/144, 'Aide-Memoire', 6 Jan. 1943.
42 John Harvey, ed., *The War Diaries of Oliver Harvey* (London, 1978), 14 Sept. 1942.

20 DIRTY WORK

1   MEC, Spears Papers, I, diary, 24 Jan. 1943.
2   MEC, Coghill Papers, diary, 31 Jan. 1943.
3   TNA, CAB 66/37/46, Casey, 'Palestine', 21 Apr. 1943.
4   Oren, *Power, Faith and Fantasy*, p. 444.
5   TNA, CAB 66/37/46, Casey, 'Palestine', 21 Apr. 1943.
6   TNA, CAB 66/37/46, Casey, 'Palestine', 21 Apr. 1943.
7   TNA, CAB 66/37/47, Resolutions of the Middle Eastern War Council on the political situation in the Middle East, 17 June 1943.
8   Gaunson, *The Anglo-French Clash in Lebanon and Syria*, p. 108.
9   GBA, Bell, diary, 11 Oct. 1919.
10 MEC, Spears Papers, III, Journal Officiel de la République Française, Débats de l'Assemblée Consultative Provisoire, 15 June 1945.
11 Catroux, *Deux Missions en Moyen Orient*, p. 94.
12 TNA, PREM 3/422/13, Spears, 'Memorandum on Anglo-French Relations in Syria and the Lebanon', n.d.
13 CADN, Mandat Syrie–Liban, Sûreté Générale I/7, 'Ingérences britanniques', n.d.
14 MEC, Spears Papers, III, Spears, draft memorandum on the elections, n.d.
15 LHCMA, Ismay Papers, 4/31/3, Spears to Ismay, 4 Jan. 1943; MEC, Spears Papers, I, diary, 2 Jan. 1943; LHCMA, Alan Brooke Papers, 6/2/46, Wilson to Brooke, 3 July 1943.
16 MEC, Spears Papers, III, Spears, draft memorandum on the elections, n.d.
17 MEC, Coghill Papers, diary, 11 Nov. 1942.
18 MEC, Spears Papers, II, W. W. Astor, staff officer, Intelligence, Levant area, to staff officer, Intelligence, Middle East Department, 18 Aug. 1942.
19 TNA, FO 684/15, 'Review of the Year 1943 in the Lebanon', n.d.
20 TNA, CAB 66/37/47, Resolutions of the Middle Eastern War Council on the political situation in the Middle East, 17 June 1943.
21 Karen Elizabeth Evans, '"The Apple of Discord": The Impact of the Levant on Anglo-French Relations during 1943' (unpublished PhD thesis, University of Leeds, 1990), p. 198.
22 MEC, Spears Papers, II, Churchill, directive, 27 June 1943.
23 TNA, PREM 3/422/13, Spears, 'Anglo-French Relations in Syria and the Lebanon', n.d.
24 TNA, PREM 3/422/13, Churchill to Eden, 12 July 1943.
25 TNA, PREM 3/422/13, Churchill, minute, 15 July 1943.
26 CADN, Londres Ambassade, C/144, 'Les Elections Syriennes', n.d.
27 CADN, Londres Ambassade, C/144, 'Les Elections Libanaises', 20 Sept. 1943.
28 CADN, Londres Ambassade, C/144, Helleu to Massigli, 4 Oct. 1943.
29 CADN, Mandat Syrie–Liban, Sûreté Générale I/7, 'Ingérences britanniques', n.d.
30 CADN, Mandat Syrie–Liban, Sûreté Générale I/7, Spears to Helleu, 24 Aug. 1943.
31 IWM, Vanson Papers.
32 TNA, FO 226/246, memorandum by the British Legation, Beirut, 28 Oct. 1943.

33 CADN, Londres Ambassade, C/144, 'Les Elections Libanaises', 20 Sept. 1943.
34 MEC, Spears Papers, III, Mideast to Spears, 11 Nov. 1943, reporting message to the prime minister.
35 CADN, Londres Ambassade, C/144, Helleu to Massigli, 4 Oct. 1943.
36 CADN, Londres Ambassade, C/144, Helleu to Massigli, 4 Oct. 1943.
37 TNA, FO 406/75, 'Lebanese Personalities', c. 1937.
38 Patrick Seale, *The Struggle for Arab Independence: Riad el-Solh and the Makers of the Modern Middle East* (Cambridge, 2010), p. 441.
39 Meir Zamir, 'An Intimate Alliance: The Joint Struggle of General Edward Spears and Riad al-Sulh to Oust France from Lebanon, 1942–1944', *Middle Eastern Studies*, vol. 41, no. 6 (Nov. 2005), p. 829.
40 CADN, Mandat Syrie–Liban, Sûreté Générale I/7, 'Ingérences britanniques – suite', n.d. The comment was made by Saeb Slam.
41 Seale, *The Struggle for Arab Independence*, pp. 512–3.
42 TNA, FO 684/15, 'Review of the Year 1943 in the Lebanon', n.d.
43 CADN, Mandat Syrie–Liban, Sûreté Générale I/7, 'Ingérences britanniques', n.d.
44 SHAT, 4H 314, Helleu to *délégués* Damas, Beyrouth, Suwayda, and counsellors Tripoli, Saida, Zahle, 13 Oct. 1943.
45 CADN, Londres Ambassade, C/144, Chataigneau to Massigli, 1 Nov. 1943.
46 CADN, Londres Ambassade, C/144, Chataigneau to Massigli, 1 Nov. 1943.

21 ANOTHER FASHODA

1   MEC, Spears Papers, III, Spears to Foreign Office, 11 Nov. 1943.
2   Spears, *Fulfilment of a Mission*, p. 227.
3   MEC, Spears Papers, III, Shone to Spears, 16 Nov. 1943.
4   Roshwald, *Estranged Bedfellows*, p. 155.
5   Spears, *Fulfilment of a Mission*, p. 225.
6   MEC, Spears Papers, III, Spears to Foreign Office, 11 Nov. 1943.
7   MEC, Spears Papers, I, diary, 26/27 June 1943.
8   MEC, Spears Papers, III, Spears to Foreign Office, 11 Nov. 1943.
9   MEC, Spears Papers, I, diary, 25 June 1943.
10 Spears, *Fulfilment of a Mission*, p. 241; Egremont, *Under Two Flags*, p. 242; MEC, Spears Papers, III, Spears to Foreign Office, 13 Nov. 1943.
11 Harold Macmillan, *War Diaries – The Mediterranean, 1943–45* (London, 1984), 17 Nov. 1943.
12 Macmillan, *War Diaries*, 19 Nov. 1943.
13 MEC, Spears Papers, III, British Legation, Beirut, to Foreign Office, 14 Nov. 1943, transmitting Casey's report.
14 LHCMA, Ismay Papers, 4/31/3, Spears to Ismay, 2 Sept. 1942.
15 Egremont, *Under Two Flags*, p. 253.
16 MEC, Spears Papers, III, HM minister Beirut to Foreign Office, 20 Nov. 1943.
17 Egremont, *Under Two Flags*, p. 215.
18 Egremont, *Under Two Flags*, p. 253.
19 MEC, Spears Papers, III, Casey, diary, 15 Nov. 1943.
20 MEC, Spears Papers, III, Casey to Foreign Office, 15 Nov. 1943.
21 MEC, Spears Papers, III, Casey, diary, 15 Nov. 1943.
22 MEC, Spears Papers, III, British Legation, Beirut, to Foreign Office, 16 Nov. 1943.
23 MEC, Spears Papers, III, Casey to Eden, 18 Nov. 1943.
24 MEC, Spears Papers, III, Casey, diary, 19 Nov. 1943.

25 MEC, Spears Papers, III, Eden to minister resident Algiers, 21 Nov. 1943, Eden to minister of state, repeated Beirut, 21 Nov. 1943.

26 MEC, Spears Papers, III, Macmillan to Foreign Office, 21 Nov. 1943.

27 MEC, Spears Papers, III, British Legation, Beirut, to Foreign Office, 30 Nov. 1943.

28 MEC, Spears Papers, III, Macmillan to Foreign Office, 1 Dec. 1943.

29 MEC, Spears Papers, III, Nancy Maurice to her father, 24 Dec. 1943.

30 *The Times*, 'Syria and the Lebanon: I – The Bid for National Status', 20 Jan. 1944.

31 MEC, Coghill Papers, diary, 28 Nov. 1943; Egremont, *Under Two Flags*, p. 255.

32 John Julius Norwich, ed., *The Duff Cooper Diaries* (London, 2005), 19 Jan. 1944.

22 FRIENDS IN NEED

1 CADN, Mandat Syrie–Liban, Cabinet Politique, I/1158, du Chaylard to Massigli, 29 Feb. 1944.

2 David Lazar, *L'opinion française et la naissance de l'Etat d'Israël, 1945–1949* (Paris, 1972), p. 221.

3 Lazar, *L'opinion française et la naissance de l'Etat d'Israël*, p. 224.

4 Dayan, *Story of My Life*, p. 46.

5 Joseph Heller, *The Stern Gang: Ideology, Politics and Terror, 1940–1949* (London, 1995), pp. 85–6.

6 IWM, Bowden Stuart Papers, Morton to superintendent, Lydda District, 13 Feb. 1942.

7 IWM, Morton Papers, 'An incomplete and inadequate account of the service of Geoffrey Jackson Morton in the Palestine Police, February 1930 to June 1943'.

8 IWM, Bowden Stuart Papers, Saunders, 'The Stern Group', 19 May 1942.

9 MEC, Coghill Papers. In his memoir Coghill did not exactly date this incident, but its timing can be inferred from the people it involved. Coghill took over command of the British security mission on 12 Mar. 1942 and B. T. Wilson, the head of SOE in the Levant, who brought the activities of his errant agent to Coghill's attention, was sacked in June the same year (Saul Kelly, 'A Succession of Crises: SOE in the Middle East, 1940–45', *Intelligence and National Security*, vol. 20, no. 1 (Mar. 2005), p. 133).

10 MEC, Coghill Papers.

11 MEC, Coghill Papers.

12 Y. S. Brenner, 'The "Stern Gang" 1940–48', *Middle Eastern Studies*, vol. 2, no. 1 (Oct. 1965), p. 6. The man arrested was Nathan Friedman-Yellin, later leader of the Gang.

13 Yaacov Eliav, trans. Mordecai Schreiber, *Wanted* (New York, 1984), p. 142.

14 TNA, WO 208/3091, Defence Security Office, Syria, summary for 1–31 Oct. 1942.

15 It is not clear what happened to the third man, Blanchet. French records suggest that he was later killed in action: on 22 Sept. 1944 the French delegate-general, by then Paul Beynet, wrote to Catroux asking for details of Blanchet's death so that they could be communicated to his 'numerous friends in the Levant': CADN, Mandat Syrie–Liban, Cabinet Politique, I/2279.

16 Shamir, *Summing Up*, p. 48.

17 Shamir, *Summing Up*, p. 48.

18 CADN, Jerusalem, Consulat-Général, C/6, *Front de Combat Hébreu*, Apr. 1944, p. 2.

19   CADN, Mandat Syrie–Liban, Cabinet Politique, I/1158, *Front de Combat Hébreu*, May–June 1944, p. 4.

20   '*Indépendance*, organe des Combatants pour la Liberté d'Israël – Groupe Stern', Jan. 1947, in Lazar, *L'opinion française et la naissance de l'Etat d'Israël*, p. 35.

21   CADN, Mandat Syrie–Liban, Cabinet Politique, I/1158, du Chaylard to Massigli, 23 June 1944.

22   CADN, Londres Ambassade, C/119, du Chaylard to Massigli, 30 June 1944.

23   CADN, Mandat Syrie-Liban, Cabinet Politique, I/1158, du Chaylard to Massigli, 18 July 1944.

24   Shamir, *Summing Up*, p. 49.

25   MEC, MacMichael Papers, Ormsby Gore to MacMichael, 15 Dec. 1937.

26   Ranfurly, *To War with Whitaker*, 6 Sept. 1944.

27   TNA, FO 141/1001, Clayton, memorandum, 14 Nov. 1944. Moyne made this remark on 18 Aug.

28   TNA, FO 141/1001, Clayton, memorandum, 14 Nov. 1944. Moyne telegraphed London on 26 Aug. Ben-Gurion's speech was made five days earlier, in Haifa.

23 TROP DE ZÈLE

1   Ranfurly, *To War with Whitaker*, 14 Nov. 1942.

2   CAC, AMEL 2/2/19, Amery, appreciation of Moyne, n.d.

3   *The Times*, 'Lord Moyne', 7 Nov. 1944.

4   Moyne, 'Walter Edward Guinness, first Baron Moyne (1880–1944)', rev. Marc Brodie, *Oxford Dictionary of National Biography* (Oxford, 2004).

5   TNA, CAB 67/9/104, Moyne, 'Jewish Policy', 30 Sept. 1941.

6   Norman Rose, *'A Senseless, Squalid War': Voices from Palestine 1945–48* (London, 2009), p. 66.

7   Heller, *The Stern Gang*, p. 123.

8   HL Deb, 9 June 1942, vol. 123, cc. 199–200.

9   Meir Zamir, 'The "Missing Dimension": Britain's Secret War against France in Syria and Lebanon, 1942–45 – Part II', *Middle Eastern Studies*, vol. 46, no. 6, p. 822.

10   CAC, Amery Papers, AMEL 2/2/19, Moyne to Amery, 21 Jan. 1943.

11   TNA, CAB 66/44/13, report of the Committee on Palestine, 20 Dec. 1943.

12   CAC, Amery Papers, AMEL 2/2/19, Amery to Moyne, 21 June 1943.

13   TNA, CAB 65/45/7, 'War Cabinet, 11th Conclusions, Minute 4, Confidential Annexe', 25 Jan. 1944.

14   TNA, CO 733/461/23.

15   TNA, FO 954/15, f. 467, Campbell, minute, 27 July 1944.

16   Stirling, *Safety Last*, p. 226.

17   CADN, Mandat Syrie–Liban, Cabinet Politique, I/2986, 'Délégation de Syrie, Section Politique, Rapport Quotidien No. 99', 2 June 1944.

18   CADN, Mandat Syrie–Liban, Cabinet Politique, I/2986, 'Note sur le Colonel Stirling', 16 Aug. 1944.

19   CADN, Beyrouth Ambassade, B 69/3615, 'Information du Colonel Stirling et du Cheikh Kamal Kassab', 11 July 1944.

20   CADN, Beyrouth Ambassade, B 69/3615, 'Information du Colonel Stirling et du Cheikh Kamal Kassab', 11 July 1944.

21   TNA, FO 371/40302, E 5442/23/89, 'Syria and Sir E. Spears'.

22 TNA, FO 371/40302, Mardam to Spears, 27 May 1944.
23 TNA, FO 371/40302, Mardam to Spears, 27 May 1944.
24 Zamir, 'The "Missing Dimension"', pp.825–6
25 CADN, Mandat Syrie–Liban, Cabinet Politique, I/2986, note of a meeting between Ostrorog and Peterson, 25 Aug. 1944.
26 TNA, FO 371/40302, Rapport Verbal: 'Résumé de la conversation qui s'est déroulée entre S.E. Saadallah bey Djabri, Président du Conseil Syrien, Djemil Mardam bey, Ministre des Affaires Etrangères, et S.E. le Général E. Spears, ministre plénipotentiaire du Gouvernement de S.M. Britannique', 5 June 1944.
27 CADN, Mandat Syrie–Liban, Cabinet Politique, I/2278, Beynet to Diplofrance, 24 June 1944.
28 CADN, Beyrouth Ambassade, B/10/159, Rapport Quotidien, No. 124, 'Déclarations du Ministre des Affaires Etrangères au sujet de 'Unité Arabe', 3 Jul. 1944.
29 Meir Zamir, 'Britain's treachery, France's revenge', Ha'aretz, 1 Feb. 2008; Zamir, 'The "Missing Dimension"', p. 827.
30 CADN, Mandat Syrie–Liban, Cabinet Politique, I/2455, 'Information, No. 330', 11 Aug. 1944.
31 CADN, Mandat Syrie–Liban, Cabinet Politique, I/2455, Beynet to Massigli, 15 Aug. 1944.
32 TNA, FO 954/15, f. 457, Eden to Cooper, 24 July 1944.
33 TNA, FO 954/15, f. 417, Cooper to Eden, 22 May 1944.
34 LHCMA, Ismay Papers, 4/31/3, Spears to Ismay, 3 July 1944.
35 TNA, FO 954/15, f. 419, Eden to Churchill, 1 June 1944; FO 954/15, f. 421, Churchill to Eden, 11 June 1944.
36 CADN, Mandat Syrie–Liban, Cabinet Politique, I/2986, response by Eden to Massigli's note of 24 Aug. 1944, 26 Aug. 1944.
37 CADN, Mandat Syrie–Liban, Cabinet Politique, I/2986, 'Négociations de Londres sur les affaires du Levant, 21 août –1er septembre 1944'.
38 TNA, FO 954/15, f. 496, Eden to Churchill, 29 Aug. 1944.
39 MEC, Spears Papers, II, Churchill to Spears, 10 Mar. 1944; FO 954/15, f. 514, Churchill to Spears, 4 Sept. 1944.
40 TNA, FO 371/40302, minute by Hankey, 5 Oct. 1944.
41 TNA, FO 371/40302, Butler, minute, 30 Dec. 1944.

24 THE MURDER OF LORD MOYNE

1 TNA, FO 141/1001, Hughes-Onslow, statement.
2 TNA, FO 141/1001, Osmond, statement.
3 TNA, FO 141/1001, Hughes-Onslow, statement.
4 TNA, FO 141/1001, 'Statement given by Eliahu Beth Tzouri and Eliahu Hakim on their examination by the Procurateur Général on 10.11.44'.
5 Norwich, ed., The Duff Cooper Diaries, 26 Nov. 1944.
6 SHAT, 4H 448, note by Vabre of the Services Spéciaux, 29 May 1943; TNA FO 371/35179, 'Notes of meeting with Massigli held in the Minister of State's room at 4.0', 15 July 1943.
7 TNA, WO 201/989A, Jago to Holmes, 27 Mar. 1943.
8 TNA FO 371/35179, 'Notes of meeting with Massigli held in the Minister of State's room at 4.0', 15 July 1943.
9 SHAT, 4H 346. 'Free French Order of Battle, 1944', 'Divers'.

10 TNA FO 371/35179, 'Notes of meeting with Massigli held in the Minister of State's room at 4.0', 15 July 1943.

11 TNA, FO 371/40349, MacKereth to Baxter, 6 Sept. 1944.

12 TNA, FO 371/40349, Hankey, minute, 21 Sept. 1944.

13 TNA, KV 4/384, A. J. Kellar, 'Visit to the Middle East' (26 Nov. 1944–2 Feb. 1945), Feb. 1945, says that the French were considering supporting the Stern Gang. Guy Liddell, the deputy director of MI5, wrote in his diary on 19 Feb. 1945: 'There is now positive evidence that it [the Gang] is receiving support from French officials in the Levant, both in the matter of arms and finance' (TNA, KV 4/196). TNA, FO 141/1001, 'Interrogation of the Two Accused in the Lord Moyne Murder Case, CID, Palestine Police, 8 Nov. 1944'.

14 TNA, KV 4/384, A. J. Kellar, 'Visit to the Middle East' (26 Nov. 1944–2 Feb. 1945), Feb. 1945.

15 TNA, FO 371/40304, 'Translation of telegram from Shukri al Quwatli to His Majesty the King [Ibn Saud]', n.d. See also Zamir, 'The "Missing Dimension"', p. 830.

16 Zamir, 'The "Missing Dimension"', p. 843.

17 CADN, Beyrouth Ambassade, B/10/159, file on Djemil Mardam Bey, 'Copie de l'Entente Secrète réalisée entre Noury Said et Djemil Mardam le 15 Septembre 1944'.

18 CAC, Amery Papers, AMEL 2/2/19, Moyne to Amery, 12 Oct. 1944.

19 SHAT 4H 382, chief of the Deuxième Bureau, 'Position et activités des Britanniques au Levant', 19 Sept. 1944.

20 CADN, Mandat Syrie–Liban, Cabinet Politique, I/2279, Francom to Maigret, Jeddah, 10 Nov. 1944, forwarded a short, ambiguous message from Alessandri to a colleague in Jeddah: 'Telegraphed you twice before in Cairo ['le Caire']. Health now very good. All, me included, send you our best wishes.'

21 CADN, Londres Ambassade, C/119, du Chaylard to Bidault, 8 Nov. 1944; Michael J. Cohen, 'The Moyne Assassination, November 1944: A Political Analysis', *Middle Eastern Studies*, vol. 15, no. 3 (Oct. 1979), p. 360.

22 TNA, KV 4/384, 'Report on Visit by Mr A. J. Kellar to SIME and CICI Organisations', May 1944.

23 De Gaulle, *Mémoires de Guerre*, vol. III (Paris, 1959), notes of meeting with Churchill and Eden in Paris on 11 Nov. 1944.

24 HC Deb, 17 Nov. 1944, vol. 404, c. 2242.

25 CAB 66/58/28, Stanley, 'Situation in Palestine', 23 Nov. 1944. Annexe IV, note by the chiefs of staff giving their views on the military implications of a wholesale search for arms in Palestine, 16 Nov. 1944; Churchill, *The Second World War*, vol. VI (London, 1954), p. 612.

26 TNA, KV 4/384, A. J. Kellar, 'Visit to the Middle East' (26 Nov. 1944–2 Feb. 1945), Feb. 1945.

27 TNA, KV 4/384, A. J. Kellar, 'Visit to the Middle East' (26 Nov. 1944–2 Feb. 1945), Feb. 1945.

28 TNA, KV 5/29, Roberts to Kellar, 11 May 1945.

29 TNA, KV 5/29, Kellar to Roberts, 21 Apr. 1945.

30 TNA, CAB 66/64/25, Grigg, 'Palestine', 4 Apr. 1945.

31 Lord Killearn, 23 Mar. 1945, quoted in Grigg, 'Palestine'.

32 Rose, '*A Senseless, Squalid War*', p. 67.

33 TNA, CAB 66/64/25, Eden, 'Palestine', 10 Apr. 1945.

34 TNA, FO 141/1001, Clayton, memorandum, 14 Nov. 1944.

25 TIME TO CALL THE SHOTS

1 MEC, Coghill Papers, diary, 31 Jan. 1945.

2 CADN, Mandat Syrie–Liban, Cabinet Politique, I/2986, 'Conférence sur les affaires du Levant tenue chez M. le Général Catroux en présence de M.M. Chauvel, Meyrier et Ostrorog, le 4 septembre 1944'.

3 CADN, Beyrouth Ambassade, B/10, Mardam to al-Atassi, 3 May 1945.

4 Antony Beevor and Artemis Cooper, *Paris after the Liberation, 1944–1949* (London, 1994), p. 56.

5 Beevor and Cooper, *Paris after the Liberation*, p. 248.

6 *DDF*, 1944, vol. II, 75, de Gaulle to Bidault, 19 Oct. 1944.

7 *DDF*, 1945, vol. I, 253, meeting on Levant affairs, 5 Apr. 1945.

8 *DDF*, 1945, vol. I, 231, Ostrorog to Bidault, 29 Mar. 1945.

9 *DDF*, 1945, vol. I, 253, meeting on Levant affairs, 5 Apr. 1945.

10 Norwich, ed., *The Duff Cooper Diaries*, 14 Sept. 1944.

11 Journal Officiel de la République Française, Débats de l'Assemblée Consultative Provisoire, 15 June 1945.

12 Kirkbride, *A Crackle of Thorns*, p. 82.

13 MEC, Shone Papers, Eden to Cooper, 27 Jan. 1945.

14 *DDF*, 1945, vol. I, 170, Massigli to Bidault, 6 Mar. 1945; HC Deb, 27 Feb. 1945, vol. 408, c. 1290.

15 CADN, Londres Ambassade, C/139, Lescuyer to Bidault, 27 Jan. 1945, enclosing a draft telegram from Paget to under-secretary of state for war, n.d.

16 SHAT, 4H 371, Noiret to chief of general staff, 7 Feb. 1945.

17 CADN, Londres Ambassade, C/139, Catroux, telegram, 17 Feb. 1945.

18 TNA, FO 226/246, Prodrome Beirut to Foreign Office, 5 Apr. 1942.

19 *DDF*, 1945, vol. I, 311, de Gaulle to Bidault, 30 Apr. 1945.

20 Norwich, ed., *The Duff Cooper Diaries*, 30 Apr. 1945.

21 Zamir, in 'The "Missing Dimension"', p. 858, quotes a telegram from Cadogan, the permanent under-secretary at the Foreign Office, to the British legation in Beirut, telling it to 'do all in your power – and this most secretly – to promote the plans in favour of the Greater Syria.' A letter from Syria's envoy to London, Armanazi, to Mardam on 27 April corroborated the impression that this was official British policy.

22 TNA, PREM 3/423/13, Churchill to Ismay, 10 May 1945.

23 TNA, PREM 3/423/13, de Gaulle to Churchill, 6 May 1945.

24 MEC, Coghill Papers, diary, 15 July 1945; MEC, Shone Papers, Shone to Bevin, 25 Aug. 1945.

25 TNA, PREM 3/423/13, Shone to Eden, 28 May 1945.

26 MEC, Shone Papers, Sophie Shone, diary, 28 May 1945.

27 MEC, Shone Papers, Shone to Bevin, 25 Aug. 1945.

28 Stirling, *Safety Last*, p. 231.

29 TNA, FO 120/525, GHQ Middle East to AMSSO, 30 May 1945.

30 Stirling, *Safety Last*, p. 231.

31 Kirkbride, *A Crackle of Thorns*, p. 151.

32 MEC, Coghill Papers.

33 Kirkbride, *A Crackle of Thorns*, p. 151.

34 *Time*, 'Who Walks in Damascus?', 18 June 1945; CADN, Mandat Syrie–Liban, Cabinet Politique, I/2986, Oliva-Roget to Beynet, 19 June 1944.

35 CADN, Mandat Syrie–Liban, Cabinet Politique, I/2986, 'Note sur le Colonel Stirling', 16 Aug. 1944.

36 'Déclarations du Général de l'Armée Beynet, Délégué Général et Plénipotentiaire de France du Levant aux Représentants de la Presse Etrangère sur les affaires de Syrie', 9 June 1945

37 Stirling, *Safety Last*, p. 232.

38 Stirling, *Safety Last*, p. 232.

39 MEC, Shone Papers, Shone to Bevin, 25 Aug. 1945.

40 Zamir, 'The "Missing Dimension"', p. 880–82.

41 Roshwald, *Estranged Bedfellows*, p. 204.

42 MEC, Spears Papers, II/A, Clarke to Spears, 15 June 1945.

43 TNA CAB 120/525, Churchill to de Gaulle, 31 May 1945.

44 *Time*, 'Who Walks in Damascus?', 18 June 1945.

45 MEC, Coghill Papers, diary, 15 July 1945.

46 DGD, vol. III, Beynet to de Gaulle, 4 June 1945.

47 TNA, PREM 3/423/14, Cooper to Eden, 2 June 1945.

48 *Glasgow Herald*, 'French Reopen Controversy over Syria: Britain Again Blamed for Trouble', 8 June 1945.

49 TNA, PREM 3/423/14, Campbell, note, 3 June 1945.

50 TNA, PREM 3/423/14, Cooper to Foreign Office, 3 June 1945.

51 Norwich, ed., *The Duff Cooper Diaries*, 4 June 1945.

52 *Time*, 'Who Walks in Damascus?', 18 June 1945

53 Stirling, *Safety Last*, p. 221.

54 Stirling, *Safety Last*, p. 236.

55 IWM, Press digests, Syria and Lebanon, 1945, *An Nasr*, 4–5 June 1945.

56 MEC, Spears Papers, III, K. M. Donald Mills to 'Robin', 20 Mar. 1946.

57 MEC, Coghill Papers, diary, 15 July 1945.

58 Zamir, 'Britain's Treachery, France's Revenge'.

59 Journal Officiel de la République Française, Débats de l'Assemblée Consultative Provisoire, 15 June 1945.

60 TNA, CAB 194/3, cabinet meeting, minutes, 13 Dec. 1945.

61 Meir Zamir, 'The French Connection', *Ha'aretz*, 3 July 2008. Zamir dates the letter to 'late June'.

62 David Ben-Gurion recorded in his diary on 8 June 1945 that representatives of both the Irgun and the Stern Gang had visited the French delegation in Beirut and that France was seeking to undermine Britain in Palestine.

63 Zamir, 'The French Connection'.

64 *DDF*, 1945, vol. I, 467, Bonnet to Bidault, 28 June 1945.

65 *DDF*, 1945, vol. II, 149, 'Visite du représentant de l'Agence juive au directeur d'Europe', 31 Aug. 1945.

66 Zamir, 'Britain's Treachery, France's Revenge'. The date of the meeting was 6 Oct. 1945.

67 *DDF*, 1945, vol. I, 253, 'Réunion du 5 avril 1945 au sujet des Affaires du Levant'.

68 Catherine Nicault, *La France et le sionisme: une rencontre manquée?* (Paris, 1992), p. 205. Du Chaylard reported Ben-Gurion's speech in Tel Aviv, on 16 May 1944.

26 GOT TO THINK AGAIN

1 Report of Earl G. Harrison on his 'Mission to Europe to inquire into the conditions and needs of those among the displaced persons in the liberated countries of Western Europe and in the SHAEF area of Germany – with particular reference to the Jewish refugees – who may possibly be stateless or non-repatriable', n.d.

2   Rose, 'A Senseless, Squalid War', p. 71.

3   Chris Wrigley, 'Bevin, Ernest (1881–1951)', Oxford Dictionary of National Biography, quoting John Colville, The Fringes of Power (London, 1985), p. 522.

4   Wrigley, 'Bevin, Ernest (1881–1951)', Oxford Dictionary of National Biography, quoting David Dilks, ed., The Diaries of Sir Alexander Cadogan (London, 1971), p. 778.

5   Roosevelt pledged to 'help to bring about' the 'establishment of Palestine as a free and democratic Jewish Commonwealth', but he also said that no decisions should be taken 'without prior consultation with the Arabs and the Jews'. The source for the estimate of the Jewish population in the United States is TNA, FO 371/61856. Official US figures for 1941 gave the Jewish population as 4,893,748, a rise of 123,101 since 1937. Assuming similar growth by 1945, the population was just over five million. The Quai d'Orsay produced a much higher estimate, of seven million, in 'Le Problème Sioniste', 25 Nov. 1945.

6   Harry S. Truman, The Memoirs of Harry S. Truman, vol. I (London, 1955), p. 72.

7   Ritchie Ovendale, 'The Palestine Policy of the British Labour Government, 1945–1946', International Affairs, vol. 55, no. 3 (July, 1979), p. 413.

8   Michael Ottolenghi, 'Harry Truman's Recognition of Israel', Historical Journal, vol. 47, no. 4 (Dec. 2004), p. 969.

9   Kenneth Harris, Attlee (London, 1982), p. 390.

10   TNA, CAB 129/2, Hall, 'Security Conditions in Palestine', 10 Sept. 1945: Annexe: 'Extracts from letter from the Officer administering the Government of Palestine (Mr J. V. W. Shaw, CMG) to the Secretary of State for the Colonies, dated 24th Aug., 1945'.

11   Wrigley, 'Bevin, Ernest (1881–1951)', Oxford Dictionary of National Biography, quoting Alan Bullock, The Life and Times of Ernest Bevin, vol. III, p. 353.

12   Harry S. Truman, The Memoirs of Harry S. Truman, vol. II (London, 1956), p. 148; Oren, Power, Faith and Fantasy, p. 485.

13   Truman, Memoirs, vol. II, p. 153. The British believed Jews made up 17 per cent of the New York population (FO 371/61856).

14   Lazar, L'opinion française et la naissance de l'Etat d'Israël, p. 70.

15   MEC, MacMichael Papers, Gort to MacMichael, 10 Oct. 1945.

16   Wrigley, 'Bevin, Ernest (1881–1951)', Oxford Dictionary of National Biography (Oxford, 2004), quoting Alan Bullock, The Life and Times of Ernest Bevin, vol. III, p. 181.

17   Eliav, Wanted, p. 216.

18   IWM, W. S. Cole Papers, WSC/3, E. H. Barker, report on 'Operation Agatha', 10 July 1946.

19   TNA, CAB 129/9, Anglo-American Committee of Inquiry, report, 20 Apr. 1946, quoting the Palestine Post, 30 Dec. 1945.

20   MEC, Crossman Papers, Singleton, 'Public Security', 9 Apr. 1946; Rose, 'This Senseless, Squalid War', p. 88.

21   Lazar, L'opinion française et la naissance de l'Etat d'Israël, pp. 44–5.

22   IWM, Windeatt Papers, diary, 10 July 1945.

23   LHCMA, Dunbar Papers.

24   LHCMA, Dunbar Papers.

25   LHCMA, Dunbar Papers.

26   David Cesarani, Major Farran's Hat: Murder, Scandal and Britain's War against Jewish Terrorism, 1945–1948 (London, 2009), p. 36.

27   TNA, CAB 129/9, Anglo-American Committee of Inquiry, report, 20 Apr. 1946.

28   TNA, CAB 194/5, cabinet meeting, 29 Apr. 1946; CAB 195/5, 15 Jan. 1947, contains Bevin's allegation that the US government steered its representatives.

29   *The Times*, 'U.S. Critics of Mr Bevin: Palestine Policy Resented', 14 June 1946.

30   TNA, CAB 195/4, cabinet meeting, minutes, 29 Apr. 1946. The typed transcript records that Bevin 'Asked Barnes why U.S. keen: found it was to prevent large Jew immigrn into U.S.'. Given the context, it seems unlikely that Bevin would have consulted Alfred Barnes, the minister of war transport, about this matter.

31   TNA, KV 4/384, A. J. Kellar, 'Visit to the Middle East' (26 Nov. 1944–2 Feb. 1945), Feb. 1945.

32   TNA, CAB 129/2, Hall, 'Security Conditions in Palestine', 10 Sept. 1945: Annexe: 'Extracts from letter from the Officer administering the Government of Palestine (Mr J. V. W. Shaw, CMG) to the Secretary of State for the Colonies, dated 24th August, 1945'.

33   *The Times*, 'Sabotage and Violence in Palestine', 25 July 1946. The article reprinted telegrams published by the government the previous day.

34   Cesarani, *Major Farran's Hat*, p. 39.

35   IWM, Windeatt Papers, 4 July 1946.

36   TNA, CAB 195/4, cabinet meeting, cabinet secretary's minutes, 20 June 1946.

37   Cesarani, *Major Farran's Hat*, p. 39.

38   Menachem Begin, *The Revolt* (Los Angeles, 1972), p. 204.

39   Rose, '*A Senseless, Squalid War*', p. 109.

40   IWM, Catling, interview.

41   CADN, Londres Ambassade, C/325, Neuville to Bidault, 12 July 1946. MI5's officer was Gyles Isham.

42   IWM, Cole Papers, E. H. Barker, report on 'Operation Agatha', 10 July 1946.

43   IWM, Morton Papers.

44   MEC, Crossman Papers, Shaw to Crossman, 2 Aug. 1946.

45   IWM, Rymer-Jones, interview, 1989.

46   CADN, Londres Ambassade, C/325, Neuville to Bidault, 24 July 1946.

47   Rose, '*A Senseless, Squalid War*', p. 117.

48   Begin, *The Revolt*, p. 228.

49   *The Times*, '39 Killed in Jerusalem Headquarters', 23 July 1946.

50   *The Times*, 'Jewish Agency and White Paper: Insinuations of Fraud', 26 July 1946.

51   Begin, *The Revolt*, p. 204. That estimate was made by Yisrael Galili.

52   TNA, CAB 195/4, cabinet meeting, cabinet secretary's minutes, 25 July 1946.

27 THE AMERICAN LEAGUE FOR A FREE PALESTINE

1   TNA, CO 537/1738, *New York Post*, 29 July 1946.

2   Truman, *Memoirs*, vol. I, p. 19.

3   Alonzo Hambly, 'The Accidental Presidency', *The Wilson Quarterly*, vol. 12, no. 2 (Spring, 1988), p. 49.

4   Truman, *Memoirs*, vol. I, p. 5.

5   Hambly, 'The Accidental Presidency', p. 55.

6   Michael J. Cohen, 'Truman and Palestine, 1945–1948: Revisionism, Politics and Diplomacy', *Modern Judaism*, vol. 2, no. 1 (Feb. 1982), p. 5. Henry Wallace recorded Truman's comment, therefore dating it to before 20 Sept. 1946, when he was sacked by Truman.

7   *The Times*, 'Statement by Mr Truman', 24 July 1946.

8   TNA, CO 537/1738, press advertisement, 2 July 1946.

9   TNA, CO 537/1738, Bergson, statement at press conference in New York, 9 July 1946.
10 Stewart McClure, 'On the Staff of Guy Gillette', 8 Dec. 1982, http://www.senate.gov/artandhistory/history/resources/pdf/McClure1.pdf
11 CADN, Londres Ambassade, C/325, Neuville to Bidault, 5 Aug. 1946.
12 TNA, CO 537/1738, British embassy, Washington, to Foreign Office, 21 Aug. 1946.
13 Rose, 'A Senseless, Squalid War', p. 122.
14 Samuel Katz, Days of Fire (London, 1968), p. 118; AJHS, I/278, 'American League for a Free Palestine, Statement of Receipts and Disbursements, Jan. 1, 1946 to Dec. 31, 1946'.
15 TNA, CO 537/1738, MI5 to Trafford Smith, 4 Oct. 1946.
16 TNA, FO 371/61856.
17 M. Ottolenghi, 'Harry Truman's Recognition of Israel', Historical Journal, vol. 47, no. 4 (Dec. 2004), p. 970.
18 Oren, Power, Faith and Fantasy, p. 488.
19 The Times, 'The Palestine Outlook: Mr Bevin on U.S. "Pressure"', 26 Feb. 1947.
20 The Times, 'U.S. Replies to Mr Bevin', 27 Feb. 1947.
21 Walter Russell Mead, 'The New Israel and the Old: Why Gentile Americans Back the Jewish State', Foreign Affairs, vol. 87, no. 4 (July/Aug. 2008), pp. 28–46.
22 John Lewis Gaddis, The Cold War (London, 2005), p. 29.
23 Gaddis, The Cold War, p 31.
24 Oren, Power, Faith and Fantasy, p. 489.
25 Katz, Days of Fire, p. 139.
26 Rose, 'A Senseless, Squalid War', p. 135.
27 Lazar, L'opinion française et la naissance de l'Etat d'Israël, p. 51.
28 TNA, CO 537/2314, 'Build Dov Gruner's Memorial'.
29 Hecht, A Child of the Century, p. 612.
30 Ricky-Dale Calhoun, 'Arming David: The Haganah's Illegal Arms Procurement Network in the United States, 1945–49', Journal of Palestine Studies, vol. 36, no. 4 (Summer, 2007), p. 31.
31 TNA, CO 537/2314, Foreign Office to Washington, 22 May 1947.
32 TNA, CO 537/2314, Foreign Office to Washington, 22 May 1947.
33 TNA, CO 967/103, Martin to Gurney, 20 Nov. 1947.
34 TNA, British embassy Washington, Chancery to Eastern Department, 13 June 1947, quoting Reuters.

28 FRENCH AND ZIONIST INTRIGUES

1   The Times, 'Terrorist Bomb in Whitehall: Woman Sought by Scotland Yard', 17 Apr. 1947; The Times, 'Bomb Hoax in London', 18 Apr. 1947.
2   TNA, KV 2/3428, Robertson memorandum, 31 Oct. 1945; Philby to Liddell, 25 June 1946.
3   TNA, KV 5/29, Roberts to Kellar, 13 Feb. 1945.
4   Calder Walton, 'British Intelligence and the Mandate of Palestine: Threats to British National Security Immediately after the Second World War', Intelligence and National Security, vol. 23, no. 4, p. 447.
5   Eliav, Wanted, pp. 237–8. Levstein later Hebraicised his name as Eliav.
6   Eliav, Wanted, p. 238.
7   Eliav, Wanted, p. 239.

8 Renée Poznanski (trans. Nathan Brecher), *Jews in France in World War II* (Hanover, 2001), p. 157.

9 Eliav, *Wanted*, p. 246.

10 Lazar, *L'opinion française et la naissance de l'Etat d'Israël*, p. 156.

11 Shamir, *Summing Up*, p. 72.

12 Lazar, *L'opinion française et la naissance de l'Etat d'Israël*, p. 55.

13 Rose, 'A Senseless, Squalid War', p. 138.

14 Eliav, *Wanted*, p. 261.

15 Katz, *Days of Fire*, p. 103.

16 TNA, CO 967/103, Robey to Bromley, 9 Sept. 1947.

17 *The Times*, 'Plot to Bomb London: Zionists under Arrest', 8 Sept. 1947; 'Terrorist Plans for London: Bombs from Fire Appliances', 9 Sept. 1947.

18 Norwich, ed., *The Duff Cooper Diaries*, 24 Mar. 1947.

19 Lazar, *L'opinion française et la naissance de l'Etat d'Israël*, p. 99, quoting *Le Gavroche*, 10 July 1947.

20 Ehud Avriel, *Open the Gates! A Personal Story of 'Illegal' Immigration to Israel* (London, 1975), p. 35.

21 Lazar, *L'opinion française et la naissance de l'Etat d'Israël*, pp. 79-80, quoting *Le Parisien Libéré*, 27 May 1947.

22 Keith Jeffery, *MI6: The History of the Secret Intelligence Service, 1909-1949* (London, 2010), pp. 689-95.

23 Rose, 'A Senseless, Squalid War', p. 156.

24 Norwich, ed., *The Duff Cooper Diaries*, 23 July 1947.

25 Katz, *Days of Fire*, p. 172.

26 Lazar, *L'opinion française et la naissance de l'Etat d'Israël*, pp. 90-1.

29 LAST POST

1 HC Deb, 18 Feb. 1947, vol. 433, c. 988.

2 TNA, CAB 195/5, cabinet secretary's minutes, cabinet meeting, 7 Feb. 1947.

3 HC Deb, 25 Feb. 1947, vol. 433, c. 2007.

4 *The Times*, 'Jewish Campaign against Terrorism: Action on Eve of U.N. Assembly', 28 Apr. 1947.

5 TNA, CAB 195/5, cabinet secretary's minutes, cabinet meeting, 15 Jan. 1947.

6 Cesarani, *Major Farran's Hat*.

7 MEC, UNSCOP Papers, 'Report of a conference between UNSCOP representatives Mr. Emil Sandström, Dr. Victor Hoo and Dr. Ralph Bunche, and the Commander and two other representatives of the Irgun Zvai Leumi, 24 June 1947'.

8 CADN, Jerusalem, Consulat-Général, C/6, Irgun, communiqué, 30 July 1947.

9 CADN, Jerusalem, Consulat-Général, C/6, Irgun, 'To All Other Ranks', Aug. 1947.

10 Rose, 'A Senseless, Squalid War', p. 167.

11 *The Times*, 'Bricks through Window: Evidence of Disorderly Crowds', 5 Aug. 1947.

12 Segev, *One Palestine, Complete*, p. 495.

13 TNA, CAB 195/6, cabinet secretary's minutes, cabinet meeting, 22 Mar. 1948.

14 Rose, 'A Senseless, Squalid War', 173.

15 Hecht, *A Child of the Century*, p. 618. See also pp. 598-9.

16 Tsilla Hershco, 'France and the Partition Plan: 1947-1948', *Israel Affairs*, vol. 14, no. 3, p. 490.

17 IWM, Cole Papers, Palestine: 'Narrative of events from Feb. 1947 until withdrawal of all British troops, by Lt Gen G. H. A. MacMillan'.

18 ISA, *Political and Diplomatic Documents*, Dec. 1947–May 1948, Jerusalem 1979, Fischer to Bonneau, 1 Dec. 1947.

19 Truman, *Memoirs*, vol. II, pp. 168–9.

20 IWM, Mayer Papers.

21 Meir Zamir, '"Bid" for *Altalena*: France's Covert Action in the 1948 War in Palestine', *Middle Eastern Studies*, vol. 46, no. 1 (Jan. 2010), p. 22.

22 Zamir, 'The French Connection'.

23 Zamir, '"Bid" for *Altalena*', p. 30.

24 Michael T. Thornhill, 'Abdullah ibn Hussein (1882–1951)', *Oxford Dictionary of National Biography* (Oxford, 2004).

25 Avi Shlaim, *Collusion across the Jordan: King Abdullah, the Zionist Movement, and the Partition of Palestine* (New York, 1988), p. 76.

26 Shlaim, *Collusion across the Jordan*, p. 101.

27 Shlaim, *Collusion across the Jordan*, p. 136.

28 United Nations Palestine Commission, 'First Special Report to the Security Council: The Problem of Security in Palestine', S/676, 16 Feb. 1948.

29 United Nations Palestine Commission, 'First Special Report to the Security Council: The Problem of Security in Palestine', S/676, 16 Feb. 1948.

30 TNA, FO 371/68648, Washington to Foreign Office, 17 Apr. 1948.

31 TNA, CAB 195/6, cabinet secretary's minutes, cabinet meeting, 22 Mar. 1948.

32 Katz, *Days of Fire*, p. 205.

33 Zamir, '"Bid" for *Altalena*', p. 46, Ariel to Boissier, 25 Mar. 1948.

34 Katz, *Days of Fire*, p. 191.

35 Zamir, '"Bid" for *Altalena*', p. 46, Lacharrière to Quai d'Orsay, 8 Mar. 1948.

36 Zamir, '"Bid" for *Altalena*', p. 23.

37 Shlaim, *Collusion across the Jordan*, p. 174.

38 Walid Khalidi, 'Selected Documents on the 1948 Palestinian War', *Journal of Palestine Studies*, vol. 27, no. 3 (Spring, 1998), pp. 74–5, quoting Bajhat abu Gharbiyya.

39 Royle, *Glubb Pasha*, p. 342.

40 Edward Henderson, *This Strange, Eventful History* (Dubai, 1988), p. 38.

41 Ilan Pappé, *The Ethnic Cleansing of Palestine* (Oxford, 2006), p. 95.

42 MEC, MacMichael Papers, Pollock to MacMichael, 27 Apr. 1948.

42 MEC, Thames Television papers, interview with Sir John Shaw.

EPILOGUE: A SETTLING OF SCORES

1 Andrew Rathmell, *Secret War in the Middle East: The Covert Struggle for Syria, 1949–1961* (London, 1995), p. 53.

2 *The Times*, 'Discontent in Syria: Denial of Vote to Beduin', 3 Sept. 1949.

3 Accounts of the attempt on Stirling's life can be found in MEC, Philby Papers, 2/3/3/19, Marygold Stirling to Philby, 22 Jan. 1951; TTA, Deakin Papers, TT/FN1/RD/1, Stirling to Deakin, 25 Nov. 1949; CADN, Beyrouth Ambassade B/69/3615, Boisberranger to MAE, 10 Nov. 1949.

4 Stirling, *Safety Last*, epilogue by Lord Kinross, p. 243.

5 Stirling, *Safety Last*, epilogue by Lord Kinross, p. 240.

6 Stirling, *Safety Last*, epilogue by Lord Kinross, p. 242.

7 Rathmell, *Secret War in the Middle East: The Covert Struggle for Syria*, p. 71.

8 L. P. Heren, *Growing Up on 'The Times'* (London, 1978), p. 26.

9 TTA, Deakin Papers, TT/FN/1/RD/1, Heren, 'Confidential Memorandum', 28 Nov. 1949.

10   TTA, Deakin Papers, TT/FN/1/RD/1, Heren to Deakin, 14 Apr. 1949.

11   TTA, Deakin Papers, TT/FN/1/RD/1, Heren, 'Confidential Memorandum', 28 Nov. 1949.

12   TTA, Deakin Papers, TT/FN/1/RD/1, Quilliam to Deakin, 3 Dec. 1949.

13   TTA, W. F. Stirling, Personnel File, Quilliam to foreign news editor, 7 Nov. 1949.

14   TTA, Deakin Papers, TT/FN/1/RD/1, Quilliam to Deakin, 28 Aug. 1949. Quilliam's view was shared by the Foreign Office: Rathmell, *Secret War in the Middle East*, p. 35.

15   *The Times*, 'Syria after the Coup: Field Open to Political Troublemakers,' 26 Aug. 1949.

16   TTA, Deakin Papers, TT/FN/1/RD/1, Giles to Deakin, 31 Aug. 1949.

17   *DDF*, 1947, vol. I, 98, Serres to Bidault, 3 Feb. 1947; CADN, Londres Ambassade, C/462, Serres to Bidault, 9 June 1947.

18   Rathmell, *Secret War in the Middle East*, p. 35.

19   TTA, Deakin Papers, TT/FN/1/RD/1, Stirling to Deakin, 16 Oct. 1949.

20   CADN, Beyrouth Ambassade, B/69/3615, Lucet to Schuman, 10 Jan. 1950.

21   *The Times*, 'Franco-British Relations', 24 Nov. 1949.

22   Rathmell, *Secret War in the Middle East*, p. 57.

23   CADN, Beyrouth Ambassade B/69/3615, Boisberranger to MAE, 10 Nov. 1949.

24   MEC, Somerset Papers, Somerset to Lord Raglan, 14 Aug. 1920.

25   MEC, Killearn Papers, diary, 13 Feb. 1945.

BIBLIOGRAPHY

1 Archive Sources

British Library, London
F. L. Bertie, 1st Viscount Bertie of Thame (Add 63039–63046)
E. A. R. Gascoyne-Cecil, Viscount Cecil of Chelwood (Add 51094)
T. E. Lawrence (Add 45914, Add 45915, Add 45983 A and B)
A. T. Wilson (Add 52455 A and B)

Centre des Archives diplomatiques de Nantes
Files from series:
Beyrouth Ambassade
Série B: various personnel files
Jérusalem, Consulat-Général
Série C
Londres Ambassade
Série B
Série C, various files
Mandat Syrie–Liban
Cabinet Politique
Services Spéciaux
Sûreté Générale

Churchill Archives, Churchill College, Cambridge
L. C. M. S. Amery
Sir W. L. S. Churchill
Sir P. J. Grigg
M. P. A. Hankey, 1st Baron

Gertrude Bell Archive, Newcastle
G. L. Bell

Imperial War Museum, London
H. Atkins (92/28/1)
M. El Baze (92/34/10)
A. Bowden Stuart
B. H. Bowring (interview, 12364)
Sir D. Brogan (92/25/1)
Sir R. C. Catling (interview, 10392)
D. W. Clarke (99/2/1–3)
W. S. Cole (07/34/6)
J. W. Dell (interview, 18269)
R. Dimbleby (reports, 1153)
L. Flanakin (07/13/1)
H. M. Foot (interview, 8937)
R. R. Griffith (interview, 18467)
H. Gunn (interview 8880)
Sir J. W. Hackett (interview, 12022)
B. Haskell-Thomas (interview, 29556)
L. H. Hill (85/2/1)
R. J. Hunting (P 339)
R. F. G. Jayne (78/15/1)
R. H. Kitson (interview, 10688)
A. Lane (interview, 10295)
A. S. Lucas (interview, 4616)
Sir T. Macpherson (05/73/1)
W. L. Mather (interview, 15326)
P. H. M. May (interview, 10419)
E. J. M. Mayer (91/32/1)
J. Moir (interview, 21554)
G. J. Morton (93/56/1)
C. P. Norman (interview, 4629)
Sir C. Norton (02/18/1)
H. Padfield (07/14/1)
A. M. Parry (67/374/1)
L. A. Passfield (87/29/1)
F. G. Peake (78/73/7, 7A–B and DS/MISC/16)
J. Pearce (interview, 831)
Press Digests, Syria and Lebanon, 1945 (Misc. 176 (2679))
R. B. Robinson (interview, 23172)
M. Rymer-Jones (interview, 10699)
D. de C. Smiley (interview, 10340)

W. F. Stirling
J. R. Stokes (99/22/1)
A. T. Ternent (interview, 10720)
R. G. Thackray (67/360/1)
B. R. Thomas (interview, 11084)
R. Usborne (interview, 8676)
Paul Vanson (06/38/1)
C. R. W. W. Wilmot (reports, 1152, 1153)
Sir H. H. Wilson (73/1/1–9)
J. K. Windeatt (90/20/1)

India Office Records, London
Political and Secret Documents from series:
L/PS/10
L/PS/11
L/PS/12

Liddell Hart Centre for Military Archives, King's College, London
E. H. H. Allenby, 1st Viscount Allenby of Megiddo
A. F. Brooke, 1st Viscount Alanbrooke of Brookeborough
L. Carr
J. A. Codrington
M. H. Coote
Sir J. G. Dill
C. W. Dunbar
Sir G. W. Furlonge
A. T. Irvine
H. L. Ismay, 1st Baron Ismay of Wormington
P. C. Joyce
A. T. O. Lees
Sir B. H. Liddell Hart
Sir W. R. Marshall
G. J. de W. Mullens
Sir E. J. B. Nelson
Sir R. N. O'Connor
Sir W. R. Robertson, 1st Bt
T. N. S. Wheeler

Middle East Centre, St Antony's College, Oxford

R. Adamson

N. Barbour

C. D. Brunton

Sir J. R. Chancellor

I. N. Clayton

Sir M. N. P. S. Coghill, 6th Bt

Sir P. Z. Cox

R. H. Crossman

J. B. Glubb

D. G. Hogarth

Sir M. W. Lampson, 1st Baron Killearn

Sir H. A. MacMichael

R. Meinertzhagen

R. F. P. Monckton

H. St J. B. Philby

Sir H. L. Samuel, 1st Viscount Samuel

Sir T. A. Shone

Sir W. A. Smart

F. R. Somerset, 4th Baron Raglan

Sir E. L. Spears, 1st Bt

Sir H. M. Stanley

Sir M. Sykes, 6th Bt

Sir C. A. Tegart

D. Tomlinson

United Nations Special Committee on Palestine (UNSCOP)

W. Yale

The National Archives, London

Files from series:

CAB 21 (Cabinet Office and predecessors: Registered Files)

CAB 23 (War Cabinet and Cabinet: Minutes)

CAB 24 (War Cabinet and Cabinet: Memoranda)

CAB 27 (War Cabinet and Cabinet: Miscellaneous Committees: Records)

CAB 42 (War Council and successors: Photographic Copies of Minutes and Papers)

CAB 65 (War Cabinet and Cabinet: Minutes)

CAB 66 (War Cabinet and Cabinet: Memoranda)

CAB 67 (War Cabinet: Memoranda)

CAB 80 (War Cabinet and Cabinet: Chiefs of Staff Committee: Memoranda)

CAB 104 (Cabinet Office: Supplementary Registered Files)

CAB 106 (War Cabinet and Cabinet Office: Historical Section: Archivist and Librarian Files)

CAB 107 (War Cabinet: Committees on the Co-ordination of Departmental Action in the Event of War with Certain Countries: Minutes and Memoranda)

CAB 120 (Cabinet Office: Minister of Defence Secretariat: Records)

CAB 128 (Cabinet: Minutes)

CAB 129 (Cabinet: Memoranda)

CAB 194 (Security Commission: Minutes, Papers and Reports)

CAB 195 (Cabinet Secretary's Notebooks)

CO 537 (Colonial Office: Confidential General and Confidential Original Correspondence)

CO 730 (Colonial Office: Iraq Original Correspondence)

CO 732 (Colonial Office: Middle East Original Correspondence)

CO 733 (Colonial Office: Palestine Original Correspondence)

CO 850 (Colonial Office: Personnel: Original Correspondence)

CO 935 (Colonial Office: Confidential Print Middle East)

CO 967 (Colonial Office: Private Office Papers)

FO 120 (Foreign Office and Consulates: Austria: General Correspondence)

FO 141 (Foreign Office and Foreign and Commonwealth Office: Embassy and Consulates, Egypt: General Correspondence)

FO 226 (Foreign Office: Embassy and Consulates, Beirut, Lebanon (formerly Ottoman Empire): General Correspondence and Letter Books)

FO 371 (Foreign Office: Political Departments: General Correspondence)

FO 406 (Foreign Office: Confidential Print Eastern Affairs)

FO 608 (Peace Conference: British Delegation: Correspondence and Papers)

FO 684 (Foreign Office: Consulate, Damascus, Syria: General Correspondence and Registers of Births and Marriages)

FO 800 (Foreign Office, Private Offices: Various Ministers' and Officials' Papers)

FO 882 (Arab Bureau Papers)

FO 921 (War Cabinet: Office of the Minister of State Resident in the Middle East: Registered Files)

FO 945 (Control Office for Germany and Austria and Foreign Office,

German Section: General Department)

FO 954 (Foreign Office: Private Office Papers of Sir Anthony Eden, Earl of Avon, Secretary of State for Foreign Affairs)

HW 1 (Government Code and Cypher School: Signals Intelligence Passed to the Prime Minister, Messages and Correspondence)

HW 12 (Government Code and Cypher School: Diplomatic Section and predecessors: Decrypts of Intercepted Diplomatic Communications)

HW 41 (Government Code and Cypher School: Services Field Signals Intelligence Units: Reports of Intercepted Signals and Histories of Field Signals Intelligence Units)

KV 4 (Security Service: Policy Files)

KV 5 (Security Service: Organisation Files)

PREM 3 (Prime Minister's Office: Operational Correspondence and Papers)

WO 32 (War Office and successors: Registered Files (General Series)

WO 33 (War Office: Reports, Memoranda and Papers)

WO 158 (War Office: Military Headquarters: Correspondence and Papers, First World War)

WO 201 (War Office: Middle East Forces: Military Headquarters Papers, Second World War)

WO 204 (War Office: Allied Forces, Mediterranean Theatre: Military Headquarters Papers, Second World War)

WO 208 (War Office: Directorate of Military Operations and Intelligence, and Directorate of Military Intelligence: Ministry of Defence, Defence Intelligence Staff: Files)

WO 275 (War Office: Sixth Airborne Division, Palestine: Papers and Reports)

WO 374 (War Office: Officers' Services, First World War, personal files)

Parliamentary Archive, London
A. Bonar Law
J. C. C. Davidson
D. Lloyd George, 1st Earl Lloyd George of Dwyfor
Sir H. L. Samuel
J. St L. Strachey

Pembroke College, Cambridge
Sir R. Storrs

Rhodes House, Oxford
Sir H. A. MacMichael

Service Historique de l'Armée de Terre, Paris
Files from series:
4H (Levant)
2N (Conseil supérieur de la Défense nationale)
6N (Fonds Clemenceau)
7N (L'Etat-Major de l'Armée)

Sudan Archive, Durham
Sir G. F. Clayton
Sir F. R. Wingate

The Times Archive
Confidential Memoranda by L. Heren and W. F. Stirling
R. Deakin (TT/FN/1/RD/1)
Managerial File: W. F. Stirling

Printed Primary Sources
Ministère des Affaires Etrangères, *Documents Diplomatiques Français*, volumes for 1944–7, Paris, 2000–7
State of Israel, *Political and Diplomatic Documents, December 1947–May 1948*, Jerusalem, 1979
United States Department of State, *Foreign Relations of the United States*, volumes covering the 1919 Paris Peace Conference and subsequent Near East affairs

2 Secondary Sources

Abitbol, M., *Les Deux Terres Promises: Les Juifs de France et le Sionisme (1897–1945)*, Paris, 1989
Abrams, L., and Miller, D. J., 'Who Were the French Colonialists? A Reassessment of the Parti Colonial, 1890–1914', *Historical Journal*, vol. 19, no. 3 (Sept. 1976), pp. 685–725
Adams, W., Brock, J. W., and Blair J. M., 'Retarding the Development of Iraq's Oil Resources: An Episode in Oleaginous Diplomacy, 1927–1939', *Journal of Economic Issues*, vol. 27, no. 1 (March 1993), pp. 69–93

Adelson, R., *Mark Sykes, Portrait of an Amateur*, London, 1975

— *London and the Invention of the Middle East: Money, Power and War, 1882–1922*, Yale, 1995

Alexander, M. S., *The Republic in Danger: General Maurice Gamelin and the Politics of French Defence, 1933–1940*, Cambridge, 1992

— and Philpott, W. J., 'The Entente Cordiale and the Next War: Anglo-French Views on Future Military Cooperation, 1928–1939', *Intelligence and National Security*, vol. 13, no. 1 (1998), pp. 53–84

Amadouny, M., 'The Formation of the Transjordan–Syria Boundary, 1915–32', *Middle Eastern Studies*, vol. 31, no. 3 (July 1995), pp. 533–49

Andréa, C., *La Révolte Druze et l'insurrection de Damas*, Paris, 1937

Andrew, C. M., 'France and the Making of the Entente Cordiale', *Historical Journal*, vol. 10, no. 1 (1967), pp. 89–105

— 'The French Colonialist Movement during the Third Republic: The Unofficial Mind of Imperialism', in *Transactions of the Royal Historical Society*, vol. 26 (1976), pp. 143–66

— *The Defence of the Realm: The Authorized History of MI5*, London, 2009

— and Kanya-Forstner, A. S., 'The French Colonial Party and French Colonial War Aims, 1914–1918', *Historical Journal*, vol. 17, no. 1 (1974), pp. 79–106

— *France Overseas: The Great War and the Climax of French Imperial Expansion*, London, 1981

Antonius, G., 'Syria and the French Mandate', *International Affairs*, vol. 13, no. 4 (July–Aug. 1934), pp. 523–39

— *The Arab Awakening*, London, 1938

Arnold, T. W., *The Caliphate*, 2nd edn, London, 1965

Avriel, E., *Open the Gates! A Personal Story of 'Illegal' Immigration to Israel*, London, 1975

Barker, A. J., *The Neglected War: Mesopotamia 1916–1918*, London, 1967

Barr, J., *Setting the Desert on Fire: T. E. Lawrence and Britain's Secret War in Arabia, 1916–1918*, New York, 2008

Bates, D., *The Fashoda Incident: Encounter on the Nile*, Oxford, 1984

Bauer, Y., 'From Cooperation to Resistance: The Haganah 1938–1946', *Middle Eastern Studies*, vol. 2, no. 3 (Apr. 1966), pp. 182–210

Beevor A., and Cooper, A., *Paris after the Liberation, 1944–1949*, London, 1994

Begin, M., *The Revolt*, Los Angeles, 1972

Bell, G., *The Desert and the Sown*, London, 1907

Bennett, G., *Churchill's Man of Mystery: Desmond Morton and the World of Intelligence*, London, 2007

Bierman, J., and Smith, C., *Fire in the Night: Wingate of Burma, Ethiopia and Zion*, London, 1999

Binion, R., *Defeated Leaders: The Political Fate of Caillaux, Jouvenel, and Tardieu*, Columbia, 1960

Binsley, J., *Palestine Police Service*, London, 1996

Bonné, A., 'The Concessions for the Mosul–Haifa Pipe Line', *Annals of the American Academy of Political and Social Science*, vol. 164, *Palestine. A Decade of Development* (Nov. 1932), pp. 116–26

Boucard, R., *Les dessous de l'espionnage anglais*, Paris, 1926

Bou-Nacklie, N. E., 'Tumult in Syria's Hama in 1925: The Failure of a Revolt', *Journal of Contemporary History*, vol. 33, no. 2 (Apr. 1988), pp. 273–90

Bowden, T., 'The Politics of the Arab Rebellion in Palestine 1936–39', *Middle Eastern Studies*, vol. 11, no. 2 (May 1975), pp. 147–74

Bowyer Bell, J., 'Assassination in International Politics', *International Studies Quarterly*, vol. 16, no. 1 (Mar. 1972), pp. 59–82

Bray, N.N.E., *Shifting Sands*, London, 1934

Brecher, F. W., 'French Policy toward the Levant 1914–18', *Middle Eastern Studies*, vol. 29, no. 4 (Oct. 1993), pp. 641–64

Brémond, E., *Le Hedjaz dans la première guerre mondiale*, Paris, 1931

Brenner, Y. S., 'The "Stern Gang" 1940–48', *Middle Eastern Studies*, vol. 2, no. 1 (Oct. 1965), pp. 2–30

Brown, M., ed., *Lawrence of Arabia: The Selected Letters*, London, 2005

Bruchez, A., 'La fin de la présence française en Syrie: de la crise de mai 1945 au départ des dernières troupes étrangères', *Relations internationales* 2005/2, no. 122, pp. 17–32

Buchan, J., *Greenmantle*, London, 1916

Burns, R., *The Monuments of Syria*, London, 1992

Calhoun, R.-D., 'Arming David: The Haganah's Illegal Arms Procurement Network in the United States, 1945–49', *Journal of Palestine Studies*, vol. 36, no. 4 (Summer, 2007), pp. 22–32

Capern, A. L.,'Winston Churchill, Mark Sykes and the Dardanelles Campaign of 1915', *Historical Research*, vol. 71, no. 174 (Feb. 1998), pp. 108–18

Casey, R., *Personal Experience*, London, 1962

Catherwood, C., *Winston's Folly: Imperialism and the Creation of Modern Iraq*, London, 2004

Catroux, G., *Dans la Bataille de Méditerranée*, Paris, 1949

— *Deux Missions en Moyen Orient, 1919–1922*, Paris, 1958

Cavendish, A., *Inside Intelligence: The Revelations of an MI6 Officer*, paperback, London, 1997

Cesarani, D., *Major Farran's Hat: Murder, Scandal and Britain's War against Jewish Terrorism, 1945–1948*, London, 2009

Challis, D., *From the Harpy Tomb to the Wonders of Ephesus: British Archaeologists in the Ottoman Empire 1840–1880*, London, 2008

Charmley, J., *Churchill: The End of Glory*, London, 1993

Charters, D. A., 'British Intelligence in the Palestine Campaign, 1945–47', *Intelligence and National Security*, vol. 6, no. 1 (Jan. 1991), pp. 115–40

— 'Eyes of the Underground: Jewish Insurgent Intelligence in Palestine, 1945–47', *Intelligence and National Security*, vol. 13, no. 4 (Winter, 1998), pp. 163–77

Churchill, W. S., *The Story of the Malakand Field Force: An Episode of Frontier War*, London, 1898

— *The River War*, London, 1899

— *The World Crisis*, London, 1929

— *Great Contemporaries*, London, 1937

— *The Second World War*, vols I–VI, London, 1948–54

Cloarec, V., *La France et la question de Syrie, 1914–1918*, Paris, 2002

Coblentz, P., *The Silence of Sarrail*, London, 1930

Cohen, M. J., 'British Strategy and the Palestine Question 1936–39', *Journal of Contemporary History*, vol. 7, nos 3/4 (July–Oct. 1972), pp. 157–83

— 'Appeasement in the Middle East: The British White Paper on Palestine, May 1939', *Historical Journal*, vol. 16, no. 3 (Sept. 1973), pp. 571–96

— 'Direction of Policy in Palestine, 1936–45', *Middle Eastern Studies*, vol. 11, no. 3 (Oct. 1975), pp. 237–61

— 'The Moyne Assassination, November 1944: A Political Analysis', *Middle Eastern Studies*, vol. 15, no. 3 (Oct. 1979), pp. 358–73

— 'Truman and Palestine, 1945–1948: Revisionism, Politics and Diplomacy', *Modern Judaism*, vol. 2, no. 1 (Feb. 1982), pp. 1–22

Colyton, H., *Occasion, Chance and Change*, Norwich, 1993

Connell, J., *The House by Herod's Gate*, London, 1947

Cook, D., *Charles de Gaulle*, London, 1984

Coulet, F., *Vertu des Temps Difficiles*, Paris, 1967

Cox, J. L., 'The Background to the Syrian Campaign, May–June 1941: A Study in Franco-German Wartime Relations', *History*, vol. 72, no. 236 (Oct. 1987), pp. 432–52

Cumming, H., *Franco-British Rivalry in the Post-war Near East*, Oxford, 1938

Dahl, R., *Going Solo*, London, 1986

Davet, M.-C., *La Double Affaire de Syrie*, Paris, 1967

Dayan, M., *Story of My Life*, London, 1976

Dekel, E., *Shai: The Exploits of Hagana Intelligence*, New York, 1959

Dorrill, S., *MI6: Fifty Years of Special Operations*, London, 2000

Doty, B. J., *The Legion of the Damned*, London, 1928

Dovey, H. O., 'Security in Syria, 1941–45', *Intelligence and National Security*, vol. 6, no. 2 (1991), pp. 418–46

— 'Maunsell and Mure', *Intelligence and National Security*, vol. 8, no. 1 (1993), pp. 60–77

Dyson, S. L., *In Pursuit of Ancient Pasts*, Yale, 2006

Duff, D., *Bailing with a Teaspoon*, London, 1953

Eden, A., *Freedom and Order: Selected Speeches 1939–1946*, London, 1947

Egremont, M., *Under Two Flags: The Life of Major-General Sir Edward Spears*, London, 1997

Eldar, D., 'France in Syria: The Abolition of the Sharifian Government, April–July 1920', *Middle Eastern Studies*, vol. 29, no. 3 (July 1993), pp. 487–504

Eliav, Y., trans. M. Schreiber, *Wanted*, New York, 1984

Eshed, H., *Reuven Shiloah: The Man behind the Mossad*, London, 1997

Evans, K. E., '"The Apple of Discord": The Impact of the Levant on Anglo-French Relations during 1943', unpublished PhD thesis, University of Leeds, 1990

Facey, W., and Safwat, N. F., eds, *A Soldier's Story: From Ottoman Rule to Independent Iraq, The Memoirs of Jafar Pasha Al-Askari*, London, 2003

Fenby, J., *The General: Charles de Gaulle and the France He Saved*, London, 2010

Ferrier, R. W., *The History of the British Petroleum Company*, vol. I, *The Developing Years, 1901–1932*, Cambridge, 1982

Fieldhouse, D. K., *Western Imperialism in the Middle East, 1914–195*[?] Oxford, 2006

Fisher, J., 'Syria and Mesopotamia in British Middle Eastern Policy in 1919', *Middle Eastern Studies*, vol. 34, no. 2 (Apr. 1998), pp. 129–70

Fitzgerald, E. P., 'Business Diplomacy: Walter Teagle, Jersey Standard, and the Anglo-French Pipeline Conflict in the Middle East, 1930–31', *Business History Review* vol. 67, no. 2 (Summer, 1993), pp. 207–45

— 'France's Middle Eastern Ambitions, the Sykes–Picot Negotiations, and the Oil Fields of Mosul, 1915–1918', *Journal of Modern History*, vol. 66, no. 4 (Dec. 1994), pp. 697–725

Forcade, O., *La République Secrète: Histoire des services spéciaux français de 1918 à 1939*, Paris, 2008

Friedman, I., *The Question of Palestine*, London, 1973

Fromkin, D., *A Peace to End All Peace: Creating the Modern Middle East, 1914–1922*, London, 1989

Fry, M. G., and Rabinovich, I., eds, *Despatches from Damascus: Gilbert MacKereth and British Policy in the Levant, 1933–1939*, Jerusalem, 1985

Gaddis, J. L., *The Cold War*, London, 2005

Garnett, D., ed., *The Letters of T. E. Lawrence*, London, 1938

de Gaulle, C., *Le Fil de l'Epée*, Paris, 1944

— *Mémoires de Guerre*, 3 vols, Paris, 1954–9

Gaunson, A. B., 'Churchill, de Gaulle, Spears and the Levant Affair, 1941', *Historical Journal*, vol. 27, no. 3 (1984), pp. 697–713

— *The Anglo-French Clash in Lebanon and Syria, 1940–1945*, London, 1987

Gautherot, G., *La France en Syrie et en Cilicie*, Courbevoie, 1920

Gilbert, M., *Winston S. Churchill*, London, 1967–88, and companion volumes

— *Exile and Return: The Emergence of Jewish Statehood*, London, 1978

— *Churchill and the Jews*, London, 2007

Gil-Har, Y., 'French Policy in Syria and Zionism: Proposal for a Zionist Settlement', *Middle Eastern Studies*, vol. 30, no. 1 (Jan. 1994), pp. 155–65

Glubb, J. B., *The Story of the Arab Legion*, London, 1948

Golani, M., 'The "Haifa Turning Point": The British Administration and the Civil War in Palestine, December 1947–May 1948', *Middle Eastern Studies*, vol. 37, no. 2 (2001), pp. 93–130

Goldstein, Erik, 'British Peace Aims and the Eastern Question: The

Political Intelligence Department and the Eastern Committee, 1918', *Middle Eastern Studies*, vol. 23, no. 4 (Oct. 1987), pp. 419–36

Gombrich, E., 'Winston Churchill as Painter and Critic', *The Atlantic*, vol. 215 (1965), pp. 90–3

Hacohen, D., *Time to Tell: An Israeli Life 1898–1984*, New York, 1985

Halamish, A., 'American Volunteers in Illegal Immigration to Palestine, 1946–1948', *Jewish History*, vol. 9, no. 1 (Spring, 1995), pp. 91–106

Haldane, Sir A. L., *The Insurrection in Mesopotamia, 1920*, Edinburgh, 1922

Hambly, A., 'The Accidental Presidency', *The Wilson Quarterly*, vol. 12, no. 2 (Spring, 1988), pp. 48–65

Hardinge of Penhurst, Lord, *Old Diplomacy*, London, 1947

Harris, K., *Attlee*, London, 1982

Harvey, J., *With the Foreign Legion in Syria*, London, 1928

— ed., *The War Diaries of Oliver Harvey*, London, 1978

Hassall, C., *Edward Marsh*, London, 1959

Hecht, B., *A Child of the Century*, New York, 1954

Heller, J., '"Neither Masada Nor Vichy": Diplomacy and Resistance in Zionist Politics, 1945–1947', *International History Review*, vol. 3, no. 4 (Oct. 1981), pp. 540–64

— *The Stern Gang: Ideology, Politics and Terror, 1940–1949*, London, 1995

Helmreich, P. C., *From Paris to Sèvres*, Ohio, 1974

Henderson, E., *This Strange, Eventful History*, Dubai, 1988

Heren, L. P., *Growing Up on 'The Times'*, London, 1978

Hershco, T., 'France and the Partition Plan: 1947–1948', *Israel Affairs*, vol. 14, no. 3 (2008), pp. 486–98

Hogarth, D., *A Wandering Scholar in the Levant*, London, 1896

Howell, G., *Daughter of the Desert*, London, 2006

Hughes, M., *Allenby and British Strategy in the Middle East, 1917–1919*, London, 1999

James, L., *The Golden Warrior: The Life and Legend of Lawrence of Arabia*, London, 1990

Jarvis, C. S., *Arab Command:The Biography of Lieutenant-Colonel F. W. Peake Pasha*, London, 1942

Jeffery, K., 'Great Power Rivalry in the Middle East', *Historical Journal*, vol. 25, no. 4 (Dec. 1982), pp. 1029–38

— 'Intelligence and Counter-Insurgency Operations: Some Reflections on the British Experience', *Intelligence and National Security*, vol. 2, no. 1 (1987), pp. 118–49

— *MI6: The History of the Secret Intelligence Service, 1909–1949*, London, 2010

Jenkins, R., *Churchill*, London, 2001

Katz, S., *Days of Fire*, London, 1968

Kedourie, E., *In the Anglo-Arab Labyrinth*, Cambridge, 1976

— 'The Bludan Congress on Palestine, September 1937', *Middle Eastern Studies*, vol. 17, no. 1 (Jan. 1981), pp. 107–25

Kedward, R., *La Vie en Bleu: France and the French since 1900*, London, 2005

Keiger, J. F. V. '"Perfidious Albion?" French Perceptions of Britain as an Ally after the First World War', *Intelligence and National Security*, vol. 13, no. 1 (1998), pp. 37–52

Kelly, S., 'A Succession of Crises: SOE in the Middle East, 1940–45', *Intelligence and National Security*, vol. 20, no. 1 (Mar. 2005), pp. 121–46

Kent, M., *Oil and Empire: British Policy and Mesopotamian Oil, 1900–1920*, London, 1976

Khalidi, W., 'Selected Documents on the 1948 Palestinian War', *Journal of Palestine Studies*, vol. 27, no. 3 (Spring, 1998), pp. 60–105

Khoury, G., *La France et l'Orient Arabe: Naissance du Liban Moderne*, Paris, 1993

Khoury, P. S., 'Divided Loyalties? Syria and the Question of Palestine, 1919–39', *Middle Eastern Studies*, vol. 21, no. 3 (July 1985), pp. 324–48

— *Syria and the French Mandate*, Princeton, 1987

Kirkbride, A., *A Crackle of Thorns*, London, 1956

Kochavi, A. J., 'Britain's Image Campaign against the Zionists', *Journal of Contemporary History*, vol. 36, no. 2 (Apr. 2001), pp. 293–307

Kulski, W. W., *De Gaulle and the World*, New York, 1966

Lacouture, J. (trans. P. O'Brian), *De Gaulle*, 2 vols, London, 1990

Lansing, R., *The Peace Negotiations: A Personal Narrative*, Boston and New York, 1921

Larès, M., *T. E. Lawrence, La France, et Les Français*, Paris, 1980

Laurens, H., 'Jaussen en Arabie', in *Photographies d'Arabie: Hedjaz 1907–1917*, Institut du Monde Arabe, Paris, 1999

Laverty Miller, J., 'The Syrian Revolt of 1925', *International Journal of Middle East Studies*, vol. 8, no. 4 (Oct. 1977), pp. 545–63

Lawrence, M. R., *The Home Letters of T. E. Lawrence and his Brothers*, Oxford, 1954

Lawrence, T. E., *Seven Pillars of Wisdom*, London, 1935

— *T. E. Lawrence to his Biographers Robert Graves and Liddell Hart*, London, 1963

— *Seven Pillars of Wisdom*, Oxford 1922 text, Fordingbridge, 2005

Lazar, D., *L'opinion française et la naissance de l'Etat d'Israël, 1945–1949*, Paris, 1972

Leclerc, C., *Avec T. E. Lawrence en Arabie, La Mission militaire française au Hedjaz 1916–1920*, Paris, 1998

Ledwidge, B., *De Gaulle*, London, 1982

Lees, G. M., 'The Search for Oil', *Geographical Journal*, vol. 95, no. 1 (Jan. 1940), pp. 1–16

Lévy, Claude, 'La résistance juive en France. De l'enjeu de mémoire à l'histoire-critique', *Vingtième Siècle. Revue d'histoire*, no. 22, numéro spécial: 'Les générations' (Apr.–June 1989), pp. 117–28

Liman von Sanders, O., *Five Years in Turkey*, Nashville, 2000

Longrigg, S. H., *Oil in the Middle East*, Oxford, 1954

— *Syria and Lebanon under French Mandate*, Oxford, 1958

Lyautey, P., *Gouraud*, Paris, 1949

MacCallum, E. P., *The Nationalist Crusade in Syria*, New York, 1928

McDonald, A., 'The Geddes Committee and the Formulation of Public Expenditure Policy, 1921–1922', *Historical Journal*, vol. 32, no. 3 (Sept. 1989), pp. 643–74

Macmillan, H., *War Diaries – The Mediterranean, 1943–45*, London, 1984

MacMillan, M., *Peacemakers*, London, 2002

Maitland, A., *Wilfred Thesiger, The Life of the Great Explorer*, London, 2006

Mangold, P., *The Almost Impossible Ally: Harold Macmillan and Charles de Gaulle*, London, 2006

Mardor, M., *Strictly Illegal*, London, 1964

Marrus, M. R., 'Jewish Leaders and the Holocaust', *French Historical Studies*, vol. 15, no. 2 (Autumn, 1987), pp. 316–31

Mattar, P., *The Mufti of Jerusalem*, New York, 1988

Mead, W. R., 'The New Israel and the Old: Why Gentile Americans Back the Jewish State', *Foreign Affairs*, vol. 87, no. 4 (July/Aug. 2008), pp. 28–46

Meinertzhagen, Col. R., *Middle East Diary, 1917–1956*, London, 1959

Messenger, C., *The Commandos, 1940–46*, London, 1985

Meulenijzer, V., *Le Colonel Lawrence, agent de l'Intelligence Service*, Brussels, 1938

Mohs, P. A., *Military Intelligence and the Arab Revolt: The First Modern Intelligence War*, London, 2008

Montagne, R., 'French Policy in North Africa and in Syria', *International Affairs*, vol. 16, no. 2 (Mar.–Apr. 1937), pp. 263–79

Morgan, K. O., 'Lloyd George's Premiership: A Study in "Prime Ministerial Government"', *Historical Journal*, vol. 13, no. 1 (Mar. 1970)

— *Consensus and Disunity: The Lloyd George Coalition Government 1918–1922*, Oxford, 1979

Mosley, L., *Gideon Goes to War*, London, 1955

Mott-Radclyffe, C., *Foreign Body in the Eye*, London, 1975

Moubayed, S., *Steel and Silk: Men and Women Who Shaped Syria 1900–2000*, Seattle, 2006

Mousa, S., *T. E. Lawrence: An Arab View*, Oxford, 1966

Neillands, R., *The Raiders: The Army Commandos 1940–46*, London, 1989

Néré, J., *The Foreign Policy of France from 1914 to 1945*, London, 1975

Nicault, C., *La France et le sionisme: une rencontre manquée?*, Paris, 1992

Nicolson, H., *Peacemaking 1919*, London, 1933

Nicolson, N., ed., *Harold Nicolson, Diaries and Letters, 1907–1964*, London, 2004

Norris, J., 'Repression and Rebellion: Britain's Response to the Arab Revolt in Palestine of 1936–39', *Journal of Imperial and Commonwealth History*, vol. 36, no. 1 (Mar. 2008), pp. 25–45

Norwich, J. J., ed., *The Duff Cooper Diaries*, London, 2005

Oren, M. B., *Power, Faith and Fantasy: America in the Middle East, 1776 to the Present*, New York, 2007

Orga, I., *Portrait of a Turkish Family*, London, 1950

Ottolenghi, M., 'Harry Truman's Recognition of Israel', *Historical Journal*, vol. 47, no. 4 (Dec. 2004), pp. 963–88

Ovendale, R., 'The Palestine Policy of the British Labour Government, 1945–1946', *International Affairs*, vol. 55, no. 3 (July 1979), pp. 409–31

Pappé, I., *The Ethnic Cleansing of Palestine*, Oxford, 2006

Paris, T. J., 'British Middle East Policy-Making after the First World War: The Lawrentian and Wilsonian Schools', *Historical Journal*, vol. 41, no. 3 (Sep. 1998), pp. 773–93

Pearse, R., *Three Years in the Levant*, London, 1949

Pichon, J., *Le partage du Proche-Orient*, Paris, 1938

Porath, Y., 'Abdallah's Greater Syria Programme', *Middle Eastern Studies*, vol. 20, no. 2 (Apr. 1984), pp. 172–89

Porch, D., *The French Secret Services: From the Dreyfus Affair to the Gulf War*, London, 1996

van der Post, L., *The Admiral's Baby*, London, 1996

Poulleau, A., *A Damas sous les bombes: journal d'une française pendant la révolte syrienne*, Yvetot, 1930

Poznanski, R. 'Reflections on Jewish Resistance and Jewish Resistants in France', *Jewish Social Studies*, New Series, vol. 2, no. 1 (Autumn, 1995), pp. 124–58

— (trans. N. Brecher), *Jews in France during World War II*, Hanover, NH, 2001

Provence, M., *The Great Syrian Revolt and the Rise of Arab Nationalism*, Austin, 2005

Puaux, G., *Deux Années au Levant*, Paris, 1952

Ranfurly, H., *To War with Whitaker*, London, 1994

Rathmell, A., *Secret War in the Middle East:The Covert Struggle for Syria, 1949–1961*, London, 1995

Rendel, G., *The Sword and the Olive*, London, 1957

Rittner, C., Smith, S. D., and Steinfeldt, I., *The Holocaust and the Christian World*, Yad-Vashem, 2000

Robins, P., *A History of Jordan*, Cambridge, 2004

Rodinson, Maxime, 'Aux origines du "Pacte National", Contribution à l'Histoire de la Crise Franco-Libanaise de Novembre 1943', *Die Welt des Islams*, New Series, Bd. 28, Nr. 1/4 (1988), pp. 445–74

Rogan, E., *The Arabs: A History*, London, 2009

Rose, N., *'A Senseless, Squalid War': Voices from Palestine 1945–48*, London, 2009

Roshwald, A., 'The Spears Mission in the Levant: 1941–1944', *Historical Journal*, vol. 29, no. 4 (Dec. 1986), pp. 897–919

— *Estranged Bedfellows: Britain and France in the Middle East during the Second World War*, Oxford, 1990

Royle, T., *Glubb Pasha*, London, 1992

— *Orde Wingate: Irregular Soldier*, London, 1995

Satia, P., 'Developing Iraq: Britain, India and the Redemption of Empire and Technology in the First World War', *Past and Present*, vol. 197, no. 1 (Nov. 2007), pp. 211–55

Savage, R., *Allenby of Armageddon*, London, 1925

Seale, P., *The Struggle for Arab Independence: Riad el-Solh and the Makers of the Modern Middle East*, Cambridge, 2010

Segev, T., *One Palestine, Complete*, London, 2000

Seymour, C., ed., *The Intimate Papers of Colonel House*, vol. III, London, 1928

Shambrook, P. A., *French Imperialism in Syria, 1927–1936*, Reading, 1998

Shamir, Y., *Summing Up*, London, 1994

Sheffer, G., 'British Colonial Policy-Making towards Palestine (1929–1939)', *Middle Eastern Studies*, vol. 14, no. 3 (Oct. 1978), pp. 307–22

— 'Appeasement and the Problem of Palestine', *International Journal of Middle East Studies*, vol. 11, no. 3 (May 1980), pp. 377–99

— *Moshe Sharrett: Biography of a Political Moderate*, Oxford, 1996

Shlaim, A., *Collusion across the Jordan: King Abdullah, the Zionist Movement, and the Partition of Palestine*, New York, 1988

— *War and Peace in the Middle East*, rev. edn, London, 1995

— *Israel and Palestine: Reappraisals, Revisions, Refutations*, London, 2009

Shorrock, W. I., *French Imperialism in the Middle East: The Failure of Policy in Syria and Lebanon 1900–1914*, Wisconsin, 1976

Silvestri, M., '"An Irishman Is Specially Suited to Be a Policeman": Sir Charles Tegart & Revolutionary Terrorism in Bengal', *History Ireland*, vol. 8, no. 4 (Winter, 2000), pp. 40–4

Simon, R. S., 'The Hashemite "Conspiracy": Hashemite Unity Attempts, 1921–1958', *International Journal of Middle East Studies*, vol. 5, no. 3 (June 1974), pp. 314–27

Singer, B., and Langdon, J., *Cultured Force: Makers and Defenders of the French Colonial Empire*, Madison, Wisconsin, 2004

Sluglett, P., *Britain in Iraq*, 2nd edn, London, 2007

Soustelle, J., *La longue marche d'Israël*, Paris, 1968

Spears, Sir E., *Two Men Who Saved France: Pétain and de Gaulle*, London, 1966

— *Fulfilment of a Mission: The Spears Mission to Syria and the Lebanon, 1941–1944*, London, 1977

Stanger, C. D., 'A Haunting Legacy: The Assassination of Count Bernadotte', *Middle East Journal*, vol. 42, no. 2 (Spring, 1988), pp. 260–72

Stein, L., *The Balfour Declaration*, London, 1961

Stevenson, D., *1914–1918: The History of the First World War*, London, 2005

Stirling, W. F., *Safety Last*, London, 1953

Stivers, W., 'International Politics and Iraqi Oil, 1918–1928: A Study in Anglo-American Diplomacy', *Business History Review*, vol. 55, no. 4 (Winter, 1981), pp. 517–40

Storrs, R., *Orientations*, London, 1937

— *Lawrence of Arabia; Zionism and Palestine*, London, 1940

Strachan, H., *The First World War*, vol. I, *To Arms*, Oxford, 2001

Sykes, M., *The Caliphs' Last Heritage*, London, 1915

Tanenbaum, J. K., *General Maurice Sarrail 1856–1929: The French Army and Left-Wing Politics*, Chapel Hill, NC, 1974

— 'France and the Arab Middle East 1914–1920', *Transactions of the American Philosophical Society*, vol. 68 (1978), Part 7

Tauber, E., *The Arab Movements in World War I*, London, 1993

Tegart, Sir C., 'Terrorism in India', lecture delivered to the Royal Empire Society, 1 Nov. 1932

Thesiger, W., *The Life of My Choice*, London, 1987

Thomas, M. C., 'The Syrian Revolt and Anglo-French Imperial Relations, 1925–27', in Kennedy, G. C., and Nelson, K., eds, *Incidents and International Relations: People, Power and Personalities*, Westport, 2002, pp. 65–86

— 'French Intelligence-Gathering in the Syrian Mandate, 1920–40', *Middle Eastern Studies*, vol. 38, no. 1 (Jan. 2002), pp. 1–32

— 'Bedouin Tribes and the Imperial Intelligence Services in Syria, Iraq and Transjordan in the 1920s', *Journal of Contemporary History*, vol. 38, no. 4 (Oct. 2003), pp. 539–61

— *The French Empire between the Wars: Imperialism, Politics and Society*, Manchester, 2005

Tombs, R. and I., *That Sweet Enemy: The French and the British from the Sun King to the Present*, London, 2006

Tournoux, J.-R., *Pétain et de Gaulle*, Paris, 1964

Townshend, C., 'The Defence of Palestine: Insurrection and Public Security, 1936–1939', *English Historical Review*, vol. 103, no. 409 (Oct. 1988), pp. 917–49

— *When God Made Hell: The British Invasion of Mesopotamia and the Creation of Iraq, 1914–21*, London, 2010

Toye, R., *Rivals for Greatness: Lloyd George and Churchill*, London, 2007

Truman, H. S., *The Memoirs of Harry S. Truman*, vol. I, *Year of Decisions*, 1945, London, 1955

— *The Memoirs of Harry S. Truman*, vol. II, *Years of Trial and Hope*, London, 1956

Tydor Baumel, J., 'The IZL Delegation in the USA 1939–1948: Anatomy of an Ethnic Interest/Protest Group', *Jewish History*, vol. 9, no. 1 (Spring, 1995), pp. 79–89

Ulrichsen, K., 'Coming as Liberators', *History Today* (Mar. 2007), pp. 47–9

Vansittart, R., *The Mist Procession*, London, 1958

Venn, F., *Oil Diplomacy in the Twentieth Century*, London, 1986

Wagner, S., 'British Intelligence and the Jewish Resistance Movement in the Palestine Mandate, 1945–46', *Intelligence and National Security*, vol. 23, no. 5 (Oct. 2008), pp. 629–57

de Wailly, H., *Liban, Syrie: Le Mandat 1919–1940*, Paris, 2010

Walton, C., 'British Intelligence and the Mandate of Palestine: Threats to British National Security Immediately After the Second World War', *Intelligence and National Security*, vol. 23, no. 4 (Aug. 2008), pp. 435–62

Wasserstein, B., 'Herbert Samuel and the Palestine Problem', *English Historical Review*, vol. 91, no. 361 (Oct. 1976), pp. 753–75

Weulersse, Jacques, *Paysans de Syrie et du Proche Orient*, Paris, 1946

Wilson, Sir A. T., *Loyalties: Mesopotamia, 1914–1917: A Personal and Historical Record*, London, 1930

Wilson, Field Marshal Lord, *Eight Years Overseas*, London, 1949

Wilson, J., *Lawrence of Arabia: The Authorised Biography of T. E. Lawrence*, London, 1989

Yapp, M., *The Making of the Modern Near East 1792–1923*, London, 1987

— *The Near East since the First World War: A History to 1995*, 2nd edn, London, 1996

Young, H., *The Independent Arab*, London, 1933

Zamir, M., *Lebanon's Quest: The Road to Statehood, 1926–1939*, London, 1997

— 'An Intimate Alliance: The Joint Struggle of General Edward Spears and Riad al-Sulh to Oust France from Lebanon, 1942–1944', *Middle Eastern Studies*, vol. 41, no. 6 (Nov. 2005), pp. 811–32

— 'De Gaulle and the Question of Syria and Lebanon during the Second World War: Part I', *Middle Eastern Studies*, vol. 43, no. 5 (Sept. 2007), pp. 675–708

— 'Britain's Treachery, France's Revenge', *Ha'aretz*, 1 Feb. 2008

— 'The French Connection', *Ha'aretz*, 3 July 2008

— 'Espionage and the Zionist Endeavour', *Jerusalem Post*, 20 Nov. 2008
— 'A Burning Ship on Jerusalem Beach', *Ha'aretz*, 22 June 2009
— '"Bid" for *Altalena*: France's Covert Action in the 1948 War in Palestine', *Middle Eastern Studies*, vol. 46, no. 1 (Jan. 2010), pp. 17–58
— 'The "Missing Dimension": Britain's Secret War against France in Syria and Lebanon, 1942–45: Part II', *Middle Eastern Studies*, vol. 46, no. 6 (Nov. 2010), pp. 791–899.
Zuccotti, Susan, *The Holocaust, the French, and the Jews*, New York, 1993

INDEX

ABOUT THE AUTHOR

James Barr has worked for the *Daily Telegraph*, in politics and in the City, and has travelled widely in the Middle East. During the research for this book he was a visiting fellow at St Antony's College, Oxford.